GARLAND STUDIES IN APPLIED ETHICS
VOL. 3

DRUGS, MORALITY, AND THE LAW

GARLAND REFERENCE LIBRARY
OF SOCIAL SCIENCE
VOL. 666

GARLAND STUDIES IN APPLIED ETHICS

ALAN GOLDMAN
Series Editor

**JUSTIFICATION AND
EXCUSE IN THE
CRIMINAL LAW**
A Collection of Essays
edited by
Michael Louis Corrado

**ETHICAL ISSUES IN
SCIENTIFIC RESEARCH**
An Anthology
edited by Edward Erwin, Sidney
Gendin, and Lowell Kleiman

**DRUGS, MORALITY,
AND THE LAW**
edited by Steven Luper-Foy
and Curtis Brown

DRUGS, MORALITY, AND THE LAW

edited by

Steven Luper-Foy
Curtis Brown

GARLAND PUBLISHING, Inc.
New York & London / 1994

Library of Congress Cataloging-in-Publication Data

Drugs, morality, and the law / edited by Steven Luper-
Foy, Curtis Brown.
        p.   cm. — (Garland studies in applied ethics ;
vol. 3) (Garland reference library of social science ;
vol. 666)
    Includes bibliographical references.
    ISBN 0–8153–0485–4
    1. Drug abuse—United States—Prevention.
2. Drug abuse—Government policy—United
States.   3. Drug abuse—Moral and ethical aspects.
I. Luper-Foy, Steven.   II. Brown, Curtis.
III. Series.   IV. Series: Garland reference library of
social science ; vol. 666.
HV5825.D87 1994
363.4'5—dc20   93–48114
                                                    CIP

Printed on acid-free, 250-year-life paper
Manufactured in the United States of America

Contents

Series Editor's Preface

The aim of this series is to make available texts and collections of essays on major moral issues. Each volume will be devoted to a single issue of contemporary interest. Such in-depth treatment will transcend the usual superficial presentation of such topics in general applied ethics texts. Background will be provided by classic statements in articles or detailed definitions in texts of the problems, and opposing sides on the issues will be given ample development.

The series will include authored texts on topics that have not been discussed extensively in the philosophical literature before, as well as contemporary advances on earlier treatments. Collections of essays will bring together articles that have previously been scattered in the recent proliferation of journals that address these issues.

The present volume fills a glaring gap in the literature of applied ethics. Given the enormous toll on the national pocketbook and national psyche of illegal drug use and the policy of war on that use, it is surprising that no volume systematically exploring the conceptual and moral issues involved has appeared until now.

These issues cry out for philosophical clarification. Common sense and policy regarding them are largely based on unquestioned assumptions that seem to conflict as often as not: For example, that use of so-called narcotics is a disease whose victims (addicts) lose the freedom to make rational choices regarding their drug habits and other actions, but that users are nevertheless responsible for their habits and actions under the influence of drugs, and may be justly punished for them; that use of ability-enhancing drugs in sports is a form of cheating, since the user's abilities are then undeserved, but that development of one's natural abilities (which are equally undeserved) is desirable and admirable; that mandatory drug testing (in place in many universities and workplaces, including my own) may be necessary to prevent work impairment in a variety of jobs, but that such impairment, to be significant, must be detectable apart from such testing.

The contributors to this volume, while taking opposing sides on these various issues relating to drug use, are well qualified to bring analytic precision to their definition and debate.

Alan Goldman

Drugs, Morality, and the Law

The Controlled Substances Act of 1970 limits the availability in the United States of many substances that have so-called abuse potential, or harmful consequences, especially when those substances do not have accepted medicinal uses. For some time the United States government has used such legislation in an attempt to eliminate or substantially reduce drug use. During the Reagan and Bush terms, the effort was accelerated greatly, not just within the country, but also outside it. The Bush Administration nearly doubled the federal drug budget, increasing it from the 1989 level of $6.6 billion to a 1993 level of $12.7 billion. Over the last 20 years, the U.S. government has spent about $70 billion on its fight against drugs.[1]

How successful has the "War on Drugs" been? It is surprisingly difficult to tell. In February of 1992, Bob Martinez, the director of the Office of Drug Control Policy (sometimes called the "Drug Czar"), testified before a House committee that the war had made significant progress. Martinez stated that, since 1989, "2 million Americans have stopped using drugs, a drop of over 13 percent. In 1988, over 2.9 million Americans were current users of cocaine. By 1991, over 1 million had stopped using cocaine, a drop of over 35 percent. The number of current users of marijuana dropped by almost 2 million, a drop of over 35 percent. Among our most critical population, young people, current use of any illicit drug has shown more than 25 percent down since 1988."[2] He added that "progress has also been made among our hard-core addict population, albeit more slowly," observing that the war on drugs is "a two-front war, the first against casual drug users and the second against hard-core drug users."[3] On the other hand, Charles B. Rangel, the chair of the same House committee, argued the following month that the available evidence "suggest[s] hard-core demand for illegal drugs is not dropping, but occasionally on the rise."[4] Among the statistics cited by Rangel were these: the price of a kilogram of heroin dropped from $65,000 in 1990 to $50,000 in 1991; the purity level of heroin increased from 78 to 87 percent; cocaine-related emergencies in hospitals increased by 31 percent from the fall of 1990 through the spring of 1991, while heroin-related emergencies increased 26 percent; and the number of weekly cocaine users rose by 29 percent in 1991. We might add that, according to the U.S. General Accounting Office, "the numbers of drug-related homicides and hospital emergency visits and deaths remain near record highs, as does drug use by arrested criminals."[5]

Are the declines in drug use cited by Martinez consistent with the figures offered by Rangel in support of his contention that the drug problem is not improving? They are, if the declines in drug use are among casual users, while hard-core use has remained the same or even increased. If, as seems likely, hard-core users purchase and consume significantly more drugs than casual users, then a drop in the number of casual users might have little impact on the overall demand for drugs; similarly, if hard-core users are significantly more likely to have drug-related medical emergencies and to commit crimes, then the statistics on emergency room visits and arrested criminals are compatible with significant declines in casual drug use.

Drug use, both of licit and illicit drugs, takes a tremendous toll on our society. The pressures it places on our health-care system, our judicial system, and our prison system are huge, and the toll in lives from health consequences of drug use and from drug-related crime is also huge. Alcohol and tobacco are responsible for hundreds of thousands of deaths a year, and the illicit drugs for a few thousand more; typical estimates of the annual economic cost of drug-related crime, lost productivity, and drug-related health-care costs run to hundreds of billions of dollars.[6] But there is little agreement about what should be done. The essays in this volume address some of the moral and legal issues in the controversy; in this introduction we will summarize some of the main points of these essays and provide background information that should be useful in thinking about the issues they raise.

Classification of Drugs

There seems to be no standard pharmacological classification of drugs which divides them exhaustively into mutually exclusive categories. Some sense of the jumble of existing classifications may be gleaned from the title of Edward M. Brecher's excellent book *Licit and Illicit Drugs: The Consumer's Union Report on Narcotics, Stimulants, Depressants, Inhalants, Hallucinogens, and Marijuana—including Caffeine, Nicotine, and Alcohol.* What a list! Here we have several sorts of classification lumped together: drugs are classified by their legal status, by their activity on the central nervous system, by their psychological effects, by their mode of administration, and by simple enumeration.

Probably the most commonly used categories are those of depressants, stimulants, and hallucinogens. Depressants are drugs which slow or impede the activity of the central nervous system. They include narcotics, such as the opiates morphine, opium, and codeine; general anesthetics such as ether, nitrous oxide, and chloroform; barbiturates; alcohol; and tranquilizers. Stimulants include cocaine, amphetamines, caffeine, and nicotine. (Oddly, cocaine is classified as a narcotic by both the Harrison Narcotic Act of 1914 and the Comprehensive Drug Abuse Prevention and Control Act of 1970, despite being a stimulant rather than a depressant.) The term "hallucinogen" was introduced into the English language in 1954 to describe "drugs that in small doses could alter perception, thought, and mood."[7] Hallucinogens include mescaline, LSD, psilocybin (derived from Central American mushrooms), and PCP.

The categories of depressants, stimulants, and hallucinogens of course are not exhaustive. They exclude a great many drugs; drugs may have effects on many of the tissues and organs of the body, including but not limited to the brain and spinal cord. It would be odd to exclude digitalis or the diuretics from a list of drugs, though the former affects the heart and the latter affect the kidneys. The classification is also extremely broad, and lumps together drugs which are quite different in their activity and effects; among the depressants, for example, the barbiturates appear to depress nerve transmission at the synapse, while alcohol affects the nerve cell membrane. Nor are the categories clearly mutually exclusive, since many drugs have multiple effects; for example, cocaine is both a central nervous system stimulant and a local anesthetic,[8] and the effects of marijuana have been described as "a combination of sedation, tranquilization, and mild hallucination."[9]

Drug Legislation

In 1970 federal drug legislation was organized by the Comprehensive Drug Abuse Prevention and Control Act, also known as the Controlled Substances Act (21 U.S.C. sec. 801). This legislation classifies drugs that are targeted for control according to factors such as their harmfulness and their accepted therapeutic value. For the purposes of regulating misuse and misappropriation of controlled substances, the "drugs and other substances" in question are graded according to five schedules. Schedule I substances are the most highly regulated, while Schedule V substances are the least regulated. Both marijuana and heroin, which have no "currently accepted medical use," are Schedule I drugs. Codeine and minor tranquilizers like valium are Schedule V drugs. A substance's position on the schedule does not correlate with severity of criminal penalty for the possession of that substance. The penalty for unlawfully possessing any controlled substance is the same: "a term of imprisonment of not more than one year, a fine of not more than $5,000, or both" (21 U.S.C. sec. 844 [a]). The specific criteria of classification are as follows:

Schedule I
A. The drug or other substance has a high potential for abuse.
B. The drug or other substance has no currently accepted medical use in treatment in the United States.
C. There is a lack of accepted safety for use of the drug or other substance under medical supervision.

Schedule II
A. The drug or other substance has a high potential for abuse.

B. The drug or other substance has a currently accepted medical use in treatment in the United States or a currently accepted medical use with severe restrictions.
C. Abuse of the drug or other substance may lead to severe psychological or physical dependence.

Schedule III

A. The drug or other substance has a potential for abuse less than the drugs or other substances in schedules I and II.
B. The drug or other substance has a currently accepted medical use in treatment in the United States.
C. Abuse of the drug or other substance may lead to moderate or low physical dependence or high psychological dependence.

Schedule IV

A. The drug or other substance has a low potential for abuse relative to the drugs or other substances in schedule III.
B. The drug or other substance has a currently accepted medical use in treatment in the United States.
C. Abuse of the drug or other substance may lead to limited physical dependence or psychological dependence relative to the drugs or other substances in schedule III.

Schedule V

A. The drug or other substance has a low potential for abuse relative to the drugs or other substances in schedule IV.
B. The drug or other substance has a currently accepted medical use in treatment in the United States.
C. Abuse of the drug or other substance may lead to limited physical dependence or psychological dependence relative to the drugs or other substances in schedule IV. (21 U.S.C. sec. 812)

The following chart shows the way some drugs are classified according to the five schedules:[10]

Category	Substance	Schedule
Hallucinogens	LSD	I
	mescaline	I
	psilocybin	I
Stimulants	amphetamines	II
	cocaine	II

(continued)

Category	Substance	Schedule
Depressants	heroin	I
	marijuana	I
	hashish	I
	opium	II
	methadone	II
	demerol	II
	barbiturates	III
	valium	IV
	codeine	V
	meprobamate (tranquilizer)	V

The classification scheme employed in the Controlled Substances Act is defective in several ways, some of which are as
follows. First, it relies on an incorrect use of the term "narcotic."
Pharmacologically, the term "narcotic" refers to sleep-inducing
or sense-dulling drugs that tend to become addictive. But the Act
defines a narcotic as any drug derived from opium, coca leaves,
or opiates.[11] Derivatives from coca leaves are stimulants, not
narcotics.[12] Second, the criteria associated with each schedule are
not listed in a way that clarifies whether they are supposed to be
disjunctive, conjunctive, or something else. Consider Schedule I:
are we to understand that substances that meet A, B *and* C are
Schedule I drugs? Must substances meet A, B *or* C? Must substances meet two out of three? The Act is not clear, and subsequent court decisions have not cleared up the confusion: "the
three statutory criteria for Schedule I classification . . . should not
be read as being either cumulative or exclusive" (*U.S. v. Fogarty*,
692 F.2d 542, 548 [1982]).[13] Third, criterion B of each schedule
refers to the (lack of a) "currently accepted medical use in treatment," without clarifying what would constitute "accepted medical use." And fourth, criterion A of each schedule refers to a
substance's "high potential for abuse" without clarifying what
constitutes "abuse."

Since 1970, most state drug legislation has been modeled
on the federal Controlled Substances Act. Forty-five states have
adopted the Uniform Controlled Substances Act, which was
modeled on the federal Controlled Substances Act. The exceptions are Alaska, Colorado, Maine, New Hampshire, Vermont,
and Washington, D.C.

The Controlled Substances Act explicitly avoids regulating the distribution and consumption of liquor. Policy concerning liquor is determined at the state level. Most states regulate the sale of drinks which have a minimum percentage of alcohol as defined by state statutes. In some cases the regulation is relaxed. For taxation and licensing purposes, exemptions are often allowed in the cases of wine made for home or religious use, and alcohol that is not to be used as a beverage. The regulation is controlled by state liquor boards and commissions. In many states, districts and sub-districts are allowed to restrict the liquor trade even more thoroughly.

States regulate primarily by issuing licenses to trade in alcoholic drinks. Most commonly, ten requirements must be met by retailers of alcoholic drinks.[14] Licensees must:

1. have U.S. Citizenship.
2. have no serious criminal record.
3. have no history of violating state or federal liquor laws.
4. have good moral character, as assessed by local community members.
5. be a minimum age of 21.
6. be the individual who actually owns or leases the retail establishment.
7. be financially responsible.
8. lack interlocking interests in other phases of the liquor industry.
9. have residence in the state.
10. not be a licensing official.

Usually alcoholic drinks may not be sold near schools or religious establishments, and some states extend these restrictions to other establishments such as colleges, prisons, military bases, and veterans' institutions.[15]

The prosecution of alcoholics for drunkenness has been problematic in a way that is relevant to the status of drug addiction more generally. Alcoholism itself was considered an illness in a Supreme Court case in the sixties. In *Robinson v. California*, the Supreme Court decided that drug addiction cannot be penalized since it is an illness, and punishing illnesses would be a violation of the Eighth Amendment prohibition of cruel and unusual punishment (370 U.S. 660 [1962]). However, in a later case,

Powell v. Texas, the Court did not follow its earlier decision (392 U.S. 514 [1968]). Citing the work of E.M. Jellinek, the Court claimed that there are insufficient medical grounds for calling alcoholism a disease:

> There is no agreement among members of the medical profession about what it means to say that "alcoholism" is a "disease." . . . There is widespread agreement today that "alcoholism" is a "disease," for the simple reason that the medical profession has concluded that it should attempt to treat those who have drinking problems. There the agreement stops. . . .
>
> Nor is there any substantial consensus as to the "manifestations of alcoholism." E.M. Jellinek . . . asserts that it cannot accurately be said that a person is truly unable to abstain from drinking unless he is suffering the physical symptoms of withdrawal. . . . In attempting to deal with the alcoholic's desire for drink in the absence of withdrawal symptoms, Jellinek is reduced to unintelligible distinctions between a "compulsion" (a "psycho-pathological phenomenon" which can apparently serve in some instances as the functional equivalent of a "craving" or symptom of withdrawal) and an "impulse" (something which differs from a loss of control, a craving or a compulsion, and to which Jellinek attributes the start of a new drinking bout for a "gamma" alcoholic). Other scholars are equally unhelpful in articulating the nature of a "compulsion."
>
> It is one thing to say that if a man is deprived of alcohol his hands will begin to shake, he will suffer agonizing pains and ultimately he will have hallucinations; it is quite another to say that a man has a "compulsion" to take a drink, but that he also retains a certain amount of "free will" with which to resist. It is simply impossible, in the present state of our knowledge, to ascribe a useful meaning to the latter statement.

The retreat from classifying alcoholism as a disease occurs in a very recent Supreme Court case: *Traynor v. Turnage*, in which the Court upheld a statute classifying alcoholism as willful misconduct, saying that

> There exists a substantial body of medical literature that even contests the proposition that alcoholism is a disease,

much less that it is a disease for which the victim bears no
responsibility. (485 U.S. 535 [1988])

Drug Use and Responsibility

Jan Narveson argues that whether people are causally determined to act as they do has little bearing on how we should
deal with criminals. For even if people are causally determined
to act as they do, they should be prevented from violating the
law, and that may mean either imprisoning them or
hospitalizing them. Lawbreakers who are responsive to
persuasion should be imprisoned, since the threat of prison
gives them an incentive to avoid breaking the law. The threat of
prison is a "supplementary appeal to reason." Lawbreakers who
are not responsive should be treated in hospitals.

Narveson divides people who want to criminalize the use
of drugs into two non-exclusive camps. The first camp argues
that drug use should be stopped because it makes people less
productive, so that others are deprived of the benefits of work
they would otherwise have done. The second argues for banning
drug use on the grounds that drug use is contrary to the interests
of the users themselves. To the first camp Narveson responds
that since people are not obligated to help others, then they cannot be forced to choose a way of life that is beneficial to others.
To the second Narveson offers a more complex response.

He begins by distinguishing an outright paternalistic argument, which says that we ought to prevent people from living
lives that are worse than they might have lived, from one that is
not obviously paternalistic: drug use undermines our autonomy.
Against the paternalistic argument he presses the liberal point
that it is impossible to offer a convincing argument in favor of
one conception of the good over all of the other possible
conceptions, including that of someone who favors the life of
drug use. As for the second argument, Narveson says that most
drugged states are similar to sleep, which is a state in which we
do not make choices. But no one would say that people should
be stopped from taking sleeping pills. What matters is whether

we can make decisions while not under the influence of drugs (or asleep). And the addict's impaired ability to choose a drug-free life seems no more serious than the opera "addict's" impaired ability to avoid the opera. Moreover, most consumers of drugs are not addicts. Many people can take drugs or leave them, "just as alcohol is consumed mostly by non addicts."

Even if addicts are less responsive than many others to persuasion, we have good reason for taking action against them when they harm others. They may be *held* responsible for taking drugs, even if drugs put them into a condition of diminished responsibility, since the probable consequences of drug consumption are known. In fact, the condition of diminished responsibility requires that we take especially forcible measures against drug users who harm others, because only such measures will be effective in protecting others. "If an addict tends to be as if asleep on the job, thus diminishing his efficiency, then stronger measures need to be taken—such as releasing him from that employment."

Jeffrey Reiman is not in favor of criminalizing the use of illicit drugs, since criminal penalties do more harm than good, and since denying people the freedom to consume drugs interferes with their autonomy. Autonomy has singular value since "the ability of people to shape their own lives according to their own judgments is the necessary condition of their living lives that are truly meaningful to them, lives that they can think of as their own accomplishment and thus in which they can take pride." Reiman thus shares with Narveson the liberal assumption that in a just society no one's conception of the good will be forced on any other sane adult.

However, Reiman argues that the typical form of drug addiction is immoral, a vice, and one for which the addict as well as society as a whole is responsible. Consequently, even though society should not prohibit the use of drugs, it ought to discourage it.

To show that the typical form of drug use is a vice, Reiman begins by arguing that addicts do not merely have a strong desire for drugs, contrary to Narveson's claim. Instead, their desire is typically such that it would persist even if they believed that satisfying it was contrary to their self-interest. Their addiction blocks their ability to pursue what they take to be their self-interest. Narveson's opera-lover's desire for opera contributes to her life, and she wants to retain her desire; yet she would drop her desire if she thought that it did not contribute to her life. But the drug addict's desire for drugs is not a contribution; instead, it is a misfortune, and the addict would eliminate the desire if it were possible to. Addiction is a vice in the sense that it is a disposition that undermines people's ability to govern their lives according to their rational judgments. Addictions are not impossible to overcome; the undermining effect of drugs merely weakens our ability to refuse the life of drug use. It does not completely destroy it. Hence addicts are typically morally responsible for their continued addictions, and for any actions or effects that are caused by their addictions, including their weakened ability to govern their own lives.

But addicts are not always responsible for their condition. They are responsible only when they live in reasonably favorable conditions, namely ones in which choosing a drug-free, worthwhile life is possible for them. Moreover, addiction is not always a vice. If addicts live in conditions (such as concentration camps) in which no worthwhile life is possible, taking drugs is a rational choice, not a vice, and the responsibility for their choosing the life of drugs is not their own, but rather that of whatever agency forced them to live under those unfavorable conditions. According to Reiman, many of the addicts who live in American inner cities have no options that would lead to their achieving a drug-free, worthwhile life. Given their regrettable circumstances, drug use is a rational choice, and it is other U.S. citizens, not the addicts themselves, who are responsible for those circumstances.

Addiction and Free Will

The term "addiction" has a long history, briefly summarized by Edward M. Brecher:

> In Roman Law, to be addicted meant to be bound over or delivered over to someone by a judicial sentence; thus a prisoner of war might be addicted to some nobleman or

large landowner. In sixteenth-century England, the word
had the same meaning; thus a serf might be addicted to a
master. But Shakespeare and others of his era perceived
the marked similarity between this legal form of addiction
and a man's bondage to alcoholic beverages; they therefore spoke of being addicted to alcohol .... The concepts
of addiction to opium, morphine, and heroin followed
quite naturally.[16]

Originally, then, addiction meant *enslavement*. Can we be
more precise about the nature of addiction? At one time it was
common to define addiction in terms of two physiological phenomena, *withdrawal* and *tolerance*. One suffers a withdrawal syndrome if abruptly terminating one's use of a drug results in
severe physical discomfort; one develops tolerance to a drug if
increasing doses are required to produce the same effect. But
these conditions are unsatisfying as a definition of addiction,
since they seem neither necessary nor sufficient. They are not
sufficient because people who develop tolerance for a drug and
would suffer withdrawal if they stopped using it are not always
classifiable as addicts. As Liska notes, "The terminally ill cancer
patient taking the Brompton Cocktail would not be considered a
drug addict. Nor would the fetus of an addict mother."[17] David
C. Lewis says that "pain killing opioids [including morphine and
dilaudid] are not usually addicting in the context of medical
practice," and stresses that "tolerance is not addiction. Addiction
is a chronic relapsing illness seen in only a small minority of
those who experience tolerance."[18] Lewis cites the 1992 report of
a Task Force on Pain by the Department of Health and Human
Services, which noted "the low risk (about 1 in 2,500) of becoming addicted following a hospital stay where surgery is performed," and concluded that "it is a myth that analgesics, including the strongest ones, the opioids, are commonly addicting
when used in medical practice for the treatment of pain." Still,
Lewis suggests, following the Task Force report, that fear of addiction has led to "a general underprescribing of pain medication," to the extent that "about half of all surgical patients suffer
unnecessarily from pain."[19]

Not only are withdrawal and tolerance insufficient for
addiction, they are also arguably unnecessary, at least as the
term "addiction" is currently used. Although some drugs, such

as heroin and the barbiturates, produce acute withdrawal symptoms, other drugs which are thought to be highly addicting do not. Cocaine and nicotine are two notable examples.[20] (Researchers have claimed in recent years that cocaine can produce withdrawal symptoms, but these "fluctuate and are neither constant nor severe enough to meet psychiatric criteria for major mood disorders."[21]) This has led some to suggest that a behavioral definition is preferable to a physiological one. A typical such definition is that of J. J. Jaffe: "a behavioral pattern of compulsive drug use, characterized by an overwhelming involvement with the use of a drug, the securing of its supply, and a high tendency to relapse after withdrawal."[22] A similar behavioral account of addiction is put in somewhat more vivid terms by Brecher: "An addicting drug is one that most users continue to take even though they want to stop, decide to stop, try to stop, and actually succeed in stopping for days, weeks, months, or even years. It is a drug for which men and women will prostitute themselves . . . . It is a drug which most users continue to use despite the threat of long-term imprisonment for its use—and to which they promptly return after experiencing long-term imprisonment."[23]

The metaphor of addiction as enslavement suggests that, just as slaves are not free to stop serving their masters, however much they may want to, so addicts are not free to stop using drugs, whether they want to or not. As Bakalar and Grinspoon put it, drugs are supposed to "have a mysterious power over the will that only coercive authority can cope with."[24] The first *National Drug Control Strategy* issued by the Office of National Drug Control Policy in 1989 strongly suggested this picture of addiction, describing "full-fledged addiction" as "a craving so intense that life becomes reduced to a sadly repetitive cycle of searching for drugs, using them, and searching for them some more."[25]

The question of whether addiction deprives us of freedom is of considerable philosophical interest. It is closely connected to the question of whether addiction should be thought of as a disease. Stanton Peele characterizes the disease theory of addiction as comprising the following theses: "(1) the addiction exists independently of the rest of a person's life and drives all of his or her choices; (2) it is progressive and irreversible, so that the addiction inevitably worsens unless the person seeks medical treatment or joins an AA-type support group; (3) addiction means the person is incapable of controlling his or her behavior, either in relation to the addictive object itself or—when the person is intoxicated or in pursuit of the addiction—in relation to the person's dealings with the rest of the world."[26] Alcoholics Anonymous and other twelve-step groups defend this conception of addiction, while writers such as Peele and the philosopher Herbert Fingarette[27] oppose it. The essays in this volume by Vihvelin and Scribner are directly relevant to this issue.

Vihvelin argues against some widely influential philosophical theories of the nature of free will. It seems at least possible that there are forms of addiction that result in a loss of the sort of freedom we normally enjoy; accounts of free will that make this impossible are therefore prima facie implausible. A natural way to describe the contrast between our freedom and the addict's unfreedom is to say that the desires of an ordinary agent influence action but do not compel it, while the desires of the full-fledged addict do compel action. *Hard determinism*, which holds that we are never free, rejects this distinction; according to a hard determinist, drug addicts are unfree, but they are no more unfree than anyone else, since desires always compel. On the other hand, *libertarianism*, which holds that our desires never compel us, also denies that there is a contrast between desires that do compel and those that do not. So, prima facie, both libertarianism and hard determinism seem implausible. Vihvelin sets out to offer an account of freedom according to which some desires compel while others do not.

What is the difference between desires that compel and those that do not? Vihvelin suggests that whether our desires compel us to action depends on our second-order desires—that is, on our desires about our own desires. For example, does my desire for a cigarette compel me to smoke? Maybe yes and maybe no. It compels me if I have two second-order desires, namely, first, the desire that my desire to smoke not be "effective," that is, that it not cause me to act, and second, that even if my desire to smoke does cause me to act, that it not be satisfied. The first second-order desire means that I want my desire to smoke not to lead me to act (for example, to reach for the cigarette pack), perhaps because it is outweighed by such other desires as my desire for good health; the second second-order desire means that I want it to be the case that even if my desire to smoke leads me to reach for the cigarette pack, I nevertheless do not succeed in smoking (because, for example, my friend quickly snatches the cigarette pack away before I succeed in removing a cigarette). If I have both these second-order desires, and nevertheless do find myself smoking, then we can say that my desire for a cigarette compelled my action. It was a desire I was not free to resist.[28]

Although Vihvelin's account offers a way in which the desire for drugs could be said to compel my action, she does not attempt to answer the question of how frequently or infrequently such desires do in fact compel drug users to act. Whether such desires compel "is an empirical question, and the answer will depend on the person, drug, and circumstances of action." She adds that she "would not be surprised if . . . there are *fewer*, rather than more, cases of unfree action than we think."

Phillip Scribner describes views like Vihvelin's as "affective" theories of the will, by contrast with his own "cognitive" theory. Scribner describes his own theory as a naturalized version of libertarianism, according to which our desires never compel us to act. Desires typically do not cause us to act directly; rather, their influence is a result of our considering them and deciding which ones to act on. Scribner thus agrees with Vihvelin that freedom has something to do with second-order attitudes toward our first-order desires, but disagrees with her claim that the relevant second-order attitudes are themselves desires. What happens at the second level is not just more desiring, but a process of rational reflection in which we decide, on the basis of our plans and our views of what is good, which desires we will allow to become effective in causing us to act. Since desires *never* remove our freedom, it must be the case in particular that desires that may be caused by taking drugs do not remove our freedom.

Are addicts, then, never unfree? This seems to fly in the face of conventional wisdom. But in fact it does not follow from Scribner's theory. Scribner argues in detail that drugs themselves cannot make us unfree, either by producing desires too powerful to control or by paralyzing the will. Nevertheless, he argues that there is a legitimate sense in which many drug addicts *are* unfree. They are unfree, he argues, not because of their desires but because of their beliefs: they cannot stop using drugs because they *believe*, falsely, that they cannot control the desires drugs induce. But this belief is caused, not by the use of drugs, but by the false propaganda associated with the War on Drugs. So, according to Scribner, the principal cause of the unfreedom of addicts is the War on Drugs rather than the drugs themselves! Scribner's view thus may provide a theoretical underpinning for the claim, made for example by Peele, that "we so often believe we have lost control because we are told so constantly about the danger that we will lose control, about the prevalence of loss of control, and about the signs that indicate that we have lost control."[29]

Ability-Enhancing Drugs

A number of drugs seem to hold out the promise of enhancing various of our abilities. Anabolic steroids are perhaps the best-known such drugs. Between 1975 and 1984, it was widely denied that steroids could affect athletic ability. This view was endorsed by the American College of Sports Medicine, the British Association of Sports Medicine, the American Medical Association, the Federal Drug Administration, and other bodies.[30] Indeed, the *Physician's Desk Reference* included the following note: "Warning: Anabolic steroids do not enhance athletic ability."[31] It is now clear, however, that anabolic steroids *can* "help increase muscle size and strength."[32] Unfortunately, steroids also have a number of undesirable side effects: they "may increase the risk of heart disease and produce liver toxicities, temporary changes in sex characteristics and reproductive functioning, possible psychological disorders, possible injury to tendons and ligaments, and stunted growth in children."[33] Concern over these side effects contributed to the passage of the Steroid Trafficking Act of 1990, which reclassified anabolic steroids from unregulated prescription drugs to Schedule III controlled substances.

Other drugs also offer to enhance our abilities. Stimulants, as their name suggests, can stimulate the central nervous system, and thereby enhance our abilities in certain respects, in particular by combating fatigue and increasing endurance.[34] Some would argue that our perceptual and intellectual abilities may be enhanced by the use of psychedelic drugs.[35] And recently so-called smart drugs have been claimed to "resuscitate memory, jump-start the intellect, fuel sex drive and even reverse the mental aging process."[36] Experts are skeptical about these assertions, but users make claims like this: "It's amazing. It's like tuning up your car, only it's your mind. You take the drugs, and you're firing on all eight cylinders again. Sometimes you're firing on nine."[37]

Is it morally permissible to use drugs for the purpose of enhancing our abilities? It is interesting to note that the American College of Sports Medicine, in its 1984 "Position Stand on the Use of Anabolic-Androgenic Steroids in Sports," stressed not only the adverse health effects of steroids, but also "the ethical issue," writing that "the use of anabolic-androgenic steroids by athletes is contrary to the ethical principles of athletic competition and is deplored."[38] Ethical issues were also stressed in a 1989 article in the *Journal of the American Medical Association*, which cited the address of the president of the Federal Republic of Germany, Richard von Weizsacker, to the West German National Olympic Committee: "Weizsacker said that he believes sport will be able to preserve its humanizing influence and contribute to human dignity only if it resists the pressure to use chemical or genetic manipulations."[39] Despite widespread concern over the morality of using ability-enhancing drugs, however, there seem to be few searching discussions of the issue.

W. Miller Brown offers a general perspective on the use of ability-enhancing drugs. He distinguishes between first- and second-order abilities. Second-order abilities are "learned competencies that can be acquired by a wide range of people," while first-order abilities are abilities to acquire second-order abilities. The use of ability-enhancing drugs typically affects primarily our first-order abilities. For example, the ability to hit a home run, the ability to kick a football long distances, and the ability to pole vault are all fairly specific. Drugs are unlikely to enhance these specific abilities directly, but steroids, for example, by enabling us to increase our muscle mass, may enhance our general, "first-order" ability to acquire these more specific abilities. Brown argues that our abilities are valuable both socially and intrinsically and thus that, other things being equal, their enhancement is also valuable. Education and training may enhance our abilities, and so may the use of certain drugs; there is no special reason to reject the use of drugs as a means of enhancing abilities.

Brown is well aware that there may be dangers in using drugs to enhance our abilities, and he discusses a number of these. There are prudential reasons not to use certain ability-enhancing drugs, including the risk of biological or psychological side effects, and the dangers of dependency and addiction. Moreover, if ability-enhancing drugs without dangerous side effects were widely available, we might need to change the nature of our sports and perhaps even of our work: "utopian drugs would call for utopian planning." But Brown rejects the idea that the use of drugs to enhance our abilities would be undesirable even if there were no danger of harmful consequences: we should not be swayed by arguments that such enhancement is "unnatural" or "cheap." Indeed, Brown concludes by arguing, following Kant, that we actually have a moral duty to develop our talents, and that in imaginable circumstances the best way to do this might include drug use.

Robert Simon raises some worries about the idea that we can evaluate the merits of certain sorts of drug use simply by weighing the costs and benefits of such use. (He is cautious, however, about attributing to Brown the view he is questioning.) We can weigh costs and benefits only relative to some set of preferences. But, supposing that the widespread use of some sorts of drugs would change our preferences, which set of preferences should we use? We need to be able, not only to weigh alternatives relative to some set of preferences, but also to evaluate the preferences themselves. And many will find unsatisfying the idea that the best set of preferences is simply the set that leads to the most satisfaction of preferences. (To use an example not mentioned by Simon, it may be that widespread use of depressants would greatly reduce our desires: a nation of heroin addicts might desire little other than a ready supply of further heroin, and as long as it was available, they might be quite happy. The citizens of such a nation might, on the whole, be more contented and less dissatisfied than we currently are. But many would argue that we should not value the preferences of the heroin addicts more highly than our own just because they are more easily satisfied. This is not, of course, an example of *enhancing our abilities* through drug use, but it does illustrate Simon's point that evaluating preferences seems to involve more than seeing whether they will lead to satisfied or unsatisfied lives.)

Simon and Brown both raise worries about the identity of the user of performance-enhancing drugs. Use of drugs raises the question of whether the abilities of the user really belong to the user. For example, the drug that makes Calvin compassionate, according to Simon, raises questions about whether *Calvin* is actually compassionate. Similarly, the strength of the drug-using athlete seems less his or her own than does the strength of the drug-free athlete. (This may be why athletes' use of steroids seems to many to be "cheating," even in contexts in which it is legal.) These considerations raise quite deep worries about personal identity. If the compassion induced in Calvin isn't really his, then what about the stability of the manic-depressive taking lithium? If there is something cheap about using steroids to increase one's strength, then why isn't there something cheap about advances in athletic equipment? As Simon notes, the question of whether Calvin as he is on drugs is the *real* Calvin is also related to the question whether Calvin after psychotherapy is the real Calvin.

Drugs and Pleasure

As Douglas Husak has noted, "for reasons that are deep and mysterious, many persons become apologetic and defensive about arguing in favor of a right to engage in an activity simply because it is pleasurable. Apparently the pursuit of fun is perceived to be so shallow and trivial that many persons feel obliged to find some other basis to defend their choice."[40] Nevertheless, pleasure is surely one of the main reasons people engage in drug use; as Husak observes, "interviews with users indicate that they are most likely to consume drugs on two general occasions. First, they use drugs to attempt to improve what they anticipate will be a good time. Hence drug use is frequent during parties, concerts, and sex. Second, they use drugs to attempt to make mindless and routine chores less boring. Hence drug use is frequent during house cleaning and cooking."[41] Quite dramatic claims are sometimes made for the pleasure of drug use; for example, James S. Lee wrote in 1939 that "all these narcotic drugs, which are commonly known as Dangerous Drugs, are really a gift of God to mankind. Instead of them doing him harm, they should really be the means of preserving his health, and making his life a state of continual happiness."[42] But even Lee conceded that drug use can be dangerous: "The life of a drug taker can be a happy one, far surpassing any other; or it can be one of suffering and misery; it depends on the user's knowledge."[43]

In her contribution to this volume, Sheridan Hough offers a qualified defense of using drugs for pleasure. Hough argues against the common view that drug-induced pleasures are somehow worse than other kinds of pleasures. She agrees that the immoderate use of drugs is a bad thing, but suggests that in this respect drug use is no different from other pleasurable activities. (It is interesting to ask whether drug use is more likely to be immoderate than other pleasurable activities. Certainly the common picture of the drug user is a picture of someone very heavily involved indeed. But in fact statistical evidence suggests that few drug users are heavy users. It appears that perhaps 10 percent of occasional users of such illicit drugs as cocaine and heroin qualify as "addicts," about the same percentage as the percentage of alcohol users who are alcoholics, and far less than the percentage of nicotine users who are heavy users.[44]) Drawing on Aristotle, she stresses that in general, we pursue pleasant activities rather than the experiences they lead to, and suggests that excessive use may be linked with pursuing the sensation caused by a drug rather than pursuing the activity of using the drug in a certain context. She suggests that drugs may be useful both instrumentally (e.g. drinking coffee to sharpen one's faculties) and recreationally, as "a diversion from work and socializing, not an enhancement of these activities." But she insists that "drugs as either instrument or diversion should hold a subordinate role in a person's life, and their pursuit should be moderate."

Rem Edwards indicates considerable agreement with Hough, but notes that his "judgment call is that drug use is much riskier than Dr. Hough seems to think." Unlike many critics of drug use, Edwards does not think there is anything morally suspicious about pleasure: "Happiness consists of pleasures of many varieties sustained over periods of time; and happiness is a very good thing." But he suggests that in general, drugs, whether licit or illicit, are not good sources of pleasure. Moderate drug use might be acceptable, but it is extremely difficult and sometimes impossible to achieve.

Edwards offers a list of explicit "criteria for identifying unacceptable hedonic drugs," or, perhaps more accurately, of unacceptable hedonic *uses* of drugs. If one's use of a drug would satisfy any one of the criteria, that is a "presumptive reason" not to engage in such use. The criteria are (in somewhat abbreviated form): that over the long run, the pain of such use will outweigh the pleasure; that the use is harmful to the user's rationality, to his or her autonomy, or to his or her "self-knowledge, self-respect, and positive self-valuation"; that the drug use will have harmful physical, psychological, or social effects on the user; that it is expensive; and that it will lead to harm to others. Edwards suggests that most drug use in fact satisfies many of these criteria.

Legalizing Drugs in the United States

The topic of legalizing or decriminalizing drugs has been increasingly widely discussed over the last several years, especially since 1988, which saw a number of highly visible defenses of legalization: an essay in the *New York Times* by David Boaz,[45] the executive vice president of the Cato Institute; an article by Kurt Schmoke, the mayor of Baltimore, in the *Washington Post*;[46]

essays by Ethan Nadelmann in the wide-circulation journals *Foreign Policy*[47] and *The Public Interest*,[48] and a number of opinion pieces in newspapers and magazines. Nineteen eighty-eight also saw two days of hearings on legalization before the House Select Committee on Narcotics Abuse and Control. Some sense of the current political feasibility of legalization may be gleaned by a look at the opening statements made during those hearings by the members of the Committee. Member after member denounced the idea of legalization; many objected even to having hearings on the issue. Lawrence Coughlin: "Having a hearing on legalization could send a wrong message to America's young people."[49] Michael Oxley: "The idea of legalization should not even be dignified with a two–day hearing by the committee . . . . My hope for an outcome to the hearings is that the book on legalization will be closed once and for all."[50] Tom Lewis: "It is contradictory that those committed to fighting drugs have agreed to give a hearing to the legalization issue."[51] Carroll Hubbard, Jr.: "I hope that the Congress will be able to lead the public and our government away from legalization."[52] And so on. The Report of the Committee includes a list of fourteen "Findings," of which the final one is: "We have not yet begun to fight the war [against drugs]. Consequently, legalization should not be considered an alternative."[53]

The years since 1988 seem to have brought no change in the climate of opposition to legalization. When in December of 1993 Dr. Joycelyn Elders, the Surgeon General, suggested that legalization was worthy of study, a number of members of Congress called for her resignation, and President Clinton's spokeswoman reported that "the President is firmly against legalizing drugs, and he is not inclined in this case to even study the issue" (*New York Times*, December 8, 1993, p. A11).

The contributors to this volume defend a variety of attitudes toward the war on drugs. All but one of those who evaluate the War on Drugs within the United States want to see it drastically scaled back or even completely stopped. The exception is James Van Wert, formerly Controller-Executive Director of the Bureau of International Narcotics Matters, Department of State, who offers a few words in defense of the domestic war before going on to argue at length in favor of the effort to stem the flow of drugs from other nations.

The most extreme position is that taken by Walter Block. We already saw Jan Narveson and Jeffrey Reiman offer brief defenses of the legalization of drugs (though the latter then argued that becoming addicted to drugs which undermine our autonomy is immoral). Arguing on libertarian grounds, Block advances a case for legalizing all drugs. Adults in the United States should be able to consume and sell any drugs, according to Block, including such drugs as heroin and cocaine.

Block is prepared to concede that the drugs he wants legalized are harmful to the health of people who use them, but he does not think that their harmfulness is grounds for banning their use. Behavior that is harmful to others is what should be discouraged by the law. Moreover, like other authors, including Nathanson, Block notes that banning such drugs as cocaine but not alcohol makes the law inconsistent: alcohol and tobacco contribute to the deaths of many people, but are legal, and almost no one proposes to ban their consumption.

Block also concedes that addictive drugs harm people other than their consumers, but he says that such harm occurs only in states that institute "socialized medicine" in which everyone is required to pay for maintaining the health of others. In such an arrangement, cigarette smoking and heroin use cause health problems for which others must pay, but instead of banning drug use we ought to maintain a free market in medicine and medical insurance.

He also suggests that the ban on addictive drugs worsens criminal behavior. The ban makes trafficking in drugs risky and profitable and hence attractive to criminals. It also converts ordinary farmers and transporters into criminals, and makes it difficult for addicts to find legitimate ways to come up with the money necessary to pay the high prices charged for drugs. Even if addictive drugs turned people into crazed, dangerous criminals (which is not the case), they should still be legal. Such people should be subject to criminal penalties for what they (threaten to) do to others, not for consuming drugs.

As to the concern that legalizing drugs would lead to widespread use, Block first denies that use would increase dramatically, then renews his plea for legalization, since even when a great number of people use drugs, they are doing so voluntarily. Meanwhile, legalization would have its advantages: there would be a decrease in crime; an improvement in people's health, partly because money spent fighting narcotics usage could be spent helping with the medical costs of curing people who are addicted; and greater protection of our civil liberties, since police officers would no longer be tempted to "ride roughshod over civil liberties in a way that occurs with regard to few if any other crimes."

It should be noted that Block's essay defends a drug policy at the opposite extreme from the current policy of completely prohibiting "illicit" drugs. Various intermediate policies are possible. Indeed, the literature on legalization has in recent years begun to articulate a wider range of alternatives than simply complete prohibition and blanket legalization. Mark A. R. Kleiman, for example, has defended such a middle ground in his aptly titled essay "Neither Prohibition Nor Legalization: Grudging Toleration in Drug Control Policy."[54] Similarly, Ethan Nadelmann has recently claimed that the term "legalization," although useful for some purposes, "exacted a stiff price with its implication that the only alternative to current policies was something resembling current US policies with respect to alcohol and tobacco. Few of those publicly associated with legalization in fact advocated such an alternative, but the misimpression has stuck in the public mind."[55] In this volume, Bonnie Steinbock defends such an intermediate position.

Steinbock raises doubts about Block's libertarian defense of legalization, and in the process implicitly challenges the defenses of both Narveson and Reiman as well. Steinbock agrees that the war on drugs has failed and that if currently illicit drugs were legalized, drug crimes would decrease. She also agrees with Narveson, Reiman and Block that banning drugs restricts people's freedom to choose how to design their own lives. But she argues that freedom is not the only value that should be protected in a just state. There is also the well-being of people to promote, including the well-being both of the consumers of drugs and of those who are adversely affected by the behavior of drug consumers, especially children harmed by people caring for them. Crack causes great harm to the children of women who ingest it during pregnancy, and such children are especially subject to child abuse, mainly in the form of neglect. Treating the ailments of crack babies is also extremely expensive: about $90,000 each for a national total of about $2.5 billion.[56]

It is a fundamental principle in the liberal tradition, traceable to Kant and Mill, that in a just society, no one ought to impose a conception of the good on others, whether privately or through the law of the land. Insofar as they do not affect others, people should be free to design their lives according to any conception of the good they choose. Narveson, Reiman and Block all appeal to versions of this principle in order to defend legalization. On Block's version, we own our bodies and so should be free to do anything to them we wish. Narveson's version has it that we own our lives and should be free to do with them what we wish. Reiman agrees that we own our lives, and adds that we may own our lives only if we are free to design and govern them as we see fit—even if that means falling into lifestyles that undermine our very capacity to govern our lives. But Steinbock thinks that the liberal principle is not incompatible with various forms of paternalism such as bans on certain drugs. She suggests that, compatibly with the liberal principle, society may act in defense of the common good defined "in terms of what Rawls calls 'primary goods': 'things which it is supposed a rational man wants whatever else he wants.'" Since primary goods are merely means to ends, acting so as to improve people's holdings of primary goods does not impose upon them any particular conception of the good.

Health is one primary good, she says, and it is important to promote health and other common goods even if doing so requires minimally intrusive sacrifices of individual liberty. She advocates a "public health approach" toward drugs, which "balances the values of liberty and autonomy against the values of health and safety." Her approach involves educating the public about the dangers and benefits of legal and illegal drugs, regulating such matters as the hours of sale of liquor, treating addicts rather than punishing them, and possibly legalizing comparatively harmless drugs such as marijuana.

Like Steinbock, Burton Leiser claims that restricting drug use is not incompatible with the liberal interest in preserving autonomy. The freedom to take drugs is not necessary if people are to be autonomous individuals. Quite the contrary: "drugs lead to abbreviated lives, to stupefaction, and in many cases, to an incessant search for more and better ways of gratifying the addict's perpetual need for the pleasure associated with the ingestion of her drug of choice." Leiser also echoes Steinbock's concern about the children who are affected by the drugs taken by their mothers. However, Leiser wants drugs legalized anyway. The concern about such children should be handled as follows:

> Introduce legislation creating a presumption that any woman who has used psychoactive drugs during her pregnancy is unfit. Such a presumption could be used to terminate the mother's parental rights. At the same time, provide facilities to which pregnant women might resort for treatment during and after pregnancy. Pregnant women who are known to be using such drugs and are unwilling to commit themselves should be subject to involuntary commitment to protect their unborn children.

Drugs and Punishment

Obviously there is a close link between the issue of legalization and the issue of whether drug users and sellers should be punished for their activities. However, opponents of legalization need not advocate punishing the consumers of addictive drugs as criminals. As Stephen Nathanson points out, opponents of legalization could argue that drug users should be rehabilitated, not punished.

To decide which users should be punished, Nathanson applies retributivist and utilitarian theories of punishment. Retributivists say that we should punish only those who deserve to be punished, and measure the degree of punishment deserved in terms of the harm done, the intention of the agent, and the difficulty of avoiding the proscribed act. However, typically drug use does not harm others, typically the user does not have malicious intent, and typically it would be very difficult for an addict to refrain. So the retributivist argument for punishing drug users is weak. The retributivist argument for punishing drug *dealers* fares no better: the seller is not really harming the buyer, since typically the former does not force the latter to buy or use drugs.

A more plausible justification for punishing drug use is utilitarian and paternalistic: (the threat of) punishment is to prevent people from doing something that harms them. Nathanson's response to this paternalistic argument is as follows: it makes sense to ban drug use only if there is a reasonable way to enforce the laws we adopt. However, to deter an addict, the punishment will probably have to be so severe that we will be making the addict worse off than she would be if we had permitted her to use drugs. Since the point of the ban was to minimize the suffering of potential drug users, it would make no sense to punish a drug user that severely. Paternalistic laws under utilitarianism "must not be so severe that they actually worsen the condition of users beyond what it would have been if they had been permitted to use drugs." In general, punishment is justifiable to a utilitarian only if it prevents the harms of drug use "without producing worse side effects." But it is unlikely that there are penalties that are severe enough to deter drug use without worsening the situations of users. Nathanson admits that punishments that worsen the situations of users might still be justified on the grounds that the extreme suffering of punished users will deter others from using drugs. His response is that "if punishment fails to have these good effects, then the suffering of those who are punished brings down the overall level of well-being in society and is therefore wrong. Many people have reached the conclusion that that is our situation."

Nathanson is skeptical about the utility of punishing drug sellers as well. It is entirely possible that punishing sellers will simply leave business to other sellers given the lucrativeness of the drug market.

Burton Leiser, who ends up favoring the legalization of drugs, nevertheless offers responses to some of Nathanson's arguments against punishing drug-related criminal offenses. One response is to Nathanson's argument against punishing drug dealers. According to Leiser, drug sellers *do* harm drug consumers. That sellers do not intend to harm consumers is beside the point, since sellers must be held accountable for the likely (hence foreseeable) consequences of their actions.

Should Mandatory Drug Testing Be Legal?

Whether we are in favor of legalization or not, we might favor the legality of mandatory drug testing. If we are against legalization, testing might be defended as a means of excluding criminals from the job force. But mandatory testing may be legitimate even if drugs are legal, for it could be used to stop employees from causing disasters that might occur if they work under the influence of drugs.

Hugh LaFollette notes that testing for drug use is entirely consistent with existing employment law and that it is constitutional in both the public and the private sectors. Testing does not violate the Fourth Amendment (concerning illegal searches) since it is not done by governmental agencies and the results are not shown to governmental agencies. Moreover, employees are warned about the tests when they accept employment.

However, mandatory testing may violate the First Amendment protection of privacy, according to LaFollette. His suggestion is that "if a belief or activity is irrelevant to job performance, it is none of the employer's business," so that only if drug use is relevant to job performance may an employer seek information concerning an employee's use of drugs. This does not mean, however, that the employer may do more than *ask* about drug use, and fire employees who admit to using drugs. To perform mandatory testing of employees, two conditions must be met: use must be "of substantial and direct risk to others," and testing must be "a reliable and relatively unintrusive way of limiting use." LaFollette thinks that his criteria for the legitimacy of testing may be met in certain actual cases, such as the testing of airline pilots. But typically they will not be met. Automakers, bridge builders, construction workers, etc., could harm others substantially if they misperform, whether under the influence of drugs or not, but "any harm which might occur, although serious, is not immediate in the sense required." Their errors should be detected through routine inspections of their work, not through intrusive drug testing.

Daniel Shapiro argues that, with only one exception, it is not possible to justify mandatory drug testing. The exception Shapiro allows is "for-cause" testing in connection with dangerous jobs. "For-cause" testing is testing "after an accident, or when there is good evidence of impaired performance or suspicious behavior on the job." Some of Shapiro's objections to more extensive drug testing are these: First, drug testing is unnecessary. To impair job performance, the level of drugs in one's bloodstream must be high enough that the impairment can be detected without blood or urine sampling. But then motor-skill testing will do the trick. Second, drug testing is unreliable. "The correlation between the amount of drugs in one's urine and impairment is very poor." (Blood tests for alcohol intoxication are reliable, but requiring them is unjustifiable since intoxication can be detected without such tests.) Third, it is possible that mandated drug testing might be abused. There would be less abuse if the decision to test were left to businesses rather than to legislators, especially since legislators will probably test for the presence of illegal drugs, which is unfair since legal ones might impair job performance as well.

Can we justify testing on grounds other than that testing prevents serious and immediate harm to people outside the company? There are three other possible justifications: (1) we must prevent all serious harm to others, even if it is not immediate, and even if they are inside the company; (2) we must prevent harm to the users themselves, and (3) we must prevent immoral behavior. Shapiro argues that none of these justifications work. A key point is that only chronic, uncontrolled use of drugs should concern us (since only chronic, uncontrolled use significantly reduces people's productivity or carefulness), but drug tests are not good at detecting such patterns. "A positive result of a drug test does not distinguish between casual or controlled use on the one hand and chronic or uncontrolled use on the other." Moreover, it is possible to detect such a pattern without drug tests.

Drugs and Foreign Policy

In "International Narcotics Control," the final selection in the book, James Van Wert describes the United States' current international drug-control policy and sketches some of the events that shaped its development. He also makes some suggestions about future policy.

According to Van Wert, U.S. policy is not one of unilateral intervention into the internal affairs of other nations. Intervention, Van Wert suggests, could not be defended on either moral or legal grounds. However, U.S. policy makers do assume that other nations can be held responsible for taking steps to reduce the supply of illicit drugs that originate from or pass through their territory. After all, there are international agreements in the form of United Nations conventions that suggest as much, such as the 1961 Convention against drug abuse and the 1988 Convention against drug abuse and trafficking. U.S. policymakers expect other nations to live up to these agreements, and are willing to apply pressure that stops short of intervention in order to pressure other nations into compliance. The pressure involves such practices as withholding foreign aid from nations that do not take (what the U.S. government considers to be) effective steps to decrease illicit drug activity in their territory. The policy is to bring about an international effort to reduce the availability of illicit drugs.

Van Wert thinks that the United States and other nations can take effective steps to foster an international cooperative effort to reduce drug trafficking, and that it is a good idea to do so. It is a good idea for the United States, he says, because the policy will decrease the availability of illicit drugs in the United States, which in turn will reduce drug-related crime. It is a good idea for other nations, too: countries other than the United States could reduce the supply of illicit drugs to their own consumer populations, and countries that supply illicit drugs could wean their economies from dependence on trafficking. Most of the steps Van Wert recommends are designed to help countries that are sources for illicit drugs to stem the flow of drugs and to redirect their economies. The steps would include more crop control, drug interdiction, trafficker immobilization efforts, area development assistance and income replacement. But the United States should also do more domestically to control the drug problem: it should rely more heavily on "education to reduce domestic demand."[57]

Curtis Brown
Steven Luper-Foy

NOTES

1. Joseph B. Treaster, "20 Years of War on Drugs, and No Victory Yet," *New York Times*, Sunday, June 14, 1992, cited by Steinbock in this volume.

2. Hearing Before the Select Committee on Narcotics Abuse and Control, House of Representatives, One Hundred Second Congress, Second Session, February 5, 1992 (Washington: U.S. Government Printing Office, 1992), p. 6.

3. Hearing Before the Select Committee on Narcotics Abuse and Control, February 5, 1992, p. 7.

4. Charles B. Rangel, Chairman, House Select Committee on Narcotics Abuse and Control, *On the Edge of the American Dream: A Social and Economic Profile in 1992* (Washington: U.S. Government Printing Office, 1992), p. 1.

5. United States General Accounting Office, "Justice Issues" (Report No. GAO/OCG-93-23TR), December 1992.

6. Some of the relevant data are summarized in Steven Jonas, "The U.S. Drug Problem and the U.S. Drug Culture: A Public Health Solution," in James A. Inciardi, ed., *The Drug Legalization Debate* (Newbury Park, CA: Sage Publications, 1991), pp. 161–82.

7. Ken Liska, *Drugs and the Human Body*, Second Edition (New York: Macmillan, 1986), p. 255.

8. Liska, p. 255.

9. Liska, p. 245.

10. Irving Sloan, *Alcohol and Drug Abuse and the Law* (Dobbs Ferry, New York: Oceana Publications, Inc., 1980), p. 36.

11. Controlled Substances Act, Section 802, Definition 17.

12. Sloan, *Alcohol and Drug Abuse and the Law*, p. 37.

13. The following criticisms are developed by Douglas N. Husak, *Drugs and Rights* (Cambridge, UK: Cambridge University Press, 1992).

14. Sloan, *Alcohol and Drug Abuse*, pp. 7–8.

15. Sloan, *Alcohol and Drug Abuse*, p. 10.

16. Edward M. Brecher and the Editors of Consumer Reports, *Licit and Illicit Drugs: The Consumers Union Report on Narcotics, Stimulants, Depressants, Inhalants, Hallucinogens, and Marijuana—including Caffeine, Nicotine, and Alcohol* (Boston: Little, Brown, & Co., 1972).

17. Liska, p. 8.

18. David C. Lewis, "Medical and Health Perspectives on a Failing US Drug Policy," *Daedalus* 121 (1992): 165–94, at p. 174.

19. Lewis, p. 175.

20. Liska, p. 7.

21. Frank Gavin and Everett Ellinwood, "Cocaine and Other Stimulants: Action, Abuse, and Treatment," *New England Journal of Medicine* 318 (1988): 1173, 1176; cited in Husak, p. 115.

22. Cited in Liska, p. 7.

23. Brecher, p. 84. Compare also the related but vaguer and milder definition of "psychoactive substance dependence" by the American Psychiatric Association: "a cluster of cognitive, behavioral, and physiologic symptoms that indicate that the person has impaired control of psychoactive substances use." American Psychiatric Association, *Diagnostic and Statistical Manual of Mental Disorders* (Washington, D.C.: American Psychiatric Association, 1987), p. 166; cited in Franklin E. Zimring and Gordon Hawkins, *The Search for Rational Drug Control* (Cambridge: Cambridge University Press, 1992), p. 29.

24. Lester Grinspoon and James Bakalar, *Cocaine: A Drug and Its Social Evolution* (New York: Basic Books, 1976), p. 187, as cited in Zimring and Hawkins, p. 28.

25. Cited in Zimring and Hawkins, p. 28.

26. Stanton Peele, *Diseasing of America: Addiction Treatment Out of Control* (Lexington, Massachusetts: D. C. Heath & Co., 1989), p. 3.

27. Herbert Fingarette, *Heavy Drinking: The Myth of Alcoholism as a Disease* (Berkeley: University of California Press, 1988).

28. Note that this is only a sufficient, not a necessary, condition of being compelled by one's desires. On Vihvelin's account, one is also

compelled if, although one does not have the relevant second-order desires, one would have acted on one's first-order desire even if one *had* had the second-order desires.

29. Peele, p. 256.

30. William N. Taylor, *Macho Medicine: A History of the Anabolic Steroid Epidemic* (Jefferson, NC: McFarland and Company, 1991), p. 29.

31. Taylor, p. 29.

32. Richard H. Strauss, "Anabolic Steroids," in Richard H. Strauss, ed., *Drugs and Performance in Sports* (Philadelphia: W. B. Saunders, 1987), p. 61. Taylor cites a good deal of evidence for this conclusion in *Macho Medicine*.

33. United States General Accounting Office, *Drug Misuse: Anabolic Steroids and Human Growth Hormone*, August 1989, p. 18 (reproduced as Appendix III of Taylor, *Macho Medicine*).

34. See e.g. John A. Lombardo, "Stimulants," in Strauss, ed., *Drugs and Performance in Sports*, pp. 69–85.

35. An interesting collection of pre-1960 pieces in this vein is John Strasbaugh and Donald Blaise, ed., *The Drug User: Documents 1840–1960* (New York: Blast Books, 1991).

36. Andrew Purvis, "Ultra Think Fast," *Time*, June 8, 1992, p. 80. An inventory of "smart drugs" and the claims made for them may be found in Ward Dean and John Morgenthaler, *Smart Drugs and Nutrients: How to Improve Your Memory and Increase Your Intelligence Using the Latest Discoveries in Neuroscience* (Santa Cruz, CA: B&J Publications, 1990).

37. Purvis, p. 80.

38. American College of Sports Medicine, "Position Stand on the Use of Anabolic-Androgenic Steroids in Sports," reprinted in Strauss, ed., *Drugs and Performance in Sports*, pp. 199–209, at p. 205.

39. Virginia S. Cowart, "Ethical, as Well as Physiological, Questions Continue to Arise Over Athletes' Steroid Abuse," *Journal of the American Medical Association* 261 (1989): 3362–3, 3367, at 3363.

40. Douglas Husak, *Drugs and Rights* (Cambridge: Cambridge University Press, 1992), p. 46.

41. Husak, pp. 44–45.

42. James S. Lee, *The Underworld of the East*, as reprinted in Strasbaugh and Blaise, *The Drug User*, pp. 1–35, at p. 9.

43. Lee, in Strasbaugh and Blaise, p. 2.

44. The statistical evidence is reviewed in Husak, *Drugs and Rights*, pp. 124–125.

45. The *New York Times*, March 17, 1988; reprinted in David Boaz, ed., *The Crisis in Drug Prohibition* (Washington, D.C.: Cato Institute, 1990), pp. 98–100.

46. Reprinted in Boaz, *The Crisis in Drug Prohibition*, pp. 9–12.

47. Ethan A. Nadelmann, "U.S. Drug Policy: A Bad Export," *Foreign Policy* 70 (Spring 1988): 1–39.

48. Ethan A. Nadelmann, "The Case for Legalization," *The Public Interest* 92 (Summer 1988): 3–31; reprinted in Boaz.

49. House Select Committee on Narcotics Abuse and Control, *Legalization of Illicit Drugs: Impact and Feasibility (A Review of Recent Hearings)* (Washington, D.C.: United States Government Printing Office, 1989), p. 5.

50. *Legalization of Illicit Drugs*, p. 9.

51. *Legalization of Illicit Drugs*, p. 9.

52. *Legalization of Illicit Drugs*, p. 10.

53. *Legalization of Illicit Drugs*, p. 5.

54. Mark A. R. Kleiman, "Neither Prohibition Nor Legalization: Grudging Toleration in Drug Control Policy," *Daedalus* 121 no. 3 (Summer 1992): 53–83; see also Kleiman, *Against Excess: Drug Policy for Results* (New York: Basic Books, 1992).

55. Ethan Nadelmann, "Thinking Seriously About Alternatives to Drug Prohibition," *Daedalus* 121 no. 3 (Summer 1992): 85–133, at p. 86. Nadelmann suggests that a better question than "To legalize or not to legalize?" is: "What . . . are the best means to regulate the production, distribution, and consumption of the great variety of psychoactive substances available today and in the foreseeable future?"

56. Howard French, "New York Sees Rise in Babies Hurt by Drugs," *New York Times*, October 18, 1989, cited by Steinbock, this volume. There are no reliable figures on the number of drug-exposed infants, or on the costs of treating them. For detailed discussion of the available figures, see the General Accounting Office report "Drug-Exposed Infants: A Generation at Risk" (Report No. GAO/HRD-90–138), June 1990. For some reservations about the evidence for effects of prenatal cocaine exposure on child growth and development, see Linda C. Mayes, et al., "The Problem of Prenatal Cocaine Exposure: A Rush to Judgment," *Journal of the American Medical Association* 267 (1992): 406–8.

57. We are indebted to Conry Davidson and James Rather for their assistance with the research for this Introduction.

Responsibility

Drugs and Responsibility

Jan Narveson

People who want drugs often want them very badly, and those taking drugs frequently and regularly are said to be "addicted" to them. For both reasons, the question arises whether they are responsible for their behavior, and more importantly whether they can be held responsible for actions committed under the influence either of the drugs themselves, or of their putatively addictive desires for them. People who committed heinous crimes under such influence may say that they "couldn't help it." Does that get them off? Persons with responsibilities at various tasks may, under the influence of drugs, be asleep or dulled to the point where they cannot perform those tasks. If their reason for taking the drugs that led to this was that they were unable to resist doing so, does that excuse them, by reason of non-responsibility? What kind of measures to control such phenomena are we, in turn, justified in taking? I shall propose answers to these important questions—answers in some respects, perhaps, rather at variance with current beliefs and practices. Doing so will require some consideration of the notions of responsibility and of freedom.

Freedom of the Will and Freedom of Action

Responsibility is thought to require freedom in some sense whose analysis has proved troublesome. The fact that one was not free to do a thing is held to diminish or remove responsibility for not doing it; and so, that one was not free not to do it, e.g. by being compelled, diminishes or removes responsibility for doing it. Do drugs remove freedom in the relevant sense? What in fact is the "relevant sense?" That is our main question here.

John Stuart Mill opened his *Essay on Liberty* by asserting that his concern was not with the metaphysical problem of freedom of the will but rather with the moral and social question of liberty of action, thought and pursuits.[1] It is, I think, a crucially important question how these are related, or whether indeed they can be satisfactorily distinguished. The proponent of liberty as a moral or political principle has a view about what we may or should *let* people do. We should, he says, allow people to do as they wish; and what we should forbid is only interference with that liberty, interference brought about by the actions of others. The "metaphysical question of free will," on the other hand, concerns choice and volition. Are my actions due to causes over which I have no control?

The distinction here, I think, is between two general sorts of sources of possible interference with what we might want to do: those due to the actions of our fellows, and those due to any other hindrances, especially to "internal" ones, psychological or physiological. The "metaphysical" question arises when we consider that whatever we do, we apparently "could not do otherwise" if our action is literally caused *at all*. Positing special kinds of "causes" that are not themselves subject to further causality seems mere grasping at straws. Positing probabilistic causality differs from such desperate maneuvers only in muddying the waters. We can be responsible for taking chances, of course; but what could it mean to say that we are responsible only if our decisions are due at least partly to chance? Yet if we could never do otherwise than we do, given identical conditions, then how can we be said ever to be free? Such has been the conundrum of metaphysical "freedom of the will."

But when we turn to the social context, it is clear enough that sometimes the reason we could not do something we might have liked to do is that somebody locked us up or otherwise got in the way, while in other cases no such reason is in sight. In those cases, my fellows may have done nothing at all to constrain my choice at the time of acting. But this apparently easy distinction is, at least on first consideration, rather obscured when we consider that perhaps the previous actions of various other people have somehow formed my choice mechanisms in ways that effectively assured that I would do whatever I now do, even so. But if one takes this line, there is a danger of relapsing into the metaphysical quagmire scouted before. *All* actions, one may reasonably suppose, are some sort of resultant of ambient social and other conditions if one includes in the ambit of relevant causes those conditions that determined that one would choose a given option, in cases where there is no evident obstacle to doing whatever one chooses from among several options.

Now, to suppose that some factor's presence in a given case of action or inaction creates an *excuse* or even a *justification* for that action is to take that factor as a *reason for treating* the subject otherwise than one would if one supposed the excusing or justifying factor absent. We normally think that some factors excuse and some do not. If Jones collided with Martha because he fell down stairs after tripping on the rug, then he cannot be blamed for it; but if he deliberately flings himself upon her, then he is guilty of assault, unless the action is for other reasons justified. In the one case, people will say, he "couldn't help it," in the other he "could." But the free-will question is thought to raise doubts about this very distinction.

Of course, there is in any case a puzzle—to put it mildly—about the alleged "metaphysical" sort of freedom. It was customary to oppose freedom to determinism. But if determinism is a matter of having causes—*any* causes—then "freedom" would on this pairing have to be a matter of having *no* causes. Now, this may or may not be intelligible in itself (I doubt it); but even if it is, the further question is raised, why it should be supposed that I am "free" if my decisions have no intelligible relation to previous events? It seems that the opposite of determinism would then be *randomness*; and it is surely strange that I should be thought "free" if I act at random in relation to any and all previous events. It is surely far more sensible to suppose that what we mean by "freedom" in the "metaphysical" sense is essentially that one is free if one acts from one's own desires, interests, and deliberations, the ones that one actually identifies with, from wherever these may ultimately have sprung. That the Afghan acts differently than an Albertan certainly argues causal influence, but it does not show *unfreedom*.

Our question is responsibility, however, and not freedom; or rather, it is freedom only in a sense of "freedom" in which freedom has a clear relation to responsibility. If we directly address the question of the relevance of the supposed analysis to responsibility, we must be struck by the result. Those who act literally at random are, we would have to conclude, *ir*responsible, and not *more* responsible than the rest of us.

Is the relation between these two questions one of identity, then? Is lack of "metaphysical" freedom an *excusing* factor? I think not. We may reasonably act in regard to our fellows on the basis of certain causative or influencing factors and not on the basis of others, *whether or not* "metaphysical freedom" obtains. If you are "compelled" by your intense hatred of me to attack me with intent to kill, I may properly ward off your onslaught by strong measures, even fatal ones, and this whether or not you could help it; and you in turn may be compelled to remain in locked quarters as a result. But if your car is slammed into by another one and in consequence runs me down, I have no quarrel with you. Or again: if you accost me on a false bit of information, which would certainly have justified you in doing so if it had been true, then I can't blame you unless you were culpably in error. And so on. These distinctions matter, whether or not we say that "in the end" your action was wholly determined by causes over which you had no control. (In the end, as Lord Keynes famously observed, we are all dead!)

Why do the distinctions matter, then? They matter because *some* of the "uncontrollable" actions you may perform do not collide with my pursuit of my interests, while others do. We will be concerned to defend ourselves against threatened damage to them, whether those threats stem from the actions of rational and autonomous agents or from those of nonrational or irrational ones. The *means* of defense may be different, but the reason is basically the same.

But the means in question are indeed different. Some conditions of persons are such that their behavior isn't susceptible to influence by what we (rightly) call "rational" means. Advancing considerations on the basis of which the agent may be moved to alter his course of action in desired ways is a useful method of approach if he is in the sort of state that makes him responsive to such; but not if he isn't. In the latter case, protection from his anticipated actions may require stronger measures. Two different kinds of "stronger measures," especially, can be employed, typified by the Prison and the Hospital.

To this point, then, I have suggested that questions of moral responsibility, and thus of freedom insofar as we speak not of "metaphysical" freedom but simply of actions from choice, purpose, and intention rather than external causes or internal causes that are not themselves matters of choice, purpose or intention, are practical questions, and it is their practical bearing on our own courses of action that makes them important. A major such bearing is exemplified in the choice of prisons vs. hospitals, in attempting to deal with persons affected by drugs.

Prisons and Hospitals

Suppose Jones attacks me and is found to be guilty of a crime in so doing; he is then sent to prison. But if he is instead found criminally insane, he is not likely to be set free, but rather to be sent to a psychiatric institution for such individuals. Either way I am protected, even though it may look and feel very different to the assailant. But what I want is that people not assault me, and this end may well be secured about as effectively in the one case as in the other.

What is the difference between them? Perhaps this: The prison is a sort of supplementary appeal to reason. We attach a certain price to the performance of certain actions, and those caught engaging in them have gambled and lost. The prospect of prison offers a rational disincentive, but its force as such a disincentive is lost if we do not in fact incarcerate those who fall afoul of reasonable requirements. The hospital, on the other hand, is not something we can intentionally choose to avoid. The actions that get one into the hospital are not the result of rational deliberations, it is supposed; one cannot act with a view to staying out of a psychiatric hospital, at least insofar as confinement there is for the purpose of treating the condition of involuntary criminal behavior. Once ensnared in the syndrome that the hospital personnel are interested in treating, we are not responsive to argument. We act in the absence of contact with reasons, in the sense that *they* weren't what got us into the pattern of motions about which others are reasonably concerned.

Of course, we do not *want* to be put into either of those places. But I am willing to concede to others a right that they put me in one of them should I behave in certain ways toward them—ways that I certainly would want to constitute ground for putting others there if that is necessary to protect me from them. We protect others by refraining from doing such things insofar as we can keep ourselves in line. We also protect ourselves by insisting that guilt or clear inability to control oneself in respect of such dangerous behaviors as assault be a necessary condition for incarceration. This is an excellent arrangement for all concerned, for it leaves us maximally free to live the sort of lives we think best.

Paternalism

There are those who think, however, that law and morals ought to do much more than protect us from each other's harmful interventions. There are two different, though related, lines of argument here. One is that drugs tend to make people nonproductive, whether or not they make them criminal. On this line, if we allow people to spend their lives on dope, then we deprive ourselves of the benefits of the work they might otherwise have performed. The other line has it that law and morals ought also to be employed in protecting people from *themselves*—to be employed in improving *their* lives. So those who accept this line of thought will make the consumption of drugs illegal even when it has no connection with crimes against others. This is what is known as paternalism.

Regarding the first, there is a clear and, I think, decisive reply: Slavery is not all right. And if it isn't, then the fact that someone might, by his or her choice of a way of life, do less for us than we might like is surely no justification for cracking down on them with threats of jail and the like.

The second is more interesting. There are, actually, two closely related ideas involved in the suggestion that taking drugs will be bad for the person who does so. (1) The outrightly paternalistic motive is that those who think this way want to help people live better lives *by preventing them from being able to live worse ones*, and they think, plausibly enough, that the life of the drug taker is a bad one. (2) But the other might be thought not to be paternalistic at all, or at least not at the same level. There is a belief that drugs involve diminution or loss of *autonomy*. This might be thought equivalent to loss of *freedom*; and thus it might be thought that we promote freedom by preventing drug use, and not just by measures called for by the preceding considerations of interpersonal protection. So the fight against drugs is hitched to a liberal moral outlook via the appeal to autonomy. Each of these important lines of thought calls for some comment.

(1) The first raises a very fundamental issue in moral theory. Is there a view of the good whose credentials are so powerful that they can justify us in overriding the differing views of individuals about their own lives when they have such views? During the heyday of Christianity in Europe and North America, enormous numbers of people were killed, imprisoned, and otherwise generally maltreated in the name of religion. Inquisitors burned heretics at the stake "for their own good"; any number of laws were passed on the ground that there was biblical justification for them. Our lives belonged, it was thought, to God and not to ourselves, so what we liked was beside the point. The Church authorities knew better than we did what was good for us.

Drugs, in similar vein, are widely regarded as putting the person who consumes them in a state of mind that is *intrinsically* bad, a state not fit for a human to be in. Differing judgments of intrinsic value are, of course, notoriously difficult to resolve. Intuitionists have long noted this, agreeing that the only thing one can do is to think again. But what do we do in the mean time? Whose view of the good are we to take as authoritative? The answer was easy for upper-class turn-of-the-century Oxbridge philosophers. And it was a snap for the dignitaries of establishment churches. And so on. And that's just the trouble, of course. This, indeed, is one of the things that liberal political philosophy is brought in to get around. The State may not side with *anybody* on matters of intrinsic value.

But there's where the putative liberal has another tactic available to him. In the case of drugs, the individual who disagrees with him about the intrinsic value of drug experiences is taken, typically, to be under the influence of those same drugs in forming it—and so his opinion *doesn't count*, despite the fact that it's his own opinion, concerning his very own life and experience. Thus the doctrine of "free will" is invoked to justify tyranny: views of yours that weren't "freely arrived at" don't count, and the rest of us get to clap you in a cell until you change your mind about the value of drug-induced experiences. And of course, if you never change it, we keep you there indefinitely. That this is a self-confirming "test" of validity is not paid much attention. Nor that the whole thing is about a matter that we have no business intervening about anyway.

Liberalism in moral theory fundamentally denies the legitimacy of the use of such judgments to justify impositions on individuals. It is essentially the view that we must deal with people on the basis of their *own* assessments of their lives—that their lives belong, so far as the rest of us are concerned, to *them*, and not to us or to a supposed god, or to the state, no matter how democratic that state may be. However well-informed our own view of what is good for you may be, the ultimate authority on your life, in the liberal view, is not us, but *you*.

Should we accept liberalism? The present essay accepts the liberal position, but obviously I cannot argue it at length here. However, one very important point about it must be appreciated. If we leave the control of your own life to you, that in no way precludes your taking the option of putting yourself, in some respect or other, under the control of others. The individual who follows the advice of a doctor does this, and often does it wisely. In innumerable ways, perfectly reasonable people assign regions of local authority over their lives to others. The issue about liberalism is whether people are properly regarded as *ultimately* subservient to that authority. Should we deprive people even of the authority to decide whether they shall accept a given authority or not? It is to that question that liberals reply in the negative. And given that negative answer, the view that we may make it illegal for Jones to do x on the ground that x would not be good for Jones is one that can't readily be accepted.

Nor, by the way, does liberalism in any way require that we abandon the very idea that some ways of life are intrinsically better than others. Of course they are. And moreover, the person who takes drugs extensively will, in all likelihood, pay a great price for this, in the way of suffering and lost opportunity. The intriguing irony of the nonliberal position about this is that the nonliberal's belief that drugs are bad is one in which he evidently has little confidence, for he won't allow others to find this out for themselves!

(2) What about autonomy, though? John Stuart Mill notably argued that the friend of liberty cannot allow people to sell themselves into slavery.[2] There is, to be sure, a certain oddity about "selling oneself into slavery": Is it really slavery if the slave retains the right to decide whether or not the master has kept his part of the bargain? And anyway, *is* an addict voluntarily "enslaving" himself? It is, certainly, an odd form of slavery in that no other individual becomes the master of the alleged slave. He is a slave to his own desires, we say. Very well, but that isn't quite the same as being subordinate to someone else's will. So without settling the question whether a right to enslave oneself should be recognized, we may doubt that the situation here is analogous.

Now, it may be argued that addiction is different from slavery in that addicts presumably lose the *capacity* for autonomy, rather than merely (and voluntarily) suppressing it or holding it in abeyance. Or do they even do that?

We make no decisions while asleep, presumably; and the addict, while under the influence of his drug, may well be functionally equivalent to being asleep. Drugs differ, to be sure, and some induce quite different behavior. But taking the more typical dreamlike states as important cases in point, they surely do not exemplify the sort of loss of autonomy that we are supposing motivates lawmakers to illegalize the consumption of drugs. Similar motives would, after all, make sleep itself illegal, as well as the sale of sleeping pills, alcoholic drinks and probably any

number of other substances. There seems, rather, to be a belief
that the drug taker's capacity to make decisions, or whatever, is
impaired even though he is awake, and impaired in a way that
constitutes a kind of enslavement.

Now, the very same states generally cause not only a
diminished capacity to make various decisions, but also a diminished likelihood of making a great many of them at all. Persons
under the influence of most drugs are conspicuously inactive.
Getting out and doing things, whether things we like or things
we don't, isn't what it's all about for the junkie. Rather, most
drugs are a means of escape, and for that matter the desire to
take them is presumably often due to a negative evaluation of
the kind of life the addict would be otherwise leading: the reality
from which he seeks escape is in his view worse than the one he
escapes into. In this new "reality" or surreality, one major feature
is the lack of need to make decisions. Existence while under the
influence is almost completely passive. One is almost entirely
spectator to one's experiences, scarcely at all an actor in control
of them.

Most of us do not think that would be an improvement.
We like normal existence well enough to prefer its challenges
and rewards, even with their attendant problems, to the passive
world of the junkie. Still, by what right do we deprive the junkie
of the option of escape, if that's what he prefers? When we
choose a certain food, say, we experience a certain sensation, and
we have no control over the relation between taking that food in
those circumstances and experiencing that particular sensation.
When we act, we quite generally submit ourselves to certain
effects of our choices. Even the very active seek out certain intrinsically passive states: the "high" of the long-distance runner,
the exhilaration at the top of the mountain, and so on. The idea
that such submission is inherently immoral actually makes no
sense whatever; there is no possibility of things being otherwise.
Choosing to diminish in some respect or other, and for some
brief time, our capacity for choice is simply a part of normal life.

It will be said that for the junkie the situation is much
worse than ours, however. For presumably his desires change in
such a way that he *can* no longer prefer going back to our real
world of action. The major area in which this claim seems plau-

sible is that of "addiction." It is not clear what to make of this claim. Let's consider it next.

Addiction

What, precisely, is an "addict?" The typical picture of the drug addict is of one who simply cannot resist the next dose. He "needs" to take it, with an intensity such that no inducement to take some other option will succeed in diverting him, so long as the option of taking the drug is open to him. And if it is not, then he will do virtually anything he can to make it open.

How does this condition compare with our normal condition with respect to things that we like? Suppose that Sheila is extremely fond of opera. She will spend her last penny on opera tickets, rather than on the necessities of life, and will sneak in behind the backs of unsuspecting ushers, despite general agreement that one should not steal. She is "hooked" on opera. Or consider Dickens' Mrs. Jellyby, who devoted herself to charitable operations in remote countries to the neglect of her children. Should we classify either of them as an "addict?" If not, why not?

We may say that Sheila or Mrs. Jellyby *could*, after all, have "controlled" their urges. But in what sense is this true? Part of it, at least, is that it is not a necessary truth, we suppose, that person K is fond of activity x. A preference for y instead is compatible with K remaining K. We can imagine K otherwise. That seems a rather thin truth, indeed. Nor is it quite so clear and obvious when we press it: how many of Jones' preferences could be otherwise without affecting our judgment that Jones remains the "same" person? When personalities change enormously, especially if the change is sudden, we might say that the subject is a "different person"; and this will be a description regarded as intelligible and reasonable if the change is sufficiently pronounced. A great deal of this has to do with the patterns of preference he exhibits.

Again, while the rest of us may imagine Jones without the taste in question, yet Jones herself may see it otherwise. Sheila may claim to be unable to imagine life without opera. More precisely, of course—since she is often not at the opera, after all—she is unable to imagine herself not having that taste and not pursuing it in every way possible.

Or is it only that she thinks life would be *worse* in the absence of such a taste? She chooses to go to the opera (and which one, if more than one is available), on the basis of her taste; and it is her taste that makes the one seem better than other options. But does she choose to have the taste that she does? Not obviously. We do speak of cultivated tastes and acquired tastes, cases in which people attempt, successfully, to induce in themselves a taste of a certain kind. Previously martinis, or snails, or Bellini, had no attraction, but by trying again we come to see something in it that we didn't see before, and end up "hooked." It is not clear what the limits of this procedure might be. Can anyone come to have just any tastes, given enough self-induced exposure? This question is worth some reflection.

There would seem to be two questions here. The first is whether one could acquire certain tastes no matter how hard one "tried." The other is: What would or could *motivate* the inducing?

It is unclear how we could attack the first question, whether there are, for each of us, tastes we simply could not acquire. In certain cases, the individual would suffer organic harms if she did what her taste would, if acquired, motivate her to do. Eating anchovies might be fatal, due to a severe allergy. It is notable that people with allergies can greatly like the things that have such effects—that's part of the problem for them, often enough. In the case of drug addictions, the drug taker is often aware that he is in for a much shorter life if he continues his habit. But he is not alone. Smokers are frequently like that: we all know individuals who agree that the evidence, overwhelmingly, suggests that they will live years less because they smoke, but who prefer the shorter life with smoking to the longer life without it. Most people, I think, agree with me that we have no business forcibly depriving those people of cigarettes on that account. We suppose that individuals may act on their preferences even if doing so will cause their earlier demise.

Martyrs refuse to alter their religious preferences even when faced with certain death if they persist in their refusal—and are widely admired for their stubbornness. And, to return to more mundane cases, no number of exposures and no amount of blandishment has been known to do anything for my own extreme aversion to rutabagas—though perhaps in a concentration camp, forced to choose between them and starvation, I would willingly eat them. It is, in short, very unclear what the limits of taste formation are; so far as ordinary experience goes, some tastes are extremely difficult to change, while others change spontaneously or readily enough given exposure to the appropriate stimuli. And the methods we would need to use to change some of them we would regard as extremely immoral—torture, for instance, or gross deception. The upshot seems to be that voluntary taste acquisition does sometimes happen, is not easy to understand even then, and probably has rather severe limits for each of us. One can never simply decide to have different tastes from those one presently has; one can sometimes undertake to expose oneself to experiences that will change one in somewhat predictable ways; but that we can willingly remake ourselves drastically and entirely seems almost out of the question.

Turning to the other question, that concerning motivation: *Why* would I undertake to become inured, let alone positively attracted, to a kind of music, or food, or whatever, that I currently very much dislike, or vice versa? It seems that one needs a motive if one is going to undertake, voluntarily, to induce in oneself a new set of motivations, namely those one has when one has the relevant set of tastes. But if we detect in ourselves no motivation to make the effort to acquire these now repulsive or eccentric-seeming tastes, then why would we make it? Can we also have a motivation to acquire the motivation necessary to make the effort? And is this iterable? Are we faced here with one of those infinite regresses so beloved by philosophers? If we are so, we at least lose all sense of what is going on once we go up a couple of levels at most. Motivation to acquire the motivation to acquire a motivation is too far out for most of us. And that strongly suggests that we are on the wrong track. The relevant sort of freedom surely does not lie in this direction.

This discussion may seem to have strayed rather far from the subject of drug addiction. But the point is to stress the continuity and comparability of drug experiences and drug takers' experiences with those of ordinary "straight" people. The tendency to treat drugs as somehow sui generis is, I believe, unjustified. We all have our problems, and we all have experiences and tendencies that we regard as unproblematic, yet seem quite comparable to the drug taker's in important respects.

Too, it is important to appreciate that addiction is not even the typical state of drug takers. There are many people who can take drugs or leave them, many who take them occasionally, and so on. Just as alcohol is consumed mostly by nonalcoholics, so drugs are consumed mostly by nonaddicts.[3] To treat all drug takers on the model of the addict is therefore misguided. Nevertheless, we must consider the bearing of drugs on responsibility, whether one is an outright addict or just an occasional user.

Responsibility

What is it to speak of responsibility? We say that people *are* or *are not* responsible for this or that; but also that they can *be held* responsible for one or another sort of thing; also that so-and-so is "a very responsible (or irresponsible) person." And that responsibility for such-and-such should be *assigned* or perhaps awarded or delegated to this or that individual. Which among these various uses is fundamental? Or if none, then which are of interest in the present context?

In asking "Who is responsible for this?" we sometimes mean "Who *did* it?" A human action occurred, and we want to know which human was the actor. This is an application of a more general question whose possible answers range over nonhuman happenings as well: *What* is responsible for this? Answers can range widely: the weather, say, or worn brake linings might be mentioned. The interest here is in establishing *causal* "responsibility," which amounts simply to causality: to say that x is causally responsible for something is to say that what caused it is x, rather than y or z. Obviously persons under the influence of drugs sometimes are the ones who did what we are inquiring about: Jethro, and not someone or something else, might have been the person who, under the influence of amphetamines, stabbed Kelly.

But in moving to the question of Jethro's *responsibility for* what he (as opposed to some other person) undoubtedly did, we need more than sheer identification of causal tracks. In wanting to know whether he can be *held* responsible, we are asking which sorts of possible response to his actions are in order: say prison, or reprimand, or the hospital, or perhaps nothing at all.

Holding responsible has a moral dimension to it. If there is no reason either to object or to hold up for praise or admiration, then it does not matter who or what is responsible, curiosity apart, and there is no point in talking of "holding" responsible. In this sense, when we raise the general question of holding people responsible for drug-related actions and passions, we are raising normative questions; we are suggesting that there is or might be something untoward or culpable about taking drugs.

But the preceding arguments show, I believe, that this is not so. That is, they show that being in the states that drugs induce is not, *as such*, properly susceptible to moral disapproval, though it is certainly subject to appraisals of a personal or aesthetic kind. Those are matters of intrinsic value; and such matters lie, I have suggested, beyond the reach of a properly liberal morality. Normal people are frequently in states that others don't like, and for that matter in states that resemble the drugged state in conspicuous respects. The ecstasies of the mystic or the saint are not far different from those of the junkie. A morality based on preferences at this level cannot embrace all moral agents; it is inevitably divisive.

Instead of the dimension of intrinsic value, then, it is certain *consequences* of drug-related activities that properly concern us. Does taking drugs increase the likelihood that the taker will perform some independently objectionable action—some crime, for instance? If so, does the fact that the crimes in question were performed under the influence of drugs excuse the agent in doing them?

It may be true at least in a practical sense—though I believe it is generally not true—that an agent under the influence of a drug literally "could not help" doing what he did. In such cases, it is clearly essential that we apply Aristotle's familiar distinction between being responsible for what one does at a certain time, and being responsible for getting oneself, at some earlier time(s), into the condition in which one would do it. If A kills B in a blind range, then we may be able to blame A for getting into that rage, e.g. by drinking a large amount of an alcoholic beverage that is known to be likely to have that effect on him. Here the importance of the addiction factor becomes clear, for A may try to defend himself by claiming that he also could not help taking the next drink; or, perhaps on psychiatric grounds, the first one either, for that matter. He is on best grounds of all if he can show that someone else slipped him the mickey while he wasn't suspecting it, or forced the brew between his unwilling lips.

We can extend Aristotle's schema in one important kind of case. What if Harry was hooked at the age of two, or even at birth, by his connection, biological or otherwise, to his addicted mother? Ever since then, he simply has had no working idea that anything else is possible. If so, we may perhaps blame the mother, and of course sometimes can go further and blame that mother's cruel or unsupportive boyfriend. Whom to blame may be important, if blame can in fact be bestowed and could do some good. But often it cannot, and the question of who bears the blame becomes the question of whom to use stronger measures on.

The Practical Aspect

Can moral responsibility be attributed, in the end, on a purely causal basis? Or is it irreducible to causal considerations? Those who suppose it is the former, I think, are insufficiently attending to the practical aspect of responsibility ascriptions. We must decide what sort of conduct on the part of others we are going to object to and what we are not, and on what basis of principle (if any). If we object to behavior of type K, then we have an interest in getting people to refrain from K-ing, and one way to do this may be to voice disapproval. The disapproval may be misguided: the claim that this sort of behavior is to be disapproved of may be refuted, e.g. by demonstrating that it causes no harm to our legitimate interests. In that case, our disapproval is *rationally* ineffective, rather than just psychologically ineffectual.

But suppose we have a good case that behavior of this sort ought not to be engaged in, and thus that expressions of disapproval strike home and could be expected to be effective with normal people. If our subject is not responsive nevertheless, then we may have to escalate. One might resort to threatening penalties of various kinds. Or one might use purely preventive measures, such as building a wall, locking a door, or even incapacitating the offender. On the face of it, none of these requires a noncausal analysis. B's expressions of disapproval might prompt A to desist; if not, his threats of adverse consequences might do so; if they do not, then a locked door may stop him; and if that too fails, then a bullet in the head will certainly do so, if an extremity is reached. Once we appreciate that our reasonable responses to others' behavior are not sheer intellectual responses to exotic spiritual conditions, but instead are practical responses, defending ourselves, our property, or our loved ones against threats, of which drug-related behaviors are sometimes cases, then abstract questions of free will and necessity are beside the point.

One main version of the question of responsibility for drugs is whether the first sort of response mentioned, that is, verbal and other communicative ones such as advice, praise and blame, can be effective in altering their behavior, if it needs altering. Are addicts beyond the reach of praise and blame? Experience suggests that they mostly are not; and certainly they are not beyond the range of stronger inducements. It also suggests that such methods are generally less efficacious than they are with persons in normal states of mind, and in that sense that persons under the influence of drugs are less responsible than others, responsibility being a matter of degree. Diminished responsibility is the general category we must apply to drug-takers, complete nonresponsibility being a limiting case. But this is shared with many other factors, such as tiredness, emotional stress, or being too busy with other things. When such an influencing factor is present, then we may need to use more forcible measures. If Alphonse is asleep, then one doesn't get him to act merely by making a request in a normal tone of voice: an alarm bell may be needed. If an addict tends to be as if asleep on the job, thus diminishing his efficiency, then stronger measures need to be taken—such as releasing him from that employment.

Are such actions justified, given the condition of the agent? Of course they are, and that they are is one of the points that anyone had better bear in mind when he considers taking to drugs. An employer hires someone to work for him for the sake of results of interest to the employer, and if those are not forthcoming, then he has no reason to continue the employment relation. Similarly, if one who takes drugs tends to resort to crime, then we are justified in taking stronger measures than the ones that are normally efficacious in inducing him to desist. People *owe* it to their fellows to refrain from violence, and we may respond to a pattern of violence by severing the offender from his "employment" as a fellow human being in society. That is an "office" that we are only entitled to hold during good behavior. Whether the offender against the requirements of elementary good behavior claims to be incapable of doing otherwise affects the kinds of measures we may take to correct the situation, but does not affect our right to take such measures.

Denying that persons on drugs are responsible for their actions, either those induced by their drugged states or those taken with a view to acquiring the drugs that induce them, is wrong because it is counterproductive. Like everyone else, the drug taker, and not other people, should be visited with the adverse consequences of his actions. If he brings harm to others, he may properly be made to pay the costs if possible, and he should be. Persons considering taking drugs should be aware that such measures will be taken; they should not be able to count on the "sympathy" they get from persons who regard them as nonresponsible. To do that is, perhaps inadvertently but nevertheless effectively, to reward the very behavior we want to extinguish.

Holding and Taking Responsibility

If we "hold A responsible" for doing x, we take it that we may deal with A in regard to x in the normal ways; if x is something to be done, then to hold A responsible is to make A liable for blame or praise, and/or other appropriate responses, according as he does or fails to do x, and does it well or badly. In particular, to hold someone responsible is to make him thus liable regarding the foreseeable consequences of doing (or, where applicable, omitting) x. Of particular interest here are values of x such that among its foreseeable consequences are dispositions to do other things that are in their turn morally consequential. If taking that potion will turn Dr. Jekyll into Mr. Hyde, then Jekyll ought to refrain from taking the potion.

Suppose that taking x will put A into a state such that there is a modest increment in A's probability of doing y, which in turn would gravely damage B. May we hold A responsible for that damage to B? If A had enough information about x to know that there was such a probability, then surely we may, indeed. If not, then there is the question of responsibility for A's state of ignorance. If it simply is not known that x might do that—x is thought to be perfectly innocuous—then there can be no penalty for A's doing x. But what about for his doing y, if he actually does it? Here it seems reasonable to hold him at least partially liable for damages imposed by y. Certainly A should feel sorry that y occurred, even if he literally couldn't help doing it at the time; the sleepwalker who murders his sister while somnolent should be concerned. And much depends on just how the y-instigation occurs. Jekyll may not, the first time, be blameworthy for becoming Mr. Hyde, but even on that first occasion Hyde is responsible for what he does: he does it in the effort to fulfill the monstrous desires that are clearly his. Had Hyde always been Hyde, then he could perhaps be incarcerated or executed in the normal way. It is the circumstances of his becoming what he then was that make us pause before reaching that conclusion.

People should have the disposition to be on the watch for things like x. The knowledge that there are possible actions with this sort of consequence makes us somewhat wary of trying out novel things. Yet an utterly conservative policy, of never trying anything new, is arguably worse than one of unlimited liberty. Perhaps the solution is a sort of insurance scheme, especially if there is enough foreseeable difference among people that it is possible to know who is more and who less susceptible to the x-result. Premiums would be adjusted accordingly. Thus we harness risk to overall good.

Drugs, however, are not in the most difficult category here, for we do have a good deal of information about what they do, and in fact they do not characteristically induce people to do what is fundamentally wrong. They do characteristically render people less capable, or in extreme cases altogether incapable, of *taking* specific responsibilities, as for work. If one delegates responsibility to addicts, one is unlikely to get good results. And they may certainly be held responsible for nonperformance, e.g. by being severed from employment or put on a disability scheme, if one exists.

Conclusions

I hope that in outline, anyway, we have covered the most important cases. Those who take drugs may be held responsible for taking them, insofar as the probable consequences of taking them are known (or sufficiently knowable) to the agents in question. Those who supply drugs to the first parties are culpable if they thereby mislead or delude their customers. Those who perform badly at required tasks under the influence of drugs may be blamed and held responsible for their bad performance, though different specific measures might be appropriate than in the case of persons in normal conditions. And as to those who engage in outrightly wrong actions under the stimulation of drugs, if there are such, we may, in the first place, take whatever measures are necessary to defend ourselves against their intended depredations at the time, and in the second, may incarcerate them involuntarily, either in a prison or in a psychiatric or other such institution, should there be no alternative method of controlling that behavior.

The general moral may be summed up in the observation that taking drugs, while an important matter in our and many societies, should not be seen as radically different from all sorts of relatively normal activities. In particular cases, they will differ in degree, but they do not in general differ in kind, and do not in general raise very special questions that do not also arise regarding these other things.

Taking drugs is a personal matter in one sense: that is, nobody may be punished by law or blamed morally simply for attempting (successfully or not) to induce one of those peculiar states of mind that it is the general purpose of taking drugs to achieve. But they may certainly be held liable for whatever adverse consequences to others may stem from their taking them, in the same way and for the same reasons that we all may and should be held responsible for our doings and nondoings.

In the preceding I have argued for, or relied on, the following four general points:

1. Responsibility is not uniquely correlated with the having of alternatives and a capacity to choose among them.
2. Persons under the influence of drugs are rarely altogether beyond the reach of normal types of moral inducements.
3. The taking of drugs is not in itself one of the things that people may properly be punished for.
4. When persons under the influence of drugs do what is morally wrong, they may always be dealt with either as patients or as ordinary offenders. In either case, our object is to protect ourselves against threats to our safety and property.

On the first point, I am influenced by the work of Frankfurt[4] as well as my own general reflections on the subject of "free will." Regarding the second, I do not claim specific expertise, but write on the basis of general information. The third point follows, I take it, from an article in the Liberal creed concerning social ethics; it is invoked without much defense here. And the fourth sums up the detailed argument of the essay. The net upshot of these points is that to refrain from holding people responsible for wrongful behavior is a mistake, rather than an appropriate response to the condition of the drug taker. Not to hold responsible is to send the wrong messages. Insofar as such behavior issues from drug taking, the right view to take is that it is basically the responsibility of the drug taker to clean up his or her act—and, if he does not, to suffer whatever ill consequences may ensue, rather than being able to visit them on others or make others bear the costs of coping with them.

A great deal depends on the work of experts in the field, especially as regards the handling of particular cases. But my main results are submitted to the philosophical reader in the belief that they will stand largely independently of what experts can contribute. If the views here advocated are accepted, then I believe it would set the stage for a much better way of dealing with drugs than the present system of suppression of drug taking and drug trading, which should be regarded as disgraceful and intolerable. If my deliberations do support such a result, they will not have been in vain. Full observance of these principles might well, I think, reduce what is now regarded as a major and pervasive social problem to a minor nuisance—just one more of life's pitfalls that the person, and thus the society, of practical wisdom can get around without great distress.

NOTES

1. See the first sentence of that famous essay.

2. *On Liberty*, Chapter 5. Everyman Edition (NY: Dutton, 1968), p. 158. "It is not freedom to be allowed to alienate his freedom." Since we do this all the time in some ways, the principle clearly needs refinement.

3. I don't mean that most drugs are consumed by nonaddicts, but rather that most consumers of drugs are nonaddicts. No doubt the specific consumption of addicts is very high.

4. Harry Frankfurt, *The Importance of What We Care About* (Cambridge, U.K.: Cambridge University Press, 1988); especially essay 1, "Alternate Possibilities and Moral Responsibility," pp. 1–10, and essay 8, "What We are Responsible for," pp. 95–103.

Drug Addiction, Liberal Virtue, and Moral Responsibility

Jeffrey Reiman

So that there will be no misunderstanding about the argument I am about to make, let me start by saying that I think that the "War on Drugs" is immoral on both consequentialist and deontological grounds. On consequentialist grounds, it is wrong because it produces more harm than the evil it aims to vanquish.[1] This is primarily because making drugs illegal has the effect of driving their prices up dramatically, due to the fact that then only those willing to risk imprisonment will supply the drug. The cocaine used daily by a heavy user could be produced and sold for pennies legally. Illegally, however, it can easily cost $100 or more a day. The effect of this is to create enormous incentives to poor people to sell the drug, to find new users, and to use deadly violence to settle bad debts or to keep competitors out of one's market. (Police attribute about a third of the many murders in Washington, DC to the work of drug-trade "enforcers.")[2] This in turn means that inner-city communities are so violence-ridden that no one will invest in them and whoever has the talent to escape will do so, with the result that both money and talent flow away from where they are needed most.

Moreover, since the drug trade is the main source of big money and the main entertainment in otherwise hopeless lives, large numbers of inner-city dwellers are involved in it at some level and thus large numbers get arrested and spend time in prison, further sapping the community of potential resources. (The prison population in the United States has more than doubled over the past decade, fueled in large measure by drug-related convictions.)[3] And this all has a kind of evil multiplier effect: With more violence, there are more strains on medical emergency resources and thus greater health expenses with less available for normal uses, such as prenatal health care. With more money tempting people to the drug trade, lives are rendered unstable and unpredictable with negative effects on the health and well-being of children. With more young men in prison, there are fewer eligible husbands and thus more unmarried young mothers. And so on. Thus, though I think that legalizing drugs has its dangers and would probably have some negative consequences, I think that these pale beside the danger and harm produced by the War on Drugs.

Deontologically, I think that the War on Drugs is immoral because I believe that a sane adult has the right to put whatever he wants in his body. The liberalism to which I subscribe, and which underlies the argument that I shall make in this essay, is of the Lockean-Kantian variety that places special weight on the capacity of rational beings to govern their own lives.[4] It holds that the ability of people to shape their own lives according to their own judgments is the necessary condition of their living lives that are truly meaningful to them, lives that they can think of as their own accomplishment and thus in which they can take pride. It is the necessary condition of people living lives that have a worth that reflects their special capacity as rational beings. Thus the right to self-governance (as far as this is compatible with the same right for all), which necessarily includes the right to control one's body, is the condition for the special dignity which humans have and the special respect to which they are entitled. Taking these rights away is treating human beings in a condescending and disrespectful manner, as if they were not capable of running their lives, as if their bodies were resources owned by the society.

Sovereignty over one's body is the sine qua non of a free society. Thus, I subscribe to what Kant called the supreme principle of morality, namely, that the freedom of each should be limited only so far as is necessary to make it compatible with the like freedom of all.[5] And I subscribe to John Stuart Mill's principle that the society has no right to restrict a sane adult's freedom except to prevent harm to others.[6]

None of this, however, implies that drug addiction is morally acceptable or morally indifferent. Kant thought that allowing bodily desires to master one's mind was a vice.[7] And, while Mill believed that we should use the law *less* to control people's behavior, he believed that we should remonstrate with our fellows *more* about what is really good and evil in life.[8] He clearly felt that what was immoral was a larger category than what could be rightly prohibited. Thus, there will be no inconsistency with the liberal views I have thus far stated when I add that I believe there is a sense, a liberal sense in fact, in which drug addiction is immoral.

To reach this conclusion, I shall sketch a theory of liberal virtue according to which drug addiction (when it possesses certain characteristics that I shall shortly spell out) is a vice. It is a vice that I think sane adults have a right to indulge, though they should not, and one that I think that the state has no right to prohibit, though they should discourage it. I shall argue, further, that the vice of drug addiction is one for which the addict is responsible, as he is responsible for the actions that result from the addiction. This notwithstanding, I shall go on to argue that insofar as drug addiction results from remediable and unfair social conditions, then society as a whole may share responsibility for the drug addictions in its midst and for the actions that predictably accompany them. This should bring to light a number of disagreements between my view and that of Jan Narveson, even though we both agree that individuals have the moral right to use drugs and that the state has no business prosecuting the War on Drugs.

Strong Addictions and Strong Desires

Narveson treats drug addiction as if it were just like any strong desire. There is nothing special about it, nothing to distinguish it from a strong desire to see operas or boxing matches. I contend that this overlooks a feature that addictions sometimes

have which other strong desires lack and which places addictions *with this feature* in a special moral category.

For Narveson, a drug addict is someone "who cannot resist the next dose," and this, according to him, makes the addict
no different from someone who cannot resist the next opera, will
spend her last penny on opera tickets, and so on. This fails to
note, however, that, when we call something an addiction, we
normally mean that it is more than simply a strong desire, but a
strong desire of a certain sort: namely, an ongoing, self-perpetuating strong desire, such that (in at least some cases) it would be
extremely hard to stop pursuing the desired object *even if one
judged that it was contrary to one's interest to continue.* The *International Dictionary of Psychology* lists among the criteria for addiction (all of which are of course disputed): "having a compulsive
inability to resist taking the drug despite the knowledge that it is
harmful."[9]

I am not suggesting that all addictions have this property.
Indeed, it is currently fashionable to stretch the term addiction
way beyond its original home in the pharmaceutical realm, to
characterize people's desires for "food, smoking, gambling, buying, work, play, and sex."[10] According to this usage, addiction
needn't involve the development of chemical tolerance with its
attendant dangers of withdrawal, needn't be to anything harmful
in itself, and may even be a beneficial process by which one
harnesses oneself to some worthwhile activity like exercise. In
the case of drug addiction, however, the implication is normally
that the continuation of the practice is contrary to the user's self-
interest and, in some sense, overwhelms his ability to pursue his
self-interest as he understands it. I think that the extensions of
the term to nonchemical substances, nonharmful practices, and
even to positive activities, feed off (draw pungency from) this
primary sense of the term "addiction."

In any event, at least some addictions have the property of
impelling the addict to continue in spite of his judgment that the
desired object is harmful and that he would be better off without
it and without the desire for it. Such addictions, I will call *strong*
addictions. Addictions which would not survive the individual's
judgment that they were contrary to his self-interest, I shall call
weak addictions. (In this category, I place my own addiction to

coffee in the morning and *MacNeil-Lehrer* in the evening.) What I shall say about the moral status of drug addiction is meant to apply only to strong addictions.

When addiction is strong, we can say that the addict's decision to take the next dose is rational in that it gives him some pleasure and forestalls the threatened pains of withdrawal. It may even give him great pleasure—though it is widely noted that the pleasure derived from addictive substances, whether heroin or potato chips, declines over time, though the strength of the desire persists.[11] By contrast, however, the addict's being or remaining addicted is irrational in that the overall amount of pleasure gained is not worth the harm done to his body, mind, work, and/or relationships, *according to the addict's own judgment*. In short, the addiction is rational in the short run and irrational in the long run. Strong addiction, then, has the effect of disabling the individual's capacity to shape his life according to his long-term best interest.

It should be evident that there is a clear and important distinction between the opera lover's strong desire and the junky's strong addiction. The opera lover's desire is itself a gift. She is better off for having the desire because it adds to the pleasure available to her. The dope addict's strong addiction is by contrast a misfortune. He would be better off without it, because having it makes his life worse overall than it could have been. To see why this distinction is morally relevant, I want to sketch a liberal theory of virtue, to which I now turn.

Liberal Virtues and Vices

The idea of liberal virtues may strike some readers as odd, even as an oxymoron, since much recent debate has been concerned with the supposed neutrality of liberalism which is thought by some to be its main selling point as a moral theory, and which seems to rule out favoring any particular set of characterological dispositions over others.[12] I think that this debate is largely otiose, since the neutrality at issue in the debate would not be desirable even if it were possible, which it isn't. It amounts to asking liberalism to be a moral position that doesn't take a moral position. There is an important and distinctive way in which liberalism is neutral, but—as I shall indicate shortly—it is not so in a way that rules out favoring certain kinds of character traits over others.

Liberalism's neutrality lies in the fact that it prohibits forcing one person's will on any other sane adult. This means that liberalism is not neutral with respect to actions (such as theft or rape) or moral doctrines (such as the sort of fundamentalism that would impose a religious orthodoxy) that involve such forcing. If liberalism were neutral on this, it would not be a moral position at all. But with this, it remains neutral in the sense that it permits all actions, lifestyles, and moral views that do not involve forcing unwanted conditions on others.

In this context it is, in any event, not surprising that the recent resurgence of interest in what is called "virtue ethics" is, in its canonical, MacIntyrean form, offered as an alternative to liberalism.[13] Virtue ethicists aim to develop an ethical theory by starting with some notion of human excellence, and showing that the components of an independently determined excellent life include behaviors that are recognizably moral. This means that they must not only develop a standard of human excellence, but do so *before* they have a standard of moral behavior. But without a standard of moral behavior and without an Aristotelian or Christian belief in an ontologically real human teleology, it is, to put it mildly, hard to come up with a standard of human excellence. MacIntyre has found no better alternative than measuring human excellence by the standards found in the culture at the time; but this sort of conventionalism offers little hope for showing that the standards are anything more than conventional prejudices about excellence.

Aristotle is sometimes taken as the model for this sort of conventionalism, since he does normally start analysis by considering (with great respect) prevailing opinions, and he does end up accepting as the virtues those that are enshrined in the conventions around him. Nonetheless, Aristotle did not in my view think that he was doing this. He thought that prevailing opinions were likely to contain truth (and not just be prevalent conventions) because he was confident in the human capacity to know reality; and he thought he could see the superiority of virtues like courage over vices like cowardice as we today think we see the superiority of health over sickness (indeed, as we see health as *health* and not just as an arrangement of bodily components).

The problem then for virtue ethics is that, insofar as it aims to derive morality from a standard of human excellence, it must provide a justification of that standard, good reasons for believing that it really is a standard of *excellence* rather than merely a conventional prejudice. But without a natural teleology to fall back on, it seems inevitable that such a justification will have to rely on a moral view—and that will undermine the attempt to derive morality from the standard of human excellence.

By way of illustration, consider the promising attempt to derive morality from human excellence that has been made by Michael Slote. His view is that excellence or virtue is a kind of strength or self-sufficiency, which he thinks is inherently admirable.[14] Slote is able to account for a surprisingly large number of common moral views by showing how forms of behavior commonly thought to be moral exhibit a kind of strength or self-sufficiency. For example, he accounts for the obligations of fairness—to do one's share in cooperative ventures from which one benefits—as exhibiting one's disposition not to be a parasite, which in turn exhibits one's self-sufficiency rather than dependence, and so on. Fruitful as this approach is, it seems to me that it does not escape the difficult circle within which all virtue ethics operates: We still need to know why strength or self-sufficiency are *good* traits, and without a natural teleology, there seems no way to do this without appealing to some standard of moral excellence—and that will make virtue derivative from a moral theory, just the opposite of the virtue ethicist's goal. Nor will it do to deny that we need to know why strength or self-sufficiency are good traits, or to claim that these are simply primitive goods or self-evidently admirable. That would effectively reduce morality to a blind attachment, in Slote's case, to something on the order of uncritical affection for John Wayne types, or "Marlboro men."

A liberal theory of virtue differs from the MacIntyrean variety and from what is normally called "virtue ethics" because it does not expect to develop a moral theory by starting from an account of human excellence. Rather, it frankly accepts that human excellence can only be identified from the standpoint of an already existing moral theory and thus that virtue is a derivative rather than a basic element of an ethics. A liberal theory of virtue takes the standard of excellence implicit in liberalism. And this, in the Lockean-Kantian version, is found in liberalism's celebration of the capacity of human beings to govern their lives by their own rational judgments.

Since the rights which liberalism thinks people have derive from their capacity for rational self-government, liberalism is hardly neutral on the worth of this capacity. If it is not taken as extremely valuable, then the argument for rights which effectively provide the space for the exercise of this capacity is undercut. To the extent that an individual fails to exercise her capacity for rational self-government, and more so to the extent that she purposely weakens that capacity, she can be said to be acting in a way that is unworthy of the rights she has. Or, if the ability to pilot one's life according to one's rational judgments is the source of the special dignity of human life, then one who fails to use or who positively subverts this ability is acting in an undignified manner.

Let us call the ability of human beings to govern their lives by their rational judgments "the sovereignty of practical reason." Then, we can say that the liberal virtues are those dispositions which promote the sovereignty of practical reason, and the vices are those dispositions which undermine that sovereignty.

This approach gives us something that is all too often missing in liberal moral theory, namely, a role for *shame*, as distinct from *guilt*. Guilt—both the status and the feeling—is normally linked to failures in one's duty to others. Shame, by contrast, is normally thought to be appropriate in cases where a person fails to be the sort of person that he or she should be. Thus, a liberal moral theory, with its emphasis on people's right to act as they wish as long as they don't violate the rights of others, seems only to have a place for guilt—the guilt that arises from violating others' rights. If, however, we add to this that liberalism must highly value the capacity for rational self-government, we get a way in which people can fall short of being the sort of people they should be *according to liberalism*. Then, a liberal can consistently hold that someone who fails to use or who positively subverts his ability for rational self-government acts in a shameful manner, even if he is guilty of no violation of anyone's rights.[15] I leave aside until a later section, the question of whether such failure or subversion is voluntary and thus something for which people can be held responsible. I shall continue to speak in the present section and the next of people subverting their capacity for self-governance and so on without meaning to take a position on whether they do so freely.

It should be noted in passing that this is not the only way in which one might try to launch a liberal theory of virtue. Separating himself from any conception of liberalism that thinks it is a neutral ideal, William Galston defends a rich and varied list of virtues as liberal.[16] He devotes most of his analysis to instrumental virtues, like tolerance or law-abidingness, which are necessary means to the preservation of liberal societies. In addition, he mentions approvingly three intrinsic liberal virtues: rational self-determination (which he attributes to Locke), ability to act on the moral law (which he attributes to Kant), and the development of individuality (which he attributes to John Stuart Mill, Ralph Waldo Emerson, and others). The first of these is the same as the sovereignty of practical reason which I take as central to liberalism. I am not persuaded that the remaining two are appropriate standards, for the following (all-too-briefly stated) reasons:

The capacity to act on the moral law is part of the capacity to subject one's actions to practical reason—indeed, for Kant it is equivalent to the capacity to subject one's actions to *nothing but* practical reason. Thus, I don't think that the second standard is really a separate standard of virtue, but rather a case of the first. As for individuality, while it may be one important excellence that can be realized in liberal societies, my own view is that liberalism insists first and foremost that one's choice be one's own—even if it is a choice to conform. Wouldn't a liberal prefer a society of people who conform because they choose to, to one where they are non-conformists because they are conditioned to be that way?

The idea that the virtues are the dispositions which support the sovereignty of practical reason is closer to the classical

doctrine than may be immediately apparent. I have argued elsewhere that this account gives us a way of explaining the so-
called "cardinal" virtues: courage, temperance, fortitude and
justice.[17] *Courage* is the ability to hold to one's rationally chosen
course of action in the face of danger, *temperance* is the ability to
hold to it in the face of temptation by pleasures close at hand,
and *fortitude* is the ability to hold to it in the face of hardship.
And, considered as a virtue, *justice* is the disposition to leave
others the same space to live according to their rationally chosen
course of life that one claims for oneself. One advantage of this
explanation of the virtues is that it overcomes the suspicion that
at least the first three of the cardinal virtues lack the generality to
be *the* virtues. Temperance, for example, seems to be part of a
particular (perhaps puritanical) moral system and not something
of value to everyone (say, to voluptuaries). But if present pleasures are recognized to have a kind of deceptively strong appeal
by virtue of their very nearness, then temperance is the ability to
withstand this deceptive appeal and weigh present pleasures by
their real value in light of one's overall life aims. Then, temperance is a means to whatever course of life one chooses. Even
voluptuaries might be tempted to overrate certain nearby pleasures (say, of security or good reputation), and thus temperance
will enable them to hold their course no less than it will help
puritans.

Moreover, this account is akin to Aristotle's, though of
course it is not an identical twin. For Aristotle, it will be remembered, the virtues are the components of a *eudaimon* or happy
life. Indeed, for Aristotle, this claim is tautological. The virtues
are the ways of living excellently, and the *eudaimon* life is an
excellently lived life. The virtues make up the excellently lived
life. Contrary to a common view, Aristotle is not a teleological
moral thinker in the sense that, say, Mill is. Aristotle of course
holds a teleological view of nature, including human nature. But,
the virtues are not simply means to happiness. Or if they are
means to it, they are in the sense in which bricks and cement are
means to a building, not the sense in which blueprints and trow-
els are means to a building. For Aristotle, the virtues stand to the
happy life as the parts to the whole, and they are means to the

end of happiness only in the way that the parts are means to the existence of the whole.

Aristotle arrives at the virtues by arguing that a happy life must be a life in which the distinctive human capacity is exercised excellently. The distinctive human capacity is reason, which in its excellent theoretical use gives us the intellectual virtues and in its excellent practical use gives us the moral virtues. The moral virtues are those ways in which people's appetites are appropriately subjected to their practical reason. A morally virtuous person is one whose desires have been trained to take their cue from reason, rather than simply go all out for satisfaction. Thus, the virtues are dispositions to *measured* passions and *measured* actions. This is how Aristotle arrives at his famous doctrine of the mean.

The mean is not an algorithm for finding virtue; it is a description of the inner life of virtuous persons. Desires or passions in themselves push for total satisfaction. But, virtuous acts share with art and athletics the property of being neither too much nor too little. This doesn't mean that the virtues are midway between total satisfaction and none at all, just that they are in between the two; and thus that the desires have been subjected to some kind of rational control. And this is all the doctrine of the mean tells us. It is not, as is sometimes mistakenly thought of Aristotle, some way of figuring out what is virtuous by first identifying excess and defect and then splitting the difference between them. Excess and defect cannot be identified prior to identifying the right amount. Thus Aristotle's mean is not a way of figuring out what virtue is, it is a characteristic of those desires and actions that are already known to be virtuous.

The moral virtues then, for Aristotle, amount to dispositions in our desires to allow themselves to be governed by rational judgment, to be felt and acted upon in a rationally measured way. To use the terms introduced earlier, we can say that the virtues are dispositions to accept the sovereignty of practical reason over one's desires. The difference between Aristotle's account and the liberal one is that Aristotle emphasizes the substantive outcomes of that sovereignty, the particular virtues which result from the subjection of desires to practical reason. The liberal view, by contrast, focuses on the preconditions rather than the results of the sovereignty of practical reason. Where, for example, on the Aristotelian view, temperance is a virtue because it is the attitude that a man of practical wisdom would cultivate, for liberalism, it is a virtue because it is a precondition for the effective exercise of practical wisdom. That the liberal theory identifies as virtues those dispositions which enable and promote the sovereignty of practical reason gives us a way of saying how some addictions are vicious.

Before taking this up, however, we should round out the discussion of the liberal theory of virtue by considering the following question: If liberalism celebrates the sovereignty of practical reason and condemns as vice dispositions that undermine this sovereignty, why doesn't liberalism allow—even demand—that law be used to prevent such vices? After all, if freedom is a value because it enables people to exercise sovereignty over themselves, why should we protect the freedom to subvert this exercise?

To this, I think the liberal has two main replies: The first is that, even if it would be good for me to be forced not to weaken my ability for rational self-governance, it is no other person's right to do this. My fate only becomes subject to other people's rights insofar as I act in ways that harm or endanger others. People do not have general rights to do whatever is good for other people whether they want it or not. The second reply is that it is not good for me, once I have become an adult, to be forced not to weaken my ability for rational self-governance. That is because what makes rational self-governance good for me is that it creates a life that is in an important way *my* life, *my* accomplishment. And this is only possible if the project of rational self-government is *my* project. While society and my parents, at least, have the right, indeed the duty, to force upon me as a child the education and rearing needed to make me into an adult capable of self-government, it is not appropriate for anyone to continue such force once I am an adult. To do so is to undermine the reality and thus the worth of the project of self-governance by stealing that project from me and making it into someone else's project for me. That the project may be subverted because I have surrendered to some vice is part of what makes the project worthwhile when it succeeds. Consequently, the liberal holds that adults have the right to indulge their vices, including vicious addictions, to which we now turn.

Vicious Addictions

As I return now to the moral status of drug addiction, bear in mind that I am speaking only of what I earlier called "strong addiction," and that I am staying neutral for the time being on the question of the addict's freedom. Strong drug addictions are ones in which the desire for the drug overcomes the addict's knowledge that it is harmful and that he would be better off without the drug and the desire for it. For each drug dose taken alone, it may be rational for the addict to indulge since he gets some pleasure and avoids a real pain (of withdrawal). However, the addict himself can see that the total package is not a good bargain. In the long run, he would gain more from not being addicted than he does from his drugs.

Strong addiction is a vice according to the liberal theory. By becoming addicted, the addict undermines his ability to govern his life in the long run (that is, the whole course of his life) by his rational judgment. This is a vice rather than a single immoral act because it is not merely an act contrary to his self-interest, but the undermining of his ongoing ability to govern his life by his rational judgment. The strong addict has (freely or not) created for himself a (more or less) permanent obstacle to his doing what it would be rational for him to do with his life. He commits a kind of treason against the sovereignty of his own practical reason.

Consequently, calling strong addiction a vice is not due to some puritanical repulsion against "unearned pleasure" or some puritanical prejudice in favor of sobriety. Rather, strong addiction is wrong in terms of the addict's own goals. Insofar as (per hypothesis) the addict gets less of what he wants in the long run from being addicted than he would without the addiction, it is in terms of his own goals that the irrationality of his addiction is measured. A strong addiction is something that persists against the addict's own "better judgment." It amounts to a kind of self-betrayal.

This shows us an additional virtue of the liberal theory. According to it, vices are dispositions to self-betrayal. This gives the liberal theory of virtue and vice its normative cutting edge. The standard theories put forth by virtue ethicists generally give some list of excellences which virtuous folks realize and vicious ones fail at. But, as such, it is far from obvious why failure at an excellence is a moral failure.[18] The burgers one grills on the backyard barbecue do not achieve the excellence of haute cuisine, but this doesn't make backyard chefs vicious. On the liberal theory, by contrast, there is a clear solution to this puzzle. The excellences that the liberal theory identifies as virtues are means to the individual's own ability to live the life which on reflection she most wants to live. Failure at those excellences amounts to betrayal of one's own aims, a kind of assault on one's own life.

That the liberal vices are dispositions to self-betrayal gives us a way to redeem (partially) Mill's dubious claim that the liberal principle (that liberty may only be restricted to prevent harm to others) prohibits selling oneself into slavery.[19] Mill contends that a principle protecting liberty cannot protect this particular freedom since it is a freedom to destroy one's liberty. This runs into skepticism because the liberal principle is normally thought to protect a sane individual's freedom to end his life. That seems like a sacrifice of more liberty than merely selling oneself into slavery, since even a life-long slave will have some occasions on which he can make free choices, which is more than a successful suicide will have.

On the liberal theory of virtue, however, we can distinguish suicide from voluntary enslavement. Insofar as suicide is the result of a rational decision about the pains and pleasures of staying alive, it is an expression of the sovereignty of one's practical reason over one's life. In a way, it is the or one of the ultimate expressions of that sovereignty since it places the size of one's very life in one's hands. Selling oneself into slavery by contrast amounts to handing over one's sovereignty to another. Suicide ends the self, while voluntary enslavement betrays the self. On these grounds, we can say that while Mill was wrong to hold that people could be rightly prevented from selling themselves into slavery, he was right in expressing a liberal contempt for those who do.

Responsibility for Vice and Addiction

It is generally held that responsibility goes hand-in-hand with free choice. A person can only be responsible for what she has chosen freely. Since vices are moral failings, and since we tend to think that we can only fail morally if we are responsible for the failure, it would seem that vices must be freely chosen to be (real, *moral*) vices. This fits with the modern tendency to exclude from the moral what people, so to speak, could not help doing (or being), and to treat the latter as a matter of nonmoral fortune. This tendency is, to be sure, part of the moral egalitarianism of the modern era, since setting aside those things which people cannot help leaves everyone, so to speak, at an equal starting point for being moral or immoral. This view of morality finds its strongest advocate in Kant, but it actually stretches back at least as far as Aristotle, who thought that virtue and vice were necessarily matters of choice.[20]

Aristotle was aware that his view led him into a very difficult tangle. Since he took virtues to be dispositions to act in certain ways (and not primarily as the acts themselves), he realized that once a person had, say, a vicious disposition, his vicious act might be said to be not a matter of choice but of the force of that disposition. Aristotle's response to this is that vicious dispositions are the result of habituation due to an accumulation of vicious acts, and those acts were products of choice. The vicious man then, if he doesn't choose his vicious acts now, did choose the acts that made him vicious and thus chose to become the sort of person who has vicious dispositions.[21] This is not fully satisfactory, since it leaves us wanting to know why such a person chose those early vicious acts, and the answer to that seems to be that he was somehow the sort of person who was prone to make such choices. But, then, it doesn't seem to be possible to say that he chose to become that sort of person, without launching ourselves into an infinite regress.

The alternative to this is simply to say that people are appropriately morally evaluated in terms of the sorts of persons they are, irrespective of how they came to be that way, even if they couldn't help it. This approach is taken most clearly by Nietzsche, who rejected free will as a myth engendered by the weak to make the strong feel guilty about their strength. Nietzsche viewed the whole of Judaeo-Christian morality as a revolt of slaves against their masters. The weak slaves succeeded in getting the strong masters to believe that their natural aggressiveness was a moral evil which they freely chose and for which they were thus responsible and guilty.

Rejecting the Judaeo-Christian view, and the egalitarianism that follows in its wake, as a kind of sickness, Nietzsche strove to recapture an ancient, pre–Judaeo-Christian ethic, whose terms of evaluation were "good vs. bad" rather than "good vs. evil." *Good and evil* correspond to the slaves' valuation of their own weakness (their tendency to turn the other cheek) and their devaluation of the master's strength (his natural predatoriness). *Good and bad*, by contrast, correspond to a valuation of the strong and the noble and devaluation of the weak and despicable. With belief in free will dismissed as a myth, this latter ethic is one that explicitly esteems qualities (such as strength) that simply characterize the sort of person someone is, without asserting that he has or even could have chosen to be that sort of person.[22]

Adapting these notions to our present purposes, we have two alternatives, which we can, with a bit of license, call the Aristotelian and the Nietzschean. The Aristotelian insists that vice must be chosen and thus that the vicious must be responsible for their vice, if it is to be vice at all. The Nietzschean holds that a natural disposition (which no one has chosen or is responsible for) can be a vice. I do not think that there is an a priori argument for preferring one of these approaches over the other. The Aristotelian fits our modern temper, but leads to a kind of puzzle when pushed to the extreme. The Nietzschean is clear and coherent, and yet it renders moral evaluation into the sort of evaluation we might make of (subhuman) animals, praising them, so to speak, as good specimens, for qualities, such as speed and grace, which are simply a matter of their makeup.

This last remark might suggest that there is some conceptual obstacle to calling the Nietzschean approach moral, since we do not normally think that moral appraisal is continuous with the sort of evaluations we make of animals. But, it is precisely this latter claim that is called into question by Nietzsche's attack on modern morality. Nietzsche is explicitly calling for a redefinition of morality, and thus no conceptual analysis of the term as we define it will settle the issue. Moreover, insofar as dispositions lead people to be better or worse members of society and the like, there is a clear sense in which they are moral dispositions and their evaluation moral evaluation, even if the dispositions themselves are not chosen.

I think, rather, that all we can say is that to take Nietzschean appraisal as moral appraisal is to mean something different by "moral" than we have come to mean by it in the modern era under the influence of the Judaeo-Christian tradition that Nietzsche is at pains to critique. Moreover, the Aristotelian approach is more in line with the liberal theory at work in this essay, with its emphasis on choice. I shall therefore assume from here on that vices must be voluntary to be vices, and thus that people with vices must be responsible for those vices. With this said, I shall take up the question of whether drug addictions can be said to be voluntary and drug addicts responsible for their addictions and the actions those addictions can be said to cause.

In raising this question, it should be noted that the main action that drug addictions cause is that of taking the next dose of drugs. It is generally untrue that drugs cause people to do violent or criminal acts. While PCP may be an exception, addicting drugs normally pacify their users. The most anti-social thing that drug use can be said to cause is lassitude or what is sometimes given the technical name "amotivational syndrome." What causes crime is not drugs but their high price which, coupled with the strong desire for the drugs, produces a powerful motivation for criminal acts. However, even if one attributes such acts to addiction, there is reason to believe that individuals who commit such acts are responsible for doing so.

Note that in making this claim, though I reach the same conclusion that Narveson does, I do not share his view that the question of responsibility is a pragmatic matter of determining the proper social response to addiction. The pragmatic problem is, of course, enormously important. Nonetheless, its solution depends on a factual question which must be answered first. The factual question is whether the addict could have acted otherwise. I believe that the answer to this is yes. This can be argued for in two ways.

First of all, there is the Aristotelian point, rightly adverted to by Narveson. Even if drug use made a person into some kind of blind robot, he would still be responsible for what he did in the robotic state *because he is responsible for taking the drug in the first place before the robotic state began.* And if it be thought that addiction makes the addict into some kind of blind robot who must take drugs, then he would be responsible for what he did in that robotic state *because he is responsible for taking the drugs that led him to become an addict which was before that robotic state began.* A drunk driver may not know what he is doing when he veers off the road and kills a pedestrian. He is thus not responsible in the way that someone is who commits premeditated murder. Nonetheless, the drunk is responsible for the harm he causes because he wasn't drunk when he started drinking, and he is responsible for starting.

But, further, neither drugs nor addiction makes one into a blind robot. Drugs may cloud one's judgment and addiction adds the pain of withdrawal as an incentive to continued use, but neither takes control of one's actions in a way that makes one into an automaton. Even drug-beclouded individuals know the difference between right and wrong, and can understand when they are hurting others and so on. And the pain of withdrawal that addicts may fear is surely less than the pain feared, say, by soldiers on a battlefield. If soldiers can still choose to do battle, addicts can hardly be thought to be unable to choose to face the pain of withdrawal.[23]

This may seem to fly in the face of the criterion for addiction which I cited earlier, namely, "having a compulsive inability to resist taking the drug despite the knowledge that it is harmful."[24] This seems to suggest that it is the very nature of addiction that addicts are unable to stop their addictions, and that in turn would suggest that addicts are not responsible for the continuation of their addictions. Note that even this leaves open the Aristotelian point that addicts are responsible for starting up their addictions (before they were addicts). And, if addicts are responsible for starting up their addictions, they are ultimately responsible for the continuation of their addictions, since in starting up an addiction one starts up something that continues. But, further, it is a mistake to think that the very nature of addiction entails that one can't stop. If that were so, we would have to say of people who do stop their addictions (and many do), that they were never really addicted! It seems more plausible to hold that addictions are very difficult to stop, but, for the vast majority of people, not impossible. This of course still leaves puzzles not unlike the one to which the Aristotelian view of responsibility for vice leads (and not unlike the related problem of weakness of the will: how people can fail to do what they recognize to be in their best interest). But these puzzles are not unique to the problem of addiction. They haunt all discussions of freedom and responsibility, without rendering these terms senseless.

It might be objected that there is a contradiction between saying that the addict can stop his addiction and that his addiction is a liberal vice, because the former implies that he has retained his ability for rational self-governance and the latter that he has surrendered that ability. But this puts the implications too strongly. The psychological truth seems to be that strong addiction is a powerful obstacle to self-control which can, with considerable effort, be controlled. Though the ability for self-governance is retained, it is voluntarily weakened, or, rather, the addict voluntarily increases the forces that work against it. This is captured in the liberal theory by characterizing vices as *dispositions* that *undermine* the sovereignty of practical reason. Dispositions, like habits, are hard but not impossible to overcome, and undermining something weakens without necessarily destroying it entirely.

Consequently, given the account of strong addiction that I have set forth, I conclude that individual addicts are (in the vast majority of cases) responsible for their addictions, for their continued drug use and thus for their continued addiction, and for any other actions that addiction may be said to cause. And this means that insofar as the strength of their desire for the drug (or the strength of their fear of withdrawal) keeps them addicted *even though they know they would be better off without the drug or the addiction*, strong addicts can be held responsible for undermining the sovereignty of their practical reason over their lives or for cultivating dispositions that undermine that sovereignty. And then their addictions are vices according to the liberal theory.

But this is not the whole story. The reason is that the discussion so far has proceeded on the unstated assumption of what might be called "normal circumstances." Strong addiction is a vice because in choosing it one undermines one's ability to subject one's life over the long run to one's practical reason. This assumes normal circumstances because it omits the possibility that undermining one's ability for self-governance may be one's best act of self-governance—an omission which makes sense in normal circumstances. Given normal conditions, people have enough to gain from subjecting their whole lives to their practical reason, that it is irrational in terms of their self-interest to surrender the capacity to do so. But, the irrationality of choosing strong addiction is not an eternal truth, independent of context. If I was, say, in a concentration camp facing constant pain and fear and small hope of ultimate survival, there would be little to recommend sobriety if drugs were available, and little reason to take the long view of my life and protect my capacity for rational self-governance against the self-induced blandishments of addiction. Then, becoming an addict in a concentration camp would not be irrational. In short, if circumstances are bad enough, then strong addiction might be the best act of rational self-governance available, and then it would not be appropriate to call it a vice.[25]

The general point is that social conditions could be so awful that preserving one's ability to govern one's life over the long run would be of little or no value. Then, strong addiction would be rationally adaptive behavior, making the best out of a bad situation. And if those awful social conditions were unjust, unnecessary and remediable, then whoever was responsible for their existence and continuation would be responsible for making what is normally a vice into, not a virtue, but a self-interestedly rational action. It is, of course, still a tragic loss. A life lived in a drug-induced cloud, driven from dose to dose by the lure of immediate pleasure and the fear of immediate pain, is still from a liberal standpoint (and just about any other) an inferior life that can only be "justified" by the extremity of the conditions to which it is a response. It is still a life in which the long-term sovereignty of practical reason—the condition for the unique dignity of human beings—has been surrendered, even if under the circumstances surrender is the individual's best alternative.

Note that such circumstances make strong addiction rational in the way that weak addictions are, although by opposite
means. In both cases, the pleasures gained from the addiction
suffice to make the addiction a rational strategy. But, since (by
definition) weak addiction is one that would not survive recognition of its harmfulness, weak addiction is rational because the
pleasures are large and the dangers small. By contrast, strong
addiction under awful circumstances is rational because the advantages of preserving long-term self-governance have diminished to a point at which the short-term pleasures of addiction
are the best alternative available.

Further, the individual who surrenders his sovereignty,
say by becoming an addict, under these circumstances makes a
choice to do so, and thus is *causally* responsible for the addiction.
He is not however, *morally* responsible for it, where this refers to
the sort of responsibility for an action that makes one rightly the
object of moral blame or praise for it. Moral responsibility for the
addict's choice passes to whomever it is who is responsible for
creating or maintaining conditions evil and awful enough to
make surrender of sovereignty rational. We can reach this in the
following way.

Conditions which are so bad must count as intolerable,
virtually by definition. But, if someone confronts me with a
choice between two alternatives where one is bad but tolerable
and the other bad and intolerable, that person *forces* me to opt for
the tolerable alternative. I am forced to hand my wallet to a
gunman though he leaves it to me to choose between my money
and my life. If addiction is chosen as a bad but tolerable alternative to (soberly facing and experiencing) intolerable conditions,
then it is forced by whomever it is who is responsible for the
intolerable conditions. And that implies that the forcer is morally
culpable for the addiction and its likely consequences.

I think that this description applies to the situation of at
least a substantial number of drug addicts in America's inner
cities. They face awful circumstances which are unjust, unnecessary, and remediable, and yet which the society refuses to
remedy. Addiction is for such individuals a bad course of action
made tolerable by comparison to the intolerable conditions they
face. In that case, I think that moral responsibility for their strong

addictions, and for the vicious betrayal of human self-governance that these entail, passes to the larger society.

NOTES

1. For more extensive discussion of the irrationality of the War on Drugs, as well as statistical evidence and citation of sources, see my *The Rich Get Richer and the Poor Get Prison: Ideology, Class, and Criminal Justice*, 3rd edition (New York: Macmillan, 1990), pp. 28–34. See also, "The War on Drugs: Is It Time to Surrender?," *QQ: Report from the Institute for Philosophy & Public Policy* (College Park, MD: University of Maryland, Spring/Summer 1989), pp. 1–5; and, Jonathan Marshall, "How Our War on Drugs Shattered the Cities," *The Washington Post*, May 17, 1992, p. C1.

2. "Capt. Alfred Broadbent, commander of the District's homicide squad . . . , estimated that as many as a third of last year's 489 homicides were tied to enforcers, an estimate that nearly matches the number of slayings police have classified as drug-related." (Pierre Thomas and Michael York, "Enforcers Are D.C.'s Dealers of Death," *The Washington Post*, May 18, 1992, pp. A1, A6).

3. See Sharon LaFraniere, "U.S. Has Most Prisoners Per Capita in the World," *The Washington Post*, January 5, 1991, p. A3.

4. I defend the liberal moral theory that underlies the present argument in *Justice and Modern Moral Philosophy* (New Haven, CT: Yale University Press, 1990).

5. Immanuel Kant, *The Metaphysical Elements of Justice*, Part 1 of *The Metaphysics of Morals* (Indianapolis: Bobbs-Merrill, 1965; originally published in 1797), p. 35.

6. John Stuart Mill, *On Liberty* (Harmondsworth, England: Penguin Books, 1974; originally published in 1859), p. 68.

7. Immanuel Kant, *Lectures on Ethics* (Indianapolis: Hackett Publishers, 1980), pp. 157–59.

8. "Instead of diminution, there is need of a great increase of disinterested exertion to promote the good of others. . . . Human beings owe to each other help to distinguish the better from the worse, and encouragement to choose the former and avoid the latter." (*On Liberty*, p.142).

9. *International Dictionary of Psychology* (New York: Continuum, 1989), p. 9.

10. *Encyclopedia of Psychology* (New York: Wiley, 1984), p. 14.

11. "Over the lifespan of the [addictive] process, the high diminishes. The individual experiences progressively less relief with increasing degrees of tolerance . . . " (*Encyclopedia of Psychology*, p. 14).

12. For more on this debate and references to the literature, see William Galston, *Liberal Purposes* (New York: Cambridge University Press, 1991). See also Charles Larmore, *Patterns of Moral Complexity* (New York: Cambridge University Press, 1987), for what might be thought of as the position of the Rawlsian camp in this debate.

13. Alisdair MacIntyre, *After Virtue* (Notre Dame, IN: University of Notre Dame Press, 1981).

14. Unpublished manuscript.

15. Perhaps this would account for the questionable moral status of professional boxing with its substantial risk of brain damage.

16. Galston, *Liberal Purposes*, pp. 213–37.

17. *Justice and Modern Moral Philosophy*, pp. 62–3, 82.

18. This, by the way, is an independent problem for virtue ethicists. Even if they succeed in demonstrating the real excellence of some standard of excellence, they still face the problem of explaining why failing to be excellent is a moral failure, indeed, why it is a failure at all for anyone who does not aspire to achieve excellence.

19. Mill, *On Liberty*, p. 173.

20. Aristotle, *Nicomachean Ethics* (Oxford: Oxford University Press, 1980), bks. ii (5), iii (1–5).

21. *Nicomachean Ethics*, iii (5).

22. Friedrich Nietzsche, *The Genealogy of Morals*, in *The Birth of Tragedy and the Genealogy of Morals* (New York: Doubleday, 1956), pp. 159–61, 178–80.

23. See Phillip Scribner's essay in this volume, which has influenced me on this point.

24. See note 9, above.

25. The same argument would suffice to show that Mill's contempt for the individual who sells himself into slavery is also only appropriate in normal circumstances. If the circumstances are bad enough, even this might be the best alternative and thus no vice. See note 19, above, and accompanying text.

Addiction
and Autonomy

Are Drug Addicts Unfree?

Kadri Vihvelin

It's commonly assumed that drug addicts are unfree in some way that distinguishes them from us. We have free will in at least this sense: we have control over whether or not we act on our desires. But the addict has a special sort of desire, a desire so strong it compels him to act. Just as someone being dragged through the street cannot resist the force that moves her body, the addict cannot resist the desire that moves him to take the drug. He is a helpless victim of his desire, and to be pitied and helped rather than blamed or punished.

But can this belief be justified? It turns out to be surprisingly difficult. On two philosophical views of freedom, there is no relevant difference between the drug addict and the rest of us. On the first view, the drug addict is *unfree*, but so is everyone else; on the second view, the drug addict is just as *free* as anyone who acts intentionally.

Someone who holds the first view might argue as follows:

The difference between the addict and the rest of us is just a difference in the kind and intensity of his desires. We note that his life is dominated by his desire for the drug, and conclude that this desire causally determines his actions. When he is in the grip of the desire, he can't help taking the drug in exactly the sense that a rock released from a window can't help falling to the ground. We think that we are different, but this is only because our desires are many and various and because we don't experience them as compulsive. But the experience of freedom is illusory. Our psychology may be more complex than that of the addict, but we are as much part of the causal net as he is. It's a mistake to think of ourselves as somehow outside the causal order, freely choosing which of our desires we should act on. If we knew enough about the laws of biochemistry, psychology, neurophysiology, and so on, and enough about the facts, we could see that we are no more free than the drug addict or the falling rock. Our genes, neurophysiology, and our environment determine our beliefs and desires, which determine our actions. Given the laws and the relevant facts, we cannot do other than what we in fact do.

The conclusion of this argument is a thesis which philosophers call "hard determinism": "determinism" because it accepts the truth of the empirical thesis of universal causal determinism and "hard" because it accepts the hard truth that determinism seems to entail—that no one is ever free or morally responsible.

Hard determinism is usually contrasted with a view called "libertarianism," which denies the universal truth of determinism and holds that while our desires may be causally determined by our genes, brain chemistry, and environment, our *will* is not. On the libertarian view, our experience of freedom is not illusory; part of us *is* outside the natural causal order and does, somehow, freely choose which of our competing desires to act on. On this view, we are never compelled by our desires; no matter how strongly a desire inclines us toward action, we have the power to refrain from acting on it.

Outside philosophy, these two positions are usually taken to be the only options there are. Either we are causally determined, and thus, like the addict, not free; or we are not causally determined, and thus free. Defense lawyers, not surprisingly, tend to be hard determinists (Clarence Darrow was notorious for using hard determinism as part of his defense strategy); while prosecutors tend to take the libertarian view.

But there is a third option, an option which challenges an assumption that the libertarian and hard determinist share. The libertarian and the hard determinist both assume that determinism and freedom are incompatible—that the former excludes the possibility of the latter.

But why should we accept this assumption? Even if determinism turned out to be true, there would still be a difference between the falling of the rock and human action. The rock has no choice about whether or not it falls because it has no beliefs and desires and thus is not capable of making *any* choices. But we have beliefs and desires, and we are capable of making choices on the basis of what we believe and want. I choose to stay at home because I want to finish a paper and because I believe that staying home will help me achieve this end. Had my beliefs or desires been different, I would have chosen and done otherwise.

And even if determinism turned out to be true, there would still be a difference between me and the prisoner who is dragged through the streets. The prisoner is like me and unlike the rock in having a will—in being capable of making choices and decisions—but he is unlike me in that his will is not causally efficacious. Whether I stay at home or not depends on what I choose, which in turn depends on what I most want to do. I stay at home because I want most to finish the paper; if I had wanted to go to the beach more than I wanted to finish the paper, I would not have stayed home. But what happens to the prisoner happens to him regardless of his will, regardless of what he chooses, regardless of how much he wants *not* to be dragged. He is the helpless victim of an irresistible force; I am not.

These are real differences, and there is a view of freedom which says that it is *these* differences which are relevant to freedom. On this view, to think that determinism is incompatible with freedom is a mistake that comes from confusing causation with compulsion. What's relevant to freedom is not *whether* what we do is caused, but *how* it's caused. We are unfree when the way our body moves does not depend on what we believe and want; we are free when what we do depends on what we believe and what we want.[1]

Even though it's virtually unknown outside philosophy, this view ("compatibilism") has been the received view in philosophy for a long time. I think that its central claim is correct; there are no good reasons for believing that causal determinism deprives us of freedom.[2]

But the simple form of the compatibilist view outlined above has a consequence that is nearly as surprising as the hard determinist's claim that no one is ever free. If a free will is just a causally efficacious will, then we lack free will when we are unable to move or when the movements of our body are involuntary (falling down stairs, a tremor of the hand, etc.), But on this view of freedom, to act intentionally *is* to act freely. For someone who acts intentionally is someone whose will is causally efficacious, someone who succeeds in doing what she most wants to do. This seems right for most cases of action, but it has the consequence that the drug addict who intentionally takes the drug is just as free as we are. For he succeeds in doing what he most wants to do.

But isn't there some sense in which the addict is *not* as free as we are? This brings us back to our starting point, which is the problem of making sense of the notion of a desire that is unlike other desires in being so strong it compels someone to act. It's possible, of course, that we are mistaken about the unfreedom of addicts. But the problem is not restricted to addicts; it's the problem of giving an account of a distinction that *seems* to make sense, a distinction that our ordinary talk of freedom and responsibility takes for granted. We invoke this distinction when we classify any intentional behavior as "obsessive compulsive" (for instance, when we call someone a compulsive gambler, a kleptomaniac, or a sex addict). Lawyers invoke the distinction when they argue that their clients are not responsible for what they did because they were victims of an "irresistible impulse." We don't always agree about how to draw the line—are "workaholics" and "shopaholics" victims of compulsive desires, or are they merely people who really like to work or shop? But we take for granted that there is a distinction between those who act freely on their desires and those whose desires compel them to act. Yet if simple compatibilism is right, there is no such distinction.

I think we can make sense of the idea that someone's desire compels her to act. Moreover, I think we can do this without assuming that determinism is false. I will offer an account which distinguishes those whose desires compel them to act from the rest of us. It's an empirical question whether drug addicts are unfree in this sense, but I think it's possible that some of them are.

To get to my view, we have to take a detour through some other attempts to explain how someone can act on her own desire, yet *not* act freely.

Addiction and Coercion: Choosing the Lesser Evil?

To be physiologically addicted to a drug is to depend on the drug for the normal functioning of one's body. Withdrawal from a drug to which one is addicted is painful.

This suggests that to be addicted is to be unfree in the way that someone who is coerced is unfree.

Someone who is coerced ("Your money or your life") is someone who acts in order to avoid a threatened evil. It would be misleading to say that the victim of the gunman hands over her money willingly or that she does it because that's what she wants to do. What she wants is to save her life; she wants to hand over her money only as a means to this end.

On this view, the physiological state of addiction is like a constant threat ("Take the drug or you will suffer terribly"). It would be misleading to say that the addict takes the drug willingly or that she takes it because that's what she wants to do. What she wants is to avoid the pain of withdrawal; she wants to take the drug only as a means to this end.

The analogy between coercion and addiction applies only to those addicts who take the drug for a particular reason—those who take the drug because, given their addiction, they fear the pain caused by not taking the drug. It doesn't apply to addicts who would take the drug even if withdrawal caused no pain, who take it because they want to experience the pleasurable state caused by the drug. This is not necessarily an objection; we should not assume that all addicts are unfree.

But there are problems with using the model of coercion to explain the unfreedom of addiction.

First, while it's often said that coercion is a paradigm case of unfreedom, it's not clear why we should think that coerced action is unfree in any interesting sense. Granted, someone who does something at gunpoint is someone who is taken advantage of by the gunman, who exploits his victim's rational fears to get her to do something she would not otherwise have done. Granted, it's bad to be used by the gunman as a mere means to serve *his* ends. But not everything bad involves a loss of freedom. So why should we think that the victim of the gunman acts unfreely?

Is it that the coerced agent is literally unable to do other than what she does, in the way the prisoner being dragged is unable to avoid being dragged? No. The options of the coerced agent are severely limited, but she has a choice. When we say that the coerced agent had "no real choice" or "no reasonable choice" we mean (depending on the circumstances) that she chose the lesser of two evils or that the choice which would have resulted in the greater overall good would have cost her more than it is reasonable to expect.

Is it that the coerced agent doesn't *really* want to do what she does? No. Granted, she doesn't want to have to make a choice in these conditions; she doesn't want to be threatened at gunpoint. But given the situation she is in fact in, she really wants to do what she does. Given that the only way to save her life is to hand over her money, she has no mixed feelings about handing over the money.

But doesn't the fact that we don't blame the coerced agent for doing what would otherwise be blameworthy (e.g., giving away the bank's money) show that we think she is unfree in the sense relevant to responsibility?

No. As J. L. Austin famously pointed out,[3] there are two very different ways in which someone might answer an accusation of wrongdoing: She might say: "It was wrong, but I didn't really do it." ("It was a mistake; it was an accident; I was pushed," and so on.) Or she might say: "I did it, but, given the circumstances, it wasn't wrong." In the first case, the person tries to *excuse* herself from responsibility by claiming that what happened wasn't an action or wasn't the action she intended to perform; in the second case, she accepts responsibility for her action, but claims a *justification* for what she did. The coerced agent defends her action in the second way, and we absolve her of blame only if we are convinced that the threatened evil justified her action. "The bank's money or your life" is a justification; "The bank's money or I'll sing annoyingly out of tune" is not.

But if the coerced agent acts freely and responsibly, then why do people think that the coerced are unfree, or at least *less* free?

I think the answer is this: We think that we are free to the extent that we have options we value having, and a coercive threat diminishes our options. Before the gunman confronted his victim, she had the option of keeping both her money and her life; now she has to choose between them.

If we are free to the extent that we have options we value having, then the gunman's threat leaves his victim less free than she was before the threat. And if the physiological state of addiction functions like a coercive threat, then the drug addict is less free than she was before she became addicted. But this is a very broad way of thinking about freedom; on this view, someone may become less free when she has an unwanted pregnancy, becomes poorer, loses a job, or loses her looks. If this is the only sense in which addiction deprives of freedom, then the addict is unfree only in the way we all are, at different times, and to different degrees. We should not take the addict literally when she complains that her desire compels her to act, that she is helpless to resist it. She's forced to take the drug only in the sense that someone with an unwanted pregnancy is forced to have an abortion or the aging actress is forced to accept a role she would not have taken in her prime.

The second problem with the view that the unfreedom of addiction is the unfreedom of coercion is that it's not clear that the prospect of withdrawal pain counts as a coercive threat. The bank clerk's choice may be described as a choice between two evils insofar as both her options involve something she regards as undesirable—handing over the money which it's her job to safeguard, or losing her life. And the choice she makes is one that both she and we regard as reasonable, given the circumstances.

But is this true of the addict? It depends on the situation and on the addict. Suppose that the addict thinks of his choice as being between these options:

1. Take drugs and feel good for a few hours.
2. Don't take drugs and feel very sick for a few days.

If this is how the addict regards his choice, then only one of his options involves an evil. If we say that his fear of pain coerces him to take the drug, then anyone who ever takes an aspirin to relieve toothache is coerced.

Another addict might think that his choice is restricted to these options:

1. Steal from my children's college fund and take drugs.
2. Don't take drugs and feel very sick for a few days.

If these are the addict's only options, then his choice is a choice between what both he and we may agree are two evils. But now it's not clear whether the threat of withdrawal pain counts as a *coercive* threat. Coercion is a normative concept. Whether a threat counts as coercive depends on whether compliance with the threat would be *justified*; that is, on whether compliance would be the lesser of two evils ("The bank's money or your life") or on whether the cost of noncompliance would be too great to expect the agent to bear. ("Give us the name of your comrades in the Resistance or we'll torture you for three more days.")

In the situation we are imagining, the addict's withdrawal pain is a considerably lesser evil than the loss of his children's college fund. And it's doubtful whether it's unreasonable to expect someone to suffer a few days of pain for the sake of his children's future. So it seems at best doubtful whether the prospect of withdrawal pain counts as a coercive threat.

The last point is this: Even if coercion involves loss of a kind of freedom and even if some addicts are coerced, this doesn't capture the picture with which we began of somebody who claims to be literally *helpless* in the face of his overwhelming desire for the drug. An addict who pleads helplessness is not defending his drug use by claiming that the pain of withdrawal is so great that it's not reasonable to expect him to quit. On the contrary, he might say something like this: "A few days of feeling very sick are not so bad, taking the long view, as a drug-free life. I agree I ought to quit. But I just can't help myself. I need the drug; I've got to have it." Such a person is *not* claiming that his action is the rational response to threatened pain; he is confessing weakness and irrationality.

This suggests another way of accounting for the unfreedom of the addict.

Addiction and Reason: Acting Against One's Better Judgment

Consider the addict who agrees that the life of addiction is not a good life, and that stealing from his children's college fund is a terrible thing to do, but who nevertheless goes ahead and does it. Unlike the addict who tries to justify his action by claiming that it's reasonable given his physiological dependence on the drug, this addict agrees there is *no* justification for what he does, and feels terrible and hates himself. This person has done what he most wants in one sense, yet we are inclined to say that there is another sense in which he has failed to do what he most wants. He has acted on his strongest desire, but he's failed to act according to what he most values and believes he ought to do.

This suggests another way of understanding the addict's plea that he is enslaved by his own desire. Perhaps the addict's helplessness lies in his failure to make his will conform to his *reason*, and, in particular, to his beliefs about what's good for him, his beliefs about right and wrong, and his beliefs about what he ought to do. Whereas the rest of us are able to conform our choices and hence our actions to what we think we ought to do, the addict's desire *overcomes* his reason.

This view, which dates back to Plato, has been revived recently by Gary Watson.[4] Watson argues that we cannot make sense of the unfreedom of the addict unless we reject Hume's account of value and his view of the role of reason in deliberation and motivation. According to Hume, it's a mistake to think that our values are beliefs about what's good, independent of our desires; to value something is just to care about it, to want it, to be motivated (in the appropriate circumstances) to try to get it. On the Humean view, we may use reason to figure out what to believe and how to most effectively get what we want. But reason has no role to play in determining what we *should* want, or what is *worth wanting*.

Watson argues that if Hume is right, then it makes no sense to say that someone acts on his strongest desire but fails to do what he most values or thinks best. For if values are just desires, then there is no difference between what we most value and what we most strongly desire. Since our strongest desire is the one that actually moves us to act (or try to act), it follows that whenever we act intentionally we act according to what we most value or think best. Despite his protests to the contrary, the addict who steals from his children does what he thinks best; his action shows that he values his short-term pleasure more than he values the future of his children.

Plato's view of value, reason, and motivation was very different. He thought that to value something is to believe it to be good and worth wanting, and he thought that reason *can* tell us what's good and worth wanting. That is, reason can tell us, not just what we ought to do given what we already want, but also what we *ought* to *want*. Since what we ought to want is not necessarily what we *actually* want, we may want something without thinking it good or worth wanting.

Watson suggests that the key to understanding the un-freedom of addicts lies in Plato's view that we may be motivated either by what reason tells us we ought to do or by mere desire. If we can be motivated either by reason or by desire, there is a possibility of conflict. We may do what we most strongly desire without doing what we think is best or most worth doing.

Watson argues that if we reject Hume's account of value, then we can retain a compatibilist account of freedom, while being able to draw distinctions Hume was unable to draw. The simple compatibilist view identifies an agent's will with what she most wants to do and says that someone's will is free when she is able to do what she most wants. If there is no distinction between someone's causally strongest desire and what she most values, as Hume thought, then simple compatibilism reduces to the view that an agent's will is her strongest desire. But if there is a distinction between wanting most in the causal sense and valuing most, then it makes sense to identify the agent's will, not with her causally strongest desire, but with her value judgment about what she *ought to do*. Given this, we can say that the addict who steals from his children acts, not just against his better judgment, but also against his will, and thus unfreely.

Watson's suggestion is appealing. While we may disagree about how to best interpret the behavior of the addict, it seems intelligible that he steals from his children despite his judgment that this is not what he ought to do, even given his need for the drug. If Hume's account of value cannot make sense of this, then we should reject Hume's account.

But is Watson *also* right in proposing that an agent's will simply *is* her judgment about what she ought to do? And is he right in claiming that someone who acts against her better judgment *thereby* acts unfreely?

Intuitively, there is a difference between someone who acts against her better judgment despite the fact that she wants to do what she believes she ought to do, and someone who *doesn't want* to do what she agrees she *ought* to do.

X lies to Customs officials. When we question him later, he agrees that breaking the law is wrong, but candidly explains that he did it because he didn't want to spend hundreds of dollars on import duties. X acted contrary to his judgment about what he ought to do. But we've got no reason to suppose he acted unfreely.

Bob is a utilitarian and thus believes that he ought to do what will maximize the greatest good of the greatest number. But sometimes when he's forced to choose between the greatest good and *his* good, or between the greatest good and the good of those near and dear to him, he does what's best for him or those he loves. It's far from obvious that *whenever* Bob fails to live up to his demanding moral theory this is because he is unable to conform his conduct to his better judgment. A more plausible explanation is that he cares more about his good and the good of those he loves than he cares about doing what he believes to be best. Or, to put it more bluntly, there are occasions on which Bob does not want to do what he believes he ought to do.

Cases like X and Bob pose a problem for Watson. There are only two ways he can respond, both unsatisfactory.

He might bite the bullet and admit that X and Bob act against their better judgment, hence unfreely. But this is wildly implausible. We shouldn't accept a view that runs so contrary to our ordinary beliefs unless there is no better account of what distinguishes free from unfree action. (I'll be arguing that there is a better account.)

Or Watson might deny that X and Bob really act against their better judgment. He might argue that X is more plausibly described as someone who thinks that breaking the law is only prima facie wrong. Perhaps X thinks that the Customs laws are absurd and should not be obeyed. If so, then X does not act contrary to his judgment about what he ought to do, *all things considered*. And he might make a similar claim about Bob. Bob acts contrary to his beliefs about what *morality* requires, but he doesn't act contrary to his judgment about what he ought to do, all things considered. Bob weighs the demands of morality against the cost to himself (or those he loves) and concludes that on this occasion morality is not worth the cost.

There is always room to argue about particular cases, including X and Bob. Despite what he says, perhaps X really believes that lying to Customs officials (in this particular case) is justified. Despite what he says, perhaps Bob believes that we are sometimes justified in doing what will not bring about the greatest good. But Watson needs to make a stronger claim, if he is to argue that, despite appearances, people like X and Bob do not act contrary to their all-things-considered value judgment. He has to argue that we must *always* disregard what people like X and Bob say and what they appear to believe, and look instead to their actions to find out what their all-things-considered value judgments are.

But now I think that Watson's account is in danger of collapsing back into Hume's. On Hume's view, there is no difference between what someone thinks best and what she wants most (in the causal sense). Watson criticizes Hume on the grounds that his view makes it impossible to make sense of someone acting against her better judgment. But if thinking best is *not* the same as wanting most, it must be possible to say, of someone, that she thinks it best (all things considered) to do x, even though her action shows that she wants something else more. Watson *seems* prepared to say this, but only in certain sorts of cases—cases like that of the drug addict and other victims of psychological compulsions. But if there is a conceptual distinction between thinking best and wanting most, this distinction should hold for *any* kind of desire, including X's desire to save money and Bob's desire concerning the well-being of those he loves. If Watson nevertheless insists that the people like X and Bob do what they think is best, all things considered, then his account does not differ, in any principled way, from Hume's.

I am persuaded by Watson's criticism of Hume; we need an account of value on which it's possible for someone to act contrary to her all-things-considered value judgment. But the cases of X and Bob suggest that it's a mistake to identify the agent's will with his judgment about what he ought to do. X and Bob fail to do what they think they ought to do, but they don't act "against" or "despite" their will. Nor do they suffer from any impairment or unfreedom of the will.

It seems then, that we must reject Watson's account of the unfreedom of those who claim that their desire compelled them to act. We must look elsewhere. Let's begin by considering another addict.

Mary is trying to quit smoking. We have excellent evidence that she's sincere not only in her claim that she thinks she ought not to smoke, but also in her claim that she *wants* to stop smoking. She's gotten rid of all the cigarettes in the house, avoids places where smokers hang out, has instructed her friends not to give her cigarettes even if she begs for them, and engages in all the displacement activity she can think of. She succeeds in not smoking for three days. But on the morning of the fourth day, she finds a cigarette in a coat pocket, and, cursing herself, smokes it.

When Mary smokes the cigarette, she acts against her better judgment. But what seems relevant to the question of her freedom (what distinguishes her from X and Bob) is the fact that she acts on a desire she wants not to be moved by, a desire she's been trying to eliminate. This brings us to our next account of the unfreedom of the addict.

Addiction and Second-Order Desires: Acting on a Desire One Wants Not to Be Motivated By

Harry Frankfurt[5] says that the key to understanding the unfreedom of the addict lies in *desires* after all. He says that simple compatibilism fails because it ignores the fact that we are motivationally more complex than young children and simpler animals. In addition to first-order desires, we have second-order desires—desires about our first-order desires. For instance, we may want to have a desire we don't yet have; we may want to get rid of a desire we have, we may want to be motivated more often by one of our desires, and so on.

Frankfurt says that we can understand freedom and unfreedom of will in terms of a certain kind of second-order desire that he calls a second-order volition. A second-order volition is a second-order desire concerning which of our first-order desires is our will (first-order motivating desire). Frankfurt's view goes something like this: Just as freedom of action is being able to do what we want, freedom of will is being able to will as we want. If we act on a desire that we want to be motivated by, then we have free will with respect to that desire.[6] If we act on a desire that we want *not* to be motivated by, then we lack free will with respect to that desire.

Let's apply Frankfurt's account to Mary. Mary is someone who has the kind of second-order desire Frankfurt tells us is relevant to unfreedom of will; she wants *not* to be motivated by her desire to smoke. When she finally succumbs to temptation and smokes a cigarette despite her second-order desire *not* to be motivated by this desire, she lacks free will with respect to her desire to smoke. It also seems plausible to say, as Frankfurt says about a similar case, that Mary acts against her will, and that she acts unfreely.[7]

This account looks promising because it allows us to bypass the difficult questions about value and motivation raised by Watson's account. We can accept Frankfurt's basically Humean account of free will, while either accepting or rejecting a Humean account of value. And it's appealing because it allows us to supplement the simple compatibilist account of freedom of action with an account of freedom of will without making any questionable empirical assumptions (e.g., that second-order desires are themselves uncaused).

But there is a problem that forces Frankfurt to revise this account.

What if we have conflicting second-order desires? Suppose I both want not to be motivated by my desire to drink coffee (I'm worried that drinking so much coffee isn't good for me) *and* want to be motivated by my desire to drink coffee (I'm convinced that it helps me work better)? If I continue to drink coffee, it seems that Frankfurt must say that I both have and lack free will with respect to my coffee-drinking desire. I have free will because I act on a desire I want to be motivated by. I lack free will because I act on a desire I want *not* to be motivated by.

So Frankfurt needs a way of saying *which* second-order desire is the relevant one. His own answer is disappointing, so I will first consider whether there is a better reply he can make.

Let's begin with a reply in the spirit of Hume: The desire relevant to questions of freedom of action is the first-order desire that is causally strongest. (Freedom of action is being able to do what you *most* want.) The desire relevant to questions of freedom of will is the second-order desire that is causally strongest. (Freedom of will is being able to will what you *most* want.)

But I don't think that this reply will help Frankfurt. The criterion of strength for first-order desires is actual or counterfactual behavior. Is my desire to eat chocolate mousse stronger than my desire to eat apple pie? That depends on which I would choose, given a choice between the two. If I'd take the chocolate mousse, then my first-order desire for mousse is stronger than my first-order desire for apple pie.

If it makes sense to talk of strength of second-order desires, then presumably a similar test applies. Is my desire to be motivated by my chocolate-mousse desire stronger than my desire to be motivated by my apple-pie desire? That depends on which *desire* I would choose to be motivated by, given a choice between the two. If I would choose to be motivated by my apple-pie desire, then my pro–apple-pie second-order desire is stronger than my pro-mousse second-order desire.

The problem with this way of revising Frankfurt is that the counterfactual test for strength of second-order desires always yields the *same* result as the counterfactual test for first-order desires. For we evaluate counterfactuals by considering the closest (most similar) worlds at which the antecedent is true. While there may be distant worlds where I am offered (and take) a pill that will miraculously rid me of my chocolate-mousse desire, these are *not* the relevant worlds. The relevant worlds are worlds very like our own, where I have the same fondness for chocolate mousse I in fact have, and where I'm offered a choice between the mousse and the apple pie. When I choose the mousse, I show by my action that my chocolate-mousse desire is the strongest. But my action also reveals that my *second-order* pro-mousse desire is the strongest. For in choosing the mousse, I also choose to be motivated by my mousse desire.

So the appeal to causal strength will not help Frankfurt. Insofar as it makes sense to talk of the causal strength of second-order desires, this does *not* yield a measure of strength independent of the strength of first-order desires. The upshot is another Humean collapse: whenever we do what we most want we are also motivated as we most want to be motivated; so we always act freely and with free will.

If the relevant second-order desire is not the causally strongest desire, then this appears to leave us with just one other possibility, one we have already considered. Perhaps what's relevant at the second-order level is what the person most *values*.[8]

Watson's account of unfreedom fails because cases like X and Bob show that acting against one's value judgment does not provide a sufficient condition of acting unfreely. Frankfurt's account is in trouble because of the problem of conflicting second-order desires. Perhaps we can combine Watson's insight with Frankfurt's as follows: Someone acts unfreely on her desire D just in case it's true both that she thinks she ought not to act on D *and* she wants not to be motivated by D.[9]

On this account, I act freely when I drink the coffee, for I don't act contrary to what I think I should do. (I don't *know* what I should do; that's why I have conflicting second-order desires.) But let's put aside the question of whether the account provides a *necessary* condition of acting unfreely on a desire, and consider the question of whether it provides a *sufficient* condition.

Suppose that I come to believe that the bad consequences of drinking coffee outweigh the good consequences. Now I think I ought not to drink coffee, all things considered. I still have conflicting second-order desires, and I continue to drink coffee. On the proposed Watson-Frankfurt account I act unfreely. But do I?

I agree that it's *possible* that my coffee-drinking desire is, like Mary's desire for cigarettes and the heroin addict's desire for heroin, a desire that compels me to act. But is this so in virtue of the fact that my action goes against my belief that it's best to stop drinking coffee and my desire not to be motivated by my coffee-drinking desire?

I presented Bob as a counterexample to Watson's original account. But I think that Bob is also a counterexample to the Watson-Frankfurt account we are now considering. Bob is a more complex creature than I made him out to be. He wants, not just to do what's right; he also wants to be a morally good person. That is, he wants to be someone who is motivated by the desire to do what will bring about the greatest overall good. But he also wants to be a good son; he wants to be motivated by the desire to do what is good for his mother. Sometimes Bob has to choose between these desires, and sometimes he does what's best for his mother *even though* he believes what his moral theory tells him—that his action is not justified. On those occasions, Bob acts, not just contrary to his all-things-considered value judgment, he also acts contrary to the second-order desire which agrees with this value judgment. But Bob still acts freely.

Consider another kind of case. The L.A. Times is a very good newspaper and I often spend the first hour of every morning reading it. I like reading the paper, but it really would be better to read it later in the day, as a break. Suppose, then, that I make the value judgment that, all things considered, I should *not* read the paper first thing in the morning, and suppose, moreover, that this value judgment causes me to have the second-order desire *not* to be motivated by my newspaper-reading desire. Nevertheless, I continue to read the paper as soon as I get up. I am probably weak willed, certainly self-indulgent. But I don't think I am unfree in the way the addict is.[10]

Up to now, we've considered two ways of revising Frank-furt's account to solve the problem of conflicting second-order desires. The first way (causal strength) has the upshot that no one ever lacks free will or acts unfreely. The second way (value judgment) allows us to say that the addict acts unfreely, but not in any way that distinguishes him from much of the rest of us much of the time. For on this view we act unfreely whenever we fail to be all that we want to be and think we should be.

This seems to exhaust the options, but Frankfurt thinks there's another way around the problem. He says that the rele-vant second-order desire is the one with which the person "de-cisively identifies."[11] Unfree action, then, is action contrary to a second-order desire with which the person decisively identifies.

If we don't think about this too much, it may seem plausi-ble. Intuitively, what distinguishes me from Mary is that Mary has made a decisive commitment to give up smoking, whereas I am wavering about whether or not to drink coffee and I only half-heartedly want to give up my newspaper habit.

But what exactly does it take for someone to decisively identify with one of her desires? Do we take her word for it? Surely not. Look to her behavior? But what behavior is relevant? And what is the behavior supposed to be evidence *for*? Frankfurt gives us no answers. But we've already seen that neither the causal strength of the second-order desire nor the fact that it accords with the person's value judgment will help him. It's not clear what's left.

I conclude that Frankfurt's answer is no answer at all, but just a label for the problem. The second-order desires that count are those with which the agent decisively identifies. That is, they are the desires which the agent somehow claims as his own and which somehow earn the right to be called the desires that count. But Frankfurt offers us no clue as to how this might be the case.

Addiction and the Ulysses Desire

Watson and Frankfurt's accounts looked appealing be-cause they promised to explain the unfreedom of the addict without appealing to any qualitative, subjective, or inherently vague and ad hoc notions like "really wanting" or "wanting most in the sense that counts." They both offered (or seemed to offer) analyses of unfree action that appeal only to the *content* of one of the person's propositional attitudes. On Watson's account, the relevant attitude is the person's *judgment* about what she ought to do. On Frankfurt's account, it's the person's second-order *desire* about which of her desires should be her will.

But when we pressed these accounts, we discovered that they do not deliver what they promise. Watson's account only gives the illusion of being able to draw distinctions Hume cannot draw. He wants to say that the unfree addict acts against his judgment about what he ought to do, but that people like X and Bob don't. But he can say this only by using a shifting and double standard for determining what someone judges that she ought to do. Frankfurt's account turned out to suffer from similar problems. In order to distinguish those who are compelled from those who are merely self-indulgent or weak willed, he needs to explain why some second-order desires about the will count against freedom and others do not. His answer sheds no light; to be told that the relevant desires are those with which the person decisively identifies is no more helpful than being told that the relevant desires are the ones that she cares about in the right sort of way.

I think that the lesson to be learned is this: We need an account that distinguishes free from unfree action by appealing *only* to the *content* of a propositional attitude. The lesson to be learned from Watson is that no belief (not even a belief about value or what one ought to do) will do the job. The lesson to be learned from Frankfurt is that the second-order desire he identified won't do it. But I think that another second-order desire will draw the right distinctions.

I want to distinguish between the effectiveness of a desire and its satisfaction. A desire is *effective* if it causes the agent to act; that is, if it's what Frankfurt calls her motivating desire. A desire is *satisfied* if the action is successfully completed or the state of affairs that is the object of the desire obtains. Since it is possible to act on a desire without attaining the object of the desire (to try, but fail), a desire may be effective without being satisfied.

On Frankfurt's original account, a *sufficient* condition for a person's being unfree with respect to the desire D that causes her to act is that she has a second-order desire which I now baptize "the Frankfurt desire": (F) the desire that D not be effective.

Does someone with the Frankfurt desire *also* want that her first-order desire D not be satisfied? It may seem reasonable to think that she does. If someone wants that her desire to eat chocolate not be effective, then this is presumably because she wants *not to eat chocolate*. Given this, it seems reasonable to describe her as someone who wants that her desire to eat chocolate *not* be satisfied.

But someone may have the Frankfurt desire without also having a *second-order desire* which I'll call "the Ulysses desire": (U) the desire that D not be satisfied, even if D is effective.

And it is the Ulysses desire that is relevant to the question of unfree action. Or so I will argue.

The Ulysses desire is the desire that explains the otherwise peculiar behavior of Ulysses. Ulysses ordered his men to bind him to the mast before they sailed by the sirens, who were notorious for the irresistible song by which they lured men to their doom:

> And if I shout and beg to be untied,
> Take more turns of the rope to muffle me.[12]

Ulysses wants *not* to be motivated by the desire that he anticipates the sirens will cause him to have. He's got the Frankfurt desire. But he also wants something more. He also wants that, *even if* the song of the sirens causes him to be moved by the desire to pursue them, that this desire *not* be satisfied. He orders himself bound to the mast because he wants that even if he tries to act on his siren-following desire, he won't succeed. He wants, if necessary, to be *stopped* from acting on his desire.

Those who have the Frankfurt desire but lack the Ulysses desire include those we call self-indulgent or weak willed. I've given several examples already. Here's another: Joe is no alcoholic but he really likes to drink, especially cold beer on a hot day after playing tennis. He's trying to lose a few pounds, though, so has decided to give up drinking beer. He's got the Frankfurt desire; he wants not to be motivated by his desire to drink beer. He stocks his fridge with mineral water, and is doing his best to acquire a taste for it. But when he's offered a beer by his tennis partner after their game, he takes it, drinks it, and snaps at his wife for reminding him that he's trying to lose weight. He lacks the Ulysses desire; given that his beer-drinking desire is effective, he wants it satisfied.

What lesson can we learn from the difference between Joe and Ulysses? I think it's this: There's a difference between being unwilling and acting *against* one's *will*. Joe is an unwilling drinker insofar as he wants not to be motivated by his desire to drink. But when it comes to the crunch, Joe doesn't act against his will. His unwillingness is conditional on the desire *not* being his effective desire. He wants to get his way; he wants the satisfaction of the desire that moves him to act.

Ulysses on the other hand, wants that his siren-following desire not be satisfied even if it is effective. If he nevertheless breaks free of his bonds and takes off after the sirens, he acts, not just unwillingly (reluctantly, unhappily, on a desire he doesn't want to be motivated by), he also acts *against* his will. His unwillingness is *not* conditional on his motivation. For even as his desire moves him towards action, he wants it frustrated; he wants his men to stop him when he can no longer stop himself. Unlike Joe, he can truly say, quoting Frankfurt, that it is "not of his own free will, but against his will" that he acts.[13]

Since what distinguishes Ulysses from Joe is the Ulysses desire, I propose that a sufficient condition for someone acting unfreely on her desire D is that D causes her to act despite her Ulysses desire concerning D. That is, she acts on D even though she wants that D not be satisfied, even if D is effective.

Ordinarily, someone who has the Ulysses desire also has the Frankfurt desire; we would question the sincerity of someone who claimed to have an unconditional desire not to succeed in acting on one of his first-order desires, but who showed no signs of trying to avoid being motivated by this desire. (For instance, someone who claims to want that his desire to sleep with his best friend's wife not be satisfied, but who makes no effort to avoid spending time alone with her.) The Ulysses desire is not *just* the desire to be stopped from acting on one's desire; it is the desire to *prevent oneself* from acting on one's desire, by whatever means possible. Since the best, and often the only, way to prevent one-self from acting on a desire is by preventing the desire from be-ing effective in the first place, someone who has the Ulysses desire will ordinarily also have the Frankfurt desire.

There may be unusual cases in which someone has the Ulysses desire without also having the Frankfurt desire. But I think that even in these cases, we will, *at the time of action*, credit someone with the Ulysses desire only if we have reason to be-lieve that she also has the Frankfurt desire.

Objection: You claim that someone may act on his desire for the drug while at the same time wanting this desire *not* to be satisfied. But to want a desire not to be satisfied is to want *not* to do the relevant action. So the unwilling addict wants *not to take the drug*. Since his desire for the drug causes him to act, he also wants *to take the drug*. But then the addict wants it to be the case that he both takes the drug *and* does not take the drug. But this is a desire for an *impossible* state of affairs, and there is no possible evidence that would lead us to attribute such a desire to anyone.

I agree that no evidence would convince us that anyone has a desire that a contradiction be true. But that's not what I'm claiming. Nor am I claiming that we should credit anyone with a desire for an impossible state of affairs. My claim is that we can have behavioral evidence for two separate *conflicting desires*, de-sires that *cannot* (logically, and not merely contingently) both be satisfied. Granted, this is irrational, in that someone with such desires *cannot* have everything she wants. But someone who is unfree *is* irrational. That's one of the reasons we think her unfree.

Objection: Granted, we have evidence that Ulysses has the Ulysses desire at the time he orders himself bound to the mast. But we've got no evidence that he still has this desire when he breaks free of his bonds and pursues the sirens. On the contrary, we then have evidence that what he wants is that his siren-following desire be satisfied.

No. When we see Ulysses pursuing the sirens, we've got evidence that his causally strongest first-order desire is to follow them. We have no evidence that he also has a second-order de-sire that he succeed in acting on this first-order desire. On the contrary, his earlier behavior is evidence that he wants *not* to succeed in what he is now trying to do. Of course it's logically possible that his earlier second-order desire vanished at the moment of action, but we have no reason to believe this. The question to ask is: "Does Ulysses want to be stopped?" (Will he thank us later for stopping him?) If the answer to this question is yes, then Ulysses still has the Ulysses desire.

Objection: Isn't your account vulnerable to the same objection you made to Frankfurt's account? What if someone has conflicting Ulysses desires?

This is not a problem for me, because my account, unlike Frankfurt's, is a pure content account. My claim is that if someone acts contrary to her Ulysses desire, then she acts unfreely, *regardless* of what other desires she has.

However, it's harder than it seems to tell a convincing story about someone with a second-order desire that conflicts with her Ulysses desire. Suppose that someone tells all her friends and even the corner grocer not to give or sell her cigarettes, but keeps one pack of cigarettes tucked away under a pile of papers at the bottom of her file cabinet. But this is evidence that she *doesn't* have the Ulysses desire; she wants her friends to stop her from smoking, but she doesn't want to stop herself.

The Ulysses desire is the desire that a first-order desire D *not be satisfied*, even if effective. Evidence for a conflicting second-order desire would have to be evidence that the person also wants that D be satisfied, if it is effective. But evidence that counts in favor of the second desire is evidence that counts *against* the first desire.

But what about Ulysses? Suppose that he fights off his men as they try to stop him from following the sirens. Isn't this behavior evidence that he has, not just a first-order desire to follow the sirens, but also a second-order desire *not* to be *prevented* from acting on this desire? If so, then Ulysses both wants to be stopped and wants *not* to be stopped from acting on it.

I agree that, at the time of action, Ulysses may have both these desires. I even agree that in such a case the question, "Does he want to be stopped?" may yield two answers: "Yes" and "No." But this doesn't bother me. *If* we are convinced that Ulysses really has the Ulysses desire, that is, if his behavior before and after the siren-following incident is consistent with this hypothesis, then I think that we should regard him as unfree.

I hope I've made it clear that the Ulysses desire, unlike the Frankfurt desire, is a relatively uncommon desire, and that cases in which someone acts contrary to a Ulysses desire are thus relatively unusual as well. It's common to fail to act on desires one wants to be motivated by (to fail to be as kind and generous as one wants to be, for instance). It's also quite common to act on desires one wants *not* to be motivated by (to be rude or mean-spirited, for instance). But it's not so common for someone to want to prevent her desire from being satisfied, and to want, if necessary, to be stopped from satisfying it.

Those who (probably) have the Ulysses desire include Mary, addicts who check themselves into drug clinics or other therapeutic programs, and the person who wrote on a New York subway wall, "Stop me before I kill again." Someone who steals under the nose of the store detective, knowing he will be caught, may have the Ulysses desire. But the addict who steals from his children does not; his shame and self-contempt notwithstanding.

Why is the Ulysses desire relevant to the question of whether someone acts unfreely on their own desire? I think it captures what was right about both the Watson and Frankfurt accounts. Why does Ulysses want to be stopped from satisfying his own desire? Presumably at least partly because he does not *value* what he knows he will try to get. When can someone legitimately claim that the desire that moves her to act is an alien force, something which does not deserve to be called her will? Only when she *disowns* the desire, by having the desire to prevent it from being satisfied.

But I think there is another reason for thinking that the Ulysses desire is the desire relevant to the question of unfree action. The sense of unfreedom we've been trying to analyze is the sense relevant to moral responsibility. The problem with all the other accounts we've looked at is that they have the consequence that agents who we think are morally responsible turn out to act unfreely.

Someone who acts on her desire D despite her Ulysses desire concerning D is, I think, someone whom we *should* regard as not morally responsible—someone to be pitied and helped rather than blamed or punished. Why? Because she is, in effect, asking *us* to assume responsibility for her actions. If she really has this desire (and of course it won't always be easy to tell if someone is sincere or faking it), then she is, in part, saying "Stop me from satisfying my own desire." Someone who sincerely says this is someone who gives us permission to treat her paternalistically rather than as a free and responsible being.

I've argued that someone who acts on a first-order desire D despite her second-order Ulysses desire concerning D is someone who satisfies a *sufficient* condition for being compelled by her desire. But is the Ulysses desire also necessary for it to be true that someone's desire compels her to act?

I don't think so. We may be more inclined to say that those who act despite having the Ulysses desire act unfreely because in those cases we have the *clearest evidence* that they were unable to do other than what they did. But an addict who lacks these desires may nevertheless be compelled by his desire to take the drug. What's relevant is whether he would still have taken the drug *if* he had had the Ulysses desire.

Consider a sailor who knows nothing about the sirens, and who is thus wholly unprepared for their seductive song. Unlike Ulysses, he has no second-order desires concerning the desire the sirens cause him to have, and he happily acts on it, thinking that he acts freely. And if we knew nothing about Ulysses, or about the other sailors who have succumbed to the lure of the sirens despite their desperate struggles not to do so, we would have no reason to think him unfree. But (on the assumption that the sirens have the same effect upon everyone), he nevertheless acts unfreely. Even though he doesn't know it, he cannot help doing what he does. For even if he had wanted the desire not to be satisfied, even if effective, he would still have acted on it.

So I propose that a necessary and sufficient condition of someone acting unfreely on her desire D is that the following counterfactual is true: Even if she had had the Ulysses desire, D would still have caused her to act. (The counterfactual may be true either because someone actually has the Ulysses desire, yet acts on D, or it may be true because at the closest worlds where she has the Ulysses desire, she still acts on D.)

People tend to take one of two extreme approaches to the question of whether someone can act unfreely on her own desire. Either they say that we act unfreely *whenever* a desire causes us to act (because only action based on reason is free), or they say that we *never* act unfreely when we act on a desire (because to act on a desire *is* to act for a reason, which is to act freely). But these extremist approaches ignore the real distinctions in how our desires may cause us to act. If we can have desires that conflict with each other in the ways I've described, then we can make sense of the idea that someone can stand in the same sort of relation to one of her desires that we stand in relation to external forces. It makes sense to say that someone is moved by a force she cannot avoid being moved by; it also makes sense to say that someone is moved to act by a desire she cannot avoid acting on.

Do the desires of addicts compel them to act? If my account is correct, then this is an empirical question, and the answer will depend on the person, drug, and circumstances of action. But I would not be surprised if it turned out to be true that there are *fewer*, rather than more, cases of unfree action than we think.[14]

NOTES

1. David Hume was one of the first to clearly articulate this view. "Of Liberty and Necessity," in *Enquiries Concerning Human Understanding and Concerning the Principles of Morals* (Selby-Bigge edition, Oxford University Press, 1902), pp. 80–103.

2. I argue this in "Freedom, Causation, and Counterfactuals," *Philosophical Studies* 64 (1991), 161–84. For the best recent defense of the view that determinism is incompatible with freedom, see Peter van Inwagen, *An Essay on Free Will* (Oxford: Clarendon Press, 1983.)

3. J.L. Austin, "A Plea for Excuses," *Philosophical Papers*, (Oxford: Clarendon Press, 1961.)

4. Watson, "Free Agency," *Journal of Philosophy* 72 (1975), 205–20. Also in *Free Will*, ed. Gary Watson (Oxford University Press, 1982). All references are to Watson, ed.

5. "Freedom of the Will and the Concept of a Person," *Journal of Philosophy* 68 (1971), 5–20. Also in *Free Will*, ed. by Gary Watson, ibid. Page references are to the Watson book.

6. This is an oversimplification, since an addict may *want* his drug-taking desire to be his will. In that case, Frankfurt tells us that the addict still acts freely and "of his own free will," but he lacks free will, since "his desire to take the drug will be effective regardless of whether or not he wants this desire to constitute his will." (p.94) I'm going to ignore the complications posed by such "willing addicts;" I will be arguing that Frankfurt's account fails even in the simpler case of unwilling addicts, like Mary.

7. ". . . the unwilling addict may meaningfully make the analytically puzzling statement that the force moving him to take the drug is a force other than his own, and that it is not of his own free will but rather against his will that this force moves him to take it." Frankfurt, p. 88.

8. Watson says that Frankfurt's inability to solve the problem of conflicting second-order desires shows that the key to the problem of unfree action lies in the desire/value distinction rather than in any distinction between lower- and higher-order desires. (p.109)

9. This may *be* Watson's account; he seems to think that whenever someone makes an all-things-considered value judgment that she ought to do x, then she both wants to do x and has a second-order desire that her desire to do x be effective and that contrary desires be ineffective. (p. 109) He thinks this because he assumes that "to think a thing good is at the same time to desire it" (p.99) I suspect that this is why Watson does not consider the possibility of people like X and Bob, whose thoughts about what they ought to do are only *contingently* connected to their desires.

10. Watson would disagree. Although he acknowledges that we think that the weak willed are free in some way that the psychologically compelled are not, he argues that we are not *justified* in drawing this distinction. ("Skepticism about Weakness of the Will," *Philosophical Review* 86 [1977], 316–31.) However, if my account of unfree action is right, then we *are* justified in drawing the distinction.

11. "Freedom of Will and the Concept of a Person," p.91.

12. Homer, *The Odyssey*, trans. Robert Fitzgerald (Garden City, NY: Doubleday Anchor, 1963), p. 214.

13. "Freedom of the Will and the Concept of a Person," p.88.

14. I would like to thank Curtis Brown, Steven Burns, Richmond Campbell, Sue Campbell, Steven Luper-Foy, Milton Wachsberg, David Zimmerman, and especially Terrance Tomkow for helpful discussion and comments on earlier versions of this paper.

Do Drugs Deprive Us of Free Will?

Phillip Scribner

Whether drugs deprive us of freedom is an important issue, because unless they do, our drug laws, indeed the whole "War on Drugs," which is currently responsible for half the convicts in federal prisons and untold terror and violence concentrated in the inner city, is an unnecessary evil. In a free society, at least, government does not limit the rights of its citizens, especially at such great cost to them, unless that is the only way to attain some greater good. In this case, the greater good is supposed to be avoiding the harm of drug addiction. This justification depends on an orthodox belief about the nature of drug addiction. The orthodoxy holds that when people take drugs, they become addicted, which deprives them of the free will they need to protect themselves from the ill effects of using drugs. Hence, the state must use its police power to prevent situations in which its citizens can choose whether to take drugs.

Although Professor Vihvelin does not mention the political significance of her position, she is defending the current drug policy, for she is trying to "make sense" of the orthodoxy. She never doubts whether drugs cause an addiction that deprives users of free will, but rather takes her project to be explaining how it does so. She holds that drugs deprive us of the ability to choose freely about using them by inducing desires in us that are so strong that they overpower our will not to take them.

I will not deny that there is such a thing as drug addiction. But I will argue that it is not the drugs that are depriving us of free will. As an alternative to Professor Vihvelin's affective theory of will, I defend a cognitive theory. I argue that *will* is a rational judgment about what one ought to do that has complete control of behavior, and that the only thing that can limit freedom of the will is reason itself. That is how I will explain drug addiction. This unorthodox explanation of drug addition has, however, the opposite implication about the justification of anti-drug laws, for, as we shall see, it implies that the only way to eliminate drug addiction is to legalize drugs.

Professor Vihvelin's Affective Theory of Will

Professor Vihvelin is a compatibilist, holding that free will is compatible with natural determinism: "What's relevant to freedom is not *whether* what we do is caused, but *how* it's caused" (p. 53). She starts by assuming that we are free because "we have beliefs and desires, and we are capable of making choices on the basis of what we believe and want" (p. 53). That is how behavior is caused when we are free. But she quickly abandons "simple compatibilism," as she calls it, because it provides no way of distinguishing the unfreedom of addicts from the freedom people normally enjoy. *Every* intentional action would be free on this account. But "we take for granted," she says, "that there is a distinction between those who act freely on their desires and those whose desires compel them to act." Thus, the problem she sets herself is "making sense of the notion of a desire that is unlike other desires in being so strong that it compels one to act" (p. 54). That is how the affective theory of will makes sense of the orthodox belief that drugs deprive us of free will.

The belief that drug-induced desires are so strong that they overpower the will about them entails the affective theory of will, because the will must be a desire of some kind for its efficacy to depend on being stronger than the desires it normally controls. Professor Vihvelin rightly rejects the notion that drug-induced desires "coerce" the addict, like an external force, because the "addict who pleads helplessness is not defending his drug use by claiming that the pain of withdrawal is so great that it's not reasonable to expect him to quit" (p. 58). The burden of withdrawal deprives one of *freedom of action*, not *freedom of will*, for it leaves the addict free to choose what to do in her difficult situation. The addict, on the other hand, lacks freedom of will, because having chosen to quit, she cannot help but take the drug. However, since the claim to lack freedom of the will does not make sense on the "simple compatibilist" version of the affective theory of will, Professor Vihvelin introduces Frankfurt's notion of "second-order desires," that is, desires *about* which first-order desires will be effective in generating behavior. On this theory, the will is free when second-order desires control which first-order desires actually cause our behavior, and it is unfree, when we act on a desire even though we have a second-order desire not to act on it. Vihvelin's example of unfreedom is Mary, a cigarette smoker who "wants *not* to be motivated by her desire to smoke": she is unfree, because she "succumbs to temptation and smokes a cigarette despite her second-order desire *not* to be motivated by this desire" (p. 64).

Frankfurt's theory of second-order desires is a form of the affective theory of will, since it takes the will to be a kind of desire. The attractiveness of the affective theory comes from the simplicity of the mechanism by which it "makes sense" of drugs depriving us of free will: it holds that the desires induced by drugs to take drugs can be strong enough to override our second-order desires not to take them. The relationship between will and desire is based on what might be called the "animal model of choice." Animals, as well as humans, have beliefs and desires, and their behavior also comes from a "choice" based on beliefs and desires. For example, a dog that waits outside the door its master has entered is making a choice on the basis of what it believes and wants: it stays there, because it believes that its master is inside and it desires to remain as close as possible to its master. To be sure, the animal's choice is simple, since it always acts on the strongest desire it has at the moment. But that is the model for the choices that humans make too. What makes humans different from other animals is having, among the desires competing for control of their behavior, second-order desires, that is, desires, about which first-order desires to act on. Second-order desires are presumably stronger than first-order desires in normal people, but human choice is ultimately, like animal choice, a matter of acting on the strongest desire at the moment. Hence, when first-order, animal desires do happen to be stronger than second-order desires, human beings lack free will.

Although the simplicity of its model for the unfreedom of drug addiction makes it attractive, that same simplicity poses a problem for the affective theory, because it does not explain how the will is formed. The will is usually assumed to be the result of a process of reasoning, but on the animal model of choice, the existence of second-order desires is simply taken as given. The failure to explain where second-order desires come from undercuts the affective theory, for without a theory of reasoning, it cannot always identify which second-order desire is the will. This problem leads Professor Vihvelin to modify Frankfurt's theory.

The problem arises for Professor Vihvelin as the possibility of conflicts among second-order desires: which one is our will, if will is just a second-order desire? To use Vihvelin's example, what does one will when one has both a desire that one's desire for coffee not be effective (for health reasons) and a desire that it be effective (for enhancing productivity)? She rejects the notion that one's will is simply whichever second-order desire is stronger. That reduces, she says, to simple compatibilism, because each second-order desire is, in effect, the desire that one or another first-order desire be the cause of one's behavior, and so there is no way to distinguish the relative strengths of second-order desires from the relative strengths of first-order desires. We simply act on the strongest first level desire, and if that is free will, the will is free whenever there is a conflict of second-order desires. Vihvelin also rejects the notion that the will can be identified as the second-order desire that we *believe* that we ought to act on for the same reason she rejects the cognitivist theory of will, which we shall consider shortly. Finally, she rejects Frankfurt's own solution, that one's will is the second-order desire with which one "decisively identifies," because she cannot make any sense of what it means to say that one decisively identifies with one of their desires.

Professor Vihvelin remains faithful to the affective theory's animal model of choice by insisting that we need "an account that distinguishes free from unfree action by appealing *only* to the *content* of the propositional attitude" (p. 69). That is, instead of identifying the will by how it is formed, say, as the conclusion of a process of reasoning, she proposes to identify the will by singling out a desire by its content. But instead of Frankfurt's second-order desire that a first-order desire not be *effective* in generating behavior, she points to the "Ulysses desire," which she defines as the desire that a first-order desire not be *satisfied*. Thus, to lack of free will in the face of a desire to take a drug, one must have not only Frankfurt's second-order desire that the first-order desire not be effective in causing behavior, but also another second-order desire, namely, the desire that the first-order desire not be satisfied, even if it is effective.

The plausibility of Vihvelin's solution to the problem of conflicts among second-order desires does not really derive, however, from taking the will to be a desire with a special kind of content. It derives from the reasoning process her affective theory of will is meant to avoid mentioning. In supplementing the Frankfurt desire with the Ulysses desire, Vihvelin is actually adding to the will the *reason* for the will. That a first-order desire not be satisfied is part of what is usually called the "reason" for not acting on it. Indeed, what other *reason* could there be for not wanting a first-order desire to be effective than that one does not want what is involved in satisfying the desire? Professor Vihvelin's attempt to show that a Frankfurt desire can occur without a Ulysses desire is, therefore, the attempt to show that we can will something without a reason for it. But her example does not demonstrate its possibility (p. 70–71). If Joe's reason for wanting (on the second order) his first-order desire for beer not to be effective is to lose weight, then he necessarily also has the second-order desire that his first-order desire not be satisfied, because that is part of the means by which his not acting on his desire for beer will lead to his losing weight. The Ulysses desire is implicit in the Frankfurt desire, because it is a necessary part of any possible reason for having the Frankfurt desire.[1]

Professor Vihvelin's solution to the problem of conflicting second-order desires exposes a basic weakness in the affective theory of will. The reduction of will to desire leads to the reduction of reasons to desires, thereby precluding any explanation of how humans are different from animals by appeal to a faculty of reason. In order to identify which second-order desire is the will, Vihvelin must point to the *reasons* for second-order desires, but since she takes those reasons to be other second-order desires, she will have to introduce yet other second-order desires to handle the problem of conflicts among Ulysses desires. And so on. Even in the end, when all the second-order desires have been mentioned, there will still be no explanation of how the will is formed or what its function is, because the desires will still be taken as given, without any explanation of the reasoning behind them. There is an alternative theory, which takes the will to be a belief about what one ought to do that follows from a process of reasoning. It is not compatible, however, with the affective theory of will, because in order for reason to serve its function, its output, the will, cannot compete for control of behavior on the animal model of choice, but must have complete control over behavior.

Professor Vihvelin's Rejection of the Cognitive Theory of Will

Professor Vihvelin's main defense of her affective theory of will is her argument for rejecting the cognitive theory of will. She considers the possibility of a cognitive theory of will when she takes up the contrast between the views of Plato and Hume. In fact, what spurs her to introduce second-order desires in the first place is the criticism of the affective theory that Gary Watson makes in defense of Plato's cognitive theory of will. Watson argues "that if Hume is right, then it makes no sense to say that someone acts on his strongest desire but fails to do what he most values or thinks best" (p. 60). She agrees that it is not possible for drug addicts to lack free will on Hume's simple compatibilist view, because "if values are just desires, then there is no difference between what we most value and what we most strongly desire" (p. 60). But she insists on the affective theory by posing a dilemma for those who believe that what opposes desire is will understood as a belief about what ought to be done.

Professor Vihvelin describes two cases in which agents act contrary to what they say they ought to do, and yet we would not say that they are unfree. In one case, X lies to a Customs official in order to avoid paying import duties, even though he agrees that breaking the law is wrong. In the other case, Bob chooses to do what is good for those near and dear to him rather than what is the greatest good for the greatest number in the situation even though he is a utilitarian who believes that one ought to do what is the greatest good for the greatest number. In both cases, the agent acts contrary to what he believes he ought to do. But in neither case does it seem that the agent is unfree. Thus, the cognitivist must either defend the thesis that X and Bob act unfreely, or else insist that, despite what they say they ought to do, neither is acting contrary to what he *really believes* he ought to do. Since there is no denying that the first horn is "wildly implausible," (p. 61) cognitivists are forced to defend the second horn, and that view, Vihvelin insists, "does not differ, in any principled way, from Hume's" (p. 63).

Professor Vihvelin does not deny that there is sometimes a difference between what people say they believe they ought to do and what they really believe that they ought to do, but she insists that cognitive theorists, like Watson, must defend a stronger claim, namely, "that we must *always* disregard what people like X and Bob say and what they appear to believe, and look instead to their actions to find out what their all-things-considered value judgments are" (p. 62). (Such an argument is given in the next section, but it might be noted here that it is not as implausible as Professor Vihvelin suggests, considering how her examples depend on a conflict between beliefs about what is morally right and self-interest. As long as there is no compelling answer to the question, "Why be moral?" it will be reasonable to doubt whether one really ought to do what one believes is morally right. And it is not so easy to find examples in which there is a conflict between what one believes is in one's self-interest and what one does, which is the case most relevant to drug addiction.) Assuming, in any case, that cognitive theorists can justify using actual behavior as the criterion for what agents really believe they ought to do, Professor Vihvelin's criticism is that the cognitive theory collapses into Hume's view that "there is no difference between what someone thinks best and what she wants most (in the causal sense)" (p. 62).

> Watson criticizes Hume on the grounds that his view makes it impossible to make sense of someone acting against her better judgment. But if thinking best is not the same as wanting most, it must be possible to say, of someone, that she thinks it best (all things considered) to do x, even though her action shows that she wants something else more.

Vihvelin goes on to argue that, since the distinction between thinking best and wanting most holds for any kind of desire, including X's desire to save money and Bob's desire to help those he loves, the cognitivist's insistence that what agents do in these cases is what they think is best, all things considered, makes their position indistinguishable from Hume's. There is no way to distinguish the unfreedom of drug addiction from the freedom of normal people.

Cognitive theorists have two ways of avoiding Vihvelin's dilemma. First, it is possible for cognitive theorists to accept this conclusion and hold that one always does what one judges best, because that does not require them to give up the *distinction* between what one thinks best and what one wants most. That distinction is the very basis of the cognitive theory, for it must recognize a difference between the rationally formed will and desire in order to hold that behavior is controlled by will rather than by desire. Thus, even if the cognitive theory implied that no one ever acted contrary to their will, and actual behavior were sufficient evidence of what one really believes about what is good, it would still be possible to *make sense* of the addict *"saying"* that her desire was so strong that she was unable to do what she believed she ought to do, because the theory recognizes a difference between rational will and desire. It is just that the addict's claim would always be false.[2] Although it is somewhat implausible to deny there is any such thing as drug addiction, its possibility makes clear that there is a difference between accepting a distinction between what we value most and what we want most and believing there are actually cases in which we act on a desire that is contrary to what we value most.

Second, and more plausibly, cognitive theorists can admit that there are cases of drug addiction, as Vihvelin says Watson *"seems"* to, but deny that addicts take drugs because they want the drugs "more" than they want what they think best (all things considered). Professor Vihvelin is assuming that the only possible explanation of why one would act on a desire that is contrary to what one judges best is that the desire is stronger than the rational will. But that is just the assumption of the affective theory of will, not the cognitive theory. Cognitivists do not have to agree with her about that, because they can explain the lack of free will by a defect internal to reason, as we shall see.

Professor Vihvelin fails, therefore, to show that there is any inherent defect in the cognitive theory of will. She does not realize that one can make sense of the distinction between will and desire even if there is no such thing as lacking free will, and she begs the question in favor of the affective theory when she assumes that the only way one can lack free will is by having an overpowering first-order desire. Hence, cognitivists are not forced to accompany Vihvelin in her attempts to defend the orthodoxy by reducing will (and the reasons for it) to second-order desires. But it is surely fair for her to ask cognitive theorists to show why we should take what one actually does in cases like X and Bob as the criterion of what they really believe is best, despite what they say.

The Cognitive Theory of Rational Will

The following theory is a naturalistic version of the traditional, cognitive theory of rational will. We may also start with the animal model of choice, since reason evolved in organisms with beliefs and desires that always act on the strongest desire at the moment. But what makes us different from animals is not second-order desires. The "second order" refers, instead, to a kind of cognition, the capacity for reflection, whose conclusions about what is good have complete control over behavior. After explaining this theory of reason, I will show that it gives us a better explanation of the struggle to control drug-induced desires and the unfreedom involved in drug addiction.

By reflection, I mean the language based capacity to *represent our desires and beliefs as causes of behavior as part of the process by which they cause behavior*. These representations are expressed by a distinctive kind of sentence, called "psychological sentences," whose predicates are verbs of propositional attitude, such as "believe" and "desire," followed by sentences indicating the proposition toward which such attitudes are taken. Desires toward objects and beliefs about how behavior will affect them are states of the mind/brain that are responsible for our behavior, as in other animals, but the capacity for reflection makes us aware that we have such mental states. Reflection is not, however, just the capacity to think about and report our own mental states; it is also an understanding of mental states which is based on a form of imagination in which we can see our mental states in terms of the kinds of behavior they would cause, other things being equal. With the use of "rational imagination," we can say not only what mental states we have, but also what effects any mental states would have on our behavior and which beliefs and desires are actually responsible for our behavior.[3]

By itself, however, reflection is just a cognitive capacity, and in order to understand its function, we must understand the role it plays in guiding behavior. The theory is that we are able, when we are reflecting on the potential causes of our behavior, to control which of those potential causes will be effective, that is, which animal desires will actually cause our behavior in the situation as we see it. This way of causing behavior is what is meant by "will," according to this theory. Will is the output of reflection as a behavior-guidance system.

Finally, in order to understand the function of reflection in controlling behavior, we must see how using it to guide behavior makes us better able to control the conditions that affect our reproduction. The capacity for reflection leads us to see ourselves as beings who are identical over time, for that is how all the explanations of particular episodes of our behavior in terms of beliefs and desires fit together coherently as a whole (given that we can remember those explanations). That is, as reflective subjects, we see ourselves as having pasts in which we have chosen to act on certain desires in certain situations with consequences we remember, and as having futures in which we know that we will have certain kinds of desires in situations yet to come. Though we choose how to behave in the present, the present is, for us, but a moment in a much longer span of time, and this perspective on our *selves* enables us to choose how to behave in the present in light of how such behavior will affect the satisfaction of many different desires that we will have in the future, even though those future desires are not felt strongly now. We can provide food today for the hunger we will not feel until tomorrow, or avoid choices that would cause us to desire later that we had made another choice. Given our desires and our beliefs about the world, in other words, we figure out *plans for moving our bodies around in space over time* that allow us to satisfy all our desires as completely and efficiently as possible. It is a creative process, what we do in figuring out how to lead our lives. But it means that, instead of acting on the strongest animal desire at the moment, rational animals must be able to do what is required by their plans. That is the role of will.[4] It enables us to act in our self-interest, rather than on the strongest desire at the moment. The ability to generate behavior that conforms to a plan is what makes rational animals more powerful than other animals. Whereas other animals are imprisoned in the immediate present and can only act on the strongest desire at the moment, rational animals can coordinate their behavior in many different situations over time to satisfy many different desires "at the same time," so to speak.

In rational animals, therefore, what causes behavior is not the strongest desire at the moment, but rather a process in which representations of desires and beliefs about the world are used to formulate a plan that connects various desires to specific ways of behaving at different places and times so that many different desires are satisfied harmoniously and efficiently over time. The desires and beliefs that cause behavior in this way are distinguished from all other causes in the natural order by calling them "reasons." Reasons are causes of behavior that are represented as causes of behavior in the planning process that connects them to certain ways of behaving in certain situations and thereby forms the will that guides actual behavior. (In a similar way, perceptions and beliefs are reasons for adopting new beliefs.)

This explains the kind of reasoning that Professor Vihvelin leaves out when she takes the "second order" to be just "second-order desires." If she recognized there are reasons for second-order desires, she would not need to add the "Ulysses desire" to the "Frankfurt desire," because the reason for not wanting a first-order desire to be *effective* in causing behavior is not wanting what is involved in its being *satisfied*. Not acting on the desire is *how* one keeps what is involved in satisfying it from happening, as required by the plan one has formulated to serve one's interest. Moreover, Frankfurt is closer to the truth in saying that our will is the second-order desire with which we "decisively identify." The closest things, on the cognitive theory, to competing second-order desires are alternative plans by which one might serve one's self-interest, and it does make sense to say that, in choosing which plan to follow, we choose our *selves*, assuming that the self includes how all the different moments of our lives fit together as a whole. Self-interested reasoning is the process by which one creates one's self.

The cognitive theory supplies, therefore, the theory of reasoning that is omitted from the affective theory, but in this context, the most relevant difference between the cognitive theory and the affective theory is not the place of reasoning in the formation of the will, but rather the relationship between the will and desires. The will, on the cognitive theory, is a plan of action that must be able to control behavior for satisfying all the desires involved over a period of time, whereas the affective theory reduces the plan of action to a set of second-order desires about how to behave in various situations that compete individually with first-order, animal desires for control of behavior that may be felt strongly at the time. The cognitive theory need not, however, deny that any desire is involved in the control that rational will exercises over animal desires. Since reason evolves in animals, it is likely that the reflective process of reasoning is given control over behavior by the evolution of a desire to do what reason concludes is best. But if it is a desire, it is one whose satisfaction is required for the normal functioning of the organism, like the desire for air. What satisfies the desire is simply locking in a mechanism that has absolute power to control behavior, regardless of any animal desires that may be felt at the moment. Reason can be conceived as a mechanism that controls how animal desires lead to behavior in much the way that turning faucets controls the flow of water through pipes: no matter how strong the animal desires may be, it is always possible for reason to control which ones are effective in generating behavior, because reason works on animal desires from the level of reflection where it has a *mechanical advantage* over them, much as workers in a chemical factory or refinery can control the flow of liquids in pipes by the mechanical advantage of turning valves, regardless how much pressure the liquids are under.

To be sure, if this mechanism is held in place by a desire, there may be cases in which that desire is not strong enough to make one act rationally or it feels like an effort is required to do so. But the failure to lock in the mechanism of rational self-control could not be caused by the greater strength of an animal desire, because its mechanical advantage over them means it does not compete with them for control of behavior. It might be caused by an injury, disease, or even a drug, although it is more likely to be a defect in the development of the neurological mechanisms involved.[5] Whatever the cause, however, the failure of the desire to lock in the rational control of behavior would put the whole mechanism out of commission, so that the rational agent is just an animal acting on the strongest desire at the moment. Thus, it would not be just a failure to do what reason wills in controlling this or that desire in this or that kind of situation. It would be a general failure of the faculty by which one formulates and carries out plans. The failure must be total, on the cognitive theory, because in order to carry out plans, rational will must be able to control how *all* immediate desires generate behavior in order to be able to control how *any* particular desire generates behavior. That makes rational will basically different from a second-order desire that can lose control of behavior in competition with the more powerful first-order desires on the animal model of choice.

This sketch of the nature and function of reason shows that there is a naturalistic alternative to the affective theory of will. It is fair to say, I believe, that the cognitive theory of will gives a better account of what makes human beings different from other animals than does the affective theory. Although we have not considered the reasoning involved in morality, it is certainly more accurate, as far as self-interest is concerned, to portray reasoning as a result of foresight and planning than simply as having Ulysses second-order desires in addition to Frankfurt second-order desires. And it does account for freedom of the will, because in order for reason to have that function, the will cannot be just one desire among others on the animal model of choice, but must have a complete control over all our desires. Indeed, it might even be argued that we can *know* that the cognitive theory is true from reflecting on our own planning and our own capacity to act on our plans despite strong, immediate desires to the contrary. But despite these advantages, defenders of the affective theory think there is decisive evidence in favor of their theory in the phenomenon of drug addiction.

The Phenomenon of Drug Addiction

The strength of the affective theory is its ability to account for the phenomenon of drug addition. There is no doubt that many people who use drugs claim that drugs have effects on them that make them unable to control their drug use. Despite efforts to quit, they continue to take drugs without any signs of getting control over their drug behavior. Although drug use may interfere with other aspects of their lives, they are generally able to formulate and carry out plans affecting other aspects of their lives. It is just that everything else in the addict's life has to be organized around obtaining and consuming drugs. Television features no end of people confessing to their inability to resist desires, that are induced by drugs, to take drugs.

The phenomenon of drug addiction is just what would be expected on the orthodox belief that drugs *cause* drug addiction. The affective theory makes sense of this orthodoxy by holding that will is just a desire that can be overpowered, on the animal model of choice, by first-order desires. There is also, as we shall see, a somewhat different way of "making sense" of the claim that drugs deprive users of free will. But however one makes sense of the orthodox view of drug addiction, the phenomenon of drug addiction seems to be compelling evidence that the cognitive theory is false.

Indeed, it must be admitted that the cognitive theory cannot account for how drugs make people unable to control their behavior. In order for reason to serve its function, on the cognitive theory, the will must have complete power over how all desires generate behavior, including those induced by taking drugs. The only cases in which the will could fail to be able to control behavior regarding the use of drugs is when it is also unable to control how other kinds of desires generate behavior. But since a general breakdown of responsibility is not what is involved in the phenomenon of drug addiction, the cognitive theory seems to be at a loss to explain it. To confirm this defect in the cognitive theory, we need only consider what it implies about the mechanisms by which the affective theory of will (and a kindred theory) makes sense of the orthodoxy about drug addiction.

To focus on the issues of will rather than morality, we will consider only cases in which the choice not to take drugs is due to self-interest, where reasoning is a matter of adopting a plan about how best to satisfy all the desires one will have in the situations one will encounter as a body in space over time, and at the extreme, a plan for one's whole life. For drugs to deprive one of free will, the drug user must have determined that continuing to take drugs is not in her self-interest and worked out a plan to quit, only to find that the drugs make her unable to carry out her plan. Let us be clear, therefore, that the mere fact of continued use of a drug is not, by itself, proof that drugs are depriving one of free will. There is no reason to deny that beings like us could decide that the experiences caused by psychoactive drugs are valuable enough to take those drugs again, and again. It could be in one's self-interest to use drugs, even if it were harmful to health in some ways (or risks such harms) or even if quitting involved severe withdrawal symptoms, because it could be part of a plan of action in which the benefits of drugs sufficiently outweigh such costs. The rationality depends on how both the continued use of the drug and the process of quitting fits into one's life. To lack free will, one must not merely not quit, but be unable to quit. But how is it possible, on the cognitive theory, for drugs to make one unable to carry out a plan of quitting drugs when one has judged that it is in their self-interest to stop using a drug, say, because they have discovered that it is harmful or not worth the costs? And how can the orthodoxy be true?

According to the affective theory, drugs work by strengthening first-order, animal desires in a way that makes one take the drugs even though one chooses not to. The drug is supposed to make the immediate first-order desire to take the drug so strong that it cannot be resisted. This is apparently what happens in heroin withdrawal: physiological addiction means that being deprived of the opiate makes one feel nausea, cold chills, nervousness and the like, which can be stopped by taking another fix. (Withdrawal from extreme alcohol addiction may be even worse, involving, as it does, delirium tremens, or "the DT's.") In either case, the power of will is supposed to be overcome by the strength of first-order desires.

However, if people really want to, they can resist such impulses, at least for a while. People can even resist torture for a while. And it need be only for a while, because withdrawal symptoms go away before long. To be sure, it takes an act of will; one must commit oneself to a plan of action, involving some suffering, by which a longer-range end that serves one's self-interest is achieved. But that is precisely what reason gives us the power to do. To exercise free will is to follow the plan one has concluded is in one's self-interest, despite animal desires, and that is possible because of the mechanical advantage that will has, like turning the faucets that determine which animal desires generate behavior. It may not be easy or pleasant, but those costs of following the plan of action have already been taken into account in deciding on a plan that is in one's self-interest.

The cognitive theory cannot explain drug addiction by the strength of the drug-induced desires, but perhaps it can explain the appearance of its happening. It may seem that reason does not have the power to control drug-induced desires, because at some point in carrying out the plan of quitting, those desires turn out to be so strong that one fails to follow the plan. But drug-induced desires are not necessarily overpowering rational will, like a first-order desire outweighing a second-order desire, because it can be explained as "weakness of will." On the cognitive theory, weakness of will is just having doubts about what is really good. That is, when the drug-induced desire is felt urgently, one comes to believe that satisfying it is more important than one had assumed in formulating the plan, and so one changes one's mind and replaces the plan on the spot with another plan that allows one to take the drug at that moment. But lack of resolution is not a case of first-order desires outweighing second-order desires. First-order desires are still only affecting behavior by way of a *belief about the strength of the desires* and the relevance of that belief to the cognitive process by which one judges what is good. One is still doing what one believes one ought to do.

Its explanation of weakness of will does not, however, enable the cognitive theory to account for drug addiction, because in the case of drug addiction, users continue to succumb to first-order desires. That is just what would be expected on the affective theory of will, because if drug-induced first-order desires are stronger than second-order desires, there is no reason to believe that second-order desires will ever be strong enough to outweigh those first-order desires. But it falsifies the cognitivist attempt to explain drug addiction by weakness of will, because weakness of will is a temporary state, a mere phase in a learning process. Rational beings may be thrown off balance in judging what is good by the surprising strength of the animal desires induced by drugs; it may happen once, twice, or even a few times. But since rational beings have the power of reflection, they cannot help but notice that drug-induced desires seem so valuable at certain moments that they abandon their plan to quit and satisfy them. This poses a cognitive problem, for they must form a stable belief about the effects and value of satisfying and not satisfying those desires. And since it is a cognitive problem, it can be solved. Rational beings eventually either revise their judgment about what is good and abandon the plan of quitting drugs as a mistake, or else they adopt the kind of plan that is required to quit, accurately anticipating all the suffering it involves. In either case, weakness of will is only a temporary state. Reason settles on some plan of action that serves one's interest, either continuing to use drugs or quitting.

It may be suggested that a subtler interpretation of the affective theory's mechanism of strong drug-induced desires would enable the cognitive theory to explain drug addiction in the orthodox way. Even Professor Vihvelin agrees that *physiological* addiction to drugs does not deprive one of freedom. She treats withdrawal symptoms as a form of *coercion* which deprives us of freedom of action, not freedom of will. Her example of drug-induced desires depriving one of free will is Mary, who tries to quit smoking cigarettes, but succumbs to the temptation to take another cigarette on the fourth day when she finds a cigarette in her pocket (p. 63).

Even this model of how drugs deprive us of freedom is not, however, compatible with the cognitive theory, for it is surely possible, on the cognitive theory, for Mary to quit. All Mary needs is to understand what subduing the craving for cigarettes requires. Intense withdrawal symptoms do not pass until after a few days or a week of not smoking, and so Mary must be prepared to suffer for a few days. This is comparable to quitting heroin, although the drug-induced desires may not be as intense. It is not so hard to get past this stage, as those of us who have been cigarette smokers know. The problem is staying quit. After the intense withdrawal symptoms have passed, a strong impulse to smoke a cigarette comes back again and again. It is brief, and if resisted for only a short while, goes away. But it is easy to be caught off guard weeks, months, or even years later, to give in to the brief impulse to smoke, and so to become addicted all over again. This is not, however, a model for how drug-induced desires override rational will, because, once again, it is just a matter of weakness of will, a form of doubt about what is good. When the impulse to smoke returns yet again, long after one had thought the desire was gone, one may doubt whether denying such impulses for so long a time is worth it and abandon the plan to quit on the spot. The reason several tries are usually required before one succeeds in quitting cigarettes is that one must learn how surprisingly long a time the plan of quitting must cover in order to succeed. But unless one decides that quitting is not worth the effort, one eventually adopts the kind of plan that will work. The trick to quitting drugs, like cigarettes, is having a long-term commitment to resisting the impulse. Acting on such a plan is what rational self-interest always involves, except that in this case, quitting must be one's *first priority* for up to a year or two, in the sense that one does not allow occasional stress, urgency of other matters, or fatigue to serve as an excuse for giving into an impulse to take the drug. Such long-term projects are not easy. But instead of working under unpleasant conditions, the cost of carrying out the plan is having to be on watch, ready to turn the faucets of desire day and night for a long period. But when one decides that quitting is worth the effort, despite this cost, there is no reason to doubt that one can act in one's self-interest. After all, millions of people have quit smoking.

If the problem posed by a short term of strong, persistent drug-induced desires is like coercion, the problem posed by a brief impulses that persist for a long time may be likened to harassment. In either case, the cognitive theory holds that drugs deprive us of freedom of action rather than freedom of will. Drug-induced desires can be resisted, and there is a plan of action that will eventually make one free of such desires, if one decides it is in one's self-interest to quit. Admittedly, the plan required to quit involves hardships. But enduring hardships for a greater good is the business we are in as rational animals. And neither strength nor persistence of drug-induced desires requires self-control any greater than what is required for other human activities, such as earning a living, living with someone, or raising children.

What might be expected to cripple rational self-control is a drug that caused intense and urgent first-order desires that persist for an indefinitely long period of time. That may be why torture is eventually successful, even when one believes that one ought to refuse the torturer's demands to the end. The will is broken, and one simply gives up. But to break the will is to break it with regard to handling desires of all kinds. It is not a matter of the will being overpowered so that only a single desire is out of control. All planning and control is lacking. Even if there are drugs that have the effect of weakening the desire that keeps the mechanism of rational self-control in place, that would not explain drug addiction, because drug addition does not involve a general loss of will. Drug addicts are basically in control of other activities in their lives; it is just that they have to organize the rest of their lives around a use of drugs that is out of control.

Although the cognitive theory cannot explain the drug addict's lack of free will in the way that the affective theory of will proposes, there is another, more subtle way one might try to "make sense" of the orthodoxy, for there is another way drugs could affect the mechanism of reflective control. Instead of inducing desires, they might alter some of the cognitive processes involved in formulating and carrying a plan of action.

A good model may be alcohol, if only because most of us are familiar with it. Alcohol weakens inhibitions and, so, allows people to do and say things that they normally would not do or say. Although drunkenness may also involve drug-induced desires, what is special about alcohol is that it impairs judgment, or at least, the immediate estimates of quantities that are required to carry out one's plan in the immediate situation. Estimates are required to carry out all aspects of one's plan, from the physical magnitudes involved in bodily coordination to the comparisons of value and importance involved in relating to other people, and thus, when those estimates are distorted, as if certain mental scales had been miscalibrated, what one wills in the current situation may be affected, at least as regards immediate behavior. This would account for drug addiction, because the distortions may affect one's judgment about whether to take another drink. Such alcoholics typically keep drinking until the rational will is totally disabled or they are physically unable to drink any more.

But even cognitive effects of drugs on the mechanism of self-control can be handled, if they are not permanent. Eventually drinkers become sober, and normal judgment is restored. Since they are reflective subjects, knowing what happens when they are inebriated may enable them to compensate for the distortions in quantitative estimates involved in carrying out a plan. Alcoholics often learn to compensate for cognitive distortions well enough to pass as sober, even though they know subjectively that they are quite drunk. The distortion most relevant to drug addiction has to do with their estimates of whether one should take another drink. Many drinkers learn not to drink as much next time. But even for alcoholics who cannot learn to discount their intoxicated judgments and always drink too much, there is a plan by which they can control their behavior. Such alcoholics must simply not drink again at all. This is possible, because being reflective means that one is not imprisoned, like an animal, in an eternal immediate present, but can choose what to do now in light of the choice's effects on one's future, indeed, on one's whole life. Alcoholics who cannot control how much they drink, once they start, can control the effects of alcohol by adopting the plan of not drinking for the rest of their lives. As long as they are not drinking, their judgment is not impaired, and so, the discipline required is similar to quitting smoking. It requires only the effort of resisting occasional impulses, albeit, perhaps, for one's entire life. Once again, however, there are millions of members of Alcoholics Anonymous who can testify that it is possible to remember one's susceptibility to alcohol and avoid the harm involved.

The cognitive theory cannot, therefore, use cognitive distortions as a model for how drugs may cause users to lack free will. It would be different, of course, if a drug like alcohol permanently crippled the cognitive mechanisms required to judge what is good, for reflection could not use experience with of the drug's effects to adopt a suitable plan to protect oneself. But that is not the kind of psychoactive drug at issue here. Such a drug would be a poison to rational nature, which makes us incapable of ever acting rationally again in any situation, and not only with regard to drugs, but all desires. There may be such drugs, but no one claims that any of the substances that anti-drug laws are meant to control are of this kind.

The cognitive theory is, therefore, unable to explain drug addiction in any of the ways used to make sense of the orthodoxy. It cannot explain the lack of free will by the strength or duration of first-order desires, unless they totally overthrow the will and the addict is unable to control how any desires generate behavior. Nor can it explain how drugs cause a lack of freedom by cognitive distortions, because reflection on the effects enables subjects either to compensate for them or to know not to take the drugs again. It does make sense to hold that drugs distort beliefs about the *value* of taking drugs, because as long as those judgments are confirmed by reflection on their value while not being under their influence, such judgments are indistinguishable from coming to prefer drugs because of the experiences they induce, which, as we have already admitted, are rational. None of the psychoactive drugs that are thought necessary to prohibit, from crack and cocaine to marijuana, "ecstasy" and amphetamines, suggest any effects by which drugs could curtail free will that are not represented by heroin, nicotine or alcohol.[6]

Defenders of the affective theory of will may argue, therefore, that the cognitive theory is false. The phenomenon of drug addiction is undeniable, and thus, if the cognitive theory cannot explain it, then so much the worse for it. They may admit that the cognitive theory has certain theoretical advantages over the affective theory. Its theory about the role of reasoning in the formation of the will and about its function in the control of behavior explains better than the affective theory how humans are different from other animals. And its view of weakness of will as a cognitive problem concerning lack of resolution about one's plan explain how people who seem to lack control of their drug behavior learn to control it. But that does not explain drug addiction, for it implies that drug users will eventually learn how to control their drug-related behavior, and that is just not what we find in the phenomenon of drug addiction. The phenomenon of drug addiction seems to show, therefore, that we have to give up the cognitive theory of will in favor of a theory of will based on the animal model of choice.

This conclusion does not, however, follow. What we have discovered is merely that the cognitive theory is incompatible with the affective theory of will and its kindred ways of making sense of the orthodoxy about drug addiction. The orthodoxy assumes that drugs cause drug addiction, and none of their explanations of how drugs deprive users of free will are possible on the cognitive theory. But as I suggested earlier, that does not mean the cognitive theory is unable to account for the phenomenon of drug addiction. There is another way to explain this phenomenon, and to see what it is, we need only notice that the same predictions about drug addiction follow from two opposite assumptions: namely, that the orthodoxy about drug addiction is *true*, and that the orthodoxy about drug addiction is *false*.

If the orthodoxy about drug addiction is true, then the effects of drugs on the will explain why people claim to be unable to control their drug behavior long after they have concluded that they ought to quit and even though they have control over other parts of their lives. That is what the affective theory makes sense of by supposing that the will is a desire that can lose control of behavior to stronger first-order desires on the animal model of choice.

On the other hand, if the orthodoxy is false, and drugs do not cause drug addiction, the phenomenon of drug addiction is explained just as well. This is the cognitivist explanation. It denies that drugs deprive users of free will. But to say that the belief they do is the orthodox view is to say that it is generally believed to be true by reasonable people, and having the belief that drugs deprive one of freedom would itself deprive one of freedom. That is, the cognitive theory implies that people who believe that drugs make it impossible for them to control their use of drugs would not be able to control their drug-related behavior. Even though they believe that it is in their self-interest to quit using a drug, it is not reasonable for them to formulate and attempt to carry out a plan of quitting, for they do not believe that that is possible. It is just not reasonable to put forth the kind of effort that is actually required to quit, if it will not succeed. The acceptance of the orthodoxy would, therefore, prevent the mechanism of rational self-control from being used in the way required to stop taking drugs, and thus, those who accept it would be unable to refrain from using drugs, even though they do not want to take them, all things considered. Hence, they would lack free will. They would have no reasonable choice but to organize the rest of their lives around drug use.

We know that the inference involved in limiting the power of will is reasonable, because our faculty of rational imagination allows us to tell what conclusions follow from having beliefs and desires of any kind. But it is important to recognize that this cognitive mechanism accounts for every aspect of the phenomenon. The fact that it is the *orthodox* belief explains why people have this false belief about the power of will to control behavior motivated by drug-induced desires. The cognitive theory of will also explains, therefore, why most addicts say that their inability to control their drug use comes from the desires they induce. That is precisely what we would expect them to *say*, if it is *actually* caused by the false belief that certain drug-induced desires are too strong to be controlled.[7] This false belief makes it *seem* that the drugs are causing the addiction to drugs. Moreover, it would explain why they continue to use drugs, even though they believe that it is not in their self-interest, long after we would otherwise expect rational beings to have learned how to control their drug behavior. The orthodoxy disposes them to learn the wrong lesson from the experience of giving in to immediate animal desire when they had chosen to stop. Instead of concluding that they had underestimated the value of satisfying the desire in formulating their plan to quit and, thus, recognizing that they must either choose to continue using drugs or adopt a more adequate plan to serve their interest, they would be confident in their belief that such desires cannot be resisted. They would not try to form a stable belief about the value of satisfying the drug-induced desire, because that would be irrelevant. They would simply stop trying to control their use of drugs and attempt only to organize the rest of lives around the use of drugs. Finally, the cognitive theory would explain why the power of the rational will is affected only with regard to controlling drug-induced desires, and not desires generally, as cognitivists would expect of anything that could put rational will out of commission from outside the faculty of reason. The false belief is a belief that only the behavior generated by drug-induced desires is out of control. Thus, even though the mechanism of rational self-control is turned off with respect to behavior involved in obtaining and taking drugs, it is still functioning normally in other aspects of people's lives. That is indeed what we find in the case of drug addicts.

The cognitive theory, therefore, explains the phenomenon of drug addiction at least as well as the affective theory (and other ways of making sense of the orthodoxy). It is possible to explain drug addiction by two such opposite theories as the truth and the falsity of the orthodoxy, because "drug addiction" does not necessarily mean "*drug-caused* addiction to the use of drugs," but can rather mean simply "addiction to the use of drugs," where that leaves open why rational beings are unable to control their use of drugs. Thus, instead of holding that the drugs cause the lack of freedom, the cognitive theory can hold that what limits the power of reason to control drug behavior is the rational agent's belief about the power of her rational will. Thus, what limits the power of reason is ultimately reason itself, not desire. The rational will is inherently free, despite the phenomenon of drug addiction, in the sense that reason would enable them to control drug-induced desires, if they understood their rational nature.

The inherent freedom of the rational will implies, by the way, that the phenomenon of drug addiction may have various causes. Complications arise, because, as mentioned above, reflection makes us aware of our power to act contrary to animal desire. Thus, some drug users who claim to be unable to control their drug use may be lying in order to avoid prosecution for violating the law. Lying also explains why drugs continue to be used even though the user is responsible in other aspects of his life. And between those who lie about their inability to quit to protect themselves from blame and those who honestly believe the orthodoxy, the cognitive theory recognizes the possibility of self-deception. There may be moments of lucidity when drug addicts recognize that they could stop using drugs and eventually free themselves from the desires they induce, if they chose to. In refusing to do so, they are, in effect, *choosing* a plan for serving their self-interest that is organized around drug use. But since, for one reason or another, they don't want to avow that choice, they deceive themselves. They quickly "forget" that they have chosen to use drugs and explain to themselves and others why they are taking drugs by their inability to resist drug-induced desires. This is a form of neurosis, with all the harmful effects entailed by neurotic behavior. That is, since they do not avow their choice to lead a life taking drugs, their use of drugs is not well integrated into a plan for satisfying all their desires over a period of time, but done in the impulsive, uncontrolled, and disruptive way, typical of neurotic behavior. That makes drug use more harmful than it would otherwise be, because overdoses are more likely and, instead of fitting drug use into an intelligent plan for satisfying all one's desires as a body in space over a period of time, the rest of one's life has to be organized around seemingly uncontrollable impulses. It is not, however, just a matter of addicts deceiving themselves, because as long as society is looking for this kind of explanation of drug behavior, society is helping addicts deceive themselves. Indeed, society may be even more deeply implicated in their self-deception, because the main reason most addicts do not want to admit that they are actually choosing to use drugs (which they recognize in moments of lucidity) may be that they do not want to admit to themselves and to society that they are choosing to violate the laws banning the use of drugs. Thus, society both gives addicts a (subconscious) reason for not admitting the choice they are actually making, and rewards them for deceiving themselves about it by treating, rather than punishing, such addicts.

The cause of drug addiction is not, therefore, simple, according to the cognitive theory of rational will. Indeed, it may be difficult to decide in particular cases whether the drug addict honestly believes that the power of rational will is limited, is lying, or is deceiving herself. But such complications do not count against the cognitive theory in deciding which theory offers the best explanation of drug addiction, because all these causes account for all aspects of the phenomenon of drug addiction. It is just that the cognitive theory can explain certain variations within the phenomenon to which the affective theory and the orthodoxy are totally blind.

Theories of Will and Their Implications for Social Policy

Although drug addiction is an undeniable phenomenon, there are two explanations of it: the orthodoxy and the cognitive theory. And it makes a difference which explanation we choose to believe, for they imply opposite social policies. The orthodox view implies that the state should ban addictive drugs and use its police powers to prevent situations in which its citizens might choose whether to use them, because once they take drugs, people are unable to stop taking them and so cannot protect themselves from the harmful effects of drug use. The cognitive theory implies, on the other hand, that drugs should be legalized. Since what deprives people of free will is *believing* that drugs induce desires (or have other effects) that rational beings cannot control, the cognitive theory predicts that if drugs were legalized (for adults) and people held personally responsible for any effects of their drug use on fulfilling their duties as citizens, parents, workers and the like, that belief would be rejected and drug addiction would be eliminated. Drugs would still be used, but only when freely chosen.

Although our social policy will depend, therefore, on which theory of will we believe, it may not seem possible to resolve this disagreement in an era that recognizes only empirical evidence as compelling. Empirical studies of drug addiction of the kind that are usually cited as showing that drugs are addicting do not choose between these two theories. Such studies simply *assume* that drugs are what deprive people of free will and then proceed to gather data about the rates at which drug addition occurs in certain populations. But they do not attempt to show that the lack of free will is caused by the drugs, rather than by the belief that the effects of drugs make it impossible to control their behavior regarding drugs. Nor does it seem possible to construct any simple and direct experiment that would test which theory is true without legalizing drugs and holding people responsible. In order to cure addiction, according to the cognitive theory, addicts must come to believe that they have the power to control if and when their drug-induced desires will be effective in generating behavior, and there is no way to be sure that condition holds as long as drugs are illegal. People tend to believe what they must assume other people believe in order to understand what others are saying and doing, and a police suppression of drugs carried on with all the urgency of a war sends the unambiguous message that people are unable to control their drug behavior by their own free will. To reject the orthodoxy would be to believe that all the violence suffered by citizens because of the police suppression of the drug market is an unnecessary harm inflicted by the government on its own citizens. Since it is hard for most people to accept such beliefs about their own government, anti-drug laws make people doubt their power to act in their own self-interest and discourages them from adopting the plan required to overcome it, thereby causing drug addiction. It is not easy to test the effect of not believing the orthodoxy, because there is no easy way of causing rational beings to have beliefs that are not reasonable.[8]

We seem, therefore, to be forced to choose between these two theories on theoretical grounds and the indirect empirical evidence theory makes relevant. On theoretical grounds, as we have seen, the cognitive theory is superior. The traditional libertarian theory about the will having complete power over desire is preserved in the cognitive theory as part of a naturalistic theory of human nature. This is superior to the affective theory, because its explanation of the nature and function of (self-interested) reasoning shows how humans are different from other animals. But it means that the will cannot be just a second-order desire that must compete with other desires on the animal model of choice, because in order for it to have the function of formulating and carrying out plans for moving an animal body around in space over time in a way that satisfies many different desires fully and efficiently, the will must be the output of a faculty that has complete control over behavior, regardless of the strength of immediate desire.

The cognitive theory also has, however, indirect empirical implications that tend to confirm it, not the least of which is what we know about rational self-control by reflecting on how the will is formed and carried out in our own case. It seems to me, at least, that I am capable of doing what I believe I ought to do, even though all the desires I feel at the moment would lead me not to. Besides such private evidence, the cognitive theory explains various public phenomena that cannot be explained by the affective theory. It explains, for example, how people who seem at first to be unable to resist drug-induced desires manage eventually to get such control over how those desires cause their behavior. The affective theory gives us no reason to believe that someone who gives into temptation will ever be able to resist it. But on the cognitive theory, weakness of will is only a temporary condition, because it is caused by confusion or lack of resolution about what is really good. Since it is a cognitive problem, it can be solved by learning.

The most telling indirect evidence for the cognitive theory is, perhaps, the practice of drug treatment centers in attempting to cure drug addiction. Although addicts are deprived of drugs temporarily, most drug counselors will admit that the only effective way to cure addicts in the long run is to bring them to recognize that they *do* have a will that can act contrary to drug-induced desires, so that they are able to take responsibility for their behavior with regard to drugs. Those who do eventually learn that they can control their drug use typically explain what kept them from doing so earlier as having "low self-esteem." Who can doubt that what they are referring to is doubts about the power of their will to do what they believe they ought to do? It is not easy, however, to teach addicts this lesson in a larger institutional context that is teaching just the opposite lesson, that is, the police enforcement of anti-drug laws.

Since the kind of evidence that would choose decisively between these two theories can be provided only by legalizing drugs, we seem to have no choice but to rely on theoretical reasons and indirect evidence. That is, however, unlikely to be sufficient to justify changing such a well-entrenched policy as drug prohibition, considering the widespread doubts about the power of theoretical reasoning to settle such disputes. There is, however, a final argument that can resolve the issue.

There are two choices. We can either continue the enforcement of anti-drug laws or we can legalize drugs. Both theories agree about what will happen in the first case: a certain portion of the population will continue to suffer from drug addiction. Where the two theories disagree is in the other case. The cognitivist predicts that legalizing drugs and not recognizing drugs as an excuse for failing to fulfill other duties and obligations of citizens, parents, workers, and the like would eliminate drug addiction, because it would disabuse them of the belief that is causing their lack of freedom. The affective theorist defending the orthodoxy predicts, however, that legalizing drugs would lead to many more drug addicts, because many more people will be exposed to drugs and be unable to control their drug-induced desires. It might seem that the *risk* of increasing drug addiction rules out legalizing drugs, but in fact, the two alternatives are on a par in that regard. Although the affective theory implies that to follow the policy of legalizing drugs recommended by cognitivists would increase drug addiction, the cognitive theory likewise implies that to follow the current policy of banning them, recommended by affective theorists, would just as surely cause drug addiction, since drug addiction would be eliminated entirely by legalizing. Thus, it may seem to be a stand off.

It is not, however, a stand off, because the kinds of addiction that these two theories are warning about are not the same and only one of them can we care anything about. Cognitivists are warning about a limitation on freedom of the will that we want to avoid, because it limits the power of reason to serve its function. The false belief about the power of will makes reason less able to formulate and carry out plans that serve our interest, and so we are less powerful. Affective theorists are also warning about limits on free will, but what they mean by lack of free will is merely that some second-order desires will be overpowered by first-order desires on the animal model of choice. If that is all that lack of freedom comes to, why should we care? Affective theories cannot hold that it is valuable to be able to act on our will because it makes us more powerful, for in order to have that function, will would have to be the output of a faculty that has complete control over behavior, and that's not compatible with explaining will as a second-order desire which must compete with first-order desires for control of behavior on the animal model of choice. In fact, no form of the orthodoxy about drug addiction can explain the value of free will as the cognitive theory does, because to admit that the will is the output of a faculty with the function reason has is to give up the belief that it can be overpowered only with regard to one kind of behavior. Thus, we have reason to avoid the unfreedom involved in drug addiction only if the cognitive theory is true. Hence, we have nothing of value to lose by legalizing drugs. And we have freedom to gain, both freedom of action and freedom of will.

NOTES

1. Moral desires may seem at first to be an example that shows the separability of these desires. When we desire not to act on a certain

first-order desire because to do so would be wrong, it may seem that we can want the desire to be satisfied without its being effective. For example, we may want to have the money, but not want to steal it, and it would apparently be satisfied without being effective, if someone gave us the money. But in this case, the first-level desire that we do not want satisfied is not *having* the money, but not *taking* the money, and that desire is not satisfied without being effective.

2. The reason Professor Vihvelin overlooks this possibility is apparently her assumption that the only way we could ever be compelled by our desires is if "part of us *is* outside the natural causal order and does, somehow, freely choose which of our competing desires to act on" (p. 52). But that is to overlook the possibility that rational will has a mechanical advantage over desire within the natural order. Indeed, I defend the theory of reason sketched in the next section by deriving it from a materialist ontology in *Knowing Matter* (to be published).

3. It is easy to see how rational imagination can be explained naturalistically. It is just the capacity to use one's own behavior-guiding processes under the constraint of certain imagined beliefs and desires. That is, when we understand those psychological sentences, we impose certain constraints on our own reasoning process, and so, by reflecting on what conclusions are drawn, we are using our own brains to simulate the inferences of others or oneself at other times.

4. This is not to say that self-interest was the original function of reason or its only function. Indeed, I would argue that moral reasons are as basic to the function of rational self-control as self-interest, but that is a complication we can ignore in this context.

5. Children lack rational will in this sense. They are protected by an overriding desire to obey parental figures they trust, but if maturation during adolescence does not give them the desire that locks in the mechanism of rational self-control, they will never acquire the ability to formulate and carry out plans that run contrary to immediate desires.

6. It is often suggested in the current political environment that cocaine and crack pose a special problem, but it seems likely that a less hysterical assessment of the effects of these drugs will eventually show that neither cocaine nor crack has addictive effects beyond those mentioned above. Bruce Alexander ("Snow Job," *Reason*, Vol. 22, No. 7, December 1990, pp. 29–34; excerpted from *Peaceful Measures: Canada's Way Out of the "War on Drugs,"* University of Toronto Press, 1990) suggests that if cocaine is different from heroin, nicotine, and alcohol, it is in being less severe. Although there are physiological effects of cocaine use (such as fatigue, brief depressions, and sleep disturbances), they are nothing like the symptoms of heroin withdrawal. Most users of cocaine

"subsequently use it intermittently and moderately" (32), but they do it voluntarily, rather than from the persistence of an irrational impulse, implying that it is easier to quit cocaine than tobacco. In-depth interviews reveal, according to Alexander, that users of cocaine have "considerable control over their patterns of use. They often use the drug casually for years without progressing to heavy use, and when use does get out of hand, they are able to cut back or stop" (30). Nor does cocaine seem to weaken the mechanism of rational self-control, like alcohol. In fact, cocaine seems to improve performance of simple tasks, especially in those who are fatigued or hungry, and to increase confidence in performances of all kinds (32). Hence, if cocaine did cause harmful overuse by weakening rational self-control, it would have to weaken it only with respect to choices about cocaine use, which is not how the control mechanism works. To be sure, crack is supposed to be more addictive than cocaine. But crack differs from cocaine only because smoking delivers more active substance to the brain more quickly, and so how much worse can it be?

7. In this context, a revealing measure of how much danger cocaine poses to free will is the small minority of people who give this reason. According to Alexander, only 3.8 percent of recent users of cocaine "reported that they had tried to stop and found that they could not." (30)

8. The virtual legalization of drugs in such countries as Holland has shown that the orthodoxy is wrong in holding that the increased availability of drugs increases drug addiction, even if we take the use of drugs as evidence of addiction. But for some reason, defenders of the orthodoxy do not take the Dutch experiment as relevant in predicting the effects of legalization on the U.S. population.

Enhancing Abilities

Ability-Enhancing Drugs

W. M. Brown

I'm not worth a thing until I've had my morning coffee.
> —*Anon*

Too much of a good thing . . . can be wonderful.
> —*Mae West*

Much of the interest in the use of drugs to affect or enhance our activities stems from the vital role they play in modern medicine. Many of our hopes for treating debilitating diseases such as AIDS, Alzheimer's disease, and various forms of cancer are linked to the development of new drugs that might alleviate or cure those conditions. We see them as holding out the hope of restoring lost capacities and competencies as well as stopping or reversing the disease processes that have damaged them. A second source of our interest, however, is the much-discussed use of drugs to enhance athletic performance. We hear much about the use of beta-blockers, growth hormones, steroids, amphetamines, and even lowly caffeine as sources of improved speed, strength, and endurance in sports. But the messages are mixed. Drugs are banned in sports; they are deplored by many as unnatural and dangerous additives to a wholesome life; their deleterious side effects seem to outweigh their promised benefits.

Yet on the face of it, the question, "Should we use drugs to enhance our abilities and thereby the quality of our behavior and activities?" seems an easy one to answer. If drugs can make us better, what reasons could we have for rejecting them? But of course, such questions conceal much that needs to be clarified.

We will need to have some idea of what we include under the rubric of 'drugs.' More importantly, we need to think clearly about what we mean by 'enhance' and what abilities or capacities (and their exercise) we might seek to alter by the use of drugs.

I plan first to examine some of these preliminary questions before discussing the kind of cases that should give rise to our concerns about drug use to enhance our abilities. These cases are largely imaginary ones in which new and startling pharmacological discoveries might enable us to transform overnight our rather plodding talents into MacArthur Foundation award-winning traits. We are primarily fascinated by the prospects of transforming ourselves beyond the normal into chemically induced geniuses or Olympic athletes. There are in my judgment few prospects for such things to happen. Because our empirical knowledge about the prospects of developing such drugs is nearly non-existent, we must resort to conjecture. But in doing so we are liable to exaggerate the likely power and effectiveness of new drugs and hold onto unreasonable expectations. We may imagine that such materials, if they were developed, would be free from the complications of side effects that would largely rule out their carefree use as if they were aspirins or vitamins. Virtually all of the drugs we know of today benefit us only in limited circumstances and only then in conjunction with other efforts by us to take advantage of their effects. Moreover, they all carry risks of harm that mitigate their insouciant use. Realistically we should consider, therefore, possible new types of drugs that are similar to ones we already know of, whose effects are likely to differ only in degree from those of drugs we now have, and whose benefits must be weighed against nearly certain risks. Nevertheless, in what follows, I will try to imagine the best-case possibilities in order to explore their implications for us of using drugs to enhance our abilities. Much would depend, of course, on what abilities are enhanced, and although I will occasionally mention an example, by and large I will discuss the use of such drugs in general.

The most general conception of what we are looking for in characterizing drugs is that of substances that affect various biological processes and thereby may enhance our abilities to perform various activities. The trouble with such a general conception is that it may include not only medicines and other pharmacologically active chemicals, but also foods including water, salt, and vitamins. (Some materials used as food, such as coffee, wine, herbs, and seasonings, are clearly biologically very active.) Further, there are various endogenous chemicals produced in our bodies that can be isolated and re-introduced into our bodies to change biological processes: insulin, testosterone, L-dopa, and many others. Legal guidelines are of little help here because they cut across so many obvious cases. Some drugs are legal by prescription, but not otherwise; some are widely used by nearly everybody, but banned for children or some athletes; some drugs are legal in one jurisdiction, but not in another. It is tempting to borrow the definitions of pharmacology texts and restrict the discussion to any "nonfood chemical that alters one or more normal biological processes in living organisms."[1] But doing this may leave out too many interesting cases (such as caffeine). And the irrelevance of food needs to be defended, not assumed.

I mention this morass of definitions because I want to stress the continuity among very ordinary substances that have profound but little-noticed affects in bettering our lives, existing ability-enhancing drugs, like caffeine or aspirin, and imagined super-drugs that might dramatically enhance abilities with unfolding consequences we can only begin to glimpse. Still, imagined chemicals that have tailored affects on our abilities offer us a way to test our intuitions and moral concerns about their possible use. So I will try to shift among these types of cases to sift out the appropriate issues and weigh our responses to them.

To enhance is to improve, to make better. When it comes to abilities it is to change for the better our actions and performances. But we need to know to what standard or norm we are appealing when we consider such favorable changes. Roughly, we may distinguish two perspectives. One is a favorable change compared to what we might normally be expected to do. This would be a better-than-normal condition. Another is a favorable change compared to some subnormal condition. Our motive here would be to enable us to perform at a capacity or level we have lost (or never had). Much depends in both types of cases on how we determine or choose the norms or standards we use for comparison. These may be norms for an individual, or for our species, or for a subclass of our species, a particular sex or age group or social community. If group norms are taken to be statistical averages, most individuals will vary from the mean. Even if we specify the normal as a range of characteristics, some people will be outside that range. For some, to normalize their conditions or capacities or behavior will be to enhance it; for others, it would be to diminish it. We could also seek enhancement in comparison to the individual's condition at some particular time, independent of any species or social norms. In this case, enhancement of the characteristics of some would be to improve toward the norm; for others, it would be to improve beyond the norm. (It is also possible to consider enhancement as tantamount to the creation of a new range of abilities. If the enhancement were successfully to increase the capacities of human performance in extraordinary ways, we would surely consider the resulting changes to be the creation of new abilities rather than merely the enhancement of old ones.)

Much of the medical use of drugs is designed to enhance in the second of these two senses, to improve people who have diminished functioning or deleterious conditions due to disease or injury, or due to congenital or genetic deficiencies. But not all of medicine is aimed at corrective enhancement. Preventive medicine is designed to maintain people at given levels of health or to improve their health above the (current) average. Here again the standards used may vary. Relative to all humans, those in a given country may be average, or already far above average. The therapeutic use of drugs to restore capacities or abilities, that is to enhance abilities that have been diminished or impaired, is not, I believe, controversial. This is because the aim and effect of such treatment is typically to restore abilities to a previous state or to one that is more nearly at an average level. Consequently, I will not be concerned with questioning the permissibility of this use of drugs.[2] Instead I will focus on the ramifications of enhancing our abilities beyond what is normal either for an individual or for groups of individuals.

Abilities are competencies, relatively long-lasting traits or capacities which manifest themselves in how we behave or perform various activities.[3] We typically acquire abilities through training or practice, learning to perform tasks, and to accomplish or attain certain goals. Some of us have acquired the ability to type, to make pasta, to manage a large company, to teach Plato to undergraduates. We can also lose abilities through disuse, aging, injury, or illness. We might call these traits second-order abilities. They are largely learned competencies that can be acquired by a very wide range of normal people with access to the relevant teaching, information, or special facilities. Most humans can, for example, learn to swim, or multiply two-digit numbers, or stalk a rabbit, or speak Chinese, when given the appropriate opportunities. Abilities of this kind are identifiable by virtue of the specific tasks and performances in which they manifest themselves.

But these abilities are themselves dependent on what may be called first-order abilities which set at a more fundamental level what it is to be a normal human being. These primary traits are our abilities to learn or acquire the secondary ones. They are largely species specific, to some extent heritable, and remarkably less amenable to formation or change by ordinary techniques of instruction and training. The character of this kind of ability is by no means certain, however. Much evidence suggests that even these very basic abilities are formed, very early in life, as a result of complex interactions of genetically regulated developmental processes and environmental stimuli. Neurological patterns of the central nervous system, for example, are by no means fixed by genetic determinants, but are strongly influenced even in early stages of childhood development by exogenous factors.

In considering how we might enhance (favorably change) our abilities, therefore, we might consider ways in which both levels of ability can and ought to be influenced by drugs. When people fantasize about improved memories or athletic prowess, they are wondering about the possibility of improving primary abilities which would allow them to change some second-order abilities to accomplish particular tasks or performances. For example, if I could drink something (in a California smart bar) that would enhance my memory, I might then be better able to write a novel based on high-tech information about computer encryption. Or, if I could enhance my ability to form fast-twitch muscle fiber, I might be better able to win the local masters indoor mile run. Drugs may well effect our abilities to do various things, not by substituting for learning and training, but by enhancing our capacities to benefit from such efforts at acquiring particular skills or performing particular actions or accomplishing particular tasks. (Steroids, for example, increase the primary ability to form muscle mass in response to exercise. They do not directly enhance one's ability to run a hundred-yard dash or play guard for the Dallas Cowboys. Neuroleptic drugs restore or enhance primary neurological capacities in order to facilitate the improvement of secondary behavioral abilities.)

We can also distinguish, roughly, among (1) abilities to develop certain largely physical skills or perform various largely physical tasks, (2) abilities to develop or perform mental skills or tasks, and (3) abilities to respond to or project emotional rapport. This latter range of abilities might include the ability to discern emotional states in others, as well as being appropriately and effectively responsive to them. We might be able to enhance our ability to feel care, sympathy, identification, rapport, and affection, to name a few "positive" types, and thereby enhance our abilities to relate to others, to respond to their needs and concerns, and to identify and facilitate complex human relationships in a variety of social and personal situations.

Finally, it is possible to distinguish valuable, beneficial, or desirable abilities from those that are in some ways objectionable. If we think of abilities as including skills for performing various nefarious acts such as the ability to garrote somebody, or the ability to embezzle large sums using computerized financial networks, then we must also consider whether enhancing such skills is ever desirable or permissible. But mainly, skills are not so specific. Even second-order abilities are focused by particular motives and opportunities but are in themselves more general than any given application. A secondary ability to tie a shoelace is acquired because of the use of shoes, but it is scarcely limited to tying shoes laces. Whether we manifest a given ability in a good, useful, or acceptable way is therefore independent of the existence of the ability itself, unless perhaps the risk of the ability's being used in a bad way outweighs its being used in other ways.

In what follows, I will concentrate on primary abilities and their possible enhancement by the use of drugs, and only indirectly the enhancement of secondary abilities. Usually it can be assumed that the enhancement of a primary ability will benefit or enhance the performance of a variety of secondary abilities or skills whose exercise is dependent on very specific circumstances. These circumstances and the abilities called into action by them are not plausibly influenced directly by biologically active substances. A drug that will enhance one's ability to remember telephone numbers will likely do so only by affecting one's general ability to remember or, perhaps, to remember numbers.

We need not restrict ourselves to how people behave or perform as a measure of ability enhancement. We use drugs to enhance many characteristics of our lives or of our activities. Analgesics may have an indirect affect on how we perform our jobs or other activities, but they are designed in the first instance to change states of our bodies, to improve how we feel and perhaps thereby how we perform or act. Or drugs may be designed to prevent some condition that would inhibit our activities, or that would prevent us from doing things that we want to do. Further, we ought to include the possibility of changing our moods and feelings as a way of enhancing our abilities to do things. It is largely the mood- or mind-altering affects of recreational (and frequently illegal) drugs like heroin or marijuana that prompt efforts to prohibit or control their use. These drugs when used recreationally have little enhancing affect on one's abilities. To the contrary, they seem largely destructive of even a normal range of human competence while fostering a debilitating dependency and loss of personal autonomy. I will have little to say about such drug use.

Our experience with drugs of certain kinds has therefore produced a justified sense of caution about their dangers and of skepticism about the possibility of a panacea. We should approach the possibility of further use of drugs to enhance our abilities and thereby our lives with similar caution. But on the whole, I shall argue, the dangers of using drugs to enhance our abilities, though real, are not new or different in severity to problems we have long faced and often overcome. Moreover, the prospect of enhancing our abilities carries with it the likelihood of benefits that may outweigh these risks. I want to divide my discussion into four main categories. The first will question whether the use of drugs to enhance our abilities is in some relevant sense unnatural or threatening to us as human beings who have evolved with a fairly fixed range of mental and physical traits. The second is a variety of prudential questions concerning the likely or at least possible effects of using drugs to enhance our abilities. Third, there are a number of important social or ethical issues concerning the control and distribution of drugs. These three kinds of issues are not easily distinguished and will occasionally overlap. And finally, I will consider several arguments for believing that the use of drugs is not only permissible but may be desirable.

In the broadest sense, what is natural is comprehensive of all existing phenomena and processes. This includes therefore human cultural and technological artifacts. But often the distinction is made between human contrivance and objects and processes that are independent of any human intervention. It is only by human attention and display that even "found objects" can take on the gloss of objects of art. Our own biological constitution is largely independent in this sense of our own control and manipulation and is therefore seen as "natural." Even though we try to modify our biological processes and structures to prevent or lessen the impact of disease, injury, and defect, our efforts are limited and often seen as interventions in the natural course of things. The use of drugs, especially those artificially tailored to perform their tasks, is a good example of this artificial effort to affect our biological natures. And this is in spite of the fact that the use of drugs to effect changes in our moods and states is probably the oldest technique for doing this known to us, one that has persisted for thousands of years of human development.

We can agree in any case that the use of drugs, whether found in herbs or other plants, prepared from fermented grape juice, or synthesized in laboratories, may be more or less artificial depending on the degree of intervention by us in purifying, preparing, processing or even manufacturing them. The most ubiquitous drugs in use today, alcohol, caffeine, and nicotine, are among the most naturally occurring and require relatively little cultivation or preparation. And these clearly are used in part because of their affect on a wide range of moods and abilities. Other substances taken from our own bodies or those of other organisms are certainly naturally occurring if anything is; it is only the procedures for acquiring them and using them that is artificial. Finally, in this spectrum of substances, there are the relatively new, artificially synthesized drugs that have been developed in the last half century. These, if any, are the most unnatural and any objection on this basis to their use to enhance our abilities will certainly focus on them.

But what objection is pertinent? Perhaps it is that only those human processes or states or dispositions, including our abilities, that develop without interference from social or technological factors are valuable. But this seems clearly false. Medical intervention, for example, in abnormal, but natural, conditions is accepted as valuable by virtually everyone. And nurturing social influences on childhood and adult development, including education and training, are universally accepted as valuable. Moreover, these influences can produce virtually permanent biological and behavioral changes in us as they account for much of what we become as competent adults. Indeed it is largely a myth that we are only the result of the unfolding of information contained in our genes.[4] Much of what we are as human beings is a complex interplay of internal and external factors, including those directly attributable to our own technology and social organization. And this has been the case surely as long as there have been recognizably modern humans.

Granted this interdependency, it may also be objected that it is unnatural to interfere in human life through the use of drugs because it is damaging to our natures, however complex they are in their development, that is, that it is likely to change what it is to be human and that this is bad or likely to be bad. This is a more cogent objection, I think, because it plays on a conservative principle of leaving things well enough alone. We may be justified in fixing what is broken or damaged to restore it to some original or normal condition, but we should not tamper with what works. But whatever traits we single out as characteristically human, we are of course only committed to them as current traits of the species that have evolved and will presumably continue to change. Even in determining those traits and deviations from them we are committed to evaluating them.[5] Still, we are proposing not to change those traits so much as we are to enhance them. So the issue is whether in enhancing them, especially various abilities and capacities, we also risk transforming them in a deleterious and harmful manner. I want to consider such risk factors separately, so for the moment, let us ask whether in the absence of such risks, it is objectionable to use drugs to enhance our abilities simply because, at least in extreme cases, they are not naturally occurring substances with a long evolving use by us as part of our species history. In the absence of the risk factors alluded to, however, I see no reason to object to ability-enhancing drug use on the grounds of their being unnatural.

If the unnaturalness lies not in the artificiality of the drugs, but rather in the enhanced traits themselves, the question is quite different. Suppose that the abilities in question are so far different from the normal range of human abilities that it is more likely that we would consider them completely new abilities. Here, too, it is not evident why that would be objectionable in itself if there were no associated risks that outweighed the value gained from the new range of abilities. In any case, the range of human abilities is so great that it is hard to imagine what plausible enhancement of normal abilities would be sufficient to better the best of already existing human abilities. We can already find examples of people whose abilities so far depart from the normal that most of us, other things being equal, would be delighted even to approach those levels.

Let me now turn to a variety of prudential issues involving risks in the use of drugs which may have the effect of persuading some people that no such use of drugs is worth these results. Among the risks is the danger of significant injury to users' biochemical processes and any subsequent incapacities to which that might lead. I believe this is a serious objection, but it depends strongly on empirical assumptions that must wait the discovery and testing of drugs of the sort we are imagining. Nevertheless, we know now that many drugs we now use medicinally or to enhance performance have potentially dangerous side effects. Few drugs that we know of today are effective without any such dangers. Among those that do seem benign are aspirin, caffeine, various substances found in herbs, vitamins, and other substances that are not usually thought of as drugs at all. Most others are dangerous to one degree or another and are used only when necessary by cautious people and only in proportion to the benefits that they confer. Human biology is so complicated and easily damaged that any drugs to enhance abilities should be used with the utmost care and with a careful assessment of their effectiveness and side effects, including temporary or permanent biological damage or imbalances in biological processes. The problem for the prudent individual is how to acquire the relevant information about such drug use and how to avoid inappropriate use. This much is important for all of us for even the most routine drug use for medical purposes. In the event of any new ability-enhancing drugs we might well regulate their use and control their availability, in spite of the further social problems this might generate.

Let us suppose, however, that such information is available for any ability-enhancing drugs we might consider, or even that negative side effects can be eliminated, that appropriate dosages are known, that individual sensitivities and peculiarities can be discounted, and that no long- or short-term physical dangers that would put off the most cautious individual are known (or exist). I disregard here also the prospect of addiction as it is usually understood: an involuntary physical dependency that we may suppose the user would wish to avoid if possible.[6]

Still there would remain some troubling prospects for us if ability-enhancing drugs were available on a broad scale for the kinds of abilities mentioned above. Foremost of these are questions about human identity and individual personality.[7] We are all to a large extent identified by ourselves and others in terms of persistent traits of character and personality which manifest themselves in our occurrent feelings and thoughts as well as by our histories and our activities and occupations. Among these traits are a variety of dispositions, capacities, and beliefs that manifest themselves in a wide range of activities. For example, we can think of personalities as William James did, as "tender-minded" or "tough-minded."[8] Or we could rely on other psychological profiles of core personality traits, such as Freud's or Jung's or more eclectic, descriptive schemes. These features of our personalities, by all accounts, form as a result of our early development and as a consequence of many years of experiences. Habits and practices form as a result both of our (relatively) inherent features and of our learning and training. During our lives we make choices that both reflect these personality traits and to some extent form or modify them. But overall, our personalities tend to be stable or slowly evolving rather than suddenly changing and erratic. This relative stability allows us to develop and maintain our sense of identity and individuality. Indeed, sudden or erratic changes in central or core features of a personality are likely to be considered pathological. They would be of concern to ourselves, if we recognized them, and to others, and would likely lead to psychotherapeutic interventions of one form or another.

But now in considering modification of some of these traits by the use of drugs we are speculating on the prospects of changing at least some of the core features of our personalities for shorter or longer terms. For example, significant changes in our abilities to remember, to concentrate, to endure physical hardship, or to relate sympathetically to others, or a combination of these, would seem to lead to a reorganization of our personalities. And this in turn raises further concern about side effects, this time psychological ones involving what might be kinds of imbalances or disharmonies in the overall economy of our personalities.[9] Even the restoration of competencies and abilities poses serious questions about personal identity. Whether this is undesirable will depend on how many such traits are modified, for how long, and in what combinations. It is conceivable that radical transformations are possible, though I think this is very unlikely. Much of our personalities, however, would remain unchanged even with the enhancement of various primary abilities such as those involving memory or physical prowess. For example, our memories themselves would presumably remain intact, our belief systems would be largely unchanged, and our values and goals, though they might change gradually as do our memories and beliefs, would not change so dramatically as to alter our various basic life projects or activities. Still we can imagine some such changes as the result of enhanced abilities and the resulting activities we engage in. But these pose no drastic threat to our identities and personalities, no more than do changes induced by other kinds of life experiences, such as education, training, marriage, or psychotherapy. We may welcome the changes in any case as enabling us to lead more productive, fulfilling, and useful lives.

We do not, however, live isolated and atomistic lives, and the changes resulting from enhanced abilities would certainly have affects on those we are most intimately related to: our families, friends, and associates. Do we threaten to change basic configurations of human relationships by the use of drugs to enhance our abilities? Are changes in social institutions also likely to be needed? Here, too, I think the kinds of changes we can plausibly envision do not pose dramatic challenges to human relationships either on an individual scale or institutionally. It may be that educational programs would need to be modified to accommodate greater learning abilities, that new and challenging types of sports activities would develop, or that work schedules and expectations would be adjusted. The challenge of such changes is not so much that they would occur at all, but that they might occur suddenly rather than gradually, allowing less time than is usual for our relationships and our institutions to change in commensurate fashions. Our autonomy and our sense of control over our own development would surely be threatened by the sudden availability of many powerful ability-enhancing drugs. And our relationships and institutions would experience similar stresses from such swift pharmacological innovation. But such rates of change are not likely, nor is the effectiveness of ability-enhancing drugs or their impact likely to be so great as we might imagine. We should argue for caution in any case, rather than wild enthusiasm. Such drugs beyond the current sorts are mostly fantasy rather than reality.

One further issue arises, however, about such drugs, namely, whether we would become in some sense dependent on them, relying on them to sustain our relationships, our jobs, and our various individual and social projects. Perhaps it is in this sense that it is most useful to speak of "addiction" rather than as a biologically causal condition. We may imagine a restructuring of our institutions and relationships so that they would come to rely on enhanced abilities and could function only relatively poorly without them. We might well become dependent on these changes in the way we have become dependent on other technologies. So we are faced with the alternatives of temporary ability-enhancement and long-term enhancement. We can imagine a slippery slope of ability-enhancement that begins with occasional use for special projects and then continuously changes into longer and longer dependency, creating a "brave new world" of drug-modified behavior.

There are genuine dangers lurking in this prospect. It leads to many concerns for loss of individual autonomy and social control that we would do well to avoid. But there are no special problems posed by the use of drugs to enhance abilities. We already enhance through education and training our abilities to run the complex institutions and technologies that comprise much of our culture. This has always been so for human society at any stage. The development of skills and the transmission of information to enhance and change those abilities have always been part of our cultural development. Our dependencies on learned and enhanced abilities are evident during periods of rapid social change or dislocation when war or other disasters disrupt our patterns of social organization. Whether the complexity of our social and technological development is desirable is a question that cuts across the particular issue of enhancing our abilities through the use of drugs or by any other means.

The two issues of autonomy and social control, however, seem to me to stand out; they are different in a curious way, though both have to do with the exercise of power. Let us assume again that some drugs do in fact enhance abilities and do so with few or no prohibitively dangerous physical side effects. Then we can suppose two opposite tendencies might arise. One is to use such drugs to exploit the behavior or working conditions of some people by others with control of the distribution of the drugs. We can imagine workers, for example, being required to take drugs to enhance their abilities to perform their jobs. The other is to create an elite class of people who restrict access to the drugs in order to provide benefits and power to themselves. This latter possibility is especially serious in the case in which the drugs are expensive and rare or arcane. A similar situation exists today in societies where scarce and expensive resources such as medical care and elite education serve to enhance the abilities of privileged classes to the exclusion of others.

It may be fairly easy to show that such situations are inherently unjust. Exploitation and the unjust distribution of power are not new to human societies; but they do not seem to be inevitable in spite of our long history of social oppression. These are general problems in our society not peculiar to the kind of case we are imagining. Nor are such conditions more likely to arise solely because of the prospects of new ability-enhancing drugs. To the contrary, it may be less likely. The drugs we would need to fear, of which there are enough already, are those that stupefy and debilitate. Furthermore, though we face serious problems in securing a just distribution of primary human goods, we do not therefore refuse to develop them rather than working to effect a more generous and equitable distribution of them.

But suppose for a moment that such drugs were as inexpensive and easily available as aspirin or caffeine or antibiotics. Suppose further that there were clear and enforceable laws against giving these drugs to other people without their knowledge and consent. Is the mere fact that such drugs are available and do in fact enhance various abilities reason enough for us to seek to control them, regulate them, or restrict access to them? My own judgment is that it is not. To the contrary, it would be reason to seek to incorporate their use in our educational and training programs, to reconfigure our sports and to restructure our work and play. Utopian drugs would call for utopian planning.

There are a number of further considerations that support the use of drugs to enhance various of our abilities. These arguments, too, depend on a prior discounting of adverse side effects of various kinds. In reality such risks must always be measured against likely benefits. And this assessment should no doubt dampen utopian hopes for benign and revolutionary changes in our lives. Nevertheless, let me now consider a number of reasons why enhancing our abilities with drugs (as much as by other means) is desirable.

Our abilities are the tools of our lives. They are what enable us effectively to make our ways through the world, warding off dangers and seeking out goods which make our lives richer and safer. Our primary abilities are a more-or-less inborn store of capacities that have evolved as traits successful in coping with our changing environments. They enable us to acquire further (secondary) skills, abilities largely learned and fostered by practice, training, and a wide range of culturally preserved educational programs. Education and other forms of nurturing are in fact our primary means of enhancing our abilities, of maximizing their effectiveness and range, and of forming and developing new specific abilities in light of our changing needs and the conditions of our lives. We know all too well how our primary abilities can be stunted early in life by poor nutrition and an impoverished and unstimulating environment. Injury and disease can also take their toll. To some extent, too, these capacities can be enhanced or at least given what we suppose to be a full, normal development by a rich and nurturing childhood. And in many ways our secondary abilities and skills can be created, developed, and enhanced by training and education. The value to us of these abilities is evident. They make us what we are and provide us with the means to achieve most of what is good (and bad) in our lives. To enhance their roles in our lives is therefore of inestimable value in enabling us to get the other things we desire.

Their social utility is therefore evident. I have already mentioned a number of concerns reflecting the possibility of the inequitable distribution of ability-enhancing drugs and of the exploitation of drug-enduced abilities. But such drugs would also have the potential for benefit for us both individually and socially. Our lives could be enriched by the safe and prudent use of drugs to enhance our abilities, just as they now are when drugs enable us to speed our recovery from disease or injury, to correct deficiencies and incapacities, and to prolong our struggle with the debilitating consequences of aging.

But we also value these abilities and their exercise for their own sake: they are of intrinsic value for us. When we exercise our abilities in performing certain tasks or engaging in certain projects there is satisfaction for us in the development of our abilities and the exercise of our skills, even when this is difficult or challenging. This is in part due to the satisfaction of improving our abilities or experiencing them being employed in a smooth and effective way. But it is also due to the fact that they represent to some degree at any time an expression of our identities and personality. By experiencing the active play of our abilities in our lives we give expression to that part of our nature that encompasses those abilities; it is a testimony to our effectiveness in the world, a projection of our choices and desires, and therefore of our powers and potentiality as human beings.

We can distinguish, however, as Aristotle did, between our satisfaction in the exercise of our abilities and the satisfactions provided by the result of applying those abilities. Sometimes people are confused by these two, allowing the satisfaction of abilities engaged well to count for the satisfaction of abilities well engaged. We need to distinguish the good of what we accomplish from the good of experiencing the process of accomplishing it. If it is a good to enhance our abilities, an intrinsic good, as I believe it is, we should not confuse that with the goods or evils achieved by their exercise. (Indeed for Aristotle, for us at our best, and for God eternally, our fulfillment lies exclusively in the exercise of our cognitive abilities!) If we enhance our abilities, we also enhance our ability to do both good and bad things. The value we may attach to the exercise of our abilities cannot override the evil consequences that may lead to. But nothing, so far as I can see, skews the use of our abilities through their enhancement toward the bad rather than the good. And this is true whether the enhancement is achieved by education or training or through the use of drugs of some kind.

Still, it might be argued, there is something cheap about drug-based enhancement. The value we associate with the exercise of our abilities, so the argument might go, is proportional to the effort put into developing or honing those abilities. What is hard won is all the more appreciated. We admire those who, though they start with relatively limited (primary) abilities, by dint of hard work and determination develop their (secondary) skills and go on to outstanding achievement. Muscles seem less impressive if partly steroid-induced than if they are the product of far more hours of grueling exercise. There is some truth in these claims, but they rest on a confusion. We do value hard work and determination, commitment and dedication. But these are additional values, commending virtues that are independent of the exercise of those competencies and abilities they may sometimes help develop. The exercise of abilities has its own value and rewards as do the achievements they may lead to. Nothing, so far as I can see, is gained by distinguishing abilities through their provenance. (My ability to give a good lecture to my 8:30 A.M. class may be enhanced by my careful preparation and by several cups of coffee, though neither may typically be sufficient by itself.)

Kant argued in the *Grounding for the Metaphysics of Morals* and elsewhere that we have duties to ourselves that are prior to our duties to others.[10] Among such duties to ourselves is a duty to develop our own talents, or, as we might put it, to enhance our own abilities. There are difficulties with the notion of duties to oneself. We can more easily perhaps understand that one might have a duty to others to develop one's own talents; but why a duty to oneself to do so? For Kant I believe the answer lies in the close connection between one's talents or abilities and one's self-esteem and a realization of one's autonomy.[11] I have already stressed the utility that abilities may have for us. Their development and exercise in the accomplishment of valuable projects and services may be not only a matter of self-interest, but also a contribution to broader community and social concerns. In many cases we may have duties to others that motivate that development and effort. But Kant alternatively argues that in developing our abilities we give fuller expression to our lives as autonomous beings sharing in a moral community of other like persons.

This duty to enhance our abilities is related to our earlier concern that doing so might threaten important features of our identities as individual persons. These features included a sense of proportion, balance or harmony that as an ideal may contribute to our effectiveness as agents and our enjoyment of a wide range of activities. Kant's concern is of course not with the promotion of self-indulgence or self-interested activities, but rather for the realization of our autonomy as moral agents. It is important for him that our assessment of ourselves be honest and objective, that it be moral and not expedient. We also, for Kant, have duties to others, such as a duty of beneficence, to improve the circumstances of others in order to further their own development as autonomous beings. Presumably a careful balance is required to avoid becoming merely a means to the development of others and to avoid using them as a means to one's own development. This balance can be accomplished in part by acknowledging the interdependence of individual and community. The development of my abilities is possible only in the context of a community of other persons where abilities can be identified and their development objectively appraised. The enhancement of my abilities, a self-regarding duty, is thus intimately linked to my duties to others as members of a society of moral agents. [12] Whatever means we employ, therefore, when we enhance our talents and abilities we thereby develop and enrich our autonomy and our capacities as moral agents. Enhancing our abilities is in this sense not only permissible, therefore, but obligatory.

Nothing I have argued for has sought to deny the probable dangers of biological technologies. But I have argued that ability-enhancing drugs, were they to be developed beyond those of limited effectiveness that already exist, would not necessarily pose special dangers. Nothing precludes our enhancing our abilities with drugs except the possible harms that might outweigh any benefits to us. Whether such harms would be likely is an empirical issue that we cannot foresee. But if such risks proved to be manageable, then on other grounds, the use of drugs to enhance our abilities would not only be permissible but desirable.

NOTES

1. David M. Grilly, *Drugs and Human Behavior* (New York: Allen and Bacan, 1989), p. 14.

2. The impact of the loss and restoration of ability can be overwhelming. See Oliver Sacks' fascinating, though extravagant, *A Leg To Stand On* (London: Duckworth, 1984).

3. For an attempt at defining 'ability' see Alvin I. Goldman, *A Theory of Human Action* (Princeton: Princeton University Press, 1970).

4. See R. C. Lewontin, "The Dream of the Human Genome," *New York Review of Books* XXXIX, No. 10 (May 28, 1992), 31–40.

5. See W. M. Brown, "On Defining 'Disease,'" *The Journal of Medicine and Philosophy* 10 (1985) 311–28.

6. But see Herbert Fingarette, *Heavy Drinking: The Myth of Alcoholism as a Disease* (Berkeley: University of California Press, 1988).

7. See Jonathan Glover, *What Sort of People Should There Be?* (New York: Penguin, 1984).

8. William James, *Pragmatism* (Indianapolis: Hackett Publishing Company, 1981), p. 10.

9. See Oliver Sacks' discussion of Tourette's syndrome in "A Neurologist's Notebook," *The New Yorker* (March 16, 1992), 85–94.

10. Immanuel Kant, *Ethical Philosophy*, trans. by J. W. Ellington (Indianapolis: Hackett Publishing Company, 1983).

11. I rely here on Margaret Paton, "A Reconsideration of Kant's Treatment of Duties to Oneself," *The Philosophical Quarterly* 40 (1990), 222–33.

12. John Rawls, *A Theory of Justice* (Cambridge, MA: Harvard University Press, 1971).

Better Performance Through Chemistry: The Ethics of Enhancing Ability Through Drugs

Robert L. Simon

New technologies create new problems even as they solve old ones. Thus, the development of techniques for transplanting organs can result in lives being saved that otherwise would have been lost. However, the problem of how scarce organs should be distributed among donors is a new one. Prior to the use of transplants, physicians were not faced with the choice of whom to save or whom to let die when the number of patients exceeded the supply of organs available for transplant.

Although this specific problem is new, its general form is not. The problem of how to distribute resources justly and fairly when there are not enough resources to go around is a very ancient one. Accordingly, although it is true to say that developments in technology create new ethical problems, these problems often are closely related to older ethical dilemmas to which extensive thought has been devoted.

In his admirable contribution to this discussion on the ethics of enhancement of performance through drugs, Miller Brown suggests that although the specific problems raised by the introduction of performance-enhancing drugs are new, they are not different in kind from other sorts of ethical problems we have faced. He maintains that once important distinctions have been raised among the kinds of problems raised by such drugs, familiar ethical tools are adequate to deal with them. In particular, the proper test to apply to the use of such drugs is the familiar one of weighing *costs* and *benefits*.

Nothing precludes our enhancing our abilities with drugs except possible harms that might outweigh any benefits to us. Whether such harms would be likely is an empirical issue that we cannot foresee. But if such risks proved to be manageable, then on other grounds, the use of drugs to enhance our abilities would not only be permissible but desirable.

I found Brown's discussion to be very helpful, and am in agreement with many of his major points. However, I suggest in what follows that the issues raised by the possible development of new and powerful performance-enhancing drugs are more complex than his reliance on evaluation of costs and benefits suggests. Interpreted narrowly, the weighing of costs and benefits often is understood along the lines suggested by the classical utilitarians, or some of their more contemporary intellectual descendants. However, the kinds of costs and benefits raised by advanced performance enhancing drugs do not easily fit within the kinds of consequentialist frameworks advocated by more traditional forms of utilitarianism. If "costs" and "benefits" are understood more broadly, however, we may have been told merely the use of performance enhancers is permissible or even desirable when it is morally better to allow their use than not to do so. This formula clearly is too general to be useful. In what follows, I will follow Brown's lead and consider some of the specific difficulties that are raised by the use of performance-enhancing drugs.

The Use of Performance Enhancers in Competition

Steroids and Sports

One area where the use of performance-enhancing drugs already has been controversial is in competitive athletics. Athletes have used anabolic steroids, synthetic forms of the male hormone testosterone, to enhance athletic performance in certain sports. The use of steroids carries with it a substantial risk of suffering sometimes severe side effects, but also allows quicker recovery from longer workouts, enhancing the development of muscle mass and strength in users. Although steroids are not "magic pills" but only provide benefits in conjunction with hard work, their use can promote some benefits for top athletes while creating significant risks for the users as well.

The leading sports organizations and authorities, such as the International Olympic Committee and the NCAA, prohibit the use of steroids to enhance athletic performance. However, many of the proposed justifications for a such a policy seem inadequate, at least when applied to competent adults. After all, why should athletes be restricted more than anyone else from taking risks to attain their goals? Assuming that the athletes are free and informed competent adults, it can be argued that sports authorities have no more right to restrict their liberty for their own good any more than any other agency has the right to restrict our own freedom for our own benefit. All of us take some risks for goods we enjoy, yet we would hardly regard paternalistic do-gooders who constantly restricted our own freedom for our own good as justified. Why should athletes have any less freedom than the rest of us?

Perhaps, however, the best case for prohibiting the use of performance-enhancing drugs in sports is not paternalistic at all but rests on the other-regarding character of competition. But what effect on others is morally relevant to the prohibition of the use of steroids? After all, differences in diet, coaching, practice facilities, and dedication in training, also can have effects on competitors, yet these effects are not regarded as illegitimate.

Perhaps what is of concern is the *fairness* of benefits gained through the use of steroids. The intuitive idea here is not simply that steroid users break the existing rules, and hence are cheating within the official framework of policies, for perhaps the existing rules should be changed. Rather, it is that a change permitting the general use of steroids would be irrational since few athletes would benefit and most would be harmed. Since rational athletes would not consent to the collective practice of steroid use, users of these performance-enhancing drugs gain unfairly by breaking rules that they themselves would support from an impartial position of choice.

Although such a line of argument is controversial, and has yet to be fully fleshed out, it may be useful to think of in terms of a hypothetical social contract. Suppose all athletes prior to participation in competition were asked whether they would support the rule, "Use of steroids by competitors in order to enhance athletic performance shall be prohibited in competition," or the alternate rule, "Use of steroids by competitors in order to enhance athletic performance shall be permitted in competition." Then let us stipulate one plausible moral restriction on their choice; namely, that they vote in ignorance of how the use of steroids would affect them personally but with knowledge of the general properties of steroids. The use of this limited veil of ignorance, suggested by Rawls's theory of justice, forces the athletes to vote impartially rather than out of self-interest. How would rational athletes vote?

According to a plausible line of argument, athletes would realize that the use of steroids would subject all users to a substantial risk of serious harm, but benefits would be unknown for each individual, and in any case would be likely to be marginal at best. Widespread use would at best yield only minimal gains for a very few users since any advantages gained by some would be cancelled out by similar advantages gained by most others. The risk of serious side effects, on the other hand, would be significant for all.

Under such circumstances, the choice of a rule permitting the use of steroids by everyone seems collectively irrational. Why risk substantial harm without knowledge of even the odds of obtaining a benefit, especially when any expected benefit is most likely to be minimal? Thus, there is good reason to believe that a rule permitting the general use of steroids to improve athletic performance would not be supported by athletes were they to deliberate under impartial conditions of choice.

This contractual approach supports the common intuition that the use of steroids to enhance athletic performance is a form of cheating, not just in the formal sense of violating existing rules, but in the broader sense of being unfair. This is because the only way significant advantages are likely to be secured from steroid use is if only a few athletes use them. But in order to insure that only a few are users, the drugs must be used covertly.

Otherwise, more and more athletes would use such drugs as a defensive measure in order to remain competitive against those who are already using them. As we already have seen, it is precisely the general use of steroids that rational impartial athletes (including those who in practice would be willing to take advantage of non-users) would prohibit. In other words, users hope to gain from the violation of rules that they themselves would support under appropriate conditions of choice.

This line of argument is hardly free from objection. But it not only provides at least some justification of the intuition that the use of steroids to enhance athletic performance is wrong, it also suggests a contractual basis for similar prohibitions in other areas.

For example, suppose some workers at a factory or office start taking a drug that allows them to work longer hours than normal at the risk of long-term harmful side effects. Given that context, other workers may prefer to also take the drug in order to enhance their work record, so as not to appear less conscientious than their drug-taking colleagues. However, while they would prefer taking the drugs in question to not taking them if colleagues were already users, they would most prefer a work environment in which they were not faced with such a choice to begin with. Moreover, as more and more workers take the drug, the gains to any one worker are likely to be minimal, especially when compared to the possible harm that is risked.

Surely it is plausible to think that if the workers did not know whether or not the drug would give them any major advantage over others, but were aware of the risks of use, they would consent to a rule prohibiting the use of the drug rather than one allowing it. Once again, the use of the drug is likely to confer an advantage only if most other competitors are not users. The practice of widespread use, however, is not likely to lead to significant gains for any specific individual, but expose virtually all to the risk of harm. If individuals were in ignorance of even whether they would be beneficiaries of such relatively minor benefits, it is hard to see why they would approve of the general practice of using potentially harmful performance enhancers in the kind of contexts we have described.

Ideal Cases and Ideal Arguments

If the contractual approach has force at all, it is because the use of drugs we have been discussing, such as anabolic steroids, can have harmful side effects. Miller Brown, however, asks us to consider the use of performance-enhancing drugs in cases where harmful side effects are either absent or minimal. Suppose, for example, that the use of steroids to enhance athletic performance had no more serious consequences than drinking a cup of coffee in the morning to increase alertness. Since use would be relatively risk-free, why wouldn't it be rational to consent to general use of the drug? Moreover, agents need not only be concerned with their own performance. For example, they might want to improve general levels of performance, that might lead to increases in productivity or (in athletics or the arts) to levels of performance they might admire, appreciate, or enjoy.

On Brown's analysis, the decision about whether to allow, encourage, or even require the use of such drugs seems to depend on weighing of the costs and benefits involved. But what counts as a cost and what counts as a benefit? If "costs" and "benefits" are understood in ways that can be broadly classified as utilitarian, they would concern the effects of use (either by a particular agent or as a general practice) that harms or helps those affected.

For example, the use by baseball players of a harmless drug that enhances hand-eye coordination so as to improve batting skills may not cause any physical harm to users. However, use by athletes may violate a widely held ideal of sport, according to which success in sport should be due to the combination of an athlete's innate skills, the dedication and hard work committed to the development of those skills, and intelligence with which they are used, as well as relevant virtues such as courage and ability to make good decisions under pressure. Adherents of this ideal might claim that use of the drug makes athletic success depend on how efficiently one's body utilizes certain chemicals, which is not a quality relevant to athletic skill. Athletic performance, in other words, should reflect traits more closely associated with our nature as *persons*, as agents, than with mere matters of bodily metabolism. Batters who have worked for years to understand the strategy of pitchers, to develop the muscle memory to swing correctly, and to "pick up" the spin on pitches, should not have their skills matched by less diligent players who merely take the right pills.

Of course, such an ideal is controversial. Critics would point out that luck plays a role in many sports. Why should the way one's body reacts to a drug be treated as any less relevant, say, than the way one's body reacts to a diet, a new training regimen, or a change of climate? What *ethically* distinguishes the introduction of a new harmless performance-enhancing drug in sports from the use of new equipment, such as fiberglass poles and graphite tennis racquets and golf shafts, that also may enhance performance?

These are legitimate questions that need to be debated by those, such as myself, who oppose the use of performance-enhancing drugs in sport, but such a debate would take us too far from the main point under consideration. What is that point? It is that if we understood "costs" and "benefits" narrowly, in the ways generally developed by utilitarians, the sort of ideal considerations represented by the appeal to respect for persons in sport would be irrelevant to the discussion, unless perhaps it could be shown that adoption of that ideal had utilitarian consequences of its own. The ideal, however, would not be evaluated on its own merits. On the utilitarian view, ideals are not morally relevant to ethical evaluation apart from consideration of the utilitarian consequences of adopting or rejecting them. Therefore, such factors as whether an ideal is noble or base, whether it accords with or conflicts with our status as moral persons, are not even considered from the utilitarian perspective.

This narrowing of the range of the discussion, which Brown may not mean to endorse, can lead us to ignore factors that ought to be considered in our evaluation of performance-enhancing drugs. These factors include our ideals about human performance, and our conception of human character and human virtue. These factors are as crucial to the debate as the more obvious kinds of utilitarian considerations, yet may be obscured by too strict a conception of cost-benefit analysis.

Performance Enhancers and Human Virtue

Narrow and Broad Costs and Benefits

Our discussion suggests, then, that there are at least two different ways of understanding Brown's claim that "Nothing precludes our enhancing our abilities with drugs except possible harms that might outweigh any benefits to us (this volume, p. 131)." According to the first or broader conception, we evaluate the use of performance enhancers by weighing all the consequences of their use, giving independent weight to a wide plurality of factors, such as their effects on our character or the quality of our relationships, that are not easily reducible to a common standard. On this view, "weighing of costs and benefits" can be interpreted so broadly as to be virtually interchangeable with overall moral evaluation. Alternately, on the second or narrower conception, we use only the criteria of harms and benefits employed by the standard forms of utilitarianism, such as equating benefits with satisfaction of preferences and harms with their frustration, and assess the value of the consequences only according to their measurement by that standard. Thus, according to the first standard, the assignment of value only to those virtues we have developed through exertion of moral effort, *independent* of their effects on the preferences of others, is a legitimate moral move (whether or not it is ultimately justifiable). However, it is ruled out of court by the second standard that assigns value to consequences only in terms of their relationship to the satisfaction and frustration of preferences.

There are substantial problems with the narrower standard of evaluation when applied to the use of performance-enhancing drugs, even apart from the general problems that have been raised with the best-known forms of utilitarianism. Consider, for example, how we are to assess the impact of a new drug that would vastly increase the musical and mathematical abilities of wide segments of the population, using some form of preference utilitarianism as our standard of evaluation. Whose preferences are we to consider? At least three possibilities present themselves.

1. We assess the impact of the drug by asking whether the present population would prefer the state of affairs following its introduction, (S_i) to the state in which its use was prohibited, (S_p).

2. We assess the impact of the drug by asking whether (S_i) would produce a better ratio of preference satisfaction to preference frustration than (S_p) among the population as it would exist given the use of the drug was *permitted*.

3. We assess the impact of the drug by asking whether (S_i) would produce a better ratio of preference satisfaction to preference frustration than (S_p) among the population as it would exist given the use of the drug was *prohibited*.

That is, since the use of the drug is likely to change the preferences of the population who uses it, supposing for example that enhanced musical ability would increase the desire to play and listen to music, both (S_i) and (S_p) might be justified by preference utilitarianism. Since the introduction of the drug might enhance our desires for musical involvement, the population that would exist after the drug was widely available might be very glad it was introduced and regard the state of affairs after the drug's introduction as superior to the state of affairs prior to its introduction. However, if use of the drug was prohibited, the population that would then result might regard its situation as superior and prefer the drug not be introduced, since its members would never have acquired new abilities and the resulting new preferences in the first place.

Of course, this is not a new problem for utilitarianism. *Any* new social policy might well generate a different set of preferences among the population it affects. For example, suppose a massive educational program extolling the benefits of vegetarianism generates widespread aversion to meat-eating. The resulting population will be far more satisfied with vegetarianism than would the original population, precisely because their preferences changed as a result of the educational campaign. Similarly, a population that otherwise would have been strongly opposed to enhancing abilities through drugs might prefer such enhancement after exposure to a sophisticated advertising campaign supporting use.

In such cases, utilitarianism presumably would recommend applying the principle of utility to the issue of which set of preferences ought to be generated. Roughly stated, the principle would require us to generate that set of preferences that over the long run would result in the best overall ratio of satisfaction to frustration.

But even if there is no paradox here, there is a problem for those of us who are not utilitarians. Many non-utilitarians are likely to think there is more to the issue of what preferences we ought to have or, more broadly, what should make us happy, then simply the issue of what set of preferences or dispositions will generate the most satisfaction and least frustration in the future. Thus, some may question whether the nobility or virtue of a set of preferences can be reduced to their role in generating more preference satisfaction than alternatives.

Consider an example from sports. One of the traits many of us presently most admire in athletes is a kind of coolness under fire; the ability to rise to the best of one's abilities and make sound decisions about how to use one's talents under the greatest pressure. This appears to be an ability that is at least partially learned since it is more likely to be exhibited by the experienced veteran than the callow rookie.

Now suppose that a drug could produce the same effect without any side effects. For one thing, it might well be a good thing that such a drug existed. It might allow us to better fulfill our potential in a wide range of areas by helping us to focus and use our abilities to the maximum. As a result of increased efficiency, the ratio of preference satisfaction to frustration might be far better than otherwise. The benefits of the new drug would exceed the harms, considered from a utilitarian framework. But note that application of the utilitarian framework does not exhaust the ethical issues raised by the introduction of the drug.

In particular, coolness under pressure is one of the features sports contests test. Developing the capacity to exhibit such resourcefulness is a goal of athletes in competitive sports, and success in developing it is an achievement. If such resourcefulness could be provided by a drug, athletes and fans would no longer have reason to admire those who exhibit it, since they would have done little else but take their medication properly. Rather, it at most would be a trait that makes competition more skillful, perhaps possessing a kind of extrinsic value. But it is at least doubtful if sport would be intrinsically better if virtually all players exhibited the kind of drug-induced resourcefulness in question.

In particular, we surely wouldn't—and in fact shouldn't—admire and respect the players who exhibit such resourcefulness in the same way we presently admire and respect players who lost important contests in their youth because of inexperience and nervousness but who have learned from their experiences and now perform at their best under pressure. Tom Watson's great victories in golf, for example, were regarded as all the sweeter both by Watson and golf fans because he had earlier been called a choker for blowing early leads in important tournaments.

This example suggests that one of the costs of inducing a kind of virtue through drugs is that we thereby lose the very qualities of the trait that made it a virtue in the first place. If Watson has acquired his resourcefulness and coolness under pressure through a medical prescription, would he have deserved admiration for his exercise of those qualities?

This kind of example suggests that there may be moral costs to the use of performance-enhancing drugs that are not captured by a narrowly utilitarian weighing of benefits and harms. But if we are to weigh benefits and harms in some broader sense, so that *any* morally relevant factor can become a benefit or a harm, the value of performance enhancers becomes more debatable. Some of the difficulties are brought out admirably in Miller Brown's discussion but the complexity of the benefits and harms at stake may be even greater than even his discussion suggests.

Enhanced Performance, Virtue, and Respect for Persons

Consider another example. Calvin, since an early age, has had a mean, sour disposition and often acts cruelly towards others. He is insensitive to the concerns of those he interacts with, and almost always places his interests, however trivial, over theirs. In addition, he seems to enjoy insulting, demeaning, and otherwise hurting others.

Now suppose a new drug is developed called *compassiomycin*, that brings about what comes to be called "the niceness effect." Through various complex bio-chemical reactions, it enhances the user's ability to relate to others and feel compassion and sympathy for their plight. Calvin is induced to take the pill and, in spite of his rather broad streak of meanness, becomes a nice guy. How are we to morally evaluate this change?

Surely our initial response is to say it is a change for the better. The people Calvin would have hurt escape harm. Still others who otherwise would have suffered from Calvin's callousness may be helped by him instead. From a roughly utilitarian conception of benefits and harms, the change surely is one for the better.

Indeed, this response may well be the correct one. However, even if the change is for the better, the moral factors involved are more complex than this initial analysis suggests. For one thing, it is far from clear that Calvin deserves to be admired or respected for his compassionate behavior. Indeed, while compassion may be a virtue, it is far from clear that Calvin is exercising that virtue in being compassionate. His compassion comes from the pills he is taking and is not a disposition of character. Calvin's twin sister who was just as mean but who resolved to improve her behavior and worked hard to implement that resolution may well deserve our admiration and respect even if she ends up less compassionate than Calvin.

Again, imagine a drug that can greatly enhance our ability to concentrate and significantly diminish fatigue. Such a drug may greatly enhance our ability to work more efficiently for longer periods of time than at present. By increasing productivity, the widespread use of this drug may make things generally better than otherwise would be the case. But even leaving aside the questions of abuse, such as whether employers might apply pressure to require workers to take the drug, other moral costs need to be considered. What would count as dedication and perseverance in a world where use of this drug was widespread?

If writers, artists, physicians, or athletes find it easy to put in the long hours necessary to perfect their skills, why admire their dedication and commitment in the first place. Perhaps, as the reporter-sleuth in a mystery series observes, "the best things that happened were the result of effort expended, like cooking the special pasta, or building a relationship, or putting together a lot of neglected facts into a really good story." Even more, aren't many of the things people do that call for our respect and admiration, and many of the traits we call virtues, important precisely because they reveal underlying commitment and sensibility that are part of the person, not the result of a performance-enhancing drug?

It is presumably concerns of this sort that lead Miller Brown to worry about whether "there is something *cheap* about drug-based enhancement." (p. 129, italics my own.) He attempts to mitigate the force of this worry by arguing first, as I read him, that we need to distinguish between the value of the exercise of an ability and the degree of virtue or admiration we assign to the bearer of the ability. In our previous example, it is valuable that Calvin exercises compassion, but it is more doubtful that he has the virtue of compassion or that he should be admired as a compassionate person. This distinction is indeed important, but perhaps it only restates the problem rather than resolves it. If our moral qualities can be enhanced by drugs, even though the world may in one sense become an overall better place as a result, the price may be that those moral qualities lose their significance or, more accurately, have less and less application as the behavior they normally generate arises instead from the use of drugs.

Brown's second and more important response is that by enhancing our abilities, we may enhance our opportunities for autonomous growth and development. Thus, the use of anabolic steroids may give an athlete the opportunity to become stronger, but skill, judgment, and perseverance are still needed if the added strength is to be applied appropriately in athletic contests. Similarly, Calvin's compassion may arise as a result of use of a drug. However, it is up to him whether he exercises it intelligently, fruitfully, and sensitively.

There is much force to this kind of reply but one wonders if it only pushes the problem back one more step. If once our abilities are enhanced by drugs, we then face new problems and new challenges, why not invent still newer and more powerful drugs that enhance our abilities even further? The problem here is not only that eventually our very identity as humans may become questionable. In fact, on utilitarian or consequentialist grounds, we may become something more than human and perhaps better. It is rather that our moral framework for evaluating and respecting persons may be undermined. If the very traits that call for respect, admiration, and honor increasingly become drug induced, what happens to such notions as character, virtue, and responsibility that are such a major and perhaps irreplaceable element of our current moral universe?

Enhancing, Restoring, and Distributing

In his paper, Miller Brown suggests what appears to be a useful distinction between enhancing performance and restoring it. This distinction may be important for reasons similar to those that lead many people to think the distinction between killing and letting die is important. That is, killing seems much more difficult to defend morally than merely letting die. Similarly, using drugs to restore people's abilities or capacities seems less in need of ethical justification than enhancing them. But is the distinction as clear as it seems? Does it have moral significance?

There seem to be cases where the distinction applies in a clear and uncontroversial way. Thus, if I break my leg, the treatment of setting the bone and protecting the leg with a cast restores the bone to its previous state. Athletically, the treatment puts me back to the level of potential performance I enjoyed before the injury, but does not enhance that potential. On the other hand, a drug that would greatly increase my strength far beyond the capacity I might have reached on my own, clearly enhances my potential.

However, in other kinds of cases, the distinction is not so easy to apply, at least not without making judgments that are likely to be controversial. For example, in golf, the replacement of wooden shafts in clubs by steel shafts might plausibly be thought of as restoring ability the golfer always had since the stronger steel did not twist as much as the earlier wooden shafts. The greater torque of the wooden shafts might be thought of as a defect removed by the introduction of steel, just as the broken bone is a defect that is repaired by proper medical treatment. However, what of the introduction of the sand wedge, a club specifically designed to cut through the sand in bunkers making recovery shots far easier than before? Did the wedge restore the ability of players to recover by replacing clubs that were defective for use out of sand, or did they enhance performance by removing much of the difficulty of a particular kind of shot? It is far from clear which response is the more plausible.

A similar problem often will arise when we consider whether a particular drug restores ability or enhances it. While many cases will be at least relatively clear, others will not. Consider a drug that promotes our ability to remember in great detail long-ago events from our childhood. Should we think of it as restoring an ability we once had, but lost through the aging process, or as enhancing an ability well beyond the human norm? Or consider our example of the nasty Calvin whose character improves after treatment with compassiomycin. Has Calvin's ability to act sensitively and compassionately been enhanced? Perhaps so, but what if the drug changes Calvin's biochemistry in a way that makes it resemble that of unusually compassionate and sensitive humans. Was Calvin's unusual original biochemical condition an impediment that blocked his true nature from emerging? If so, didn't the drug really restore his true nature, rather than enhance what little compassion and sensitivity he may have possessed prior to treatment?

Miller Brown points out that whether we consider treatment by a drug as restoring or enhancing an ability may well depend on the base with which we make the comparison. (p. 115) Is the restoration or enhancement relative to the way the person was at some earlier time, relative to what is normal for the species, or to the way the person should have been if not for some condition we regard as an impediment?

How we conceive of the baseline of comparison to be used to determine if a drug is restorative or enhancing will depend upon complex and controversial judgments. These may include judgments about human nature, the true nature of specific individuals, and what counts as an impediment to normal development rather than an aspect of it. Since these are likely to be controversial themselves in many cases, it is doubtful if the distinction between a drug that restores an ability and one that enhances it is likely to be of great moral significance, at least in cases that are morally difficult in the first place. Rather than helping resolve difficulties, the restoring-enhancing distinction is only likely to add to them in hard cases.

If the restoring-enhancing distinction is not likely to be a particularly useful tool of moral analysis, some of the problems mentioned by Brown are likely to be even more complex than even he suggests. Thus, the distinction will be of little use in helping us determine whether a drug that enhances an ability is morally desirable. For example, compassiomycin, which turns nasty Calvin into nice Calvin, may seem a good thing to many of us. However, from the point of view of others, it may transform Calvin from a crusty but refreshing cynic to an interfering do-gooder who is never willing to let others make their own mistakes. A defense of the use of compassiomycin might be based on the principle of restoring Calvin to what he would have been in the absence of his unusual biochemical makeup. But if that distinction itself is unclear it is unlikely to be helpful in such a case. Has the true Calvin been restored or replaced by the use of the drug? How are we to tell? Does it morally matter?

If the distinction between restoring and enhancing abilities is unlikely to be useful in helping us to draw moral lines in controversial cases, the question of access to performance-enhancing drugs is likely to become central. If the effects of the drugs are morally controversial, and there is no easy way to draw even preliminary lines, should such drugs be made available? Available to whom? Who decides?

Suppose we assume, along with Brown, that such drugs will not have clear physical or psychological side effects so that we can focus on the moral issue of distribution. Should such drugs be generally available? Should people be free to use them as they choose? Should moral or even legal pressure be exerted to promote use of especially beneficial drugs? Can drug use even be *required*? Imagine, for example, a drug that vastly reduced the probability of the user initiating violence. Should everyone be encouraged to take them or only the violence-prone? Should the latter be required to "take their medicine"? Should "nasty" people who refuse to take their compassiomycin be treated any differently than the rest of us?

If we adopt a kind of libertarianism and maintain that competent informed adults ought to make their own choices, one set of problems arises. The libertarian would leave it up to competent adult individuals as to whether or not they took any particular performance-enhancing drug.

A world in which the libertarian principle applied might be less good than it otherwise might be if people chose not to take drugs that would have beneficial effects if taken. On the other hand, if many people chose to take such drugs, the kinds of problems of autonomy and personal identity to which Brown alludes have special force. For example, does Calvin's future spouse have the right to know that Calvin's sympathetic character that she so admires is the result of the drug he is taking? Should she be informed about the "real" Calvin? Which Calvin is the real one? Does Calvin have a right to privacy in this area?

What about those people who refuse to enhance their abilities through drugs? Will they be regarded as subnormal and be subject to discrimination? Will people feel they have been pressured to take drugs to keep up with their competitors, just as some athletes today believe they must take steroids simply in order to remain competitive with other athletes who already are users?

But if libertarianism faces difficulties, the corresponding difficulties of government regulation are also great. If the state is to remain neutral towards different conceptions of the good, as some liberals have argued, how is it to distinguish between permissible and impermissible forms of enhancement? If it is permissible for me to take coffee so I can give a better lecture to my early morning class, why isn't it permissible to take compassiomycin so that I will remain sympathetic to my students who interrupt my research with what I regard as minor problems. But if we encourage use of performance enhancers on a wide scale, we eventually may be unable to identify the original "I" whose performance we wanted to enhance, or remain within the moral universe of discourse that generated the problems we hoped to resolve in the first place.

Presumably, at some point, we will do our best to weigh the benefits and harms that are likely to accrue from the general use of different performance-enhancing drugs, just as Miller Brown suggests. The problems with such use, as he points out, are not completely new in principle. Just as we can ask in our hypothetical future scenario if the real Calvin is the old nasty version or the drug-enhanced nice version, we now can ask if the real Calvin is the neurotic we knew before psychotherapy or the self-confident adult who emerged from it.

What I have tried to argue, however, is that while the problems raised by the introduction of performance-enhancing drugs are not new in principle, they are likely to be exceedingly complex. Moreover, the costs and benefits involved should not be interpreted as might be suggested by the narrower forms of utilitarianism and consequentialism if we are to get a full picture of the moral issues involved. Rather, as Brown points out, the use of performance enhancers raises deep questions about personal identity, human nature, autonomy, virtue, and respect for persons. Indeed, if the kinds of drugs he discusses ever are developed, the problems raised are likely to be far more complex and serious than even he indicates. Considering costs and benefits might serve us well, but only so long as we do not think of the weighing of costs and benefits simplistically. Rather, we need to understand the problems that might arise in even identifying the real costs and benefits of the use of performance enhancers and the changes they might make in the moral framework within which we think and act.

Pleasure

The Moral Mirror of Pleasure: Considerations About the Recreational Use of Drugs

Sheridan Hough

> Meanwhile the wineglasses had flushed yellow and flushed crimson; had been emptied; had been filled. And thus by degrees was lit, halfway down the spine, which is the seat of the soul, not that hard little electric light which we call brilliance, as it pops in and out upon our lips, but the more profound, subtle and subterranean glow, which is the rich yellow flame of rational intercourse. No need to hurry . . . no need to be anybody but oneself . . . how good life seemed, how sweet its rewards, how trivial this grudge or that grievance, how admirable friendship and the society of one's kind, as, lighting a good cigarette, one sunk among the cushions in the window-seat.[1]

Virginia Woolf's paean to spiritual pleasures, both conversational and alcoholic, is familiar enough: she celebrates not only what Aldous Huxley has called the "chemical vacation"[2] but, more importantly, the civilizing aspects of drug use. Sharing a good bottle of wine may revive and renew our appreciation of self and other, perhaps (as Woolf seems to suggest) enhancing the network of relations that sustain and bring together human endeavors (an insight that no doubt informs, e.g., the annual Philosophy Department cocktail party: collegial relations are meant to improve in an atmosphere of release).

But what of these amusements? Even when rendered in the most flattering light, the heightened experience provided by drugs seems dangerous, a glamorous invitation to a host of potential ills and evils. Given the unquestionable possibility for abuse, is it ever morally permissible to use drugs for pleasure?

Of course, any discussion about drugs must cope with the very different sorts of issues raised by legal and illegal substances. Those who moralize in the popular media usually treat "drugs" as a uniform list of substances when in fact many legal, medical and social distinctions obtain. Certainly, illegal drug use involves a host of moral concerns other than the status of the pleasures of drug taking. An inquiry about recreational drug use is undoubtedly complicated enough without the additional burden of related moral issues generated by legal matters: therefore, I will focus primarily on licit drug use; some of the moral difficulties at work in the use of legal substances may have some bearing on the use of illegal drugs.

But de-emphasizing the pleasures (and, moreover, pains) of illicit drug use only highlights an exceedingly important fact of the matter, namely, that the scope of licit drugs is a contingent and culturally relative determination. Different cultures often see the same drug in a very different light; moreover, individual cultures do not maintain stable rosters of licit and illicit drugs. The varying treatment of marijuana is a standard example of cultural differences in drug use: while still criminalized in the United States, it remains a licit drug in the Netherlands and in Thailand. The differences between cultures concerning the same drug (as well as one culture's changing attitudes over time towards a particular drug)[3] is a telling interpretive phenomenon, and one that I will address in the latter part of this essay.

In order to evaluate the moral status of drug use for pleasure, some important clarifications must be made. First, we should consider the ordinary distinctions we make between drugs and kinds of drug use: the perceived differences are often confused and sometimes deeply incoherent. The values of a culture are inevitably revealed in its recommendations and prohibitions about drugs.

Next, some thoughts about one prominent attitude towards drugs, specifically: any drug use for pleasure is morally questionable, even licit and moderate use; a society that can do without drugs is better off than one that tolerates use. What is it about drug use that seems problematic as such? Perhaps the physical sensations created by drugs are considered base, or perhaps the activity of taking drugs is (somehow) morally compromising. I will argue that drug taking is much like other pleasurable activities in that it is usually governed by contextual guidelines for moderate and responsible use; however, drugs are particularly vulnerable to de-contextualization, viz., the user can pursue a physical sensation apart from relevant contextual concerns. The latter kind of behavior may lead to immoderate use, and it is this immoderate, decontextualized use that should concern the moralist.

These distinctions in place, we can consider the particular benefits of appropriate recreational drug use. Finally, we will return to our initial observation that many of our attitudes about drugs are not reflectively worked out, but "inherited" from our culture: attachment to custom lives in an uneasy balance with rational consideration of the effects of drugs.

I.

The discriminations and distinctions we use in thinking about drugs are always relativized to a particular set of local concerns: even the most "dangerous" drugs can have, in the appropriate amounts and at the appropriate times, salubrious uses. The list of psychoactive drugs is quite long; it includes any substance that alters consciousness or affects mood.[4] These psychoactive substances are generally divided into four classes: prescription drugs such as codeine and Demerol; over-the-counter medications such as cough syrup and antihistamines; legal non-medical substances such as alcohol, nicotine, and theobromine (the active ingredient in chocolate); and, of course, illegal drugs such as LSD, heroin and marijuana.[5] Although our focus is on the third group of substances, it may be useful, later in the essay, to consider cultural reservations about the recreational use of drugs that are still illegal in the United States.

Even this brief classification indicates the vast differences in our attitudes towards psychoactive substances. Both marijuana and codeine have medical and nonmedical uses; codeine is an opiate derivative used primarily as an analgesic (also as a cough suppressant), while marijuana is used to treat glaucoma, asthma and as a treatment for a host of nervous system disorders.[6] Nonetheless, marijuana is widely regarded as a merely recreational drug, whereas codeine (a drug that is regularly abused) is usually seen as "medicinal" and hence relatively harmless. It is not the case that our attitudes neatly attach to objective data about the harmfulness of the substance in question. Alcohol is perhaps the best example of a commonly abused drug that has been both praised as the "good creature of God"[7] and condemned as a dangerous commodity, the "open sore of this land."[8] The scope of our characterizations of alcohol are revealing: the same drinker can be alternately described as either "fun loving" or "diseased." The drug in question does not alter, but our sense of the user of that drug may shift dramatically, depending on the account of his use.

Depictions of drug use in the popular media and in literature are valuable, for they usually reflect deeply held, perhaps deeply incoherent, views about the drugs used by a culture. The portrayal of fictional detective Lord Peter Wimsey is a good example of some of the subtleties at work in the distinctions made about drug use. Lord Peter, by late–twentieth-century American standards, is a heavy drinker: the port is perennially at table, dinner is accompanied by the wines that will complement it, champagne denotes the successfully concluded case. Lord Peter, however, is an oenophile—his manservant Bunter is often found wrapping the vintage port in eiderdown and worrying about excessive speeds in its transport[9]—and readers are clearly meant to differentiate between Lord Peter's appreciation of drink and the vile, destructive habits of the (occasionally) alcoholic criminals he pursues. Does this depiction tell us anything useful about the effects of alcohol, or does it simply provide a lesson in British class structure of the earlier part of this century? Are there legitimate differences between "kinds" of alcohol use, and, if so, what is their basis? For example, the followers of Alcoholics Anonymous argue that there is only one distinction between drinkers, namely, between those who have the disease of alcoholism and those who do not. The status of perceived differences is an important question, and one we will return to momentarily.

In *Heavy Drinking: The Myth of Alcoholism as a Disease*, the philosopher Herbert Fingarette provides an excellent account of how American drinking behaviors have been radically re-interpreted. He argues that Americans have moved from a benign view of drink[10] (held in the colonial period) to the "classic disease concept" of alcoholism, a view largely created and promoted by Alcoholics Anonymous in the earlier part of this century. The disease concept is indeed familiar:

> Alcoholism is a specific disease to which some people are vulnerable. Those who are vulnerable develop the disease if they take up drinking. From apparently normal social drinking, they progress to drinking ever greater amounts . . . to developing an increased tolerance for liquor. . . . Most crucially: those afflicted by the disease inevitably progress to uncontrolled drinking because the disease produces a distinctive disability—"loss of control.". . . Abstention is the only hope, because the disease is incurable.[11]

Familiar as these remarks are, however, they have little basis in current scientific research. Fingarette reviews much of the most recent work in biology, physiology and psychology, and reports their collective rejection of the classic disease concept: "One researcher puts it quite baldly: 'There is no adequate empirical substantiation for the basic tenets of the classic disease concept of alcoholism.'"[12] Indeed, the most cherished of AA beliefs failed to pass the tests set by researchers. For example, the disease concept insists that alcoholics are unable to "tolerate" alcohol, and that even one sip will precipitate a "loss of control." This idea that taking a drink invariably cripples the alcoholic's ability to control his or her drinking has been tested in several famous studies; surprisingly, the diagnosed alcoholics of these experiments were able to *moderate* as well as abstain from drinking. William Miller writes:

> In the most thorough review of this issue to date, Scottish psychologists Heather and Robertson (1981) summarized the findings of now numerous studies examining loss-of-control phenomena . . . they conclude: "When allowed to determine the volume and pattern of their own drinking, alcoholics do not drink to oblivion but do clearly demon-

strate positive sources of control over drinking behavior . . . "[13]

Both Miller and Fingarette cite the experiment of Marlatt et
al. (1973) in which

some alcoholics were led to believe they would be drinking alcohol, whereas others were told they would receive a
nonalcohol drink. Within each of these two groups, half
actually received alcohol disguised in a mixer and half did
not. Thus there were alcoholics drinking alcohol and not
knowing it, others drinking a beverage they falsely believed to contain alcohol, and still others drinking only
mixer and knowing it. *Alcoholics drank more of the beverage
when they believed it contained alcohol, whether or not it did.*[14]

Experiments of this sort cast doubt on the notion that alcohol
triggers some sort of biochemical "loss of control" in the alcoholic: instead, expectation, deliberation and choice seem to be
playing an important role.

Attempts to find a single cause for chronic heavy drinking
have likewise met with failure. Fingarette reviews the favorite
culprits: genetic tendency, metabolism, the development of
"physical tolerance" for alcohol, the "alcoholic personality":[15]
none of these alone can adequately explain the behavior of the
heavy drinker. As he states, "Thus the best answer we have to
the question, What causes the disease of alcoholism? is: There is
no such single disease and therefore there is no cause."[16]

Evidently, our culture is more comfortable with the notion
of a disease that afflicts a minority, rather than a psychosocial
phenomenon with no simple indicators and virtually no
potential for a swift and assured remedy. Fingarette remarks,
". . .cultural values, rather than careful observation or scientific
evidence, have been decisive in determining our beliefs about
alcohol."[17] This conclusion is important for our own discussion,
because it highlights the scope of interpretation at work in the
"facts of the matter": our values determine what facts we will
marshal in order to evaluate our beliefs and practices. Researchers can continue to produce evidence that undermines the prevailing disease concept of heavy drinking, but none of that
evidence will have much impact until one current (largely
American) view of "human being," viz., the "sick," or "addict-

ed" model of understanding human behavior, loses some of its force. Miller remarks,

> ... there does seem to be reasonable agreement on several points in the U.S.: a). true alcoholism is a primary disease rather than being secondary to other problems, b). the cause of the disease is not the alcohol itself, because many people drink without having problems. c). Alcoholism likely has a biomedical etiology ... It is clear that these assumptions are not shared throughout Europe ... Social policy in Sweden focuses on the control of alcohol consumption and the unhealthy consequences of overdrinking, seeking social causes and solutions. ... The assertion that alcoholism (read: negative consequences of overdrinking) is not caused by alcohol would be met there with puzzled bemusement.[18]

These remarks point out something that should have been obvious: there is no international agreement about the cause, treatment or, for that matter, the definition of habitual heavy drinking.[19] But even the most elementary survey of cultural practices will produce this rubric: if the drinking patterns (and the attendant accounts of those patterns) of, e.g., the French, the Finns, and Americans are compared (and, moreover, compared over time), a vast array of subtle distinctions and differences come to light.[20] A culture naturally distinguishes between acceptable and unacceptable drinking practices given a relevant set of environmental and social constraints: thus a "lush" in one culture may well be a "celebrant" in another. The classic disease concept turns out to be one more version of delineating unacceptable drinking practices, standing in no better relation to scientific data about alcohol use than other methods of defining acceptable drinking habits.

What, then, of Lord Peter's elevated drinking habits: is there really a difference between his schedule of liquor-induced pleasures and the lager-lout's beerswilling? A first observation about the difference in question is that it is an *interpretive* one: it reveals social disparities and inegalitarian treatment, rather than what inevitably happens if a person drinks beer instead of Pol Roger. Nonetheless, to say that the difference is "interpretive" is *not* to say that no difference obtains: behaviors are shaped, governed, and identified by a set of values; identifiable differences in behavior are the work of some prevailing evaluation.[21] But the question remains: what is the composition of a "healthy" drinking practice? Specifically, what is a good recreational use of any drug? Are there any features that can be reliably identified despite cultural differences?

II.

> Sugar then seemed the center of all satisfaction, and I am inclined, now, to regard it as a symbolic substance . . . well, not as a substance, but as the ultimate adverb of value.[22]

Our sense of the drugs we ingest, legal or otherwise, is itself an indicator of deeply held (albeit sometimes incoherent or seriously confused) cultural views. An analogous remark can be made about what we take pleasure in (and, moreover, what we feel we should find pleasurable): these sources of pleasure are also important indicators of how we view ourselves.

Prevailing sensibilities in the United States about legitimate sources of pleasure are quite revealing. In an article about current drug sensibilities, Jacob Sullum reports, "'The drug problem, even in some of its most difficult aspects, is getting better,' acting drug czar John P. Walters said. For Walters the 'drug problem' is this: people use drugs."[23] Furthermore, Charles Schuster, Director of the National Institute on Drug Abuse, remarks that the United States should move towards a "'drug-free' society."[24] These recommendations give voice to a widely shared condemnation of all drug-induced pleasures (although the nature of the condemnation at work cannot be taken at face value, since e.g., drugs used in medical treatments are surely not included in this purge). Why are many popular moralists inclined to damn drug use as such: why not praise the moderate use of legal substances? We should extend the scope of the question: what is it that makes some pleasures benign, or even healthy, and others, such as those that are drug-induced, pernicious?

Before considering what a "moral drug pleasure" might be, and certainly before we can speculate about the status of the use of drugs for pleasure, we should make some observations about pleasure itself.

An obvious place to start is with the view of the ethical hedonist, who claims that pleasure alone has intrinsic value. Although I will not defend ethical hedonism in this essay, a short review of some versions of hedonism will be instructive.

The ethical hedonist believes that pleasure, and only pleasure, should be the focus of our pursuits.[25] Obviously, this view as such must be agnostic about the sources of our pleasure. So described, the ethical hedonist cannot consistently object to the pleasures of drug use in and of themselves; however, distinctions can be made on a quantitative basis: so, for example, a source of pleasure can be preferred because of its greater intensity, duration, or because of its proximity in time. Quantitative ethical hedonists typically distinguish between "higher" and "lower" pleasures in this way. According to Henry Sidgwick, the pleasures of sex and food are lesser pleasures: not because these sources are somehow intrinsically less "worthy," but because they are quantitatively deficient in comparison with the pleasures of the intellect. Sidgwick writes,

> And often when we say that one kind of pleasure is better than another—as (e.g.) that the pleasures of reciprocated affection are superior in quality to the pleasures of gratified appetite—we mean that they are more pleasant.[26]

John Stuart Mill famously adds a wrinkle to this formula: he claims that pleasures differ not only in quantity but in quality: some pleasures are qualitatively better than others. Rem Edwards, in his account of Mill's view, remarks, ". . . there are, according to Mill, two more ways in which the experienced pleasures differ. They differ psychologically, as qualities of feeling, and also normatively, in desirability."[27]

These two versions of ethical hedonism introduce important refinements: first, Sidgwick's account of getting pleasure embeds the pleasure in the activity that is its source: thus, the emphasis falls not so much on the pleasure itself but on the preferred pleasure-producing activity. Mill's insistence that pleasures differ in psychological quality is sympathetic to the intuition that pleasures are very different, e.g., the pleasure of having sex is quite different from the pleasure of doing philosophy. Although I will have nothing further to say about these versions of hedonism, these theoretical refinements are nonetheless illuminating. From them we might borrow two "intuitions about pleasure": to call something "pleasurable" is to indicate a disposition to engage in an *activity* because of its associated feeling; moreover, the activities a person takes pleasure in are distinctively different in affect.

These intuitions are crucial in thinking about the use of drugs for pleasure, and it will be useful to investigate them in that light. First of all, it is important to get clearer about the composition of a "drug pleasure." In remarking that a person's choice of a "drug-induced pleasure" reveals a preference for the felt qualities of drug use, it must be acknowledged that the "felt qualities" of a particular drug pleasure *are not usually the product of a chemical agent alone;* rather, the "sensations" a person enjoys are often shaped by a drug activity, a drug ritual. It is widely documented that the efficacy and effects of most psychoactive drugs can depend in large measure on the environment in which they are taken (and here "environment" can include the surroundings of the user as well as the psychological state of the user).[28]

Not only do the environs shape and inform a drug experience; it is often the case that a *kind of activity* is in fact what is being desired by the user, rather than a simple drug sensation as such. One example of this is the study in which diagnosed alcoholics showed a much higher tendency to drink and to crave drink in a "bar-setting" furnished with liquor bottles and hors d'oeuvres than in a clinical setting, such as a lab.[29] A preference for drug-induced pleasures is not always simply an expression of a desire for the substance in question: a person's expectations and her or his surroundings all contribute to a person's sensations; also, the accouterments of the drug ritual, the social context of the drug activity, etc., all serve to create a "drug pleasure."

These are two rather different observations about the nature of drug-taking (viz., what sort of activity it is). The first is a remark about a characteristic feature of ingesting drugs: a person takes X and the taking of X is influenced by factors besides biochemistry; the person's beliefs and desires, her or his emotional state, the environment in which the drug is used, all play a part. (Indeed, placebos can quite often produce drug "experiences" (and their associated behaviors) on the basis of the user's expectations). The second observation, however, has to do with a person's dispositions: a person will be more disposed to take X in a favored context (e.g., a lounge setting) because the desired effect is constituted in large measure by that context.

Both of these elaborations on the act of drug-taking emphasize the murky nature of what is being preferred in choosing to take a particular drug. A person may indeed desire a bodily sensation: but the "bodily sensation" is itself a complex admixture of beliefs and desires, caused in part by the setting in which it occurs.

Much more could be said in this regard; however, it is sufficient here to simply point out that choosing to take a drug is not always the same as choosing to have a particular sensation as such: rather, it is choosing to engage in a particular activity in which sensations play some kind of role. Thus, "drug-induced pleasure" can usually be taken to mean "pleasurable drug experience." The latter expression emphasizes the heterogeneous nature of ingesting drugs: biochemical activity, the beliefs, desires, and attendant dispositions of the agent, and a host of environmental features all work to produce a "drug-pleasure," a pleasure not usually reducible to a physical sensation alone. In most cases, the drug used is necessary—but not at all sufficient—to account for the pleasurable affect.[30]

Having thus amplified our first "intuition" about pleasure, viz., that it is the pleasure it is within the context of an activity, we may turn to our second "pleasure intuition" (prompted by Mill's qualitative distinctions between pleasures): we readily distinguish between pleasures, normatively as well as psychologically, on the basis of the activities that produce them. Indeed, in focusing on drug-induced pleasures, we often find these distinctions at work; we habitually, and easily, distinguish between various kinds of drug pleasures. Let's return to our former exemplar, Lord Peter. A reader may see no contradiction in admiring Lord Peter's appreciation of fine drink on the one hand and being shocked by the wino's consumption of meths on the other:

what is the basis, legitimate or otherwise, of this difference? The reader might observe that one pleasure is "refined," while the other is "driven" (or "merely appetitive," or what have you). What in turn does *this* distinction rest on? Perhaps it means that the pleasurable sensations in question—that is, what Wimsey feels versus what the wino feels—are different. This sort of distinction, however, is troubling: it is notoriously difficult to identify a sensation as such. Our previous discussion is relevant here: if the sensations are different, how much of that is produced by the environment in which the sensation is habitually felt? Gilbert Ryle points out a difficulty in the usual treatment of pleasure: any sensation, he argues, can be either pleasant or unpleasant, depending on contextual features. Furthermore,

> It always makes sense to ask about any sensation or feeling whether or not its owner enjoyed having it, disliked having it, or did not care one way or the other about it . . . even though what a person has felt is properly described as a thrill of pleasure or, more specifically, as a tickle of amusement, it is still a proper question whether he not only enjoyed the joke but also enjoyed the tickled feeling it gave him. Nor should we be much surprised to hear him reply that he was so much delighted by the joke that the "tickled" feeling was quite uncomfortable; or to hear someone else, who had been crying from grief, admit that the crying itself had been slightly agreeable.[31]

Suppose we ask both Wimsey and the wino about their sensations, and they report roughly the same list: tingling, warmth, a feeling of "lightness." Would we thus be tempted, on this basis, to conclude that they are having much the same experience?

The word "experience," with its ambiguous sense, in ordinary usage, of being either privately held or contextually shared (or both) is, of course, the key: clearly the *activities* of each are very different. In comparisons such as this we are usually interested in an analysis of the pleasure-giving activities themselves: the content of a person's sensations is, for the most part, moot (unless we are hedonists who are interested in the measurement of such things). Because Lord Peter is engaging his intellectual as well as his gustatory predilections, in a social context and in a non-physically dependent manner, the reader will probably prefer his drinking habits, regardless of whether or not the attendant sensations are similarly "elevated." Likewise, Mill feels that pleasures must be evaluated on the basis of the activities that produce them: if one pleasure exceeds another in quantity, we may still choose the other on the basis of its "quality" (which depends, of course, on the nature of the activity in question.)[32]

These two intuitions—that pleasurable sensations are always part of a larger set of experiences, and that we often distinguish between the activities that produce pleasure, rather than between sensations alone—imply the following: in thinking about the pleasures of drug taking, it is important to distinguish "drug pleasure" from the physical sensations created by drugs. "Drug pleasure" will include a variety of elements, and will be understood to be the pleasure it is given a psychological and cultural context. Does this conclusion give us any way to respond to the view that all drug use for pleasure is wrong? First, we need to consider what the heart of this categorical objection might be. Perhaps it is the *sensations* of drug use that are objectionable: the distortions and enhancements created by drugs are considered base, and indulgence in them immoral. As we've already noted, it is difficult to reliably pick out a "drug-sensation" as such: characteristic affects of drug use, such as tingling, tickling, euphoria, giddiness, are feelings that can accompany a host of activities. Windsurfing and a large dose of caffeine can both make the heart race, or create a feeling of tension: but, as readers of Mill would be quick to point out, the *pleasure* of windsurfing is nothing like the pleasure of drinking coffee. Separating a "drug sensation" from its activity is misleading, because it eliminates the very features that make those sensations part of a "drug-induced pleasure."[33]

Perhaps, then, this view condemns drug pleasures on the basis of a drug activity: thus the *activity* of taking drugs for pleasure is immoral. Certainly this view is widely held in the case of illegal substances, but what about legal drugs? The objection to using licit substances for pleasure must hold that the activity itself compromises a person's "moral health," as it were. "Moral health" will include standard concerns of the good for persons, viz., the importance of autonomy; the need for developing and using the intellect, both in practical as well as theoretical concerns; involvement in human relations, personal, social, and political; and so forth. This essay is not the place to elaborate on the particulars of "the good for persons"; still, this crude list serves to illustrate why the possibility of drug-induced addiction or immoderate behavior are so frightening: these behaviors can constitute a serious erosion of autonomy, of social skills, of the intellect. Any drug user displaying these behaviors could well be said to have poor "moral health." On the other hand, *any* pleasure-seeking activity that erodes a person's autonomy or impairs his involvement in human relations would have serious moral implications. Consider the excrescences regularly pilloried in tabloid coverage (and, indeed, in other sorts of reporting as well): the person addicted to sex, or love, or work, or abuse, etc., is a current media staple. All of these various sufferers report a loss of autonomy and compulsive behavior akin to actual physical dependence (although, in the midst of this proliferation of addictions, the American Psychiatric Association declared "addiction" no longer a diagnosis: terms such as "obsession," "compulsion" and "dependence" are used instead).

Perhaps the categorical rejection of recreational drug use has to do with the potential for physical distress and damage: using drugs may compromise a person's physical health. Those who hold this view may argue that the risk of abuse and dependence outweighs the pleasures of use. Certainly, scientific evidence contributes to our understanding of the physical toll taken by drugs; e.g., nicotine is now known to be a tremendously addictive substance.[34] Information about the physical toll of a particular drug should certainly play a role in a society's view of that drug. Of course, even the mildest substance can be excessively used, and that excess may also create physical problems: e.g., a person who craves the stimulant present in chocolate may well eat far too much of it; although such behavior is not truly a case of physical dependence, it may certainly be bad for a person's health.

Both moral and physical concerns about recreational drug use focus on moderation: immoderate drug use may well interfere with a person's social, intellectual and physical capabilities. Moderation is no doubt a fundamental notion of the good for persons: although cultural and personal differences will be present in defining the boundaries of moderate use, the notion of moderation will stipulate than a given activity must not present any serious disruption of autonomy, social skills, intellectual capacity or physical function.

In order to see the case of drug use more clearly, we might consider other pleasurable pursuits that can also be excessively pursued. A person can immoderately ski, scuba dive, ride roller coasters, or bungee jump; a person can also study French literature or do mathematics to excess. "Immoderate use" normally means that a person engages in an activity too frequently, and/or for too great a duration each time. In many cases, when we question the immoderate pursuit of a pleasure, we question the frequency and duration, not the activity itself. A usual recommendation is to "cut down" on the activity, rather than give up the activity altogether. This sort of advice assumes that the source of pleasure is not intrinsically bad, but that the pursuit of that pleasure has gone wrong. Why isn't it the case that drug use receives the same treatment, specifically: like other pleasure-seeking behaviors, we applaud being a moderate and responsible seeker of licit pleasure?

Nonetheless, doubts about the value of using any drugs for pleasure assuredly remain; some thoughts about this lingering unease are in order. First, to review the steps thus far: we considered what it is that makes up a "drug pleasure," and proposed that a drug pleasure is not merely a "drug sensation," since such pleasures are composed of environment, disposition, and expectation informing a physical sensation. We then focused on the activity of drug taking: perhaps some feature of that activity is troubling as such. A central concern of both moral and physical objections to drug taking is moderation; still, this concern is equally relevant to other sorts of pleasure-seeking activities: that is, standard concerns about the good for persons apply. The activity of drug-taking, like other enjoyable activities, should not e.g. seriously disrupt a person's autonomy, impair her social attachments, or cripple her intellect.

Even so, moderate drug-use for pleasure will still have, for many people, a lurid taint. This "taint," I will suggest, is created by an all-too-common result of drug taking. For example: a person may take up the pleasurable activity of drinking wine, and discover that he has an insatiable appetite for the "sensations" created by alcohol, over and above the activity of having a drink itself. In this instance the person has psychologically "subtracted" the sensations created by alcohol from their context: so, this person may begin drinking inordinate amounts of any drink, in any setting, in order to have the sensation itself, regardless of whether he is actually enjoying himself or, more to the point, finding the sensation pleasant. Indeed, many addicts report that their drug use is not in the least enjoyable.[35] The danger of drug-induced pleasures is that a person can, and somtimes will, pursue a sensation rather than an activity. And, of course, it is here that the familiar language of dependence and addiction becomes relevant.

Recall the difficulty in distinguishing a "sensation" from its behavioral context; in noting these problems, we concluded that it is perhaps more fruitful to focus on drug behaviors. Now the importance of this qualification becomes much clearer. Consider the person who drinks alcohol in order to have a particular sensation: as the research discussed in this essay reveals, that drinker may not even be doing what he takes himself to be doing (e.g., Marlatt's study, in which alcoholics drank excessive amounts of tonic water, believing it to be mixed with vodka, and moderate amounts of what they believed to be water, when it actually contained vodka). In other words, a certain kind of behavior is problematic, and it is that behavior, i.e., the pursuit of a bodily sensation (regardless of the actual composition or context of that "sensation") that can be a troubling feature of some drug users.

We should note here an interesting connection between the pursuit of a mere sensation and a particular kind of excess. A person who desires a drug sensation alone will often disregard the context in which the drug is taken; thus the usual contextual constraints may no longer apply. The usual contextual cues that govern many drug activities (such as time of day, the surroundings, the other drug users involved) are less likely to shape appropriate behavior ("appropriate" given the event in question) if the drug user is merely concerned with having a physical affect. Of course, this is merely the difference between, e.g., a person drinking in order to celebrate an occasion, and one who drinks to feel drunk. When the contextual boundaries for use are eliminated, the temptation to use the substance to excess may be overwhelming. One reason why this sort of excess is perhaps easier in the case of drugs than in other pleasurable pursuits is because the physical effect is produced by a convenient and (often) easily obtained apparatus.

A legitimate—and difficult—question is thus raised: how does the excessive pursuit of a physical sensation differ from the excessive pursuit of a drug activity (e.g. throwing too many cocktail parties or taking too many coffee breaks)? Obviously, there are no hard distinctions at work here, but one important difference should be clear. The immoderate use of a drug to produce a physical sensation is focused on the consuming of that drug; excessively pursuing an activity, such as giving (or attending) too many cocktail parties is probably concerned with something very different, such as "improving one's social standing." The difference between the eager socialite and the habitual drunk is at least the difference between the motives for their behavior. In the case of the socialite, such behavior may ultimately interfere with living a complete and whole life, but his problem is very different in kind from that of the drunkard.

Having reviewed these concerns, it is easier to appreciate the common sense of Aristotle's approach to the pursuit of bodily pleasures. Aristotle's account emphasizes the inherent dangers of the pleasures of "touch", which include sex and food as well as drink. Pleasure itself, Aristotle argues, is properly associated with an activity: it is not attained in the way that the goal of movement is attained (viz., as an "end" that completes it). Instead, pleasure supervenes on an activity and, so to speak, "perfects" it: pleasure is the hallmark of an "unimpeded activity."[36] Furthermore, the pleasure that "completes" an activity is virtually indistinguishable from it: "the pleasure is close to the activity, and so little distinguished from it that disputes arise about whether the activity is not the same as the pleasure."[37] Each activity has its appropriate pleasure, and the worth of the activity determines the worth of the pleasure that accompanies it: " . . . each activity has its own proper pleasure. Hence the pleasure proper to an excellent activity is decent, and the one proper to a base activity is vicious . . . "[38]

What, then, is the status of bodily pleasures? Aristotle treats the pleasures of touch and taste differently from other kinds of pleasure; he remarks,

> Temperance, then, will be about bodily pleasures, but not even about all of these. For those who enjoy what they notice through sight, e.g. colours, shapes, a painting, are called neither temperate nor intemperate, even though it would seem possible to enjoy these both in the right way. . . . The same is true for hearing. . . . The pleasures that concern temperance and intemperance . . . are touch and taste.[39]

Because touch and taste (touch in particular) allow an "excess of pleasure,"[40] temperance is their particular virtue. In his discussion of Aristotle's *Ethics*, J. O. Urmson remarks on the singling out of touch:

> *It is the feelings that are enjoyed by the intemperate, not the activities that engender them.* But Aristotle fails to make this point explicit in his analysis of pleasure; he persuades himself that the intemperate pleasures are to be distinguished from others because they involve the sense of touch, and thus fails to see that what he needs is a distinction between *the enjoyment of activities*, whether of touch or other sense or of intellect, as such and *the enjoyment of the feelings and sensations that they may produce.*[41]

Urmson's analysis of Aristotle is useful for our purposes (whether or not we agree with his reading of Aristotle), for his remarks about the intemperate pleasures of "touch," sensation, also underline a singularly disquieting feature of drug use. Urmson claims that the intemperate person does not enjoy an activity that involves a particular sensation, but is instead focused on the feeling alone.[42] Certainly, drugs can be taken simply in order to produce a certain sensation apart from a "drug activity," and it is *this* sort of drug use, intemperately pursued, that strikes most people as "base," not the temperate pursuits of the chef or oenophile, or, indeed, the usual taking of drink at weddings and parties.[43] Thus, we might attempt a preliminary sketch of an "appropriate" use of drugs for pleasure: an appropriate use will be (in some as yet unspecified way) a kind of enjoyable drug-taking activity, pursued moderately, rather than an intemperate substance use as a mere means to a sensation.

Those who object to the pursuit of drug-induced pleasures as such may believe that all drug use ultimately reduces to the pursuit of mere sensation; such use is thus never, despite appearances, truly the enjoyment of an activity. In order to evaluate this view, some distinctions need to be made in the various uses of drugs for pleasure.

III.

> Now the bodily goods allow excess. The base person is base because he pursues the excess, but not because he pursues the necessary pleasures; for all enjoy delicacies and wines and sexual relations in the same way, though not all in the right way.[44]

Drug use for pleasure is formally comparable to other pleasure-seeking activities: like these, the pleasures of drugs should be pursued moderately and responsibly. Of course, as I noted in the previous section, pleasurable pursuits can vary widely in their affect and concern. Can anything be said in defense of the particular pleasures offered by drug use?

Before proposing any benefits of drug use, we must describe the particular ways in which drugs are used. I will describe two broad categories of recreational drug use; each may be healthful or deleterious to the agent, depending on the way in which the kind of use in question is pursued.

The first sort of use may be called "instrumental." A drug taken in this way is intended to facilitate goods other than the immediate sensations of the drug itself. Indeed, a person may be drawn to a drug in an explicitly instrumental fashion: so, for example, a person drinks coffee in order to feel focused and energetic, in order to complete the essay she is writing. Here the goal is not the pleasant feeling of heightened concentration, but the writing of the essay.

The use of drugs for pleasure may also be implicitly instrumental: e.g., a person drinks coffee simply in order to feel
energetic, and discovers that she is able to work with good cheer
on her essay as well. The quote from Virginia Woolf at the outset
seems to be a case of an implicitly instrumental use: she drinks
the wine in order to feel relaxed, and inadvertently discovers
that her ability to appreciate her colleagues has also increased.

The implicit use of drugs for pleasure is reminiscent of a
program described by the priestess Diotima in Plato's *Symposium*. Diotima's subject is not, of course, the altered condition
created by drugs, but the altered condition brought on by love.
Diotima tells Socrates about a "ladder of loves" that a person
must ascend in order to (perhaps) glimpse the Beautiful itself. A
person begins by being drawn to a beautiful body, but discovers
that the beauty that attracted him is shared by all beautiful bodies; and so, in being attracted to a succession of loves, first
beautiful bodies, then beautiful souls, beautiful acts, and the
beauty of knowledge, a person draws closer to the Beautiful
itself.[45] In each case, the person is drawn to the beauty of a
particular person or activity, but eventually realizes that those
particular attractions have led to other, higher, goods. Thus, the
value of an initial physical love is instrumental: its particular en-
ticements are valued (ultimately) for drawing the lover towards
other goods.

This program is also dangerous, for a person may well
become "stuck" on a particular form of beauty, such as the
beauty of a person, and find himself unwilling or unable to
"use" that love to generate other goods. (In the *Symposium*,
Alcibiades is clearly in this predicament.) Certainly, an analogous form of this danger is at work in the implicit instrumental
use of drugs: a person may use a drug to feel a certain way, but
ultimately fail to exploit those feelings, in her working or socializing, by becoming too enamored of the drug experience itself.

This apparent "failure" (from the perspective of the instrumental view) is, in fact, the alternative category of recreational drug use. Certainly, many people do not "use" their
drug-induced pleasures, explicitly or otherwise, to effect some
other end: the pleasurable activity is an end in itself. This second
kind of drug use emphasizes the separation often created by

drugs between the person and his or her environment. The pleasant dissolution caused by, e.g., alcohol is, in this view, a diversion from work and socializing, not an enhancement of those activities. Nietzsche's writings often acknowledge the attractions of a comparable kind of respite:

> Zarathustra spoke thus to his heart: "Soft! Soft! Has the world not just become perfect? What has happened to me? . . . Just see—Soft! old noontide sleeps, it moves its mouth: has it not just drunk . . . an ancient brown drop of golden happiness, of golden wine? . . . Thus—does a god laugh. . . . Precisely the least thing, the gentlest, lightest . . . little makes up the quality of the best happiness. Soft! What has happened to me? Listen! Has time flown away? Do I not fall? Have I not fallen—listen! into the well of eternity?"[46]

Zarathustra's respites from preaching the coming of the Übermensch are often punctuated by moments of disaffection, intoxicated divestments of his usual concerns. In describing these "rests," Nietzsche often compares the experience of being drunk with psychic disassociation as such: the result in either case is a release from the ordinary burdens of life.

This sort of drug use further highlights the difference between pursuing a sensation rather than an activity: the person seeking respite is still doing so with a context of *other* concerns and activities; the person who wants to produce a physical sensation is not engaged in "respite" from other concerns, but is instead wholly focused on the pursuit of a physical affect (hardly a rest at all in the case of someone who is physically dependent on a substance; at best this person obtains a moment's ease from the need to have the effects of that drug).

The difficulty with using drugs as a "rest" from other cares, obviously, is that the diversion may become more inviting, and its sensations more valuable, than the life it is meant to occasionally relieve. The pleasures of escape may well begin to outweigh other goods. Indeed, Zarathustra seems tempted to extend his stay in this disaffected *Augenblick*, moment: "Let me alone! . . . Has the world not just become perfect? . . . when, well of eternity? serene and terrible noontide abyss! When will you drink my soul back into yourself?"[47] The narcotic pleasures of disengagement can ultimately overwhelm the other activities that constitute a complete life: obviously, this sort of drug use is no longer, properly speaking, a respite. The pleasures of drugs should be a diversion, not the goal of a person's labors.

What value can be ascribed to these two kinds of recreational drug use? An instrumental use of drugs can enhance a person's social or intellectual life; drugs as "respite" may be a joyful release from the quotidian. Both can add variety and vigor to a life. The inappropriate use, in either case, will involve the use of drugs to produce a sensation alone, pursued, moreover, regardless of the context of that use.

It is important to remember that drugs can, and often do, play these useful roles, and in quite unremarkable ways: a coffee break (or the British variant of "tea time"), a cocktail party, an enticing dessert, are all perfectly ordinary instruments of social intercourse; moreover, the glass of cognac late at night is an unremarkable method of shedding the day's cares. It is the abuse of these pleasures, rather than their use, that draws our attention, for the abuses are often disastrous. But Aristotle's characterization is nonetheless apt: It is the *pursuit of the excess* (construed as, at least in part, as the intemperate pursuit of a sensation apart from the activities associated with it) rather than the desire for, or the use of, such pleasures, that is base. Drugs as either instrument or diversion should hold a subordinate role in a person's life, and their pursuit should be moderate.

Of course, one might still object that the potential for excess is far greater than the enjoyment to be had by moderate drug users. A stronger defense of the value of recreational drug use may be provided by reconsidering an initial restriction of this essay.

IV.

Direct self-observation is not nearly sufficient for us to know ourselves: we require history, for the past continues to flow within us in a hundred waves; we ourselves are, indeed, nothing but that which at every moment we experience of this continued flowing.[48]

The distinction between licit and illicit drugs that has been used thus far in the essay now needs to be examined. What has been stated, but by no means explored, is that this distinction is wholly relative to a particular culture's concerns. The *Consumer's Union Report on Narcotics* makes this introductory point with admirable clarity:

> People tend to categorize . . . drugs in various ways—as "licit" or "illicit," "good" or "bad"—and some drugs are treated as if they were not drugs at all . . . the boundaries of those categories have little justification; they vary from generation to generation and from country to country.[49]

If the moderate and responsible use of drugs for pleasure has any value, which I have argued that it does, why restrict that use to licit drugs?

Obviously, the fact that a particular drug is legal in late–twentieth-century North America is by no means an indication that the drug in question is somehow "better" or more life-enhancing that an illegal drug. Furthermore, and more importantly, it by no means indicates that the roster of licit drugs is "safer" than illicit ones: the disfigurement and death caused by drunk driving, cancers of the lung and esophagus, fetal alcohol syndrome, etc., are frightening testimony to the contrary.

If they are not "better" or "safer," why focus on licit drugs?

The first, largely programmatic, reason has already been mentioned. Any user of an illicit drug is supporting the illicit traffic that supplies that drug: moral questions about aiding and abetting the smuggling, extortion, murder, and social mayhem that characterize that trade are inevitable. In order to clearly see the moral issues surrounding drug-induced pleasures, it is necessary to look at those pleasures apart from the extensive moral issues that attach to illicit drug use.

As a result, my discussion has focused on currently licit drugs; however, it is important to note that my remarks do not concerns those drugs particularly: any drug, if deemed licit, may be enjoyed in a moderate and responsible fashion. Thus, even though this analysis has focused on alcohol, caffeine and nicotine, this does not mean that these drugs are better at accomplishing either an instrumental or diversionary sort of pleasure:

it simply means that these are the drugs our culture currently deems acceptable.

Are we to conclude, therefore, that culture is somehow "right" about the drugs it endorses? And what could the force of "right" possibly be? Every drug has, at one time or another, been alternately embraced, tolerated, or rejected by the societies that use it: no drug has been universally endorsed. The history of the use of caffeine is chequered in this way: when first introduced in Arabia, coffee was used to keep Mohammedans awake during religious observances; coffee was later condemned in the Koran as an intoxicant, only to later regain cultural approval.[50] The Consumers Union Editors also report the following condemnation of caffeine in the United States in the earlier part of this century:

> A typical medical attack can be found in *Morphinism and Narcomanias From Other Drugs* (1902) by T.D. Crothers, M.D. . . . Dr. Crothers classed coffee addiction with morphinism and alcoholism. "In some extreme cases delusional states of a grandiose character appear. . . . Often coffee drinkers, finding the drug to be unpleasant, turn to other narcotics of which opium and alcohol are most common." . . . To many, the above indictments will seem incredible . . . yet caffeine can be a dangerous drug. Contemporary scientists echo several of the early allegations made against caffeine.[51]

The dangers of caffeine, real or otherwise, are not an issue here. Rather, two features of the drugs we use need to be observed. First: the history of a particular drug's use will usually reveal a host of different accounts of its effects and appropriate uses (often wildly contradictory); furthermore, the interpretation worn by a particular drug is by no means the final word on the matter: given changes in the cultural climate, a drug may climb to favor or fall from grace.

Two examples that illustrate this latter point are marijuana and tobacco. In the United States, the decriminalization of marijuana is still being argued, and it is certainly conceivable (though not likely in the near future) that the drug will become legal. Tobacco, on the other hand, is still legal; nonetheless, its cultural image has been severely tarnished by the medical evidence concerning its effects on the body. In many workplaces its use is being banned all together, and a common sentiment—even among smokers—is that smoking is probably more trouble than it is worth.

The first reason for largely ignoring illicit drugs in this discussion is that these drugs carry an additional moral burden—albeit a contingent one—that makes them difficult to consider on the basis of pleasure alone. The second reason for focusing this inquiry on licit drugs is very different. We might call it, for lack of a precise term, an "interpretive" reason. The thesis at work here is mundane, yet crucial: the drugs used by a culture, for good or ill, play a deep and important role in that culture. Consider the contrast case of a widely used yet still illegal drug, marijuana: what must change in order for marijuana to become legal? First and foremost, the attitude of many people towards that drug must change; what is less clear is the nature of that change of heart. Will it involve a change in our habits? (Which ones?) Religious practices, perhaps? A slower economy, or a slower pace of life? Many of those who write about drug use remark that marijuana and the American mind-set are simply inimical: the kind of relaxation provided by marijuana will always be perceived as a threat to the aggressive American psyche.[52]

These speculations aside, it is nonetheless clear that a society is reflected in the drugs it uses; a culture's history is shaped by its drugs: the tea it imports, the vines it cultivates, the countries it colonizes, the land it appropriates, the industries and art-forms created on behalf of a drug (bottling, cooperage, etc.) This history is often a tale of egregious abuse and manipulation. Still, the production and use of licit drugs also reveals deeply held, perhaps deeply confused, notions of what will constitute at least part of a good life. Those views are borne out in the institutions of a society: the café, the public house, the neighborhood bar, the tobacconist and confectioner all generate and support a host of behaviors that in turn articulate the lives of those who use their products and who frequent their establishments. Feelings about drug use are not only deeply connected to the history of a drug, and its place in the culture: they are also, ultimately, a reflection of how a society views itself.

The drugs we use are not simply substances, chemicals, but part of the way we see ourselves. But that vision is not always clear: empirical evidence and critical analysis may reveal that some favored drug habits are dangerous, or improperly enjoyed. When we eliminate the use of a particular drug, we also eliminate a way of life. In considering whether or not society will tolerate a particular drug habit, we might ask ourselves: how much do we value a particular behavior that we have "culturally inherited?" The balancing of evidence against known pleasures (and displeasures) will always be controversial: the data will be contested, habitual users will protest, those in the business of supplying a drug will rush to protect their interests, and so forth. Even the most time-honored drugs are vulnerable to condemnation: and this is how it should be, reflection about our behaviors being weighed against the traditions we inherit. Because a society's sense of what will constitute the health and well-being of its members is never absolutely established, the list of appropriate drugs will always be open to alteration.

These speculative and admittedly sketchy remarks frame the second reason for focusing primarily on licit drugs: these drugs can, if appropriately used, connect its users to other members of a society, provide them with a common currency of release and relaxation. This is also, obviously, another reason for finding value in the use of drugs for pleasure as such. Those who use the drugs of their culture will understand themselves, like those from whom their habits were inherited, as creatures who crave the shared release of bodily pleasure; perhaps users obtain a measure of enlightenment by so seeing themselves. And, finally, in accepting that some of its members enjoy using drugs, a society may avoid the hubristic error of thinking that it can eradicate either the sources of drug-induced pleasure or the desire for such pleasures.

As such, the pleasures of drugs appear to be ones that we would be advised not to try to do without. Recall the lesson that Pentheus receives from Dionysos in the *Bacchae*: in attempting to evict the god from his kingdom, Pentheus is himself seduced by "vine-worship," and is ultimately torn to bits by the god's worshippers. Dionysos is a ready emblem for the two-edged pleasures of drug taking: he is not only a god of intoxication and dissolution, but a civilizing god as well.[53] Indeed, even the maenads are quietly weaving and dancing before Dionysos urges them into a murderous frenzy.

The same drug that can heighten our senses, that can intensify our ability to provide articulations of ourselves, can also stupefy, stun, dismantle. This is a danger with which Nietzsche was familiar: too much worshipful "love of the vine" could push one into the "well of eternity," a suspension of life that becomes a kind of death in life. The anodyne can be dangerous indeed. And so we are right to be respectful of the substances that can both liberate and betray, their seductions verging on traducements; still, consider the maenads as they are before their Bacchic frenzy, a gathering able to wisely celebrate its humanity.

NOTES

1. Virginia Woolf, *A Room of One's Own* (New York: Harcourt, Brace Jovanovich, 1981 [1929]), p. 11.

2. Aldous Huxley, *The Doors of Perception* (New York: Harper and Row, 1963 [1954]), p. 64.

3. *The Consumers Union Report on Licit and Illicit Drugs* notes that while the effects of a drug on mind and body are "relatively stable decade after decade . . . the effects of laws, policies, and attitudes . . . may vary from decade to decade." (Edward M. Brecher and the Editors of Consumer Reports, *Licit and Illicit Drugs: The Consumers Union Report on Narcotics, Stimulants, Depressants, Inhalants, Hallucinogens and Marijuana—including Caffeine, Nicotine and Alcohol* (Boston: Little Brown and Company, 1972) p. x.

4. A standard definition, cited by Oakley Ray in *Drugs, Society and Human Behavior* (Saint Louis: Mosby, 1972), p. 11.

5. Oakley Ray, p. 13.

6. Oakley Ray, p. 430.

7. Increase Mather, as cited in Herbert Fingarette's *Heavy Drinking: The Myth of Alcoholism as a Disease* (University of California Press, 1988), p. 13.

8. N.H. Clark, *The Dry Years: Prohibition and Social Change in Washington* (Seattle: University of Washington Press, 1965), p. 66.

9. Dorothy L. Sayers, *Busman's Honeymoon* (New York: Harper, 1960 [1937]).

10. Fingarette reports, "In those days, drinking was considered essential to daily sociability. . . . Americans in the colonial period did not associate drunkenness with violence, crime or even rowdiness. . . . 'Habitual drunkenness'—some of which we would today call alcoholism—was not viewed in terms of 'loss of control' or the onset of a disease. It was a matter of consuming too much of a good thing." (*Heavy Drinking*, p. 15)

11. Fingarette, p. 3.

12. Marlatt, "The Controlled Drinking Controversy," (1983), 1107, as cited by Fingarette, p. 8.

13. William Miller, "Haunted by the Zeitgeist: Reflections on Contrasting Treatment and Goals and Concepts of Alcoholism in Europe and the United States," *Alcohol and Culture: Cultural Perspectives from Europe and America* (New York: The New York Academy of Sciences, 1986), p. 115.

14. Ibid.; emphasis mine. Fingarette recounts several of these fascinating experiments in Chapter Two of his book.

15. These hypotheses are reviewed in Chapter Three.

16. Fingarette, p. 51.

17. Fingarette, p. 13.

18. Miller, p. 113.

19. Fingarette, p. 65.

20. Miller relates the following anecdote: the "problem drinkers" he treats in his research, all of whom consume 40–50 drinks a week, were greeted very differently by different audiences: in Sweden and Norway they were shocked by these amounts; in Germany and Scotland, however, the audiences wondered if this group wasn't within the range of normal (albeit heavy) drinking. (p. 111)

21. Cf. Nietzsche's observation: "A table of values (eine Tafel der Guter) hangs over every people . . . " and that "table" can be easily discerned in our views about drugs. (*Thus Spake Zarathustra*, "Of the Thousand and One Goals," R.J. Hollingdale, trans.)

22. William H. Gass, "Sweets," *The Review of Contemporary Fiction*, Fall 1991.

23. Jacob Sullum, "What's the Problem?" *Reason*, Vol. 22, March 1991, p. 8.

24. Ibid.

25. This view is different than psychological hedonism, which claims that only pleasure is intrinsically desired. William Alston provides a good review of the varieties of hedonism in his article "Pleasure" in the *Encyclopedia of Philosophy*, Paul Edwards, ed., (New York, Macmillan, 1967).

26. Henry Sidgwick, *The Methods of Ethics* (Chicago: University of Chicago Press, 1962), p. 94–5. The merits of this argument are not my concern here; a quantitative account may not work (although it admittedly deserves a better hearing). Rather, Sidgwick's emendation of the standard hedonist view reveals a basic intuition about pleasure that is important.

27. Rem Edwards, *Pleasures and Pains: A Theory of Qualitative Hedonism* (Ithaca: Cornell University Press, 1979), p. 32. Edwards presents an interesting and extensive analysis of qualitative hedonism (most of which exceeds the immediate concerns of this essay).

28. The so-called non-specific factors in drug effects.

29. Ludwig, Wikler and Stark, 1974, as cited by Fingarette, 1989.

30. Again, placebos are an interesting exception: in their case, only the agent's *beliefs* about what he is ingesting are necessary to produce an effect.

31. Gilbert Ryle, *The Concept of Mind* (Chicago: University of Chicago Press, 1984), p. 109.

32. Mill's "test" of quality is whether a competent judge (a person acquainted with a range of pleasures) would prefer one pleasure to another; roughly, the "higher" pleasures are mental ones, while the "lower" are physical. Mill, of course, would find Wimsey's pleasure in drink to be a very low one indeed.

33. I am omitting the ethical hedonists' view that a drug pleasure is base because it is a localized bodily one: this view places a lower value on the pleasure (via whatever means, quantitative or qualitative) but still holds that it has some value since it is a pleasure-creating activity. The view that I am interested in addressing holds that drug pleasures are universally worthless.

34. Brecher and eds., Ch. 25, passim.

35. Brecher and eds., p. 13.

36. Aristotle, *Nicomachean Ethics*, Terence Irwin, trans. (Indianapolis: Hackett Publishing Company, 1985), 1153a 13–15.

37. Aristotle, 1175b 33.

38. Aristotle, 1175b 27–30.

39. Aristotle, 1118a 2–25.

40. Aristotle, 1154a 13–15.

41. J.O. Urmson, *Aristotle's Ethics* (New York: Basil Blackwell, 1988), p. 107; emphasis mine.

42. Presumably, Urmson also believes that focusing on a particular physical sensation, rather than on the activity that produces it, often produces intemperate behavior.

43. Indeed, Aristotle makes this very point in his discussion of bodily pleasures (1118a 25–30).

44. Aristotle, 1154a 15–20.

45. Plato, *Symposium*, 210b.

46. Friedrich Nietzsche, *Thus Spake Zarathustra,* R.J. Hollingdale, trans., IV, #10.

47. Ibid.

48. Nietzsche, *Human, All Too Human,* R.J. Hollingdale, trans. (Cambridge: Cambridge University Press, 1986), #223.

49. Brecher and eds., p. 195.

50. Brecher and eds., p. 196–9.

51. Ibid.

52. Cf. Oakley Ray, p. 457.

53. Hans Oranje, *Euripides' Bacchae: The Play and Its Audience* (Leiden: E.J. Brill, 1984), p. 104.

Why We Should Not Use Some Drugs for Pleasure

Rem B. Edwards

By "pleasure" I will mean "any quality of feeling that we normally wish to cultivate or sustain in experience for its own sake," and by "pain" I will mean "any quality of feeling that we normally wish to avoid or eliminate from experience for its own sake." Mill was right; there are many qualities of pleasure; and this definition of pleasure allows for all kinds. I will defend the view that there are *some* drugs that we should not use for pleasure, which leaves open the possibility that there are others that we may use for pleasure.

In developing and defending the view that we should not get our pleasures from some drugs, I want to steer a middle course between the extremes of what Gerald L. Klerman called "psychotropic hedonism" and "pharmacological calvinism."[1] The former is the view that any source of pleasure is admissible, that if it feels good, we may do it. The latter is the view that if anything is pleasant, it is bad for us and morally wrong to use it.

On a theoretical level, my views are much closer to psychotropic hedonism than to pharmacological calvinism. However, with respect to the actual use of drugs for pleasure, I think that the latter has the edge because many if not most "recreational" drugs are in fact very bad for us, especially when used to excess. We have not yet discovered the "perfect drug" like the soma of Aldous Huxley's *Brave New World*, which had "All the advantages of Christianity and alcohol; none of their defects."[2]

I unequivocally reject the view that pleasure is a bad thing in itself or that enjoyment is inherently wrong, sinful, degenerate, or effete, so I am not for these reasons practically inclined toward pharmacological calvinism. Unlike Cleanthes the Stoic, who believed that to experience pleasure is the worst thing that can happen to a person, I am convinced that it is one of the best. I think that Nietzsche was just being obtuse and chauvinistic when he suggested that only effete Englishmen desire pleasure, not real men.[3] Happiness consists of pleasures of many varieties sustained over periods of time; and happiness is a very good thing.

Nevertheless, we should choose our sources and qualities of pleasure carefully. Life affords us myriads of "innocent" (i.e. harmless) pleasures, some of them chemically induced, e.g. from a caffeinated soft drink or a good cup of tea or coffee; but many chemically caused enjoyments are not innocent. Some, like cocaine, heroin, marijuana, alcohol, peyote, LSD, amphetamines, barbiturates, and tobacco are very likely to result in a clear preponderance of pain over pleasure in the long run for users and/ or for others whose lives are affected profoundly by users. These same drugs are also very likely to destroy other important human goods that it is rational to want and to choose—like health or rationality itself and the ability to choose for oneself. Other persons are likely to be affected extremely adversely by one's irrational and irresponsible drug-induced behaviors. It is neither prudent nor moral to use such drugs, except perhaps in great moderation. Since they are addictive, moderation is extremely difficult; and for many persons it is impossible. Moderation is much easier said than achieved.

I am convinced that some drugs, like the modest quantities of caffeine found in cola drinks, tea, coffee, and the theobromine found in chocolate bars, are quite acceptable as sources of pleasure, though even these can be overdone. The third edition of the *Diagnostic and Statistical Manual of Mental Disorders* (hereafter *DSM-III*) of the American Psychiatric Association recognizes "Caffeine intoxication" as a mental disorder and makes a convincing case that excess caffeine consumption can be quite troublesome.[4] Other drugs like cocaine, heroin, marijuana, nicotine, and alcohol—minus moderation, are clearly unsatisfactory.

Criteria for Identifying Unacceptable Hedonic Drugs

Responsible persons will draw the line somewhere between acceptable and unacceptable uses of hedonic drugs, though not necessarily where I would draw it. Rational line drawing requires criteria for distinguishing acceptable hedonic uses of drugs for pleasure from unacceptable hedonic uses. I propose the following criteria, each of which is a presumptive reason against hedonic drug use, though they vary in significance or strength. In *unacceptable* hedonic uses one or more (usually more) of the following conditions are fulfilled.

(1) The resulting pain outweighs the pleasure over the long run for the user.

Rational prudence requires that one's choices be likely to result in more pleasure than pain over the long run, and it forbids choosing the pleasures of the moment and ignoring the ensuing pains. There are many reasons why some hedonic uses of drugs result in the long run in the preponderance of pain over pleasure. Some hedonic drugs result very quickly in "bad trips," i.e. in horrifying hallucinations, thoughts, and perceptual distortions; prolonged use of alcohol to excess results in the terrors of delirium tremens. Some hedonic drugs produce considerable bodily pain in a relatively short time span associated with hangovers, nausea, vomiting, headache, gastric disorders, elevated blood pressure, sweating, shock, depressed respiration, convulsions, comas, etc., depending on levels of tolerance and quantities consumed. Most available hedonic drugs result rather quickly in a dull or confused state of mind and may eventually produce the psychological pains involved in agitation, restlessness, irritability, delusions, depression, and paranoia. Some cause grave and frustrating social alienation and social withdrawal. Some result rather quickly in delayed reaction time and reduction of motor control, and this can have serious adverse consequences when driving or operating machinery. Some, after lengthy use, cause painful diseases and frustrating psychical and physical debilities. Some kill. Some do many or all of these things at once. All things considered, their pleasures are not worth their price of suffering.

Hedonic drugs like alcohol or crack are often used, not so much for pleasure, but primarily to relieve pain, e.g., the pains of low self-esteem, loneliness, jealousy, hopelessness, anxiety, or depression, all of which may result from a great variety of social, psychological, and physical causes. However, hedonic drugs are grossly inefficient means of alleviating these pains and are more than likely to compound the suffering over the long run. Certainly, they do nothing to remove the real causes of such pains of soul, which must be corrected if a war on drugs is to be won. Those who really want to win a war on drugs must attack the real causes of despair in our society.

(2) The pleasure drug is destructive of the user's rationality, either temporarily or more permanently.

Many pleasure drugs stupefy and seriously interfere with a variety of cognitive abilities such as the ability to perceive without distortion, to think clearly, to remember, to pay attention, to concentrate on the task at hand, and to be creative. Other persons can see this easily, though intoxicated persons often cannot. When they sober up or dry out, they can see what fools they have been; but by then it is too late. The damage has been done. Many intoxicated persons mistakenly believe themselves to be brilliant conversationalists, but sober persons listening in know better. Under the influence of drugs, many people have a powerful but false sense of intellectual achievement and immense creativity; but when they return to reality, the marvelous results just are not there. Ralph Waldo Emerson wrote in "The Poet" that the quest for "extraordinary powers" is "the reason why bards love wine, mead, narcotics, coffee, tea, opium, the fumes of sandalwood and tobacco, or whatever other procurers of animal exhilaration." He warned, however, against "quasi-mechanical substitutes for the true nectar."[5]

> But never can any advantage be taken of nature by a trick. The spirit of the world, the great calm presence of the Creator, comes not forth to the sorceries of opium or of wine. The sublime vision comes to the pure and simple soul in a clean and chaste body. That is not an inspiration,

which we own to narcotics, but some counterfeit excitement and fury.[6]

Emerson's extreme condemnation may be a bit exaggerated, but it is not far removed from the truth. I have found that moderate coffee drinking does enhance both creativity and intelligence and results in better philosophy through chemistry. Other drugs do more harm than good, however, in my limited experience.

When I ask myself why I indulge so little in hedonic drugs, I find that drug-induced stupidity, even if relatively temporary, is inconsistent with the great value that I attach to my own intelligence, the extensive time and intense effort that I have devoted to its development, the serious commitment that I have to making informed choices, and the lifetime of effort that I have expended as an educator to make these qualities available to others. This does not mean that I think that all of life should be spent in intellectual pursuits—only that rationality should be available for use, when needed, in all of life. When one is sufficiently intoxicated, rationality simply is not available; judgment is severely impaired.

(3) The pleasure drug is destructive of the user's autonomy (ability to choose), either temporarily or more permanently.

Drug-induced obtuseness is inconsistent not only with the rational part of rational choice, but with the choice or self-control part of it as well. Hedonic drugs give pleasure at the price of autonomy, self-control and will power; and under their influence we cannot and do not make the self-interested or the other-regarding choices that we otherwise could and should make. Under their influence, we may do terrible things to ourselves or to others, are often dangerous to self or others, for we lack the capacity to make prudent and moral choices. Not only weakness of will, but ill will, aggressiveness, and the worst in us easily prevail under the influence of hedonic drugs.

Vulnerability to control by others is the other side of the coin of lack of or loss of rational choice by self. Peer pressure, social and political manipulation, and sexual exploitation easily dominate persons who are spaced out on hedonic drugs. Aldous Huxley recognized the political vulnerability of persons on drugs when he later commented on the fictional "soma" that dominated the lives of the citizens of *Brave New World*. According to Huxley, soma was:

> . . . one of the most powerful instruments of rule in the dictator's armory. The systematic drugging of individuals for the benefit of the state (and incidentally, of course, for their own delight) was a main plank in the policy of the World Controllers. The daily soma ration was an insurance against personal maladjustment, social unrest and the spread of subversive ideas.[7]

In our society, systematic political drugging has not reached the proportions that it had in *Brave New World*. On a lesser social scale, however, we easily recognize that persons who cannot control themselves are easily dominated and exploited by unscrupulous others. After sobering up, they realize that this is no fun.

(4) The pleasure drug is destructive of the user's self-knowledge, self-respect, and positive self-valuation, either temporarily or more permanently.

In pluralistic value theories, there are other intrinsically good things besides pleasure, and their worth may outweigh that of some or all kinds of pleasures, especially soporific, drug-induced ones. Prudence tells us: "Know thyself; respect thyself; cherish thyself." Excessive drug users sacrifice self-knowledge, self-respect, and the intrinsic value of themselves as unique conscious centers of experience and self-initiated activity for the sake of what, in Biblical terms, might be called "a mess of pottage," pun intended. Hedonic drugs that are presently available may give pleasure, of sorts, or at least some temporary release from pain. Unfortunately, they also extinguish the intensely personal goods of self-knowledge, self-respect, and self appreciation at the same time. The small pleasure is really not worth the price.

(5) The pleasure drug is likely to have irreversible or not easily reversible harmful physical, psychological, or social effects on the user.

Many of the harmful psychological and social effects of hedonic drugs are covered above or below. These effects can be difficult if not impossible to reverse.

Let us concentrate for the moment on the fact that prolonged use of different hedonic drugs have enduring and not easily reversed physical effects that are quite harmful to the user. Addiction to any drug is itself a serious physical effect, not easily undone. Specific effects may differ from drug to drug, though many have common drawbacks. Tobacco is the number one cause of emphysema and lung cancer and is a major factor in coronary diseases and heart attacks. Cocaine has recently been linked to many coronary hemorrhages and strokes. Most other hedonic drugs will cause cardiac arrhythmias and arrests and respiratory paralysis and failure when ingested in sufficient quantities. Under their influence, judgment about "when to say when" is severely impaired. They also cause neurological damage, and mental hospitals are now flooded with patients with severe drug-induced psychoses involving brain damage. Prolonged consumption of alcohol causes cirrhosis of the liver, peptic ulcers, chronic gastritis, and turns the brain to mush in Korsakoff's syndrome. Consumption of relatively small quantities of alcohol destroys millions of brain cells and/or synaptic connections. Who can afford to lose them?

(6) The pleasure drug is expensive, in large part because buying, selling, and/or possessing the pleasure drug is illegal. Obtaining it consumes an inordinate share of the user's and/or society's financial resources and is likely to involve criminal behavior.

Unfortunately, many pleasure drugs that are currently available fit the above description. Though alcohol, caffeine, and tobacco are legally available, many pleasure drugs are illegal controlled substances. The law and its penalties must enter into any hedonistic calculus; and as long as laws against the sale or use of controlled substances are on the books, the consequences of doing so must be taken into account. However, millions of persons are apparently willing to run the risks and sell and consume illegal controlled substances. For many inner-city residents, the drug economy offers the only jobs available, the only way to enjoy middle-class material and social amenities, the only way to get rich, the only way to gain social power, status and respect. This is a sad commentary on our present social order and its lack of opportunities for the poor and powerless. A really successful attack on drugs must be a war on poverty, prejudice, ignorance, and unemployment.

Whether the law and its penalties should be considered in deciding upon a course of action is one thing. Whether the law is a good law is quite another. The drug trade is so lucrative precisely because so many hedonic drugs are illegal. Drug users zealously make converts both for their social support and camaraderie and because they can sell drugs to converts to support their own incredibly expensive drug-use habits. Many women are driven to prostitution to pay for costly drug consumption.

Anyone who buys illegal drugs contributes to the enrichment of the international drug lords and street gangs and to gang wars, murders, violence, theft, prostitution, and exploitation. Middle-class individuals who use drugs in great moderation are the very ones who collectively are making the drug lords rich. Though each makes only small purchases, there are so many of them that they are the primary source of wealth from drugs.

In my opinion, the most effective way to end the drug trade is to take the money out of it. The most effective way available to significantly reduce drug consumption is to legalize drugs and make them available in government-owned or regulated stores at prices with which the drug lords cannot compete. Monies so derived, together with monies now being squandered on our current ineffective War on Drugs, should then be spent on education, treatment, and rehabilitation.

After legalization, many drug users will remain, just as many abusers of alcohol persist after the repeal of prohibition. However, the powerful incentives of extreme wealth and exalted social status in the drug subculture would be removed. Only the intrinsic hedonic appeal of the drugs themselves would remain—to be balanced against their liabilities. Legalization would be risky, no doubt. Many persons would be lost to drugs, just as many are already lost both to illegal drugs and to legal drugs like alcohol and tobacco. However, incentives to make converts to support drug habits would disappear; and risks to the rest of us of auto and property theft, mugging, and organized criminality to support drug habits would be eliminated. Let's face it: No society can prevent some of its members from being fools and destroying themselves. If some people will not respond to the best that can be offered in education, counseling, and rehabilitation services, then they will just have to suffer the consequences. There is no need for the rest of us to be destroyed along with them, however, especially if we really have done our very best to provide them with alternatives.

It is entirely possible that cheap and legal hedonic drugs would prove to be so appealing that massive numbers of persons would succumb to them and become pawns in the hands of unscrupulous manipulators. Aldous Huxley asked how a dictator could "get his subjects to take the pills that will make them think, feel and behave in the way he finds desirable," and he answered:

> In all probability it will be enough merely to make the pills available. Today alcohol and tobacco are available, and people spend considerably more on these very unsatisfactory euphorics, pseudo-stimulants and sedatives than they are ready to spend on the education of their children.[8]

For his schemes to succeed, a tyrant would have to deny his subjects the educational and rehabilitational services that I envision. Where these services are available, some would doubtless capitulate anyway. If most members of a society actually succumb, I suppose that they would get what they deserve; but I have more faith in people than that, especially if they have a fair chance in life.

(7) Persons under the influence of pleasure drugs are likely to do things that are very harmful to other persons, especially those close to them, which they would not do in their "right state of mind," and which they would and should regret when they return to their right state. The resulting pains and other harms outweigh the resulting pleasure over the long run for other persons affected by the user's drug-related behaviors.

Morality requires that we consider the effects of our actions, including our pleasure-seeking behaviors, on other people.

It is really very difficult to find self-regarding activities that do not also affect others quite significantly. Some of our hedonic uses of drugs do affect others adversely, at times quite momentously. Persons "under the influence" frequently have accidents at home and at work that injure others as well as themselves. Intoxicated drivers maim and kill thousands of persons on our highways every year, devastating their lives and the lives of those who love them, and causing immense physical and mental pains. Families and friendships are destroyed. Social withdrawal and estrangement are commonplace. Jobs are lost. Fortunes are squandered. Dependents, especially children, are denied the economic resources that would lift them from distressing and oppressive poverty and ignorance. Degrading and criminal behaviors like prostitution, theft, and mugging are frequently necessary to support drug habits. Criminal behaviors like assaults, murders, rapes, spouse beatings, and child abuse occur frequently under intoxication, as do many other grave moral and social indiscretions. As *DSM-III* tells us,

> Highway accidents are a major complication of Alcohol Intoxication. At least half of all highway fatalities involve either a driver or a pedestrian who has been drinking. Intoxication also results in falls and numerous household and industrial accidents. Moreover, it is frequently associated with the commission of criminal acts. More than one half of all murderers and their victims are believed to be intoxicated at the time of the act. One study indicates that about one-fourth of all suicides occur while the individual is drinking alcohol.[9]

Physical injury to others results from drug consumption in many ways. Drugs ingested by pregnant women do permanent damage to their developing fetuses. Thousands of infants are born every year with Fetal Alcohol Syndrome. Thousands are addicted to alcohol and other drugs even before they have drawn their first breath. Thousands still in the womb are permanently stunted both physically and mentally by mothers who smoke, drink, and do drugs. After birth, children suffer the same effects from "secondary" inhalation from their parents' smoke. People who inflict comparable harms on children in other ways would be prosecuted for heinous crimes, but this sanction would be ineffective for drug users. What they really need is greater moral sensitivity, moral education, counseling, job training, and economic opportunity.

Under the influence of hedonic drugs, not only do users harm innocent others, but they also fail to contribute positively and creatively to the well being of others. Time and energy are consumed that could be better spent. Drugs easily become an all-consuming religion to which devotees give all their hearts and souls and minds and strengths—with nothing left over for others. Interestingly, one of the principle objections that Sigmund Freud had to alcoholism was that it "wastes a large quota of energy which might have been employed for the improvement of the human lot."[10]

Of course, it can be said that any pleasurable diversion takes time and energy away from helping others. All of us really are entitled to the pursuit of happiness, and that includes pleasurable diversions. It is unreasonable and pointless to moralize the whole of life and require that every moment of our existence be devoted to promoting the greatest good of the greatest number, often to the neglect of self. It is reasonable to expect, however, that happiness be pursued through means that do not inflict significant injury on self and/or others in the long run.

In conclusion, the case against hedonic drugs is very strong. The disadvantages of drug use for hedonic purposes are too great, especially when, with the slightest bit of education, imagination, and a little bit of luck, we can find innumerable alternative sources and varieties of enjoyment that are harmless and innocent. Without drugs, life can be a "natural high" if we give it a chance.

A Response to Sheridan Hough

After reading Dr. Hough's defense of drug use, I was struck by how little we really disagree. Our differences are largely those of emphasis. She defends the moderate use of drugs, and I attack the immoderate use of drugs. I largely agree that the moderate and responsible use of drugs is acceptable, and she agrees that the immoderate and irresponsible use of drugs is unacceptable. I find many of her comments to be exceptionally illuminating. The line between what counts as moderate and immoderate use really is fuzzy and culturally variable. We agree that pleasure is a good thing. She skillfully develops the ideas that pleasures are bound to activities and colored by expectations and by the social and physical situation in which they are generated. I too have serious doubts that alcoholism is a disease. I try to be very explicit about criteria for drawing the line between responsible and irresponsible uses of drugs, and she actually appeals to most of my criteria in the course of her discussion. I had expected a more radical defense of drug use, but her defense is so qualified and temperate that it is difficult to disagree with her.

There are some minor differences between us, however, though these seem to be mainly differences of emphasis, or differences in judgment calls in marginal situations.

First, I think that we do not really get to the heart of the matter by focusing on ambiguities in the concept of moderation, or on whether alcoholism and drug use are diseases. No matter what our conventions are with respect to concepts of "moderation" and "disease," the crucial thing is that at some point, uses of drugs become harmful to self and/or others in the many ways I have detailed in the preceding discussion. The focus needs to be directly on these harms. The harms are real, no matter what our social conventions are with respect to moderation and disease. A rational theory of moderation would focus directly on the harms, but often there is little rationality in our social conventions.

Next, Dr. Hough stresses that moderate drug use can make a positive contribution to constructive social intercourse and to knowing and appreciating self and others; but my emphasis has been on the large extent to which drug use destroys desirable social relations and is incompatible with knowing and appreciating self and others. The difference is primarily one of emphasis, but on the whole I judge that the harms involved in these matters far outweigh the benefits.

Next, Dr. Hough correctly emphasizes that we frequently indulge immoderately, i.e. harmfully, in other kinds of pleasure-seeking activities. I certainly agree that we can indulge harmfully and excessively in such things as skiing, scuba diving, roller-coaster riding, bungee jumping, studying French literature, or doing mathematics. It does not follow, however, that drug use is any less harmful just because other things are also harmful. Also, it does not follow that illegal drugs are any less harmful simply because legal drugs are just as harmful.

Finally, my judgment call is that drug use is much riskier than Dr. Hough seems to think. She seems to presuppose that moderate and responsible drug use is easy to sustain, but it seems to me that it is extremely difficult to use pleasure drugs so minimally that significant harm does not result from their use. In her opinion, the risk is worth running that harmless alcohol consumption will not spill over into harmful uses; but I have serious doubts. Too many people who have believed that have been seriously mistaken. I do think that the sale and use of alcohol and drugs currently classified as controlled substances should not be illegal; nevertheless, the use of most drugs for hedonic purposes is ill advised for both prudential and moral reasons.

NOTES

1. Gerald L. Klerman, "Psychotropic Drugs as Therapeutic Agents" (*Hastings Center Studies*, Vol. 2, No. 1, 1974), p. 91.

2. Aldous Huxley, *Brave New World* (New York: Harper & Row, 1965), p. 42.

3. Walter Kaufmann, ed., *The Portable Nietzsche* (New York: Viking Press, 1954), p. 468.

4. American Psychiatric Association, *Diagnostic and Statistical Manual of Mental Disorders, Third Edition* (Washington, DC: American Psychiatric Association, 1980), pp. 160f.

5. Ralph Waldo Emerson, *The Complete Works of Ralph Waldo Emerson* (Boston: Houghton Mifflin Co., 1903), Vol. III, p. 27.

6. Ibid., p. 28.

7. Aldous Huxley, *Brave New World Revisited* (New York: Harper & Row, 1965), p. 56.

8. Ibid., p. 60.

9. American Psychiatric Association, pp. 130, 131.

10. Quoted by Ernest Wallwork in *Psychoanalysis and Ethics* (New Haven: Yale University Press, 1991), pp. 247–8.

Legalization

Drug Prohibition: A Legal and Economic Analysis

*Walter Block**

Introduction

This paper shall argue the case for the legalization of addictive drugs such as marijuana, cocaine, and heroin. In section two the claim is defended that there are no "market failures" which could justify a banning of these substances. Section three makes this point with regard to the libertarian theory of law. In section four several objections to this thesis are explored and rejected, and section five concludes with an analysis of the benefits of legalization.

Economics

There is nothing in the tenets of value-free economics that would preclude the legalization of drugs. On the contrary, the presumption from this quarter is that a free market in marijuana, cocaine, heroin, and other such substances will enhance economic welfare.

This somewhat startling conclusion emanates from the axiomatic nature of the proposition that there are always gains from trade. Whenever any two persons engage in commercial activity—whether it be barter, or for employment, or the purchase or sale of consumer goods or intermediate products—both must gain in the *ex ante* sense. That is, neither party would agree to take part in the endeavor did he not expect to be made better off as a result of it. If I purchase a newspaper for fifty cents, I do so only because I predict that I will enjoy its perusal more than any other usage of this money; conversely, the vendor prefers the coins I give him more than the paper and ink he must give over to my possession.

The claim being made here, strictly speaking, is *not* that a free market in drugs (or anything else for that matter) will enhance economic welfare *ex post*, but rather only in the *ex ante* sense. When one views a trade *ex ante*, he does so from a time perspective before it actually takes place; he anticipates that he will benefit from it. And that is the reason he agrees to take part in it in the first place. Economic welfare from the ex post sense is from the perspective of after the trade occurs. For him to have gained in this regard, the participant must continue to regard himself as better off because of it.

There is indeed a strong presumption that trade benefits both partners in both senses. However it must be acknowledged that every once in a while a consumer regrets making a purchase; perhaps the price has fallen in the interim between the point of sale and the *ex post* evaluation. Or a vendor later regrets selling an item, because he now thinks it was of higher quality than he estimated when he agreed to the sale.

If this insight applies to ordinary trades, it holds no less in the case under consideration. Were I to sell to you an ounce of cocaine for $100, it must be true that at the point of sale, I value the money more than the opiate, and that you rank the two items in the inverse order. Since trade is a positive sum game, we both gain.

It cannot be denied that third parties to this arrangement will often feel themselves aggrieved. There are legions of decent citizens who are sometimes affronted when consenting adults engage in voluntary capitalist acts. Temperance leagues object to alcohol sales, health nuts are enraged at cigarette advertising, and, for all we know, there may be people who are in principle opposed to the publication, sale, and reading of newspapers. None of this, however, vitiates our original economic insight. The market, the concatenation of all voluntary trades, still enhances the welfare of all participants (Rothbard, 1977). These objectors may be participants in other market activities, but as third parties, their misgivings are simply not included in our welfare calculations.

There are several good reasons for disregarding the welfare of third parties.

First, a praxeological reason. According to the old saw, "talk is cheap, action is what counts." Any third party is free, of course, to verbally oppose any given trade. For example, feminists and conservatives oppose the sale of pornography; teetotalers argue against the purchase of intoxicants; Jews and Muslims decry markets for pork. The point is, however, that these opponents are limited in their opposition, to talk; there is no action which necessarily reveals their true assessment. At least they cannot demonstrate their preference in the manner in which the trade of the two parties to the transaction indicates a positive evaluation of the item received compared to that which is given up.

Second, a pragmatic one. In theory, *no* trade can escape this criticism. There can always be found at least one person who will object to each and every trade ever made. Died in the wool Marxists fit this bill; they see commercial activity as necessarily exploitative. Additionally, those who favor self-sufficiency and carry this to its logical conclusion, are in principle committed to disputing the propriety of all exchanges. This applies as well to those who think that we ought to be giving each other presents instead of buying and selling to one another. However, it is rather an unfair hurdle to expect a market defense of legalized drugs to satisfy a philosophy, which can even call into question the pedestrian exchange of fifty cents for a newspaper.

Third, a reason that clarifies the claim being made in the present paper. We are not affirming that the market makes everyone on earth better off; on the contrary, it merely enriches those who take part in it. Third parties, by definition, do not, in the specific and limited contexts in which they are third parties, take part in market transactions. Therefore, no benefit accrues to them on those occasions. Our interest is not in maximizing overall welfare; merely that of market participants. Anyone of course, is free to enter the market, and offer goods or services in trade. On such occasions, their economic welfare can or will be enhanced. But the welfare of third parties qua third parties cannot be counted, since we do not contend that they will be enhanced.

Law

There are basically two kinds of law in this context: normative and positive. The latter is confined to actual legislative enactments, and judicial interpretations. Since the bottom line on this literature is that certain drugs are now illegal in the U.S., a discussion of this aspect of law would be uninteresting and unedifying.

Instead, we concentrate on the former. In particular we focus on the libertarian legal code, insofar as this is one philosophy consistent with full legalization, the position we wish to defend. In this John Locke–based perspective, man is the owner of his own body, since he, in effect, "homesteaded" it, and likewise of all parts of the natural world with which he has mixed his labor. Given that he legitimately owns these properties, he can do with them whatever he wishes, provided that he respects the equal human and property rights of all other people. Thus, a man can use his domicile for target practice, provided he keeps the bullets confined to his own premises; if ever they stray onto the property or bodies of other persons, his actions are no longer consonant with the libertarian legal code.

Under such a regime, a man can properly attain new property by any legitimate noncoercive means (Nozick, 1974): inheritance, gambling, work, and, particularly relevant to our concerns, trade. That is to say, if A homesteaded some land, and grew marijuana plants on it, and B earned some money in any other legitimate occupation, then it is entirely legitimate for B to purchase this commodity from A. Even more important, it is then proper (e.g., it *should* be legal for B) to use this item in any manner, shape, or form which does not violate the right of others to use their persons and property in a manner of their own choosing. That is to say, B is allowed under the libertarian legal code to ingest or smoke the marijuana, but not to use it as a projectile to throw at his (unwilling) neighbor.

The implication of an interference with this right of marijuana use is (partial) slavery. The problem with this "curious" institution is that the control of each of us over our own bodies is abrogated. Are we being hysterical in categorizing present drug law as a form of slavery? It is all a matter of degree; there is never total abrogation. For example, in the epoch of U.S. slavery before the close of the Civil War, slaves were denied the right to come and go as they wished, and to work for any willing employer. Rather, they were typically confined to one particular plantation, and owned by other people. However, they did have a certain limited control over their bodies: they were allowed to sleep; they were allowed to eat; they were allowed to engage in their other bodily functions.

It is no different with the prohibition of dope, except in the matter of degree. In both cases our control over our bodies is restricted. In slavery, this occurs almost but not quite totally; in the present case, the limitations concern merely the right of ingestion of illegal substances. But insofar as interference with our control over ourselves is proscribed, we are to that extent enslaved.

Objections

1. Addictive materials are physically harmful to the person who uses them. They should therefore be banned.

Given the purely economic perspective, we are entitled to deduce from the fact that a man buys narcotics the conclusion that he values them more than their cost. And that is all. It cannot be shown, as attempted by Stigler and Becker (1977) that there are "beneficial" and "harmful" addictions, according to whether or not they enhance, or detract from, the earning of income in the future. Why is it necessarily "beneficial" ("harmful") to engage in activity which promotes an upward (downward) sloping lifetime-earnings profile? Whether the individual chooses an example put forth by these authors in the former category (e.g., classical music) or in the latter (alcohol), the value-free economist cannot categorize them as beneficial or harmful. All he can conclude is that, in the view of the economic actor, at the time the decision was made, the choice of consumption, whether alcohol or Amadeus, was made in order to enhance his welfare.

If pure economic theory cannot support this distinction between "good" and "bad" addictions, even less so can it be used in behalf of the case for interdiction. For even if it could somehow be established that heroin is a harmful addictive substance, in the absence of a value judgment it by no means follows that it should be outlawed.

The paternalistic argument (bad addictive materials should be legally prohibited) undoubtedly rings true from a health point of view, in that if there were any such substances, ending their use would be a medical accomplishment. But this is irrelevant to public-policy analysis, at least from the libertarian legal perspective. There are many other things that are deleterious; for example, chocolate, ice cream, hang gliding, ice skating, boxing, fatty foods, automobile racing, fried chicken. Were we to accept this argument in the present case, logic would require that we forbid all such items, and activities. But this would surely be an infringement on self-ownership rights.

Let us now concede for the sake of argument that heroin is harmful. Even so, injury is a relative, not an absolute concept. Harmful, but compared to what? Alcohol? Tobacco? Many more people—even proportional to actual use—die of the latter two than of the former. If foreclosure is indicated, it is thus by no means clear as to which item it should be applied. Further, legal suppression does not improve, but rather exacerbates the health problem. This is because of the potency effect of prohibition: the mere existence of prohibition, and the more severely it is administered, the stronger will be the potency of the ensuing drugs. A smuggler would rather risk transporting a suitcase full of cocaine than marijuana, because of its greater value. The same phenomenon occurred with alcohol in the early part of the twentieth century: beer manufacture declined, while that for hard liquor increased. This, too, is the explanation for the most recent generation of chemical substitutes: crack, ice, PCP, etc.

If anything is harmful for human consumption, rat poison and carbon monoxide fit the bill. And yet our society has not so far legally excluded these items from commerce. There are some people who even go so far as advocate entrenching into law the right of suicide. These individuals, as in the case of the pro-choicers, are logically obligated to support repeal. For at worst addictive drugs are a (slow) form of suicide. If we do not advocate disallowing these other death aids, nor even doing away with oneself, how then can we logically proscribe substances such as heroin?

2. Addictive drugs are financially harmful to the persons other than the one who uses them. They should therefore be forbidden.

This is true, but only under a regime of socialized medicine. There, we are indeed each "our brother's keepers." If you overeat, and contract heart disease, I, along with everyone else, am forced to pay for it. If I smoke cigarettes and fall victim to cancer, you, and all other citizens, must foot the bill. We therefore each have a clear and focused interest in the health habits of everyone else. The individual is a "clear and present" financial danger to the group. In such a situation, there certainly is a case for the injunction of addictive material: the rest of us can save money if we can reduce the incidence of use.

But why accept this context as a fact of nature? Coercive medical insurance schemes have many shortcomings, not the least of which is the problem of moral hazard, which encourages all parties to overuse scarce health services since they are priced at subsidized costs. Given a free market in medicine, this reason for restraint of drug markets all but vanishes.

Further, alcohol and tobacco, as we have seen, are far more harmful than addictive drugs. To the extent that this objection has any merit, we should first enact legislation against the former, and only then prohibit the latter.

In contrast, this Hobbesian war of each of us against the other does not occur under a market regime. There, it is to the financial interest of private medical insurance companies to set prices which reflect the best estimated risk of future health-care needs. For example, if a person smokes, or drinks, or engages in any number of dangerous activities such as chocolate, ice cream, hang gliding, ice skating, boxing, fatty foods, etc., their insurance premiums will tend to take this into account. In equilibrium, the risk of these dangers will be fully incorporated, no more, no less: the charges cannot be any higher than the levels predicted by these activities due to competition from other firms; they will not be any lower, since bankruptcy will eliminate such practices.

But what of the objection that insurance companies do not currently charge lower rates to non-alcoholics? There are several replies to this. First of all, we do not at present have an insurance industry based fully on free-market principles. There are simply too many barriers to entry—regulations, prohibitions against foreign carriers in the local market, domestic entry restrictions—for that. Were there no barriers to entry, and if it were profitable for companies to discriminate against alcoholics, the presumption is that this is precisely what would occur. Secondly, ill health is now dealt with by the courts as a handicap, and handicap is now in the process of becoming a status against which it is illegal to discriminate. If alcohol is interpreted as more of a protected handicap than tobacco, due, perhaps, to secondary effects, this may explain why insurance companies are loath to apply their cigarette policy to liquor. If there were absolutely no law against discrimination, insurance companies would likely be able to ensure that one person need not subsidize another's indulging in chocolate or fatty-food consumption: they could measure the blood pressure, height and weight, etc., of their clients. They could subject them to other medical tests: heart-beat rate after five minutes on a treadmill. They could ask them to sign a statement attesting to the fact that they do not engage in activities such as skiing or hang gliding: violations would annul insurance coverage. Needless to say, any such market responses (which would tend to make our lives safer) would be severely dealt with by the courts (Epstein, 1992).

3. Addictive drugs promote crime, and should therefore be banished.

This is perhaps the weakest objection of all so far, in that it is the suppression of narcotics that leads to criminal behavior, not these substances themselves.

If left to the market, the prices of heroin, cocaine, marijuana, and all the rest would be exceedingly modest. After all, they are based for the most part on very hardy plants, which cost little to harvest and process. The reason they are so expensive at present is because of their legal status: it is highly risky to bring them to market. The high prices they can fetch, however, create vast profits. These attract people whose adherence to the niceties of the law are less than totally thorough.

Crime comes about in three ways based on this scenario. First, the farmers, refiners, transporters, street vendors, etc., involved in the practice are per se considered criminals, since they break the law. But this is not "real crime," since there are no victims of these commercial interactions; all the way from planting the seed to final consumption there are only willing participants involved.

Second, because of the exorbitant costs of the drugs, addicts must resort to crime (burglaries, auto theft, assault and battery, etc.) in order to obtain the funds necessary to feed their habits. Here, there is at last real crime, since the victims by no stretch of the imagination can be considered to have given their permission to the burglar.

Third, there are those who pay the ultimate penalty as a result of gun battles in the streets between different gangs contending for turf. These "mushrooms" are also entirely innocent, and lose their lives not because of drugs in and of themselves, but rather due to the law. This is because it is not possible for an aggrieved drug gang member to utilize the courts and police; rather, he must "take the law into his own hands." A similar situation occurred during the epoch of alcohol prohibitionism, and the same people then as now are ultimately responsible for the deaths of the innocents: the legislators who enacted the law, and the police and jurists who administer it.

Despite the foregoing, there are claims to the effect that narcotic usage creates crime in a very different way: by turning the addict into a crazed, enraged lunatic, uncontrollable in his lust to lay waste to the countryside, and all who reside in it. This "Godzilla" effect is entirely erroneous when applied to the traditional opiates. There are three bits of evidence which can be adduced in behalf of this claim. One is the British experience with legalization, where doctors in hospitals would not start newcomers out on this path, but would administer the drug to confirmed addicts. The finding from this source (Judson, 1974) is that the recipients of this medication were able to lead normal lives without any extraordinary involvement in criminal activity. Second are the opium dens of Chinese origin. The denizens of these establishments, too, were not given over to violence; if anything, the very opposite was the case. This substance induced lethargy, if anything. And third is the example of the one segment of U.S. society which now has almost full access to such material at cut-rate prices: physicians. Experience has failed to show enraged, antisocial behavior as a result.

However, let us consider the contrary-to-fact-conditional. That is, let us assume, if only for the sake of argument, that there is indeed an addictive (or even non-addictive) "Godzilla" drug. Should it be prohibited? The answer, at least from the realms of value-free economics and the libertarian legal code, is no. From the former perspective, we must still deduce from the sale of this product that both parties gained economic welfare in the *ex ante* sense. From the latter, it is still unjustified to initiate violence against non-initiators, and the imbiber of "Godzilla" will, by stipulation, not begin his crazed rantings, ravings, and waves of murder until at least a few seconds after ingestion. Thus, there is no case for prior restraint on these grounds. It would not be unreasonable, however, for the forces of law and order to carefully monitor such people. Then, as the early stages of this mania begin to take effect (pounding on the chest, drooling, snapping of teeth, whatever) the police can subject him to the fullest penalties of the "real" criminal law as soon as he makes even a slight aggressive move in the direction of a victim. There might be some slight risk of criminal behavior under these circumstances, but it would be far less than in the present situation, where public policy truly unleashes the whirlwind.

A few words of clarification on this matter.

At what point would it be all right for officers of the law to intervene? They could do so as soon as there were any indication whatsoever that the person taking this drug were about to go on a rampage. In the extreme case, if we knew with absolute certainty that the Godzilla pill lead necessarily to mayhem (we can never know this, since it is an empirical matter) it would be justified for the police to open fire on the person as soon as ingestion took place. Just as the police may fire at a gunman in order to protect innocent victims long before his bullet has left the pistol chamber, so may they act against "Godzilla" before he actually commits violence.

The only difference between the system of legalized drugs advocated in this paper and the present legal regime would be in the motivation of the forces of law and order. They would be executing a murderer, not a drug taker; they would be killing a person not because he took drugs, but because he was about to commit murder, and in order to prevent him from so doing. This might not matter, much, to the user of the Godzilla drug, but this places in stark contrast the difference between prohibition of drugs and prohibition of murder.

We wouldn't hesitate to impose prior constraint to prevent people from swallowing a nuclear bomb. But cannot the Godzilla pill be looked upon akin to a thermonuclear device? No, there is a relevant difference. If a nuclear device blows up, it is beyond the power of the police, or anyone else, to prevent harm to innocent persons. In contrast, if a person swallows the Godzilla pill, the forces of law and order will be able to stop him in his tracks the moment he gives any indication on incipient violence. At most, then, this analysis can support a law calling on purveyors of the Godzilla pill to notify the police of an upcoming sale; it cannot justify prohibition. With the bomb, things are very different; the clear and present danger it constitutes (to say nothing of the fact that it is intrinsically an offensive weapon and should be prohibited on that ground alone) provides reason for its proscription.

Of course, if the Godzilla pill makes the person who takes it all but omnipotent, as well as murderous, then and only then is there a case for prohibition. But in this scenario, Godzilla has left the realm of (addictive?) drugs and entered that of atom bombs.

4. If narcotics are legalized, they will gain an imprimatur from the state. Their present legal status should therefore be preserved.

The problem with this objection is that legalization does not imply sanction. If it did, extant law with regard to tobacco, alcohol, and gambling would suggest that the government favored these goods and services. And yet they are usually subjected to extra taxes, e.g., "sin" taxes. As well, there are many other disreputable activities which are nonetheless legal, at least at present. For example, lying, gossiping, disloyalty to employers, jilting fiancees right at the alter, disrespect to parents, nose picking, cheating at solitaire, not keeping ones lawn trimmed, cutting corners, not taking regular baths, breaking promises to children. If it were true that a failure to legally interdict these activities is reducible to approval of them, then our society, insofar as it does not fine or imprison perpetrators, actually recommends and esteems them. Needless to say, nothing could be further from the truth.

5. The elasticity of demand for narcotics is very high. Small reductions in price will call forth large increases in demand. The gigantic fall in price likely to emerge with legalization would create a stupendously gigantic elevation in use. Were these agents to be legalized, the whole society would become drugged out of its gourd.

Although posed in a rather exaggerated form, this objection is a very powerful one indeed. Even ardent advocates of repeal such as Friedman (1989) would change their position on the issue were this elasticity claim to be proven correct. Fortunately for the position taken in this chapter, however, the evidence suggests that the elasticity is likely to be far lower than that depicted in the doomsday scenario. Why?

First of all, the elasticity for drugs in general is very low. This is because such items are usually seen by their consumers as necessities, not luxuries. While one might severely reduce demand for the latter in the face of an increased price, or even give it up entirely in the extreme, this does not apply to the former. But if such behavior is characteristic of most drugs, it applies even more so in the case of addictive substances. For at least in the mind of the addict, these are the most difficult of all from which to refrain.

Secondly, the effect of legalization—in markedly reducing profits—will be to greatly decrease the incentive for "pushing." No longer will it pay for addicts to go to school yards, offering free samples, in an attempt to "hook" children into a life of addiction in order to support their own habits. With a free market, where these products will be exceedingly cheap, there will be no temptation to resort to these extraordinary means of salesmanship.

Third, even if quantity increases, potency will fall, as we have seen above. Given this effect, a greater amount of total drugs may be less harmful to the population than what is presently consumed, as heroin and cocaine begin to take the place of the more deleterious chemical derivatives, and as marijuana begins to replace those two.

Given this wealth of evidence, we must conclude that it is extremely unlikely that elasticity will prove very high at all. A much more reasonable expectation is that when prices fall due to legalization, quantity will not increase much if at all.

We must, however, squarely face the Armageddon scenario. Suppose for argument's sake that evidence to the contrary notwithstanding, what will really happen upon repeal is accurately portrayed by the exaggerated fears of the objection under consideration. Assume, for instance, that 75 percent of the population, just to pick a number out of a hat, were to become addicted. We still maintain that there is again nothing in the realm of positive economics, nor of normative libertarian political theory, that can serve as the basis for prohibition. It will still be true that all parties concerned will gain, in their own subjective estimates, from their participation in the drug market. It will still be true that the industry will be a totally voluntary one, with no one forced to take part. Hence, libertarian theory still proscribes interdiction. To be sure, G.N.P. will not be as high under such a regime, at least at the outset; but this calculation is a very imperfect estimator of economic welfare, which will be maximized by allowing people to freely choose their consumption patterns. In any case, for those inordinately fond of G.N.P. cal-

culations, there is a consolation. If addiction really is the killer
feared by some, the likelihood is that in the long term G.N.P. will
rise at least on a per-capita basis, as the death by slow suicide of
the addicts raises the average productivity of those who remain.

Advantages

1. Decrease in crime

As legalization takes the vast profits out of the drug business, the incentives toward criminality will tend to disappear
pari passu. And this is no accident, since the one stems from the
other. According to some estimates (Trebach, 1978), this factor
alone accounts for some 50 percent of crime in urban America. In
addition, with fewer criminals, there will be less overcrowding
of prisons; expenditures in this direction will fall. Another
saving will be in terms of the monies now expended on crime
prevention. Less money will have to be wasted on locksmiths,
burglar alarms, gated communities, and fewer ulcers will be
generated due to fear and worry about crime.

This point highlights the reason for the difficulty of
"fighting the War on Drugs." Every time a battle is won in this
"war," paradoxically, the enemy is strengthened, not weakened.
If one ton of cocaine is seized, the price of this commodity increases; but this subsequent higher value only succeeds in raising the profit incentives attendant upon production. Thus, the
more vigorous and successful the activities of the Drug Enforcement Agency, the greater the strength of the illicit drug industry.
The way to "win" the war is not by fighting the alligators, but by
draining the swamp. As jurists and law enforcement agents in
South American and Asian countries have long known, and as
their counterparts in the U.S. are in the process of ascertaining
for themselves, these alligators, the drug gangs, have very sharp
teeth indeed. Better to ruin their business by deflating the profit
balloon than by acting in a way (prohibition) which only supports them. The present drug war is so far from being won that
the authorities cannot even stop their spread in prisons, where
civil liberties niceties do not play any nugatory role, and their

control is as total as it will ever be in any sector of society (Thornton, 1991).

2. *Better health protection*

If even a small part of the money now fruitlessly spent on banning narcotics were instead allocated to the *medical* problem of curing people of the malady of drug addiction, the average level of health in this country would be vastly improved. *This* battle is a winnable one, as shown by the great strides made recently in fighting the depredations of alcohol and tobacco. The lowered use of these commodities, especially in the upper classes, which usually set consumption patterns for the rest of society, is a pattern which can and must be emulated for narcotics.

In addition, there is the problem of AIDS. Drug prohibition plays its part in the tragic spread of this dreaded disease because of shared needles. Like so much else, this is a result of the outlawry, not of the narcotics themselves, as can be seen from the fact that insulin addicts (diabetics, that is) need never resort to shared needles. On the contrary, they can avail themselves of the finest medical care that our society can offer. Were we to reverse matters, that is, legalize narcotics but prohibit insulin, there is no doubt that the results would be reversed as well. Crazed and enraged insulin junkies would then commit crimes and spread AIDS through shared needles, while heroin addicts would lead relatively calm and unthreatened lives.

The health of addicts would moreover improve. Lenny Bruce died not from an overdose of heroin, but from impurities in the sample with which he injected himself. This is the modern equivalent of "bathtub gin." If Squibb, Pfizer, Upjohn, Ciba-Giegy, Glaxo, Merck, and their ilk were in charge of production instead of a bunch of fly-by-night outfits, there is little doubt that the quality-control safeguards would be immeasurably enhanced. Suppose you were about to die and had a child addicted to narcotics. Would you prefer a situation where he had to run around like a half-crazed wretch, doing all sorts of unspeakable things in order to raise the requisite funds for his habit, never knowing where his next fix was coming from, nor what would be in it, or one where he could be given an injection in safe, comfortable, clean hospital surroundings, under the care of a physician?

3. *Civil liberties*

Because drug sales are a victimless crime, the police labor under a disadvantage compared to auto theft, rape, assault, arson, etc. There is no formal complainant. Therefore, if they want to solve the "crime," they must often resort to tactics and techniques which would otherwise prove unnecessary and repugnant. This is why they ride roughshod over civil liberties in a way that occurs with regard to few if any other crimes. As a result, we have witnessed teen curfews; "zero tolerance," where boats and automobiles have been seized upon the finding of minuscule amounts of marijuana; strip searches; National Guard patrols on our city streets; and legal prosecutions for the parents of teen addicts. Political leaders have gone so far as to advocate flogging, cutting off a finger for each drug conviction, the death penalty, and sending the U.S. military to foreign countries to interdict supplies. The civilized world was properly outraged by the shooting down by the Russians of the Korean Airlines commercial jet which strayed from its flight path; what are we to make in this context of the suggestion of Customs Commissioner William von Raab (Bandow, 1989) that planes suspected of carrying illegal drugs should be shot out of the sky?

As well, drug legalization—of possession, use, sale, transport, "trafficking," merchandising, advertising, etc.—is a litmus test for the philosophy of civil liberties. One can hardly be a civil libertarian and favor prohibitionism. Advocacy of legalization, or at least decriminalization, is a necessary albeit not sufficient condition for a civil libertarian.

NOTES

[*]Nothing in this article should be taken as an indication that the present author favors the use of the drugs discussed herein. Actually, the very opposite is the case. While he opposes prohibition, he advocates all noncoercive methods—arguments, counseling, advertising, etc.—which lead to decreased or zero usage of these pernicious and immoral material and substances.

REFERENCES

Gary Anderson and Walter Block, "The Economics and Ethics of Paternalism: A Reply to George Akerloff," mimeo, 1992.

Doug Bandow, "Once Again, a Drug-War Panic," *Chicago Tribune,* March 22, 1989.

Walter Block, *Defending the Undefendable,* New York: Laissez-Faire Books, (1976) 1991.

Walter Block, *The U.S. Bishops and Their Critics: An Economic and Ethical Perspective* (Vancouver: The Fraser Institute, 1986).

David Boaz, ed., *The Crisis in Drug Prohibition* (Washington, DC: The Cato Institute, 1990).

Richard Epstein, *Forbidden Grounds* (Cambridge: Harvard University Press, 1992).

Milton Friedman, "An Open Letter to Bill Bennett," *Wall Street Journal,* September 7, 1989.

Ron Hamowy, ed., *Dealing with Drugs: Consequences of Government Control* (San Francisco: The Pacific Institute, 1987).

Hans Hermann Hoppe, *A Theory of Socialism and Capitalism* (Boston, Kluwer, 1989).

Horace F. Judson, *Heroin Addiction in Britain* (New York: Harcourt Brace Jovanovich, 1974).

Robert Nozick, Anarchy, *State and Utopia* (New York: Basic Books, 1974).

Murray N. Rothbard, *For a New Liberty* (Macmillan: New York, 1973).

Murray N. Rothbard, *The Ethics of Liberty* (Humanities Press: Atlantic Highlands, N.J., 1982).

Murray N. Rothbard, "Toward a Reconstruction of Utility and Welfare Economics" (San Francisco: Center for Libertarian Studies, Occasional Paper #3, 1977).

George Stigler and Gary Becker, "De Gustibus Non Est Disputandum," *American Economic Review* 67 (March), pp. 76–90.

Thomas Szasz, *Ceremonial Chemistry: The Ritual Persecution of Drugs, Addicts and Pushers,* red ed. (Holmes Beach FL: Learning Publications, 1985).

Mark Thornton, *The Economics of Prohibition* (Salt Lake City: University of Utah Press, 1991).

Arnold Trebach, "The Potential Impact of 'Legal' Heroin in America," in *Drugs, Crime and Politics,* Arnold Trebach, ed. (New York: Praeger, 1978).

Drug Prohibition:
A Public-Health Perspective

Bonnie Steinbock

The Drug Problem

It is estimated that over six million Americans are heavy drug users.[1] Between 1986 and 1988, the number of cocaine addicts in New York City more than tripled, with an estimated total of 600,000 in 1988, most addicted to crack.[2] Although middle-class cocaine use in the United States as a whole is on the decline—it has dropped 22 percent since 1988—Federal officials say that 6.4 million Americans used cocaine last year. In the poorest neighborhoods, cocaine smoking and snorting is on the rise, and a flood of potent heroin is creating new addicts.[3] Drug abuse has caused problems for individuals, families, and society as a whole for years, but the introduction of crack cocaine has made things much worse. Let me mention just a few of the effects attributed to crack in New York City.

- Drug-related crime is far worse than it was twenty years ago. From 1987 to 1988, the number of murders in New York rose 10.4 percent. Police say that drugs, in particular, crack, played a role in at least 38 percent of the 1,867 murders in 1988, compared with a generally constant rate of 20 percent for years.

- Crack contributed to a tripling of cases in which parents under the influence of drugs abused or neglected their children. In 1987, 73 percent of the deaths in abuse and neglect cases resulted from parents abusing drugs, up from 11 percent in 1985.[4]

• Between 1986 and 1988, the number of newborn children in New York City testing positive for drugs—mostly cocaine—almost quadrupled, going from 1,325 to 5,088. Because of crack, in some inner-city hospitals, the number of babies going directly from the hospital into foster homes has risen from 2 percent to 15 percent.[5] Urban child-welfare workers estimate that 70 percent of children they see are raised by grandmothers or other relatives after parents abandon them for drugs.[6]

The impact of the crack epidemic on children is perhaps the most heartrending aspect of the drug problem. Other effects of crack, such as the tremendous increase in the prison population—up from 9,815 in New York City in 1985 to over 17,500 in 1989—can be laid to the fact that crack is *illegal*. Legalize addictive drugs, and drug arrests (1.2 million a year in the United States), which are overwhelming the criminal justice system, causing overcrowding in the prisons, and costing billions of dollars, would disappear. Moreover, according to Ira Glasser, Executive Director of the American Civil Liberties Union (ACLU) and a proponent of legalization, three-quarters of "drug-related" homicides are caused by territorial disputes and other incidents relating to the criminal trafficking system. "Only 7.5 percent of the homicides were related to the effects of the drug itself, and two-thirds of those involved alcohol, not crack."[7]

By contrast, the effects of crack on children, both pre- and postnatally, will not be diminished by legalization. Dr. Linda A. Randolph, director of the State Office of Public Health, says that, because of drug abuse, particularly crack, "we are seeing dramatic increases in infant mortality, in congenital syphilis, and in the number of AIDS-infected women who are giving birth."[8] Intensive hospital care for *each* crack baby costs about $90,000. That translates into $2.5 billion annually for the nation.

Crack can have devastating effects on the nervous systems of newborns. T. Berry Brazelton describes the clinical manifestations this way:

They are either limp and unresponsive or are hyper-sensitive and behave chaotically. They have difficulty receiving and responding to the stimuli of a soothing voice or face. When they are cuddled or rocked, they react with piercing wails and jerky motions. Few people could love these babies. They are likely to suffer later from learning disabilities and to be either hyperactive or emotionally flat. They also tend to be at the mercy of their impulses. The social programs required to educate them will cost billions of dollars.[9]

It should be noted that, although crack is ingested during pregnancy, the harmful effects are imposed on the newborn, the infant, and even the older child. The pregnant crack addict does not risk harm only to herself, but also to the baby she will bear, if she decides not to abort. The term "fetal abuse," often used to describe the use of drugs during pregnancy, is something of a misnomer, since the damage is not confined to the fetus, but is done also to the born child. However one views the fetus, born children have full legal rights, including the right not to be injured prior to live birth.[10] That is why there is no logical contradiction in supporting the right to abortion and maintaining that women have an obligation not to harm their not-yet-born children through ingestion of drugs during pregnancy.[11]

While there is debate among the experts about how bad and long-lasting the physical damage is to children born to crack users, there is agreement that these babies are especially susceptible to child abuse. They suffer from neglect because, as one article put it, ". . . people who hardly bother with food for themselves can't be expected to give up precious crack to feed a baby, can they?"[12] And they are at risk for child abuse because their screaming and nonresponsiveness make them unattractive and difficult to care for. As Brazelton asks, "What would an addicted parent in an addicted environment do to such a baby? The ingredients for child abuse were all there."[13]

The Libertarian Approach

Even this brief recounting indicates a major social problem, something with which society is entitled—even obligated—to concern itself. Yet the libertarian perspective offered by Professor Block suggests otherwise. He holds that people gain when they are able freely to buy the drugs they want. And if both parties gain, what possible justification can there be for interfering with the liberty of the parties to trade? Block's advocacy for the legalization of addictive drugs follows from "the axiomatic nature of gains from trade":

> Whenever any two persons engage in commercial activity—whether it be barter, or for employment, or the purchase or sale of consumer goods or intermediate products—both must gain in the *ex ante* sense. That is, neither party would agree to take part in the endeavor did he not expect to be made better off as a result of it. . . . If this insight applies to ordinary trades, it holds no less in the case under consideration. Were I to sell to you an ounce of cocaine for $100, it must be true that at the point of sale, I value the money more than the opiate, and that you rank the two items in the inverse order. Since trade is a positive sum game, we both gain. (pp. 199–200; all references to Block are to his essay in this volume.)

Block is aware that "third parties" may feel affronted when consenting adults engage in voluntary capitalist acts, but so what? "The market, the concatenation of all voluntary trades, still enhances the *welfare of all participants*."

Strictly speaking, the claim is merely that a free market (in drugs or anything else) enhances welfare only in the *ex ante*, not in the *ex post*, sense. Block maintains that there is a strong presumption that trade benefits both partners in both senses, although he concedes, somewhat grudgingly, that "every once in a while a consumer regrets making a purchase" and therefore does not benefit in the *ex post* sense. However, it is benefit in the *ex post* sense that is essential for his argument, for the argument in favor of a free market is premised on the notion that, in such a market, everyone actually benefits, and not merely expects to benefit. Since everyone benefits, there is no justification for intervention. However, we cannot assume that people will gain when they expect to gain, without making further assumptions. One important assumption is that the buyer has adequate and truthful information about the item purchased. Unfortunately, sellers do not always provide such information; sometimes they even make false claims. Trades made under these conditions are neither voluntary nor fair. Intervention in the free market to assure that consumers have the information they need to make rational and voluntary purchases is entirely justified. It is for this reason that we have such agencies as the Better Business Bureau and the Food and Drug Administration (FDA), and laws requiring "truth in advertising." Even libertarians should welcome such laws, as the constraints they place on manufacturers ensure that capitalist acts are genuinely voluntary.

The FDA goes beyond laws requiring "truth in advertising." It has the power to prevent drugs that have not been shown to be effective or that are harmful from being put on the market. From a libertarian perspective, this is unjustifiable. So long as people have the information they need to make a voluntary choice, their choices should be unconstrained. However, we may question the plausibility of the libertarian view. Most people acknowledge that they have neither the knowledge to make judgments about the safety or efficacy of medications nor the time to research the issues. Most of us are willing to sacrifice the liberty to buy useless or dangerous medications in return for increased safety.[14]

Absence of knowledge is only one factor that prevents trade from being a positive sum game. Another is coercion. If one is forced to trade ("Your money or your life"), then one does not gain, even in the *ex ante* sense. How does this relate to the sale of narcotics? Some drugs, such as crack cocaine, are highly addictive. The choices of addicts are not fully voluntary, perhaps not voluntary at all. They are constrained, comparable to the "choice" of a person who has a gun to his head. However persuasive the economic analysis may be in the case of voluntary transactions, it is of limited application in the case of addictive drugs. For these reasons, economic axioms about commercial activity do not support non-intervention into the drug market (legalization).

However, the economic analysis is only part of Block's argument. In addition, he espouses a libertarian philosophy that regards the value of individual liberty higher than any other value. The libertarian principle can be traced back to John Stuart Mill, who argued in *On Liberty* that the only purpose for which it was permissible to restrict individual freedom was to prevent harm to others. A person's own good was never sufficient warrant. Mill's principle has been applied in all sorts of ways: from opposition of seatbelt and helmet laws to opposition to closing gay bathhouses in an effort to stop the spread of AIDS.[15]

Mill attempted to defend his absolute prohibition against paternalistic intervention on utilitarian grounds, but this has been notoriously unsuccessful. There is no reason to think that the harm of paternalistic intervention will necessarily outweigh the benefit to be attained. Philosopher Gerald Dworkin persuasively argues that it was not utilitarian calculation that led Mill to his absolute rejection of paternalism, but rather a non-contingent, non-utilitarian argument about what it means to be a person, an autonomous agent. Dworkin says, "It is because coercing a person for his own good denies this status as an independent entity that Mill objects to it so strongly and in such absolute terms."[16] Dworkin goes on to argue that some paternalistic intervention can be justified, even on Millian grounds, namely, restrictions that preserve a wider range of freedom for the individual in question.

The Public-Health Approach

Whereas Dworkin can be seen as attempting to justify very limited paternalistic measures, within a Millian perspective, Dan Beauchamp, a professor of public health, is a more outright critic of Mill. Beauchamp notes that some restrictions on individual liberty result in considerable social gain. Consider the example of seat belts. Each year roughly forty-five thousand people in the United States are killed in car crashes. Laws requiring the wearing of seat belts or making air bags compulsory would save roughly ten thousand lives a year. That's a lot of lives, a considerable social good. Libertarians object to seat-belt laws as being objectionably paternalistic. Why shouldn't I decide for myself whether to buckle up? Refusing to buckle up doesn't cause "harm to others" and so laws forcing people to use seat belts are not warranted on Millian grounds. But Beauchamp argues that, since the infringement on individual freedom is minuscule, and the social good so great, the intrusion is warranted. He supports "reasonable, minimally intrusive restrictions that yield significant gains in the health and safety of the public."[17]

I think that Beauchamp's public-health approach is far more useful in thinking about the legalization of drugs than the libertarian approach.[18] The libertarian insists that there isn't a drug problem, since trade is a positive sum game, and both parties gain. No one who has any experience with drug abuse and the social upheaval it has caused will agree with that conclusion. Instead of insisting, on ideological grounds, that individuals should have the right to buy whatever they want, regardless of the social costs, we should examine carefully the costs of prohibition and the costs of legalization. This means that the argument about legalization is not primarily a philosophical one. Rather, it is an empirical argument about the likely consequences of different strategies for dealing with the drug problem.

While the public-health approach rejects Mill's absolutist antipaternalism, it entirely agrees with Mill on one thing: the rejection of moralism. Mill argued that legal or social prohibitions on behavior could never be justified simply on the ground that the behavior in question was regarded by the majority as wicked or sinful. He insisted that infringements on individual liberty have to be justified by demonstrating that the conduct in question was likely to cause harm to others.

Of course it is not always easy to settle the question of whether an activity will cause harm to others: the example of violent pornography is a case in point. However, the rejection of moralism at least makes it clear what *kind* of argument is necessary to support coercive intervention. Empirical evidence of injury or the risk of injury is essential. Simply referring to moral principles, no matter how widely accepted, or moral feelings, no matter how strongly held, will not do. Someone who takes a public-health perspective may be willing to consider closing gay bathhouses *if* it is reasonable to think that this will slow the spread of a deadly disease, but will not be willing to infringe on individual liberty because the activities in such places are viewed by many as nasty or evil.

Why does the public-health perspective reject moralism? After all, if it is willing to acknowledge collective or communal values, such as health, why not acknowledge that there can be collective or communal *moral* values? Indeed, aren't free speech, equal opportunity, and the democratic process, which are essential to a democratic republic, *moral* values? Of course. The rejection of moralism does not consist in rejection of or neutrality toward all moral values. Rather, the rejection of moralism consists in opposition to coercion (as opposed to education and persuasion) to eradicate sin and vice or to make individuals morally better.

It might be objected that a public-health approach is based on a false distinction between different kinds of values. On a public-health approach, some government coercion is acceptable for the sake of certain values (for example, those connected to public health) but not others (for example, those related to private sexual behavior). A libertarian might argue that if it is permissible to infringe individual liberty for the sake of social goals, there is no principled reason for insisting that the goals to be achieved must be of a certain kind. If the majority in a society thinks that homosexuality is bad for society, then why shouldn't it pass laws against homosexuality? What justifies coercion for some social goals, but not others?[19] The answer has to do with a certain conception of the common good. The common good should not be understood in terms of whatever the majority values or wants. Such a conception would indeed threaten individual liberty through, in Mill's phrase, "the tyranny of the majority." Rather, I suggest that we think of the common good in terms of what Rawls calls "primary goods": "things which it is supposed a rational man wants whatever else he wants."[20] Health is an example of a primary good. By restricting our conception of the common good to primary goods, we avoid imposing goals and values on individuals that they do not happen to share. However, it may be objected that, even if it is true that everyone has reason to value his or her own health, it does not follow that everyone has reason to value the health of the community. (This was the mistake that Mill is supposed to have made in his proof of the principle of utility.) What if I am not interested in saving ten thousand lives a year? What justifies forcing me to buckle up?

I am not sure that it can be demonstrated that not caring about aggregate welfare or the good of society as a whole is *irrational*. However, the communitarian or republican morality of "We're all in this together" seems to me infinitely preferable to the extreme individualism which is concerned only with individuals' interests and rights. Republican morality balances individual virtues like self-reliance and individual responsibility against community virtues like beneficence, cooperation, and justice. As Dan Beauchamp puts it:

> Beneficence means that we wish the good and welfare of others as well as ourselves, while cooperation and justice mean that we as citizens are disposed to see that the common welfare is extended to all alike and do not allow our private interests to frustrate achievement of the common good. While the principles of individuality and community can often pull in opposite directions, both principles are needed to assure the fullest development of the individual and his dignity both as an autonomous person and as a member of the political fellowship.[21]

Recognition that there is a common good, as well as the separate welfares of individuals, does not preclude controversy over its nature. Moreover, even when individuals acknowledge a collective good, such as disease prevention, they may differ as to its importance relative to other collective goods. A public-health approach does not demand that we value life and health above all else. It merely supports minimally intrusive restrictions on individual liberty to promote the common good.

A related objection holds that even if it is possible to differentiate among social goods, so that infringement of individual liberty is restricted to primary collective goods, such as health, there is still a danger of imposing majoritarian moral views on individuals, because there is no morally neutral way to characterize even basic goods. All people may want to be healthy, but one's conception of health depends on one's particular moral or religious views. Whether one regards drug use, for example, as "unhealthy" depends on one's views about the body, altered consciousness, pleasure, industriousness, and, in general, the right way to live. It is this inability to characterize, in an objective fashion, basic goods that leads the libertarian to maintain that the assessment about what is worth pursuing should be left to individuals.

I think we can agree that there is an overlap between health and morality without conceding that it is impossible to distinguish the two. Individuals from widely divergent religious and moral backgrounds can agree on whether someone is sick, what disease he or she has, and whether something is a health risk. This suggests that there is a difference between health and morals, which makes it possible, in general, to distinguish arguments and reasons based on health considerations from those based on moral and religious values.

It must be admitted that much of American drug policy has been drenched in moralism. This moralistic attitude is revealed both in regarding addiction as a failure of willpower ("Just say no") and in wildly exaggerated descriptions of the effects of addiction. Here is a description of the effects of heroin from a concurring opinion by Justice Douglas in a 1962 United States Supreme Court decision:

> To be a confirmed drug addict is to be one of the walking dead. . . . The teeth have rotted out; the appetite is lost and the stomach and intestines don't function properly. The gall bladder becomes inflamed; eyes and skin turn a bilious yellow. In some cases membranes of the nose turn a flaming red; the partition separating the nostrils is eaten away—breathing is difficult. Oxygen in the blood decreases; bronchitis and tuberculosis develop. Good traits of character disappear and bad ones emerge. Sex organs become affected. Veins collapse and livid purplish scars remain. Boils and abscesses plague the skin; gnawing pain racks the body. Nerves snap; vicious twitching develops. Imaginary and fantastic fears blight the mind and sometimes complete insanity results. Often times, too, death comes—much too early in life. . . . Such is the torment of being a drug addict; such is the plague of being one of the walking dead.[22]

Similar lies were propagated about LSD in various newspaper stories, and about marijuana in such films as *Reefer Madness*. The effect, ironically enough, was to persuade a generation that any warnings about drug usage were likely to be completely untrustworthy.

Moralism about drugs is often coupled with hypocrisy about legal drugs. Schoolchildren are taught about the evils of illicit drugs, but the dangers of legal drugs are downplayed or ignored. A recent ad on television depicts a father confronting his child with marijuana found in his room, asking, "Who taught you to do this?" only to be told, "You did, Dad!" The announcer solemnly intones, "Parents who use drugs will have children who use drugs." Yet we don't see ads warning, "Parents who smoke and drink will have children who smoke and drink," despite the fact—as Professor Block notes—that far more people die from cigarettes and alcohol than from illegal drugs.

A public-health approach is pragmatic and non-ideological. It rejects moralism, and insists on sound empirical evidence for its claims. It recognizes the values of liberty and privacy, and supports the right of people to make their own choices about how they will live, free from governmental interference. At the same time, it recognizes that private acts can have social consequences.[23] Thus, a public-health approach balances the harm to individuals of coercive laws against the social good to be achieved. It is willing to sacrifice some individual liberty in order to achieve important collective goals, such as the saving of thousands of lives or the eradication of disease.

Implications for Drug Policy

The Failure of the War on Drugs

There is wide consensus on one thing: the penal approach to the drug problem has been a dismal failure. The United States has poured nearly $70 billion into fighting drugs in the last twenty years,[24] with very little to show for it. The reasons for the failure of the War on Drugs are primarily economic. Illicit drugs are big business. Seventy-nine billion dollars are generated every year by the sale of illicit drugs.[25] Only the Exxon Corporation has higher annual revenues.

In many less-developed countries, drug trafficking, which has provided a new way to earn vast sums of hard currency, is transforming whole economies. In poor Third World countries, coca is one of the few cash crops that grows well, much better than coffee or oranges. In Colombia, Bolivia, and Peru, many farmers have turned from growing food crops to growing marijuana and coca, which make them three or four times as much money a year.[26] In Bolivia, cocaine is estimated to generate as much as ten times the amount of Bolivia's leading official export, tin. Drug traffickers are at least as powerful as the government. They have more money than—and weapons and equipment as least as good as—the armed forces or the police. Moreover, drug traffickers are regarded by much of the populace as benefactors, not criminals. Even with the best will in the world, the government can do little to enforce laws that run counter to the vital economic interests of large numbers of its citizens. And that will is not always present. Mathea Falco, former Assistant Secretary of State for International Narcotics Matters, writes:

> It is very difficult to convince a foreign government to take the serious political and economic risks that are entailed by an all-out campaign against, say, cocaine production when the American public's predilection for cocaine is so well known. And it is virtually impossible to persuade foreign growers of marijuana to stop producing when one American in four has tried the drug—and billions of dollars in profits are being made by marijuana growers in the United States.[27]

Occasionally, the U.S. government has been able to solicit the cooperation of foreign governments to stop production, but often with unexpected results. In 1975, the Mexican government, with American assistance, began a program to eliminate the marijuana crop by spraying it with paraquat. Mexico, then a major supplier to the U.S. market of relatively cheap, low-potency marijuana, effectively destroyed much of the crop. Jamaica and Colombia, previously only minor suppliers of marijuana, quickly stepped up production, producing a plant of much higher potency. In addition, American domestic production of marijuana began to boom. Marijuana is currently the second-largest cash crop in the United States, just after corn and ahead of soybeans.

Throughout the 1980s, the Reagan and Bush administrations acted aggressively in mobilizing the agencies of the federal government in a coordinated attack on the drug supply from abroad and the distribution of drugs within the United States. Total federal spending on the War on Drugs rose from approximately $1 billion to $9 billion during the 1980s.[28] The crackdown yielded record numbers of drug seizures, arrests, and convictions. The Drug Enforcement Administration (DEA), the FBI, and Customs seized nearly half a billion dollars in drug-related assets in 1986. That year, the DEA arrested twice as many drug offenders as in 1982. From the end of 1980 to June 30, 1987, the prison population soared from 329,021 to 570,519. Roughly 40 percent of new prison inmates are incarcerated for drug offenses.

Should we conclude that the War on Drugs was a success? Not at all. None of this activity had any impact on either drug consumption or the drug market. Domestic marijuana cultivation took off and the black market in cocaine grew to record size. As the result of an abundant supply of cocaine, prices plummeted. "In 1980–81, a gram of cocaine cost $100 and averaged 12 percent purity at street level. By 1986, the price had fallen to as low as $80 ($50 in Miami), and the purity had risen to more than 50 percent. It rose to 70 percent purity in 1988. Around the nation, crack was marketed in $5 and $10 vials to reach the youth and low-income markets."[29] In hospitals, cocaine-related emergencies rose from 4,277 in 1982 to more than 46,000 in 1988. That trend began to go down in late 1989, but a new Federal report shows a 13 percent increase in hospital emergencies attributed to cocaine in the third quarter of 1991 and a 10 percent increase in emergency room visits from the use of heroin.[30]

This rapid expansion of supply and decline in price occurred despite President Reagan's increasing the federal anti-drug enforcement budget from $645 million in fiscal year 1981 to over $4 billion in fiscal year 1987. A third of that budget was specifically devoted to interdiction. Commenting in 1987 specifically upon the interdiction budget, the Office of Technology Assessment concluded:

> Despite a doubling of Federal expenditures on interdiction over the past five years, the quantity of drugs smuggled into the United States is greater than ever. . . . There is no clear correlation between the level of expenditures or effort devoted to interdiction and the long-term availability of illegally imported drugs in the domestic market.[31]

In 1992, the Bush Administration spent nearly $12 billion on drugs, more than double what was spent in Mr. Reagan's last year in office, two-thirds of it going to interdiction. "It reminds me of that cartoon," says Dr. Herbert Kleber, professor of medicine at Columbia University and a former deputy director of the Office of National Drug Control Policy who quit when he couldn't get more money shifted to treatment. "This king is slamming his fist on the table, saying, 'If all my horses and all my men can't put Humpty Dumpty together again, then what I need is *more* horses and *more* men.'"[32]

Why has the government continued to pour money and other resources into a failed policy? For the same reason, I suspect, that we stayed in Vietnam. In *The March of Folly*, Barbara Tuchman suggests that "Woodenheadedness . . . plays a remarkably large role in government. It consists in assessing a situation in terms of preconceived fixed notions while ignoring or rejecting any contrary signs. It is acting according to wish while not allowing oneself to be deflected by the facts."[33]

The War on Drugs has not simply failed. It's made things much worse. Steven Wisotsky writes:

> It has spun a spider's web of black-market pathologies, including roughly 25 percent of all urban homicides, widespread corruption of police and other public officials, street crime by addicts, and subversive "narco-terrorist" alliances between Latin American guerrillas and drug traffickers. In the streets of the nation's major cities, violent gangs of young drug thugs armed with automatic rifles engage in turf wars. Federal agents estimated in 1988 that more than 10,000 members of "posses" or Jamaican drug gangs were responsible for about 1,000 deaths na-

tionwide. Innocent bystanders and police officers are among their victims.[34]

Another negative effect of the War on Drugs has been a reduction in civil liberties.[35] The Supreme Court has upheld searches without probable cause, warrantees searches of automobiles, adopted a "good-faith exception" to the exclusionary rule, and authorized search of "open fields" adjacent to a residence. The power of the police to stop, question, detain, investigate, and search vehicles has expanded significantly. Wisotsky comments, "The net result of the War on Drugs is gradually, but inexorably, to expand enforcement powers at the expense of personal freedom."[36]

The War on Drugs mentality has prevented doctors from making authorized use of many controlled substances having valuable therapeutic applications. In 1984, the House of Representatives killed a bill that would have made injectable heroin available to dying cancer patients suffering severe, intense and intractable pain, when other drugs were ineffective. In California, patients with extremely debilitating cases of rheumatoid arthritis exhibited remarkable pain-free ability when they smoked freebase cocaine. Nevertheless, the government ended the experiment.

Most recently, the fight has centered around the use of marijuana as a medicinal drug. In March 1992, the Drug Enforcement Administration refused to reclassify marijuana as a Schedule II drug so doctors could prescribe it for patients suffering from glaucoma, cancer, muscular sclerosis, and AIDS.[37] A Federal appeals court had ruled the previous April that the government was using illogical criteria in prohibiting the use of marijuana for medical purposes, because the agency had based a conclusion that marijuana had no "currently accepted medical use" on factors like the drug's general availability, its use by a substantial number of doctors, and recognition of its use in medical texts. Since the drug is illegal, the court said, meeting these criteria would be all but impossible.

Robert C. Bonner, chief of the DEA, said that marijuana had not been shown to be as safe and effective as legal alternatives, such as Marinol, a synthetic form of THC, the active ingredient in marijuana. In his response to the appeals court,

Bonner said, "Beyond doubt, the claims that marijuana is medicine are false, dangerous and cruel. Sick men, women and children can be fooled by these claims and experiment with the drug. Instead of being helped, they risk serious side effects." Although made in the guise of scientific information, this is pure moralism. As Dr. Lester Grinspoon, an associate professor of psychiatry at Harvard Medical School who is the author of several books on marijuana's medicinal uses, says, "It's absolutely extraordinary that our government is behaving the way it is toward cannibis. They see legalizing it for medical use as a Trojan Horse for recreational use."[38]

There has been a surge in the last year in requests for medical marijuana by AIDS patients, and some advocates argue that this inspired the recent Government actions. "The government is not doing this to protect patients," said Kennington Wall, a spokesman for the Drug Policy Foundation in Washington, which advocates a liberal national drug policy. "They're doing this to protect their political agenda."[39]

Should Drugs Be Legalized?

If the War on Drugs has been a disaster, should drugs be legalized? A simple "yes" or "no" is impossible, partly because different drugs may require different responses, and partly because there are factual issues yet to be resolved. For example, what would be the effect of legalization on access and consumption? Some argue that legalization would have little impact on access, because illegal drugs are already easily available. More than half the high school seniors questioned by University of Michigan researchers in 1991 said that finding cocaine was "fairly easy" or "very easy." Nearly 40 percent said the same for crack and about a third for heroin.[40]

Others are convinced that, even if illegal drugs are already easy to obtain, legalization would make drugs even more accessible. This would lead to higher addiction rates, and thus worsen the already massive problems faced by the inner city. Many advocates for inner-city communities view illegal drugs as one aspect of the dominant society's oppression of their communities. Legalization "is construed as an expression of disdain for and dismissal of the misery that drugs bring to inner cities."[41]

Block thinks that legalization will not increase the number of addicts for three reasons. First, although the price of drugs can be expected to go down, this will have little effect on the behavior of addicts who regard drugs as a necessity, not a luxury. Second, there will be little incentive for addicts to try to "hook" others to support their own habits. Third, even if quantity increases, potency will fall. Prohibition leads to stronger and stronger drugs, which are both more concentrated and have higher value. Therefore, even if greater amounts of drugs are consumed under legalization, they are likely to be less harmful to the population.

Block may be right about the effect of legalization on consumption and addiction. Still, it should be remembered that *three times* as many Americans abuse alcohol as use illegal drugs. Why? Because alcohol is legal, it is easy to buy, it is an accepted part of our culture. If addictive drugs were legal, it seems likely that entrepreneurs would cultivate or manufacture them, package them, and advertise them, just as they do alcohol. And it is reasonable to believe that this would result in higher consumption, greater abuse, and a higher rate of addiction.

If the end result of legalization is higher addiction rates, this is a serious argument against legalization, from a public-health perspective. Astoundingly, it has no bearing at all on a libertarian view. Block says:

> Assume, for instance, that 75 percent of the population, just to pick a number out of a hat, were to become addicted. We still maintain that there is again nothing in the realm of positive economics, nor of normative libertarian political theory, that can serve as the basis for prohibition. It will still be true that all parties concerned will gain, in their own subjective estimates, from their participation in the drug market. It will still be true that the industry will be a totally voluntary one, with no one forced to take part. Hence, libertarian theory still proscribes interdiction. (p. 211)

However, this is less an argument for legalization than an argument against libertarianism. When a theory has absurd results—

in this case, a total disregard for the disastrous effects of addiction on society—the adequacy of the theory must be questioned.

Sometimes the argument in favor of legalization is based on claims about what we learned from Prohibition. It is often said that Prohibition "didn't work": that people went right on drinking in speakeasies, which facilitated the rise of organized crime and led ordinary citizens to lose respect for the law. In fact, by public-health standards, narrowly construed, Prohibition was a success. Consumption of alcohol fell by more than two-thirds, and cirrhosis rates fell to half the level that obtained in 1910. Two years after repeal, total consumption of alcohol was only one-third of the 1910 level.[42]

Nevertheless, Prohibition was a failure, because it was unduly moralistic, restrictive, and repressive. Moreover, it was unnecessary. As Beauchamp says, ". . . most of what we could accomplish in health and safety under Prohibition could be achieved through more stringent regulation of alcohol. Prohibition is something like ringing a doorbell with a cannon."[43]

It might be argued that it is equally unnecessary to ban addictive drugs, even if one is concerned about their impact on the nation's health and safety. Perhaps we could legalize or decriminalize the sale of addictive drugs, while keeping their availability severely restricted. However, there is an important difference between alcohol and illicit drugs, and that is simply that alcohol is currently legal. Millions of Americans have grown up regarding alcohol as a normal and socially acceptable part of life. Having wine in a restaurant, champagne at weddings, and beer at picnics are pleasures of which many Americans would resent being deprived. Prohibition of alcohol is politically impossible.

Because narcotic and opiate drugs have been illegal since the beginning of this century, they aren't viewed by most people as something to which they have a right. *Keeping* drugs illegal would not engender widespread anger and resentment, as *making* alcohol illegal would. The question faced by policy-makers and ordinary citizens is whether we should opt for changing the law, and legalizing addictive drugs. The risks and harms posed by addictive drugs provide a powerful argument against changing the status quo. No doubt it is for this reason that Beauchamp supports "a policy that combines legal suppression of supply, both here and abroad, with more humane and compassionate treatment of users and addicts, even offering some form of maintenance as an alternative to obtaining drugs in illegal settings."[44]

Interestingly enough, Block does not seem so far from Beauchamp on this matter. He says, "Suppose you ... had a child addicted to narcotics. Would you prefer a situation where he had to run around like a half-crazed wretch, doing all sorts of unspeakable things in order to raise the requisite funds for his habit, never knowing where his next fix was coming from, nor what would be in it, or one where he could be given an injection in safe, comfortable, clean hospital surroundings, under the care of a physician?" (p. 213–214) Here, Block seems to drop his libertarian stance. As he acknowledges in endnote 11, a real libertarian is committed to allowing drugs to be advertised and marketed, like alcohol. In suggesting something along the lines of the British model, where registered addicts receive drugs by prescription, Block is adopting something that resembles a public-health approach. This approach recognizes that an all-out War on Drugs and a completely free market are not the only two possibilities.

A pragmatic approach also requires us to distinguish between drugs. The case for keeping cocaine and heroin illegal is much stronger than the case for keeping marijuana illegal. Marijuana is not addictive, that is, there is no physical dependence or withdrawal. Psychological dependence appears to be minimal or nonexistent.[45] Sixty-two million Americans have tried marijuana at least once, and roughly 18 million use it regularly.[46] While marijuana is not risk-free (especially for adolescents and pregnant women), there is considerable evidence that it is much less harmful than alcohol. Yet there are approximately one-half million arrests per year for marijuana, almost all for simple possession or petty sale offenses.[47] It is hard to see what social goals require that the criminal justice system be overburdened in this way.

A public-health approach toward drugs would require various measures. First and foremost, it requires continuing education about the benefits and dangers of both legal and illegal drugs. But a public-health approach goes beyond mere education. It supports getting tough on the legal drugs by such measures as getting rid of cigarette vending machines so that cigarettes are not so readily available to minors; restricting the hours of sale of liquor; and levying raising taxes on these items, commensurate with their social costs—billions of dollars in property damage, disease, and lost productivity.[48] At the same time, the respect for individual choice and the rejection of moralism that are part of the public-health approach[49] require that we remain open to the possibility that some currently illegal but comparatively harmless drugs, such as marijuana, should be legalized. And even if we decide to keep cocaine and heroin illegal, the emphasis should be on treatment. For most of the Reagan years, only about 20 percent of the budget went to treatment and education. This rose to about 30 percent under Bush. Despite Clinton's campaign rhetoric, it is still woefully inadequate, according to many experts. Studies indicate that present prevention and treatment efforts reach only 10 percent of alcohol and drug abusers.[50] In addition, there is also very limited research on which prevention and treatment programs work. Dr. Herbert D. Kleber, a former deputy director in the Federal Office of National Drug Control Policy and one of the organizers of the recently created Center on Addiction and Substance Abuse in Manhattan, jokes about the "four-two-one" syndrome in medical school, meaning that in four years of medical school, students get two hours of instruction on the nation's No. 1 health problem, drug abuse. Obviously, this lack of attention must be addressed if we are to combat effectively the drug problem.

Conclusion

This paper does not attempt to answer the complex question whether drugs should be legalized. The answer to that question hinges on various empirical issues, such as whether legalization would increase addiction rates. Instead, my aim has been to show that the right approach to the problem of drug addiction is a public-health perspective, as opposed to the libertarian analysis provided by Professor Block. Whereas the libertarian insists on absolute freedom of choice, regardless of social costs, the public-health approach balances the values of liberty and autonomy against the values of health and safety. It rejects the uncompromising stances characteristic of both moralism and libertarian ideology. Above all, a public-health approach insists that policies must be based on an honest appraisal of the problem and accurate empirical evidence about what does and does not work to solve it.[51]

NOTES

1. Joseph B. Treaster, "Hospital Visits Show Abuse of Drugs Is Still on the Rise," *New York Times*, May 14, 1992, A16. According to other estimates, 2 million Americans are addicted to cocaine; 1 million use heroin; 18 million have drinking problems or are alcoholics, and 10 million abuse barbiturates or other prescription drugs. (Kathleen Teltsch, "3 Joining to Start Center Against Substance Abuse," *New York Times*, May 18, 1992, B3.)

2. Michel Marriott, "After 3 Years, Crack Plague in New York Only Gets Worse," *New York Times*, February 20, 1989, A1.

3. Joseph B. Treaster, "20 Years of War on Drugs, and No Victory Yet," *New York Times*, Sunday, June 14, 1992, E7.

4. The above facts come from Michel Marriott (see note 2). There are signs that the crack epidemic, which peaked in 1988, is beginning to abate. A decline in the use of cocaine by pregnant women, combined with improved prenatal care, helped significantly reduce infant mortality in New York City in 1990 for the first time in four years. (Celia W. Dugger, "Infant Mortality in New York City Declines for First Time in 4 Years," *New York Times*, April 20, 1991, p. 1.)

5. Anna Quindlen, "Hearing the Cries of Crack," *New York Times*, October 7, 1990, E19.

6. Editorial in *New York Times*, May 28, 1989, E14.

7. Letter to the Editor, *New York Times*, November 20, 1989, A22.

8. Howard W. French, "New York Sees Rise in Babies Hurt by Drugs," *New York Times*, October 18, 1989, B1.

9. T. Berry Brazelton, "Is America Failing Its Children?" *New York Times Magazine*, September 9, 1990, p. 90.

10. The right of a surviving child to recover in a civil suit for pre-natally caused injuries has been upheld in the United States since the landmark case of *Bonbrest* v. *Kotz*, 65 F. Supp. 138 (1946).

11. For a fuller discussion of this point, see my *Life Before Birth: The Moral and Legal Status of Embryos and Fetuses* (Oxford University Press, 1992), especially Chapter 4, "Maternal-Fetal Conflict."

12. "Hour by Hour: Crack," *Newsweek*, November 28, 1988, p. 75.

13. Brazelton (see note 9), p. 90.

14. This argument for limited paternalism works only when there are alternative safe medications. If conventional medicine can do noth-ing for someone who is going to die, it is rational to want access to new treatments, even if they are unproven and potentially dangerous. This kind of argument is often heard from terminally ill cancer patients and AIDS activists. However, even AIDS activists do not want to abolish the FDA, only relax some of its standards for new drugs to treat AIDS.

15. See Richard D. Mohr, "AIDS, Gays, and State Coercion," *Bioethics* 1:1 (1987), pp. 35–50.

16. Gerald Dworkin, "Paternalism," *The Monist* 56:1. Reprinted in Ronald Munson, ed., *Intervention and Reflection: Basic Issues in Medical Ethics*, 4th edition (Belmont, CA: Wadsworth, 1992), pp. 276–87, at p. 282.

17. Dan E. Beauchamp, *The Health of the Republic: Epidemics, Medicine, and Moralism as Challenges to Democracy* (Philadelphia: Temple University Press, 1988), p. 89. Actually, Beauchamp objects to character-izing laws requiring the wearing of seat belts as "paternalism." The rea-son is that, in this case, the individual is not coerced for his *own* good—the chance of any one individual being killed in a car crash is minuscule. Rather, the good to be achieved is a communal or collective good, namely, a reduction in aggregate levels of death and injury.

18. For a detailed application of a public-health approach to the drug problem, see James F. Mosher and Karen I. Yanagisako, "Public Health, Not Social Warfare: A Public Health Approach to Illegal Drug Policy," *Journal of Public Health Policy* (Autumn 1991), pp. 278–321.

19. This objection was suggested to me by Betty Daniel.

20. John Rawls, *A Theory of Justice* (Cambridge, MA: Harvard Uni-versity Press, 1971), p. 92.

21. Dan Beauchamp, "Life-Style, Public Health and Paternalism," in S. Doxiadis, ed., *Ethical Dilemmas in Health Promotion*, Chapter 7 (John Wiley & Sons Ltd, 1987), p. 71.

22. *Robinson* v. *California*, 370 U.S. 660, 672 (1962) Douglas, W.O., concurring.

23. *Private Acts, Social Consequences* (The Free Press, 1989) is the title of a book about AIDS by Ronald Bayer, professor of public health at the Columbia University School of Public Health.

24. Treaster, "20 Years of War on Drugs" (see note 3).

25. Mathea Falco, "The Big Business of Illicit Drugs," in Robert Emmet Long, ed., *Drugs and American Society* (New York: The H. W. Wilson Company, 1986), p. 8.

26. Ibid., p. 10.

27. Ibid., p. 15–16.

28. Steven Wisotsky, *Beyond the War on Drugs: Overcoming a Failed Public Policy* (Buffalo, NY: Prometheus Books, 1990), p. xviii.

29. Ibid., p. xix.

30. Treaster, "Hospital Visits Show Abuse of Drugs Is Still on the Rise" (see note 1).

31. Cited in Wisotsky (see note 28), p. xx.

32. Treaster, "20 Years of War on Drugs" (see note 3).

33. Barbara Tuchman, *The March of Folly: From Troy to Vietnam* (New York: Ballantine Books, 1984), p. 7.

34. Wisotsky (see note 28), p. xx.

35. In light of this, it is ironic that Mill thought that the preventive function of government was more dangerous to liberty than the punitory function. Beauchamp argues that Mill had this exactly backward (see note 21, p. 77).

36. Wisotsky (see note 28), p. 125.

37. Joseph B. Treaster, "Agency Says Marijuana Is Not Proven Medicine," *New York Times*, Thursday, March 19, 1992, B11.

38. Katherine Bishop, "Marijuana Still a Drug, Not a Medicine," *New York Times*, March 22, 1992, E5.

39. Treaster, "Agency Says Marijuana Is Not Proven Medicine" (see note 37).

40. Treaster, "20 Years of War on Drugs" (see note 3).

41. Although they do not accept this analysis, Mosher and Yanagisako acknowledge that it is a widely held view among advocates for inner-city communities. (See note 18), p. 314.

42. Beauchamp (see note 21), p. 179.

43. Ibid., p. 189.

44. Ibid., p. 196.

45. James C. Weissman, *Drug Abuse: The Law and Treatment Alternatives* (Anderson Publishing Company, 1978), p. 89.

46. National Institute on Drug Abuse, "Highlights of the 1985 National Household Survey on Drug Abuse: National Institute on Drug Abuse," *NIDA Capsules* (November 1986).

47. Wisotsky (see note 28), p. xxv.

48. Ibid., p. xxviii.

49. For a detailed defense of the view that respect for privacy and autonomy are not opposed to, but part of, a public-health approach, see Beauchamp, *The Health of the Republic* (note 21).

50. Kathleen Teltsch (see note 1).

51. I would like to thank Professor Dan E. Beauchamp of the School of Public Health at the University at Albany, Professor Steven Burton of the University of Iowa Law School and Professor Betty Daniel of the Economics Department at the University at Albany for helpful comments on an earlier version of this paper.

Punishment

Should Drug Crimes Be Punished?

Stephen Nathanson

In approaching the question whether "drug crimes" should be punished, I have in mind two kinds of actions. The first involves the use of presently illegal drugs like marijuana, cocaine, and heroin, or the possession of these drugs for private use. The second involves the production, transportation, or sale of these drugs to others. For brevity, I will refer to "use" and "sales" as the acts I have in mind. My question, then, is whether the use and/or sale of these illegal drugs ought to be punished.

This question, in turn, is related to the question whether the use and sale of drugs ought to be illegal. Indeed, one might think that these questions are identical. After all, if one favors making these acts illegal, then one is willing to enact legal prohibitions of them, and what puts teeth into such prohibitions is that a penalty is attached to their violation. Without the threat of punishment, a legal prohibition amounts to no more than a recommendation and hence is not a prohibition at all. For this reason, it looks as if asking whether drug use and sales should be illegal is the same as asking whether they should be punished.

Likewise, if one opposes making these acts illegal, thinking (for example) that people have a right to use drugs if they wish, then it would be odd to think that people ought to be punished for using drugs. To favor punishing them would, on this view, amount to favoring the punishment of people for actions they have a right to perform.

Nonetheless, the legalization question and the punishment question are not identical. It is possible, for example, to favor drug prohibition and to oppose punishing drug users on the ground that rehabilitation is preferable to punishment. In addition, it is possible to oppose the passage of laws against drugs and yet to believe that if such laws are passed, then as long as they are on the books, they should be enforced and people who violate them should be punished.

So, the question whether drug use and sales should be illegal is not identical with the question of whether people ought to be punished for using and selling drugs. Nonetheless, these questions are closely related. Even if one favors rehabilitation rather than punishment, such rehabilitation has a coercive aspect to it, and refusal to take part would presumably lead to punishment. Moreover, while there are many forms of undesirable behavior, one way of testing whether we favor legal prohibition, as opposed to other means of discouraging such behavior, is to ask whether we think it appropriate to punish people who engage in such acts. If we do not think punishment appropriate, that may indicate that legal prohibition is the wrong strategy.[1]

In this paper, then, I will address the question of whether it is morally appropriate to punish people who use or sell drugs, with the hope that this will shed some light on the question of whether drug use and sales should be legal or illegal. I will investigate the punishment issue primarily by asking what the traditional retributive and utilitarian theories of punishment imply about punishing people for using or selling drugs.

Retributivism and the Punishment of Drug Use

Retributivist theories of punishment constitute a family of ideas about the justification of punishment and the determination of which punishment is appropriate.[2] In analyzing and justifying punishment, retributivists focus on the notion of desert. A person should be punished only if she deserves to be punished. The paradigm cases of morally justified punishment involve acts that are harmful to others and that are deliberately initiated with malicious intent *(mens rea)*. In these paradigm cases, one person harms another and does so in a way that leads us to believe that the agent deserves to be punished. In determining how much punishment a person deserves, retributivists take a number of different approaches, but they tend to focus on the degree of harm to the victim, the intention of the agent, and other factors such as the ease or difficulty of avoiding the action.

In applying the retributivist perspective, some people focus exclusively on the harm done to the victim, using it as a criterion both for justifying punishment and for determining its severity. People who focus on the amount of harm done tend to support either the "equality retribution" ideal expressed in the familiar biblical saying, "an eye for an eye and a tooth for a tooth," or the "proportional retribution" view that the suffering to be imposed on the offender should be proportional to that imposed on the victim. According to these views, it is legitimate to impose a result on the criminal that is equal or proportional to the harm done to the victim.[3]

When we seek to apply these ideas to drug use, it is immediately clear that they are ill suited to it, just as they are ill suited to other "victimless" crimes. In typical cases of drug use, there is no direct harm done to others. A person uses a forbidden substance and may harm herself, but her action need not impose any harm on anyone else. Hence, if we are to apportion punishment according to harm done, then using this approach would lead us to deny that any punishment is appropriate.

In special circumstances, others may be harmed by one's personal drug use. A pregnant woman who takes drugs, for example, may harm a fetus, or a railroad engineer may endanger passengers. I ignore these cases here in part because anti-drug laws were not passed with these kinds of effects in mind. Similarly, I ignore other nonstandard cases in which currently illegal drugs would have medical value, easing the pain of patients who would otherwise suffer badly. If our concern were with the collateral effects of drugs, we would treat drugs much differently than we do, not banning them entirely but making their use illegal only when others were endangered.

Now one might say that it doesn't matter whether the person harmed is oneself or someone else. Kant argued that we had duties to respect the humanity in ourselves just as we do to respect it in others.[4] Even if one puts aside the lack of another person as victim, however, the "eye for an eye" approach does not get us very far. Applied literally, it would require us to punish drug users by making them use more drugs (doing to them what they have already done to themselves). Needless to say, this is not quite what advocates of prohibition have in mind.

We encounter other problems if we focus on the intentions of the drug user in order to determine desert. Typically, a drug user has no malicious intent. He or she is seeking pleasure, relief, escape, or satisfaction of need. Even if the user believes that drugs are harmful, the act of taking the drug is not usually done with the intention of bringing about this harm. Whatever harm occurs is an unintended but foreseeable result. Borrowing a military term, we could say that it is the "collateral damage" that accompanies drug use, but it is not the point of taking drugs.

Finally, in assessing desert, we often ask how easy or difficult it is for a person to do or avoid an action. From this perspective, for example, a poor swimmer who risks her life to rescue a drowning child would deserve more moral credit than an expert swimmer who knows she can save the child easily. Likewise, a person who commits a crime under extreme duress (e.g., someone who steals a loaf of bread to avert starvation) would be considered less blameworthy than a well-fed thief.[5]

Looking at drug use from this perspective, we get the result that an addicted person is either minimally deserving of punishment or not blameworthy at all. If refraining from drug use requires extraordinary efforts, then succumbing to use occurs under a degree of duress which either excuses or mitigates the blameworthiness of the act. From this perspective, addicts might be less blameworthy than novices or other non-addicted users.

Even in the latter cases, however, one might want to assess the person's total situation.[6] One image of the drug user is the person whose life is dismal and provides few sources of deep gratification. The temptation to use drugs is powerful because they provide a form of deep satisfaction that is otherwise lacking in the user's life. As James Q. Wilson, an advocate of drug prohibition, acknowledges, "The simple fact is that heroin use is intensely pleasurable, for many people more pleasurable than anything else they might do."[7] If this is true, it would be a strong mitigating factor against punishment.

Opponents of retributivism often suggest that it provides no real grounding for punishment or that it reduces to a desire for revenge against wrongdoers. One can construct a coherent retributivist rationale for punishment by following a suggestion of Herbert Morris and claiming that the point of punishment is to take away the ill-gotten gains of the criminal.[8] According to Morris, when people break the law they get extra advantages that other citizens forego. Punishment is justified because it restores things to a moral equilibrium by offsetting the ill-gotten gains of the criminal with the losses imposed in punishment.

Applying this model to drug use, one could say that the reason that drugs are prohibited is to prevent people from experiencing illicit pleasures. People who use drugs and gain these pleasures acquire an unfair advantage over law-abiding citizens who deny themselves these pleasures. On this model, unlike the "eye-for-an-eye" model, punishment does not seek to return evil for evil done. Rather, it seeks to offset illicit goods through imposing licit harms.

While Morris succeeds in providing a coherent, overall defense of the retributivism, his account fails to provide a plausible rationale for punishing drug users. Applying his model to drug use neglects entirely the concerns people express about the harmfulness of drugs, and yet this appears to be a central reason for prohibiting them. From the perspective of Morris's model, the dangerous ill effects of drugs have nothing to do with the punishment. Drugs are prohibited for the pleasures they produce rather than the harms they do, and punishment seeks to balance out these illicit, drug-produced pleasures. From this perspective, laws against drug use are like laws against homosexual sex and are quite different from laws against using laetrile or driving without a seat belt. In the latter cases, the law protects people from harms that they might not protect themselves from and not from pleasures that we do not want them to enjoy. If we punish people because we regard the pleasures their drug use produces as illicit, then we are not trying to prevent them from harming themselves, and the ill effects of drugs become irrelevant. Yet their ill effects seem to be a central concern and provide the basic rationale for drug prohibition.[9]

Second, if drugs really are harmful, then the illicit pleasures of users will not add up to a net gain for them over other
citizens. The pleasures of drug use are, in Bentham's terminol-
ogy, "impure" pleasures.[10] They tend to be followed automatically by negative consequences which can be seen as a natural
punishment for the illicit pleasures gained. Further punishment
is unnecessary to restore the moral equilibrium because the
scales are naturally rebalanced. Law-abiding citizens continue to
be better off than drug users even without the intervention of the
law.

Overall, then, retributivism seems ill suited for justifying
the punishment of drug use. This is because a major component
of the justification for prohibiting drugs is the paternalistic justification. It is claimed that drug use harms people and that we
need laws to prevent people from harming themselves. The
problem in applying a retributivist model to justify punishing
drug users is that the retributive model is not well suited to
violations of paternalistic laws. All of the central ingredients that
enter into the paradigm on which retributivism rests are missing.
In typical cases of drug use, there is neither harm to others nor
malicious intent, and the notion of doing to the offender what
the offender has done to the victim simply makes no sense in this
context.

Retributivism and Drug Sales

One might think that if we move from drug use to drug
sales, then some of the problems about justifying punishment
retributively will disappear. If a person knowingly provides
harmful drugs to another person, then the provider harms the
user. Hence, on retributive grounds, one might think that some
equivalent harm could legitimately be imposed on the seller.

Even here, however, the justification of punishment runs
into difficulties. Granting that drugs are harmful, it does not follow that it is the seller who harms the user or who is primarily
responsible for the drug's ill effects. For, in typical cases, the
seller does not force the user to obtain or use drugs. Nor need
the seller withhold information about the drug's effects from the

user. If the user knows about a drug's positive and negative effects and voluntarily purchases it, it is not clear that we can hold the seller responsible for harming the user. The user is harming himself.

In some cases, the claim that the seller harms the user is more plausible. If the user is a child or someone ignorant of the effects of the drug or if the seller forces the user into taking drugs, entices the user into trying a drug by describing its pleasurable effects but not its damaging ones, or provides impure drugs that are especially threatening without informing the user, then we could classify the seller's actions as cases of harming the user. But if the seller is no more than a source of something that the user wants and fully understands, then the responsibility for harmful effects would appear to rest primarily with the user rather than the seller.

Note, too, that the seller might intend no harm to the user and might even be acting under conditions of psychological duress, needing to sell drugs to support his own addiction. If the seller has no other ways of paying for his own supply, it might be especially difficult to refrain from selling drugs. In such cases, whatever punishment the seller might deserve would be mitigated by the magnitude of the effort required to refrain from selling drugs to support his own habit.

Whether the seller deserves punishment, then, depends on the role that the seller plays. If he or she is merely a provider of drugs to people who already want them, then retributive grounds for punishment seem to be lacking. In other cases, the seller may be an enticer, causing people who otherwise might not use drugs to find them appealing and thus playing a more significant role in generating drug use. As enticer, the seller bears a greater responsibility for causing drug-related harms and may be a legitimate target of punishment. The more vigorous the efforts at enticement are, the more responsibility falls upon the seller.[11]

In making these points, I do not mean to condone the act of selling drugs. I am interested in assessing the blameworthiness of people who sell drugs and not the rightness of their actions. Perhaps surprisingly, it turns out that a careful look at drug selling from a retributivist perspective does not lead to blanket approval of punishment for this act. Punishment is appropriate where the seller is chiefly responsible for the harmful effects by virtue of using coercion, intentionally misleading users about the effects of the drug or providing them to children. In other cases, a retributive analysis does not appear to support the claim that sellers ought to be punished.

Utilitarianism and the Punishment of Drug Use

Utilitarianism aims for the highest level of well-being that we can produce. It supports the imposition of punishment when (and only when) punishing produces better results than not punishing.[12] People who favor prohibition of drugs because of their ill effects probably assume that prohibition and punishment of drug use produce better results than legalization. After all, it is plausible to suppose that prohibition and punishment will diminish the amount of drug use and drug-related harms, thus preventing evils that would occur under more permissive policies.

This is certainly one possibility, but it is not the only one, and, if there is one striking thing about utilitarianism, it is the way the theory stresses the importance of contingency. If punishing drug users maximizes utility, then utilitarians will be all for it, but if other policies produce better effects, utilitarians will simply abandon prohibition. Some may see this as moral fickleness, but utilitarians defend it as the essence of a rational morality.

In addition, since utilitarians stress the value of pleasure, they will tend not to deplore the pleasures of drug use. For Bentham and many other utilitarians, a pleasure is a pleasure, and it can only be criticized if the way of bringing it about brings pains that are greater. Utilitarians will not support the kind of puritan attitudes that make some people skeptical about the use of drugs as a means of obtaining pleasure.[13]

The most powerful utilitarian argument for punishing drug use is that it would prevent the damage and suffering that drug use can produce. Since this damage is typically self-inflicted, prohibition is best justified on paternalistic grounds.

The utilitarian threatens punishment to prevent people from harming themselves. If the threat works, then all is well. No harmful punishment has been imposed, and no harmful drugs have been taken.

But what if the threat of punishment does not work? Here things become more complex. Surprisingly, recent defenders of paternalism do not consider this question. Unlike Bentham, they are only concerned with deciding whether there are good utilitarian grounds for over-riding a person's own desires, and appear not to worry about the negative effects of enforcing paternalistic laws.[14] This question needs to be addressed, however, if we want to consider legal paternalism as opposed to other informal forms of deterring self-inflicted harms.

If we ban drug use, then, in order to protect people from self-inflicted harm, what should we do to a person who ignores the law and uses drugs? Suppose the user has worsened her situation through drug use and that we now impose a punishment. Though we began with benevolent motives, we are now worsening her situation by punishing her. This is not the result we wanted. Our aim was to protect her from harm, but our punishment for drug use only compounds the harm already done.

Whether punishment is actually counterproductive in this way depends very much on the severity of the punishment. If a light punishment is sufficient to discourage further use, then the benefits of discontinuing drug use may justify the punishment. The problem is that the desire for drugs is often very strong, so a light punishment is probably not sufficient to deter use. The desire to deter use will probably lead, then, to the imposition of severe punishments. Unfortunately, in order for the punishment to be severe enough to have a realistic chance of deterring future use, it may have to be so severe that it makes the punished user much worse off than she would have been if she had been permitted to use drugs.

This is more than a hypothetical possibility. There are now thousands of people serving prison terms and suffering grievously in ways that probably surpass whatever damage drugs might have done to their lives. Any utilitarian analysis of our current policies must take these negative effects into account.

In other cases of paternalistic laws, we treat people quite differently. A cancer sufferer, for example, who desperately seeks out laetrile treatment may actually be harming himself. We would pity such a person and would not want to make his situation worse, even though the law prohibits this treatment. While we might favor punishing those who administer laetrile, I doubt we would favor punishing those who wish to use it. Likewise, we may impose small fines on people who ride in cars without seat belts or ride motorcycles without helmets, but it would be strange to impose severe penalties (such as prison terms) on them under the rubric of trying to prevent them from suffering harm.

If we think about punishing people who violate paternalistic laws from a utilitarian perspective, then, we are led to the conclusion that while punishments may be justified, they must not be so severe that they actually worsen the condition of users beyond what it would have been if they had been permitted to use drugs.

At this point, one might properly object that we need to measure the value of the punishment not simply by looking at its effects on individual users but by looking at the overall effects of either punishing or not punishing drug use. While a particular user may be worse off than he would have been under a permissive law, his example and the general practice of punishing users may deter a sufficiently large number of people from using drugs and thus protect them from drug-related harms. So, even though some individuals are worse off under prohibition, the overall level of well-being may be higher. This is because of the general deterrence value of punishment. One person's suffering sets an example for others, deterring them from drug use and thereby sparing them from the harmful effects of drugs.

This general deterrence scenario is quite reasonable from a utilitarian perspective, and if things work out this way, utilitarians would approve the imposition of punishment on drug users. But suppose they don't work out this way. Suppose that in spite of the punishment of some, many others continue to use drugs. Or suppose that other negative side effects of prohibition become significant—large expenditures of government money, the growth of black markets and criminal enterprises, spiraling violence among drug sellers, corruption of police and other government officials. If these negative effects occur or if deterrence simply fails, then the punishment of those drug users who are caught and convicted will not be justified.

The crucial thing about punishment and deterrence from a utilitarian view is that punishment is only justified if it actually works, where "works" means succeeds in preventing the harms of drug taking without producing worse side effects. If punishment fails to have these good effects, then the suffering of those who are punished brings down the overall level of well-being in society and is therefore wrong. Many people have reached the conclusion that that is our situation.[15] They believe that drug prohibition does more harm than good. If they are right, then punishment of drug users is not only lacking in justification; it is in fact a grievous moral wrong.

These same points apply to sellers as well as users. The punishment of sellers is justified only if it leads to a better balance of well-being over ill-being. From a utilitarian perspective, the punishing of sellers rather than users is more attractive because punishing one seller might protect many users from drug-related harms. This is both more efficient and more humane than punishing individual users.

This view, however, presupposes that punishing individual sellers will diminish the number of sellers and make drugs harder to obtain. This might not happen, however. If the incentives to sell drugs are sufficiently large and people's alternative options are restricted or unappealing, then new sellers may appear, hydra-like, for every one who is prevented from selling.

Utilitarians, then, will favor the punishment of drug crimes, but only if doing so actually reduces drug-related harms without producing other significant negative consequences. To the extent that a "war on drugs" fails and is known to be a failure, the punishment of anyone as part of such an effort will not pass the utilitarian's test for a justified punishment.

It is worth noting that Bentham was extremely skeptical about the use of punishment for paternalistic purposes or, as he put it, to enforce "the dictates of prudence." He writes:

> With what chance of success, for example, would a legislator go about to extirpate drunkenness and fornication by

dint of legal punishment? Not all the tortures which inge-
nuity could invent would compass it: and before he had
made any progress worth regarding, such a mass of evil
would be produced by the punishment, as would exceed,
a thousand-fold, the utmost possible mischief of the
offense.[16]

This is a warning that others who seek the general happiness
need to take seriously.

The Problem of Arbitrariness

There is a final test that is worth considering when we
evaluate the legitimacy of punishments. When we ask whether
the punishment of a person is just, we need to consider not simply what that person has done or deserves but also how other
people who have acted in similar ways have been treated.[17]

Several members of the Supreme Court invoked this principle in the 1972 case of *Furman v. Georgia*. The court ruled that
the death penalty, as then administered, was unconstitutional
because it was imposed in an arbitrary and capricious manner.
Whether a convicted murderer was sentenced to prison or to
death appeared to be a purely arbitrary fact that in no way
correlated with facts about the nature of his or her crime. Of
those who were deserving of death, only some were sentenced to
die and others were not, and this occurred for no good reason.

The lesson of *Furman* is that a person can be unjustly
punished even if he is guilty and deserves to be punished. This is
the case if other people are equally deserving and for no good
reason receive lesser punishments or none at all.[18]

This principle is relevant to the drug case in the following
way. We know that while some harmful substances (heroin, cocaine, etc.) are legally prohibited and some people are punished
for selling and using them, other extremely harmful substances
(tobacco and alcohol) are legally permitted. People are permitted
to drink alcohol and smoke cigarettes, even though these are
quite damaging to health. Likewise, people are permitted to sell
these substances, in spite of the grievous harmful effects they
produce.

Hence, drug users can legitimately complain about being punished on the ground that others are not punished for engaging in behavior that is similar in the relevant respects, using harmful substances to produce pleasure. Likewise, drug sellers can legitimately complain about being imprisoned while purveyors of cigarettes and alcohol are not punished, make large profits, and even hold high-status positions in society.

There is surely both irony and injustice in punishing those who use and sell heroin, cocaine and other drugs on the grounds that these are harmful while, at the same time, those who use and sell alcohol and tobacco suffer no similar penalties. Alcohol is estimated to be the direct cause of 80,000 to 100,000 deaths per year in the United States, a contributing cause in another 100,000 deaths, and the source of annual financial costs to the U.S of over $100 billion. In addition, in the U.S., it is estimated that tobacco use causes 320,000 premature deaths each year.[19] Yet, use and sales of these substances are widely accepted as legitimate activities, and no one is punished for either personal use or sales.

Others who have debated about legalization have often pointed out these arbitrary features of our policies but have accepted them with resignation. For example, after raising this point, James Bakalar and Lester Grinspoon write that "It is useless to protest against this in the name of abstract consistency and rationality. . . ."[20] What is missed in this resigned dismissal of the arbitrariness problem is that these inconsistent policies are a source of serious injustice. As a result of them, some people are severely punished for engaging in actions that are quite analogous to other actions that people are permitted to perform without interference. It is as if people who played baseball were left alone while those who played tennis were imprisoned.

No legal system is perfect, of course, and complete consistency cannot be expected. Nonetheless, when widespread and systematic forms of arbitrariness characterize a practice that involves severe punishments for some and none for others, this constitutes a serious injustice.

Conclusion

This paper is in no way a defense of drug use or drug sales. I believe that these are activities which ought to be discouraged, just as I believe that cigarette smoking and excessive use of alcohol ought to be discouraged. The question concerns what means we ought to use to do this.

I have suggested that one way of testing the belief that legal prohibition is the best means is by asking whether we can justify punishing people who use or sell drugs like marijuana, cocaine, and heroin. Having investigated this question from several perspectives, my conclusion is that punishing the use and sales of drugs is much harder to justify than one might have thought. A full treatment of this issue would require more discussion of the actual effects both of drug use and of prohibition, and I am in no position to provide that here. Nonetheless, the burden of proof is clearly on those who wish to impose punishment, and if my arguments are correct, they face a formidable task.[21]

NOTES

1. This is precisely Bentham's criterion for legislation. For his discussion, see *An Introduction to the Principles of Morals and Legislation* ch. 17, par. 9.

2. For a brief description of retributivism, see Martin Golding, *The Philosophy of Law* (Englewood Cliffs, NJ: Prentice-Hall, 1975), ch. 5. For some representative statements of the view, see Gertrude Ezorsky, ed., *Philosophical Perspectives on Punishment* (Albany, NY: State University of New York Press, 1972).

3. For a famous statement of "equality retributivism," see Immanuel Kant, *Metaphysical Elements of Justice,* John Ladd, trans. (New York: Macmillan, 1965), 101f. Andrew von Hirsch defends "proportionality retributivism" in *Doing Justice* (New York: Hill and Wang, 1976). For a critical discussion of both views, see my *An Eye for an*

Eye?—The Morality of Punishing by Death (Savage, MD: Rowman and Littlefield, 1987), ch. 6.

4. See, for example, his discussion of the second form of the categorical imperative and its application to suicide in his *Grounding for the Metaphysics of Morals,* James Ellington, trans. (Indianapolis, IN: Hackett Publishing, 1981), p. 36.

5. For an excellent discussion of this aspect of desert, see Elizabeth Beardsley, "Moral Worth and Moral Credit," *Philosophical Review* 66 (1957), 306–7. I defend the importance of this perspective in *An Eye for an Eye?,* ch. 7.

6. For the difficulties of such "whole life" assessments of desert, see W.D. Ross, *The Right and the Good* (Oxford: Oxford University Press, 1930), pp. 58–9.

7. *Thinking About Crime,* revised edition (New York: Vintage Books, 1985), p. 200.

8. For Morris's view, see "Persons and Punishment," *The Monist* Vol. 52 (1968).

9. For a valuable discussion of related issues, see Dan W. Brock, "The Use of Drugs for Pleasure: Some Philosophical Issues," in T. Murray, W. Gaylin, and R. Macklin, eds., *Feeling Good and Doing Better: Ethics and Nontherapeutic Drug Use* (Clifton, NJ: Humana Press, 1984), pp. 83–106. In the same volume, see James Bakalar and Lester Grinspoon, "Drug Abuse Policy and Social Attitudes to Risk-Taking" for comparisons between drug prohibition and a variety of other laws.

10. Cf. *An Introduction to the Principals of Morals and Legislation,* ch. 4.

11. From this perspective, consider the massive advertising campaigns whose purpose is to entice people to use tobacco and alcohol, including sophisticated efforts to target specific groups of potential users.

12. For the classic statement of the theory and its application to the question of punishment, see Jeremy Bentham, *An Introduction to the Principles of Morals and Legislation,* chs. 1, 13, 14, 15. For a brief discussion, see Martin Golding, *The Philosophy of Law,* ch. 4.

13. J.S. Mill defends the view that pleasures vary in quality and worth in *Utilitarianism,* ch. 2. For a sophisticated utilitarian criticism of drug-related pleasures, see Dan Brock, op. cit., 102–104.

14. While I did not conduct a thorough survey, I did find that none of the best-known philosophical articles or books on legal paternalism discusses the question of punishing people for violating paternalistic laws.

15. See, for example, John Conrad, "Controlling the Uncontrollable," in Murray et al., eds., *Feeling Good and Doing Better*, 49–64; and Ethan Nadelman, "The Case for Legalization," *Public Interest* 92 (1988), 3–31; reprinted in James Inciardi, ed., *The Drug Legalization Debate* (Newbury Park, CA: Sage Publications, 1991). For a contrary view, see the same volume for James Inciardi, "The Case Against Legalization," 45–79.

16. *An Introduction to the Principles of Morals and Legislation*, ch. 17, par. 15.

17. Joel Feinberg raises this issue, distinguishing between "comparative" and "noncomparative" desert in "Noncomparative Justice," in his *Rights, Justice, and the Bounds of Liberty*.

18. For a defense of this reasoning, see Charles Black, *Capital Punishment: The Inevitability of Caprice and Mistake*, 2nd ed. (New York, 1981). The Furman argument is criticized in Ernest van den Haag, "The Collapse of the Case against Capital Punishment," *The National Review*, March 31, 1978. For a further defense of Furman and criticisms of van den Haag's arguments, see my "Does It Matter if the Death Penalty Is Arbitrarily Administered?," *Philosophy and Public Affairs* 14 (1985), 149–64, and my *An Eye for an Eye?*, chs. 4,5.

19. These statistics come from Ethan Nadelman, "The Case for Legalization," in J. Inciardi, *The Drug Legalization Debate*, p. 37. According to Richard Daynard, Director of the Tobacco Liability Project at Northeastern Law School, tobacco-related deaths in the United States actually number over 400,000 annually.

20. In Murray et al., eds., *Feeling Good and Doing Better*, p. 13.

21. My thanks are due Curtis Brown, Richard Daynard, Nelson Lande, and John Post for their helpful comments on previous versions of this paper.

Drugs, Crime, and Punishment*

Burton M. Leiser

Assuming that drugs are relatively harmless entertainments accomplishes nothing toward determining whether drug users or sellers should be punished. Some drugs may in fact be nothing more than that, as the advocates of marijuana legalization have argued.[1] But others certainly pose extreme, potentially lethal hazards, at least to those who consume them and perhaps to others as well. Whatever the joys of cocaine might be, for example, excessive use leads to listlessness, anxiety, irritability, and symptoms of paranoia. The auditory, visual, olfactory, and tactile hallucinations that sometimes result are so terrifying that some users, in order to kill the roaches, ants, or spiders they believe are crawling under their skin, have mutilated themselves with knives and razors. Sniffers develop eczema and infections that lead to perforation and destruction of the septum. Heavily addicted persons have turned to prostitution, theft, embezzlement, forgery, burglary, armed robbery, and murder. And heavy intoxication can cause convulsions, coma, and death.[2] Anyone who has worked in a hospital emergency ward for any length of time has seen the ravages of cocaine, heroin, and PCP[3] abuse, and many of us have either suffered the loss of loved ones to these and other drugs, or are close to people who have.

Despite these facts, it is often argued that the use of narcotic drugs should be decriminalized because such use is a "victimless crime." Since those who purchase and ingest the drugs do so voluntarily, it is said, the sellers too ought to be free to ply their trade without interference from the criminal law.

Applying John Stuart Mill's libertarian principle,[4] some people argue that social controls should not be employed paternalistically so as to interfere with anyone's freedom to act as he wishes so long as no one else is harmed. It follows, so it is said, that people ought to be permitted to purchase and use drugs without governmental interference, and correlatively, that other people ought to be permitted to sell them. After all, it makes no sense to say that I have a right to drink wine when it is illegal for anyone to grow grapes or ferment them, to transport the finished product, or to sell it to me. No right is worthy of the name if no one is legally permitted to exercise it. Thus, if drug use is to be decriminalized, then those who produce and sell drugs should not be subject to criminal penalties either.

Legitimate questions may be and have been raised about Mill's principle. Indeed, Mill himself was quick to recognize that it was not quite as absolute as he had suggested, for he immediately added that children and primitive persons, "those backward states of society in which the race itself may be considered as in its nonage,"[5] among others, could not expect to enjoy the same blessings of liberty as adults and more advanced (civilized, educated) persons could. He went so far as to state that "[d]espotism is a legitimate mode of government in dealing with barbarians."[6] In any case, those actions that *do* cause injury to others *could* be prohibited by society and punished, either by such informal sanctions as social ostracism or by penalties prescribed by the criminal law.

In view of Mill's own qualifications, one might legitimately ask whether Sir James Fitzjames Stephen, who wrote a critique of Mill's theory soon after Mill's essay was published, might not have been correct when he wrote:

> Men are so constructed that whatever theory as to goodness and badness we choose to adopt, there are and always will be in the world an enormous mass of bad and indifferent people—people who deliberately do all sorts of things which they ought not to do, and leave undone all sorts of things which they ought to do. Estimate the proportion of men and women who are selfish, sensual, frivolous, idle, absolutely commonplace and wrapped up in the smallest of petty routines, and consider how far the freest of free discussion is likely to improve them.[7]

Ask anyone who has gotten drunk, Stephen suggested, whether he did so upon concluding, after full deliberation and free discussion, that it was wise to get drunk. If he is at all truthful, Stephens concluded, the drunk will reply, "I got drunk because I was weak and a fool, because I could not resist the immediate pleasure for the sake of future and indefinite advantage."[8]

Those who argue for the decriminalization of drugs often do so on the basis of Mill's principle of liberty or something like it. They rarely consider the important qualifications Mill placed upon his theory or the serious critiques of the theory itself. They appear to assume, as if it were axiomatic, that any society that places any restrictions upon the conduct of any of its members with respect to self-regarding actions falls short of being a *free* society. One of the purposes of this article is to raise this fundamental question: What *are* the self-regarding actions that ought to fall under Mill's libertarian principle, and who ought to qualify as entitled to exercise the freedoms associated with that principle?

In this article, I shall argue first that drug use is *not* victimless, and that even under the most liberal interpretation of Mill's libertarian principle, a liberal, civilized society may be fully justified in prohibiting it by banning the sale of selected dangerous drugs and by punishing those who violate the law. In Part II, I shall examine the consequences of doing so under the social conditions currently prevailing in the United States and most, if not all, other industrialized nations. In Part III, I will suggest that despite the fact that society *may* justifiably punish drug users and sellers, it would be more prudent, under present circumstances, not to do so; that as the world is today, laws governing so-called drug crimes ought to be repealed, and we ought instead to be seeking other ways of dealing with the horrifying consequences of drug addiction. And finally, I shall conclude by offering a few brief comments on Professor Nathanson's article.

Drug Use as a Non-Victimless Crime

Victimless Crimes Generally

It is more difficult than it is sometimes thought to determine just what so-called victimless crimes are. Courts and commentators have compiled a rather considerable list of such crimes, but it takes an active imagination to conjure up circumstances under which the crimes perpetrated do not harm *someone*. The most popular examples among advocates of a liberal approach to such offenses are those that appear to involve only a single individual who abuses herself in some way (e.g., masturbation or suicide), or those that occur between two or more individuals who mutually consent to participate in the forbidden activity (e.g., prostitution, homosexual relationships, adultery, aiding and abetting suicide). But other examples have arisen in recent years that raise serious questions about the meaningfulness of the concept itself. A few of them may be worth pondering:

- A sham marriage entered into by an American citizen and an alien in order to enable the alien to acquire permanent residence in the United States.

- Insider trading—i.e., buying or selling corporate shares on the basis of inside information that is not available to the general public.

- Privately viewing child pornography in one's own living room.[9]

- Money laundering.

- Stealing examinations that will be used for making promotion decisions.[10]

- Illegal possession of a firearm.[11]

- Dwarf tossing.

- Ticket scalping.

- Abandoning a refrigerator with its door intact.[12]

- Tax evasion and failure to file a tax return.

Each of these offenses might properly be called victimless, for in none of them can any particular victim be identified. Nevertheless, an injury is done to *someone* whenever any of these offenses is committed. Even if it is impossible to identify any specific individual person as the victim of any specific instance of such a violation, there is some loss to the community as a whole, and ultimately to some of its members when laws against these actions are broken. Injury to *individual* victims may be indirect, but collective injury to the *community* is direct and cumulative. Consider just a few examples:

- Persons who enter into sham marriages in order to circumvent the nation's immigration restrictions skew the statistics and may contribute to the enactment of lower quotas, thus preventing more scrupulously honest applicants from being admitted.

- Although no particular investor can be named as an individual inside trader's victim, everyone who buys or sells shares during the time the insider engages in his unlawful activities is at a disadvantage relative to him, and is more likely than not to lose a portion of her investment.

- A firefighter who steals a copy of an examination that is to be administered to applicants for promotions puts all of the other applicants at a disadvantage relative to himself and to others to whom he distributes the examination.

- The tax evader, together with all other tax evaders, deprives the government of money to which it is entitled, increases the burden on more honest taxpayers, contributes to disillusionment with government, and because of her contribution to a general reduction in revenue, is responsible, in part, for reduced services to those who need them and would otherwise benefit from them.

- It is impossible to identify any specific individual as victim of an abandoned refrigerator unless some child suffocates in it. But the community is a victim, even if no mishap occurs, since its law, designed to protect innocent children, has been broken and its children have been put at risk.

As Lord Devlin put it in his essay on the enforcement of morals, "Society is not something that is kept together physically; it is held by the invisible bonds of common thought. If the bonds were too far relaxed, the members would drift apart."[13] Even though an apartment dweller who tosses garbage from her window onto the street may not have spread her filth on any one of her neighbors, her action has nevertheless defiled the neighborhood. Her community has been wronged and damaged, and to some extent, so has each person who lives in it. They are *all* victims.

At one time, it was axiomatic that every person owed certain duties to the king: to pay his taxes, to take up arms in defense of the kingdom, and so on. Suicide was a felony[14] because it deprived the king of one of his valuable assets. Today, with so much emphasis on individual rights, duty—and most especially duty to the state—is virtually excluded from consideration. The presumption that individual rights far outweigh the rights of the state or the community has become so deeply ingrained that whenever the two come into conflict, the conclusion that the claims of the individual should prevail is virtually automatic.

The examples enumerated above do *not* prohibit acts that totally lack victims, for they were enacted in order to protect the community as a whole from perceived evils, from acts or conditions that were deemed by the legislature to be likely to lead to injury to or degradation of the community, its institutions, and the people within it.

Drug Use Is Not a Victimless Crime

Congress enacted the various Food and Drug Acts, which are today compiled under Title 21 of the United States Code, to correct what it perceived to be grave threats to public health and safety. Food products sold to the public were often contaminated with dangerous bacteria. They were adulterated, misrepresented, unwholesome and hazardous to the consumers' health. Congress was prodded into action in part by Upton Sinclair's 1906 novel, *The Jungle*, which graphically depicted the squalid conditions in which Chicago's giant packing houses prepared meat products that were sold throughout the nation: sausages contaminated with the carcasses of ground up poisoned rats, hogs dead of cholera rendered into a fancy grade of lard, steers found by government inspectors to be infected with tuberculosis were nevertheless being shipped to food markets.

Worthless nostrums were palmed off on a gullible public as effective for the relief of everything from halitosis to tuberculosis. Quacks made fortunes selling preparations laced with ingredients that were ineffective or worse, for they were often harmful or poisonous. Labels and advertising claims bore no relation to the truth.

Pharmaceutical testing was haphazard and unscientific. Consequently, people whose ailments might have been cured or ameliorated by proper medical treatment were misled into believing that over-the-counter preparations that had no scientifically verified efficacy were better for them than anything their physicians could prescribe. Since many of these products contained large quantities of alcohol, opium, or cocaine, the victims often *did* feel better, for a time at least. But meaningful treatment, if there was one, was deferred or entirely foregone, at a tremendous cost to the public.

The Federal Food and Drug Administration (FDA) was created in an effort to protect consumers against being unwitting victims of schemes designed to defraud them by playing upon their fear of disease and death, their lack of scientific sophistication, and their inability to detect harmful substances, contamination, or adulteration, without sophisticated laboratory equipment. Thus, Congress enacted legislation designed to compel drug manufacturers and distributors to test their products under careful, scientifically controlled conditions; to label and advertise them in accordance with strict guidelines; to make no claims for them that could not be scientifically verified; and to completely avoid using certain substances, which had been found to have especially deleterious effects upon human beings, or to use them only under the most rigorously controlled conditions.

There is ample evidence that these laws and the agencies that Congress created to regulate the food and drug industries have contributed significantly to public health and safety. Food and drug products in the United States are generally safe and effective for their stated purposes.[15] Despite flaws and weaknesses and occasional lapses on the part of industry, the professions, and the regulators, the system seems to work reasonably well. Unsafe products are kept off the market. Consumers are well informed through regulations that require full disclosure on packages and labels and in advertisements. Tests of new drugs and medical devices are carefully monitored, and products that do not meet rigid standards of purity, healthfulness, and efficacy are forced off the market.[16]

All of this is admittedly paternalistic. It is designed to protect the consuming public against becoming victims of dangerous or ineffective products, whether those products are purveyed by unscrupulous charlatans, by well-meaning but misguided healers, or by manufacturers who are not sufficiently attentive to quality control. Mill's arguments against paternalism come up against a well-entrenched government program that has won the respect and admiration of people around the world who have not forgotten how the scrupulous care of an FDA official prevented thousands of American women from giving birth to children who would have suffered the terrible deformities associated with Thalidomide.

If Mill's arguments for individualism and against paternalism were offered in support of the right to consume drugs, they would be utterly beside the point. His principal argument was that to acquiesce in "rigid rules of justice for the sake of others" simply dulled and blunted one's whole nature. "Whatever crushes individuality," he wrote, "is despotism,"[17] for genius can breathe freely only in an atmosphere of freedom.[18] But to suggest that the consumption of drugs contributes anything at all toward the flowering of individuality or the sharpening of anyone's genius is to step well beyond what is justified by the evidence and possibly even beyond the bounds of reason. One of the principal goals of the libertarian principle was to enable those who have the requisite gifts to make those original contributions of which they are capable, despite the fact that originality "is the one thing which unoriginal minds cannot feel the use of."[19] It was to enable those capable of it to overcome the collective mediocrity that afflicts the great mass of mankind.[20] But there is not the slightest evidence that drug consumption contributes toward that end. On the contrary, drugs lead to abbreviated lives, to stupefaction, and in many cases, to an incessant search for more and better ways of gratifying the addict's perpetual need for the pleasure associated with the ingestion of her drug of choice.

With regard to so-called victimless crimes, Mill's clearest statement is the following:

> But with regard to the merely contingent or . . . constructive injury which a person causes to society by conduct which neither violates any specific duty to the public, nor occasions perceptible hurt to any assignable individual except himself, the inconvenience is one which society can afford to bear, for the sake of the greater good of human freedom.[21]

This seems almost to be an *a priori* judgment. Mill offered no argument to bolster it. He treats "human freedom" generically, as if every form of freedom was of equal value and ought to be given the same protection as every other. But of course there is no reason to suppose that there are no differences among the things people want to do. Some liberties are worth fighting and dying for—like the freedom to speak and write and think that Mill so eloquently defends. Such freedoms are indeed crucial to the development of human society. But surely there is a world of difference between them and the desire of some people to engage in dwarf tossing, to discard refrigerators, to view pornographic photographs of children, and to get high on cocaine. One can scarcely imagine anyone seriously trying to devise a rational argument equating such claimed freedoms with those of free speech and a free press.

Thus far, I have not mentioned those cases in which there are innocent, direct victims of drug use, including most especially infants born with grave symptoms of exposure to cocaine or other drugs. Such cases are no longer rare. Neonatal intensive care units are swamped with babies seriously affected by exposure to drugs during gestation. Infants suffering from cocaine exposure during their mothers' pregnancy are five to ten times as likely to die of sudden infant death syndrome than drug-free babies.[22] Such infants are likely to experience withdrawal, to be addicted at birth, and to have developed disabling abnormalities in various organs, such as malformed kidneys and genitals, missing fingers, missing portions of the digestive tract, and defects of the neural tube.[23] During development, fetuses whose mothers are using cocaine are likely to suffer impeded brain development and other symptoms resulting from direct exposure, through the placenta, to the cocaine itself, and indirectly because of drug-induced abnormalities in the maternal circulatory system. After birth, such children often have such serious physical and psychological symptoms as vomiting, rapid weight loss, diarrhea, excessive tension, rapid mood swings, and autism. As a rule, they suffer severely retarded development. There is evidence that women who consume other drugs—including heroin and alcohol—cause similar damage to the children they bear. Such damage is neither indirect nor without identifiable victims. The number of infants born with such problems is increasing at a constantly accelerating rate. Their mothers are either unwilling or unable to care for them. The expense of lengthy hospital stays, special education, and general support for these children inevitably falls upon the taxpayers, who are informed that any interference with a woman's pregnancy or her pursuit of pleasure through drugs is an unconstitutional intrusion upon her right of privacy.

To sum up:

1. Despite the widely held assumption that supposedly self-regarding and consensual actions are victimless, in actual fact many of them harm other persons, directly or indirectly, and therefore may not be protected by Mill's libertarian principle.

2. The collective harm inflicted upon a community by actions that cause no direct harm to identifiable individuals should not be ignored in determining whether such actions should be discouraged by informal sanctions or by criminal penalties.

3. The consumption and sale of narcotic drugs are potentially so damaging, both to communities and to the persons living within them, that it is reasonable to advocate the maintenance of criminal sanctions against them. Such a position is not at all inconsistent with a firm belief in and support of the most liberal policies in such areas as free speech, freedom of the press, freedom of religion, freedom of conscience, and the like.

The Consequences of the War on Drugs

The War on Drugs, as it has been called by American political and law enforcement leaders, has had no perceptible effect upon the pattern of consumption of forbidden drugs. Since the arrest and prosecution of drug users and drug dealers became a high national priority, drug use in the United States has increased. One might argue that the increase would have been even greater if the government had assumed a more lenient stance, but that proposition is not susceptible of proof.

The efforts of the Drug Enforcement Agency (DEA) and other government agencies, including the military, have nevertheless had some results that may readily be observed or inferred from the available evidence. Successful interdiction of large quantities of illegal drugs being transported into the United States from abroad, and the seizure of tons of domestically produced drugs have reduced the supply from time to time. The supply has occasionally been so radically diminished that street sellers and their customers have been moved by at least one law which they cannot disobey: the law of supply and demand. The government's success in reducing supplies has led to the adulteration of those drugs that were available, and to significant upward adjustments of their prices. Seriously addicted, unemployed users have resorted to ever more dangerous crimes in order to satisfy their insatiable cravings, advancing from prostitution and petty larceny to grand larceny, burglary, robbery, and murder.

As the drug trade has become more lucrative, it has become easier to recruit people who were eager to earn the big money it was possible to make in it. The risks are great but remote, while the profits are immediate and sizable enough to lure impoverished young people into the business. Expensive clothes, jewelry, and motor vehicles that would otherwise remain far beyond their reach suddenly become the nearly certain rewards that every young person can aspire to without the tedium of school, the discipline of maintaining regular hours, or the odium of keeping account books and paying income taxes. There are the added pleasures of high adventure, with advancement up the ranks conferring ever greater power upon young and hitherto impotent young men—including the power of life and death over their subordinates, their suppliers, and their customers. All of this and more—for they also enjoy the sense of power that comes from defying the law with relative impunity, inasmuch as very few of their number are caught. Even those who are apprehended can generally count on relative immunity from hostile witnesses, who are intimidated by the threat of capital punishment that is meted out with a swiftness and certainty that make the threats of lawful authorities pale into insignificance. Informal "penalties," such as severe beatings and murder, are to be expected when these "merchants" have no law but their own to turn to for enforcement of the rules of their illegal marketplace. Those near the top of the hierarchy know that there is an endless supply of new dealers whenever the law or their own enforcement actions terminate the careers of the older ones.

But the costs to society do not end there. As the penalties become more severe, the price to the public goes up as well. Immense numbers of prisoners have been jammed into the nation's jails and prisons. Each of them must be fed and housed and given medical and dental treatment at public expense. Most of them also benefit from publicly supplied legal counsel. And all of them are tended by large staffs of guards, counselors, and other persons who are essential for running large, crowded penal institutions. The cost to New York State's taxpayers for each inmate is estimated to be in the neighborhood of $30,000 per year. If that money could be turned to other uses, it would be possible, for example, to offer every poor student in the state a full-tuition scholarship and room and board at any of the finest universities in the land.

In addition to the financial costs of current policies, there are the social and moral costs. A recent study nicely sums up the problem:

> The availability and use of illicit drugs may have substantial effects on the social organization of urban areas, and these aspects of social organization can in turn have a very important impact on levels of predatory crime. For example, a thriving illicit drug economy in a slum neighborhood may weaken the power and influence of legitimate

social institutions. There is a seductive appeal to a drug economy in a community when drug dealers are driving expensive cars. And when they are virtually the only persons driving expensive cars, the credibility of teachers and police and legitimate business people may be undermined in the eyes of the young, and the morale of conforming segments of the population may suffer. An atmosphere of demoralization can thus set in, making all forms of illegitimate activities seem both more attractive and less credibly stigmatized.[24]

Finally, constitutional rights have suffered. Police, prosecutors, and courts have become inured to the large numbers of criminal defendants whose crimes are directly or indirectly related to drug abuse. The criminal justice system has become so jammed in some cities that it is difficult to resist the temptation to move cases along with minimal attention to the niceties of the Fourth, Fifth, and Sixth Amendments. The penalties enacted by Congress and state legislatures become empty, meaningless threats when the logjam in the courts induces judges and prosecutors to help defendants fly swiftly through the system on the wings of plea bargains.

The well-being of drug users must also be brought into the equation, for they too are human beings entitled to decent treatment and reasonable consideration. Many of them have been caught up in a situation which they would gladly escape, if only they could. Treatment programs are not always successful. Although it is easy to blame users for making the wrong choices, blame does precious little to help them escape from the habit that threatens their health and their lives. The current system automatically increases the risks that they run. Instead of seeking treatment, they seek to avoid it, for fear that they may be arrested and disgraced. Unable to find unadulterated products with properly measured doses, they purchase whatever they can buy on the street, not knowing what poisons may have been introduced into the mixture, or what dose is appropriate for their needs. Thus, they put their lives at risk every time they consume a dose of the drug upon which they have become dependent, and their families are too often left to mourn the results.

The linchpin of the "War on Drugs" is the system of criminal penalties supposedly to be imposed upon those who violate the laws, designed to protect the public against the evil effects of narcotics and other forbidden drugs. But the system itself appears to be causing incalculable damage to the nation by contributing to the incidence of drug-related crimes (i.e., those that are committed in order to enable drug users to pay the high prices being charged for the drugs they crave because of the government's "success" in interdicting the supply, and to protect the drug pusher's business); by weakening the protections of the Bill of Rights; by geometrically expanding the economic burden of law enforcement and penal institutions; and by increasing the risks of physical harm to those who become dependent upon such drugs—all without the slightest evidence that drug use has been reduced or deterred, but with constant growth in the number of drug users throughout the land. Under such circumstances, it is reasonable to ask whether some other approach might be more in keeping with our ethical and legal traditions.

Some Possible Alternatives

The foregoing discussion clearly leads to the conclusion that the "War on Drugs," with its philosophy of punishing drug users and especially drug dealers, is fundamentally misguided. This is so, not because there is anything intrinsically wrong about punishing wrongdoers—and I am willing to grant that drug dealers are wrongdoers—but rather, because the practical effect of doing so has been just the opposite of what is intended, or at least so it appears to be. Drug use has increased despite the billions of dollars spent to curtail it. There has been an increase in the number of deaths due to drug overdoses, in the number of infants suffering from drug-induced syndromes, in the number of drug-related crimes, and in all of the other evils associated with this epidemic. If the remedy were working, we should have seen *some* improvement by this time; but instead, the situation has become steadily worse.

Once a well-intentioned government program is put into place, the spirit of scientific reason is often replaced by political and bureaucratic inertia. Social programs are self-perpetuating. Their efficacy becomes an article of faith that is defended in the face of all the evidence to the contrary. A half-century of failure is defended on the ground that the program was never "really" given a chance: "If only we would have spent *more* money," goes the refrain, "*then* you would have seen what an excellent program it is." The drug war has been tried for long enough. The United States has gone so far as to send guided missile cruisers into action to intercept drug shipments bound for American shores from Latin America and Caribbean islands. It is time to try a new approach—*not* because drug dealing is an honorable calling, for it is not; but because the harm being done by treating drug dealers and users as criminals appears to be far greater than what a freer market in drugs might do.

I therefore propose the following:

1. Provide ready access to *all* currently banned drugs through pharmacies, preferably upon the prescription of a physician or a clinic. The only exceptions would be those drugs that cause reactions that are likely to result in direct harm being done by the user to other persons, as PCP is reputed to do.

2. Permit responsible pharmaceutical manufacturers to package such drugs in carefully controlled doses so that anyone who has a habit may obtain the dose that he or she needs with minimal danger of taking an overdose.

3. The pharmaceutical manufacturers providing such drugs would be required to prepare them under the same rigid controls and standards as are imposed by the FDA upon the manufacture of other drugs. The purity and quality of the drugs dispensed by the pharmacist to the consumer would thus be assured.

4. Stop all interference with the agricultural policies of those nations that currently produce the raw materials from which the drugs are currently manufactured. They are generally impoverished nations without many other products that are readily exportable. If their farmers can make a living by growing opium or cocaine, let them do so and compete in an open market.

5. Mount an educational campaign designed to persuade as many people as possible that the use of such drugs is

or can be harmful. Point out truthfully and graphically the hazards that they represent.

6. Strictly enforce laws forbidding driving or operating dangerous machinery under the influence of any psychoactive drug. Forfeiture of an automobile driven under the influence would be a powerful deterrent to future offenses, and imprisonment for a second offense would be quite appropriate. (There is no reason why similar penalties should not be attached to driving under the influence of alcohol.)

7. Release all persons currently incarcerated for drug use or drug sales. (Those who have committed other crimes related to drug use, such as robbery, burglary, or murder, should of course serve the terms imposed on them for those crimes.) Recidivism would not be a problem since drug use would no longer be illegal, and they would be unable to compete with the legal sales of drugs in pharmacies.

8. Deal with harm caused to other people because of drug use as we do in all other cases—through the civil courts, by way of actions in tort where that is appropriate, or through family court if that is what is called for. If a drug user harms another, the victim should be compensated by insurance or by attaching the tort-feasor's assets. Where necessary, victims might seek other remedies, such as injunctions.

9. Any person committing an intentional tort through the administration of a drug to a nonconsenting person (as by spiking a drink with a drug) should be subject to appropriate criminal and civil penalties.

10. Impose a small tax on the sale of each dose of every psychoactive drug. A portion of that tax should be kept in a fund that would be used to compensate victims of drug abuse and to establish and maintain drug treatment clinics and research institutes.

11. Hold anyone who serves drugs liable for injuries suffered by third parties as a result of ingestion of the drug by his or her guests. This would be analogous to the dram-shop rule, which many states have enacted to hold the owners of bars and other establishments that

serve liquor liable for injuries their inebriated customers cause to third parties. This rule would apply to private hosts as well.

12. Introduce legislation creating a presumption that any woman who has used psychoactive drugs during her pregnancy is unfit. Such a presumption could be used to terminate the mother's parental rights. At the same time, provide facilities to which pregnant women might resort for treatment during and after pregnancy. Pregnant women who are known to be using such drugs and are unwilling to commit themselves should be subject to involuntary commitment to protect their unborn children. Of course, if a pregnant woman had an abortion, she would be free to go on her way, since the sole purpose for involuntary commitment would be protection of the unborn child.

If these proposals were adopted, say, for a ten-year trial period, I would predict that the following results would ensue:

1. Prices of psychoactive drugs would drop substantially. Everyone who wanted to purchase them could do so, but would have to approach a professional intermediary first.

2. Far fewer deaths from overdoses or impurities would occur.

3. Addicted users would more readily seek professional assistance in coping with their addictions, because they would no longer have to face possible criminal prosecution for their activities.

4. Because drugs would be readily and inexpensively available, relatively few users would become prostitutes, thieves, robbers, or murderers in order to sustain their habits. The rate of violent crime related to drugs would decline precipitately.

5. The enormous tax burden associated with the War on Drugs would be greatly alleviated, and the money thus saved could be spent on other worthy projects—including drug education.

6. The number of crack babies and babies born with fetal alcohol syndrome would decline significantly.

Theories of Punishment and Drug Use

Professor Nathanson's excellent analysis leaves very little for me to add. He is quite right, for example, in noting that drug laws were not passed with the fetuses being carried by pregnant drug users or the passengers of railroad trains in mind. It is not clear, however, that this is a reason to argue against criminal penalties for such persons. The fact that the legislature over-looked some of the evil consequences in passing laws to forbid wrongful behavior is not a very good reason for doing away with punishment of the wrongful behavior. On the contrary, it merely reinforces the conclusion that the legislature acted wisely in the first place.

Nathanson is certainly correct in arguing that paternalism is a major factor in anti-drug legislation. But one of the principal functions of government has always been to protect the community and its members from some of their more unworthy inclinations. It is simply not true that we cannot legislate morality. We can, we have, and we do. A large part of virtually every aspect of our law is infected, if that is the right term, with morality. There is no *a priori* reason to suppose that that is wrong.

Retributivists need not insist that the wrong done by the offender must be revisited on him. In some cases that would be patently ridiculous. They argue only that the harm done to the offender must be proportioned to the evil she has done. A few years in prison or a sound thrashing might be proportional to an offense that has nothing to do with either imprisonment or battery.

Although it is true that the drug user harms himself, it is most emphatically *not* true that drug sellers do not harm drug users. Of course they do! It may be difficult to determine the precise proportion of responsibility the seller has for the harm done to the user, just as it is often difficult in automobile collisions to decide how much responsibility each driver bears for the damage sustained; but courts and juries weigh the evidence and make such determinations every day. Moreover, the fact that the seller "intends" no harm to the user is irrelevant, at least in the law, and I would suggest that it ought to be equally irrelevant in morals. In the law, "subjective intent," or what the perpetrator has in mind when he commits a criminal act, has virtually nothing to do with the matter. A person is held to intend *the consequences that a rational person would know are likely to follow from his actions.* The defendant in a murder trial claimed that all he intended to do when he shot at the victim was to "wing" him, by shooting him in the elbow, but that he had no intention to kill him. Unfortunately, the bullet exploded when it struck the victim's arm bone, and fragments of lead and bone blew a large hole in his chest. The court held that whatever the defendant may have *thought* at the time, he *should have known* that the victim might die as a result of being shot—and therefore, under the law, he *intended* to kill him. The defendant was convicted of first degree murder.

If Nathanson's theory is correct, a gun dealer, knowing that the buyer intends to shoot the president, would not deserve to be punished for the president's assassination, for he merely provided a gun to a person who wanted one. Even Cephalus[25] saw how unsound that argument was.

Finally, Professor Nathanson correctly points out that people who use different psychoactive, harmful substances (alcohol, tobacco, narcotics) are treated differently. He concludes that drug sellers and users can "legitimately" complain that they are punished for doing what others may do with impunity. In defense of the legislative bodies that have drawn these distinctions, one must realize that many factors properly go into making laws on such complex issues, including moral, social, political, economic, and historical considerations, and a host of practical considerations as well. The people who live on the upper west side of Manhattan may park their cars on the street during the day, while those who live in areas adjacent to Time Square may not. I suppose the denizens of Times Square might "legitimately" complain about their relatively worse treatment, but the municipal government had excellent reasons for drawing the lines as it did, and everyone concerned has a duty to obey or suffer the consequences. Lovers of alcohol, tobacco, coffee, and chocolate are relatively freer to indulge their tastes than lovers of marijuana and crack, but legislators have committed no injustice in drawing the distinctions they have drawn—though Professor

Nathanson and I would agree that the time has come for them to draw them differently.

NOTES

1. See, for example, National Organization for Reform of Marijuana Laws (NORML) v. Bell, 488 F. Supp. 123 (D.C.D.C. 1980), in which NORML argued, among other things, that the Controlled Substances Act, which prohibits the private possession and use of marijuana, violates the Constitution's guarantees of privacy and equal protection and its prohibition against cruel and unusual punishment. In arguing its case, NORML contended that since marijuana is a relatively harmless drug, its classification as a controlled substance violated the Equal Protection Clause of the Constitution, since neither tobacco nor alcohol, whose deleterious effects are well known, was so classified. The court concluded, however, that because there was evidence that marijuana impaired the circulatory, endocrine, and immune systems of the body, altered chromosomes, changed cell metabolism, and might possibly induce "marijuana psychosis," it was not irrational for Congress to include it in the list of prohibited substances. Since there is a rational basis for its inclusion, the statute stands up under the accepted constitutional test.

2. See, for example, Gabriel G. Nahas, Cocaine: The Great White Plague (Middlebury, VT: Paul S. Eriksson, 1989), 50 ff. and passim.

3. Phencyclidine, commonly known as "angel dust."

4. In his book, On Liberty, Mill expressed his principle as follows: "The sole end for which mankind are warranted, individually or collectively, in interfering with the liberty of action of any of their number is self-protection, . . . to prevent harm to others. His own good, either physical or moral, is not a sufficient warrant." On Liberty, ed. C. V. Shields (Indianapolis: Bobbs-Merrill, 1956), p. 13.

5. Ibid., p. 14.

6. Ibid.

7. James Fitzjames Stephen, Liberty, Equality, Fraternity (Chicago: University of Chicago Press, 1990), p. 72. (Stephen's essay was first published in 1873, about fourteen years after Mill's essay was first published. The Chicago edition is a reprinting of the second edition of Stephen's essay.

8. Ibid., p. 70.

9. For the United States Supreme Court's leading decision on "kiddie porn," see New York v. Ferber, 458 U.S. 747 (1982). The Court concluded that publications that include lewd photographs of children could be banned under the Constitution because selling or purchasing them contributed to the unlawful exploitation of the children whose photographs appeared in them.

10. Stotts v. Memphis Fire Dept., 858 F.2d 289 (6th Cir. 1989).

11. Bernhard Goetz, who shot several assailants while riding in a New York City subway late at night, was convicted of unlawful possession of a firearm despite his acquittal of other charges on the ground that he had acted in self-defense. In Re Goetz, Slip Opinion, State of New York Crime Victim Board, March 17, 1988.

12. Abandoning a refrigerator was not a crime under the common law. It became a criminal offense only after statutes were enacted forbidding it, because of the large number of children who had suffocated after crawling into abandoned refrigerators and been unable to open the doors from inside.

13. Sir Patrick Devlin, The Enforcement of Morals (Oxford: Oxford University Press, 1964), p. 10.

14. Felonies were punishable by death. This may seem laughable, for it was obviously quite impossible to execute a person who had committed suicide. But felons also forfeited all their worldly goods to the Crown. This would not have been very amusing to the suicide's survivors.

15. Of course, some drugs are inherently dangerous, but their use is licensed because the diseases or conditions they are intended to alleviate are so serious that on balance, the FDA has determined that the benefits outweigh the potential hazards.

16. See Weinberger v. Hynson, Westcott and Dunning, Inc., 412 U.S. 603, 93 S.Ct. 2469 (1973) for a good review of the standards imposed upon drug manufacturers before their new drugs will be approved by the FDA. Justice William O. Douglas explained that a drug must be shown to be both safe and effective for its intended use. The burden is upon the manufacturer to provide "substantial evidence" that a new drug is effective. Such evidence must consist of "adequate and well-controlled investigations, including clinical investigations, by experts qualified by scientific training and experience to evaluate the effectiveness of the drug involved, on the basis of which it could fairly and responsibly be concluded by such experts that the drug will have the effect it purports or is represented to have under the conditions of

use prescribed, recommended, or suggested in the labeling or proposed labeling thereof." (Citing 21 U.S.C. § 355[d].) The FDA's regulations outline in considerable detail the protocols of acceptable scientific investigation. They specifically exclude uncontrolled or partially controlled studies, "isolated reports, random experience, and reports lacking the details which permit scientific evaluation." (Citing 21 CFR § 130.12[a] [5] [ii] [c].) Justice Douglas concluded that the FDA's "strict and demanding standards" precluded anecdotal evidence, such as the fact that doctors "believe" in a drug's efficacy. "Impressions or beliefs of physicians, no matter how fervently held, are treacherous," he concluded. (412 U.S. at 619, 93 S.Ct. at 2478.)

17. Mill, op. cit., p. 77.

18. Ibid., p. 78.

19. Ibid.

20. Ibid., p. 80.

21. Ibid., p. 100.

22. National Association for Prenatal Addiction Research and Education, A First: National Hospital Incidence Survey, Substances Most Commonly Abused During Pregnancy and Their Risks to Mother and Baby (1989).

23. Bingol, Fuchs, et al., "Teratogenicity of Cocaine in Humans," Journal of Pediatrics 110: pp. 93–6 (1987).

24. Franklin E. Zimring and Gordon Hawkins, The Search for Rational Drug Control (Cambridge, England: Cambridge University Press, 1992), p. 149.

25. Plato, Republic, Book I.

Drug Testing

Mandatory Drug Testing

Hugh LaFollette

By some estimates one-third of American corporations now require employees to be tested for drug use. These requirements are compatible with general employment law while promoting the public's interest in fighting drug use. Moreover, the United States Supreme Court has ruled that drug-testing programs are constitutionally permissible within both the public and the private sectors. It appears mandatory drug-testing is a permanent fixture of American corporate life. (Bakaly, 1990)

The legal roots of mandatory drug testing are found in the common law doctrine of "employment at will." That doctrine states that either party to an employment contract can terminate the contract for any reason, at any time, unless the contract specifies otherwise. As the Court held in *Adair v. United States*, (208 U.S. 161, 175–6, 1908) the employer "was at liberty, in his discretion, to discharge [the employee] from service without giving any reason for so doing."

In unqualified form, this doctrine would give employers effective control over employees. Employers could establish any requirements they wished for prospective and current employees. They could decline to hire employees who refuse drug tests. They could likewise decline to hire people with characteristics, beliefs, or behavior they dislike. Employees must endure these requirements or seek employment elsewhere. However, since most people have limited job opportunities, they will be forced to "accept" these requirements, no matter how objectionable. Courts and legislatures have since recognized the abuses this principle could engender. During the last thirty years they have placed numerous constraints on employer's rights.[1] The Civil Rights Act of 1964 states that it is illegal to refuse someone employment because of "race, color, or national origin" (42 U.S.C. at 2000). Later courts likewise prohibited discrimination based on sex and religion.

Nonetheless, elements of the "employment at will" principle are alive and well. Consider a recent Texas Court of Appeals ruling rejecting an employee's challenge to her employer's drug-testing program. In siding with the employer the court said: "Generally, when the employer notifies an employee of changes in employment terms, the employee must accept the new terms or quit. If the employee continues working with the knowledge of the changes, he has accepted the changes as a matter of law." (*Jennings v. Minco Technology Labs, Inc.*, 765 S.W.2nd 497, 1989) Although not in the same unqualified form, the doctrine is similarly evident in several U.S. Supreme Court cases discussed later. Given the staying-power of this doctrine—albeit in attenuated form—it is easy to see why mandatory drug testing does not run afoul of the Constitution as interpreted by the Reagan/Bush court. Employers can make extensive demands on employees, simply because it is their pleasure.

Mandatory drug testing is also underwritten by potent political considerations. The public wants to curtail the growing use of illegal drugs. The Supreme Court specifically noted this concern in upholding the mandatory testing of Customs Service employees. The use of illegal narcotics, it ruled, is "one of the greatest problems affecting the health and welfare of our population." (*National Treasury Employees Union v. von Rabb* 109 S.Ct. 1384, 1989). The public wants drug use stopped, and they are willing to use virtually any means to achieve that result.

Concerns about Testing

Even those who endorse widespread mandatory drug testing do—or should—fear an employer's unbridled intrusion into the private lives of its employees. The Supreme Court, in upholding testing programs, recognized that mandatory testing involves invasions of privacy which cannot be constitutionally ignored.

"Because it is clear that the collection and testing of urine intrudes upon expectations of privacy that society has long recognized as reasonable . . . these intrusions must be deemed searches under the Fourth Amendment." (*Skinner*, at 1413). The Fourth Amendment reads: "The right of the people to be secure in their persons, houses, papers, and effects, against unreasonable searches and seizures, shall not be violated, and no Warrants shall issue, but upon probable cause, supported by Oath or affirmation, and particularly describing the place to be searched, and the persons or things to be seized." In effect, the Court ruled that unless a testing program is reasonable under the constraints of this Amendment, then it would be unconstitutional.

It is not evident, however, that the Fourth Amendment is relevant. In fact, by focussing exclusively on this amendment, the courts have made the case for mandatory drug testing too easy. The primary functions of the Fourth are to insure that governmental agents cannot criminally prosecute someone using evidence obtained "unreasonably," and that neither people nor their property can be examined without warning, unless an independent magistrate determines an unannounced search is necessary. (Israel, 1975, p. 86)

Drug testing does not run afoul of any of these functions.[2] First, testing programs are not governmental actions in the sense required by this amendment. Even when the federal government is also the employer (as in *National Treasury* discussed later), it demands qua employer—not qua government agent—that employees be tested. Second, test results are not made available to law enforcement officials, and, hence, cannot be grounds for criminal prosecution. Third, since employees know when they accept certain jobs that they will be tested, then they will not be searched without appropriate warning. In short, such tests are not unconstitutional searches under the meaning of the Fourth Amendment. At least that is what the Court ruled. I am inclined to agree.

However, even if drug testing does not violate the prohibition against unreasonable searches, mandatory testing may still be morally impermissible. There are moral limits on an employer's discretion: no employer should be able to control the private lives of her employees.

These moral limits are also constitutional limits—albeit not ones the Court majority recognized in any of the cases cited. (They do, however, feature prominently in the dissenting opinion by Justice Scalia, discussed later in the paper.) In particular, the Constitution's protection of privacy, recognized in the Court's landmark ruling in *Griswold v. Connecticut* (381 U.S. 476, 479) is sufficient to throw mandatory testing in doubt. There the Court held: "specific guarantees in the Bill of Rights have penumbras, formed by emanations from those guarantees that help give them life and substance." For instance, "the First Amendment has a penumbra where privacy is protected from governmental intrusion." This right "conferred as against the government, the right to be let alone—the most comprehensive of rights and the right most valued by civilized men."

In light of the constitutionally recognized right to privacy, more is at issue than whether mandatory drug tests are illegal searches under the meaning of the Fourth Amendment. Even if drug tests are not impermissible searches, they are, at least at first glance, invasions of privacy that merit protection. Thus, we must still determine whether employers can require employees to take drug tests that intrude into employees' private lives. This way of putting the matter, however, assumes that the use of drugs is indeed private—beyond the scope of legitimate inquiry by potential employers. Yet that we have not shown. Thus, our search to determine if mandatory drug testing is permissible requires us to inquire more generally about the demands that employers can legitimately make of employees.

Employers Demands on Employees

In deciding what employers can legitimately demand of employees, we must consider the interests of employers as well as those of employees. In our efforts to protect workers, we should not decree whom employers must hire nor mandate what they may expect of workers.[3] To do so would intrude inappropriately into *their* lives. For the purposes of our present inquiry, however, we need not prescribe whom employers must hire nor dictate employment practices. Rather, we need only establish limits to employer discretion. We must find ways to protect employers' prerogatives without intruding unduly into employees' private lives.

Here's my suggestion. If a belief or activity is irrelevant to job performance, it is none of the employer's business. She cannot rightly prescribe or proscribe it, nor can she even inquire about it. If privacy is to mean anything, it must mean at least that. The following example, I think, illustrates this principle. Suppose an employer wants to examine an employee's blood, not to detect illegal drugs, but to determine if she has elevated serum cholesterol. Anyone with elevated levels is given three months to lower her cholesterol to appropriate levels. If she fails, she is dismissed. Moreover, let us stipulate, what is likely true, that elevated cholesterol does not directly affect an employee's job performance. The employer recognizes that. She just refuses to retain people who are unhealthy. Under these circumstances such tests would be unreasonable and their unreasonableness would not be exhausted by the Fourth Amendment's prohibitions on unreasonable searches. In fact, as I argued earlier, it is doubtful whether the Fourth Amendment is directly relevant to the present inquiry.

Likewise, employers should not be able to control employees' behavior which, although marginally related to job performance, is primarily private. For instance, elevated serum cholesterol may be remotely relevant to job performance: people with elevated cholesterol are more likely to suffer heart attacks and die. The employer must subsequently train a replacement. That is expensive. Even so, permitting employers to specify an employee's serum cholesterol fails to draw an appropriate distinction between the public and the private. If testing were permissible under these circumstances, employers could also forbid their employees to smoke, drink, climb mountains, drive race cars, and eat fried chicken—or any other activity which might shorten their lives. That, however, would give employers extensive control over employees' private lives. And most assuredly *that* limits employees' privacy in ways which should horrify us.

We return to the original question: what may employers demand of employees? Can they legitimately force employees to hold particular religious beliefs? Can they require employees to have a particular diet or exercise regimen? Can they enforce dress codes? We cannot answer these questions in the abstract. Such matters are not invariably subject to employer control, nor are they always beyond its legitimate reach. Whether these are reasonable demands depends on the nature of the job. If what is being required is obviously and directly related to job performance, then the requirement is arguably permissible.

For instance, it is generally impermissible to require employees to have specific religious beliefs. In most circumstances such beliefs are unrelated to job performance. Nonetheless, having specified religious beliefs is an eminently plausible requirement for parish priests—and arguably relevant for teachers in parochial schools. And, although diet is typically irrelevant to job performance, perhaps it is reasonable to expect employees in a vegetarian grocery store to be vegetarians.

Fortunately, for our present purposes we need not determine exactly what are reasonable requirements for every job. Nor do we need a comprehensive theory of employment—although for other purposes such a theory would be highly desirable. The only answer we need for the present inquiry is suggested by the previous examples. If normally private information is irrelevant to a job's performance, then the employer cannot legitimately expect it or even inquire about it. Thus, in circumstances where drug use is irrelevant, or only marginally relevant, to the performance of a job, then the employer could not ask applicants or employees about their drug use. This principle seems only too obvious if an employer wanted to ask applicants and employees whether they use Tylenol.

On the other hand, if drug use (or any other behavior, for that matter) were demonstrably relevant to the performance of an employee's assigned duties, an employer may reasonably inquire about such use (or behavior).

Someone might object that no one should have to disclose details of her private life, even if those details *were* relevant to job performance. To ask that they do is to violate the Fifth Amendment's protection against self-incrimination. Not so. For the Fifth

Amendment—like the Fourth—primarily functions to protect people (potentially) engaged in criminal proceedings. As previously argued, employee drug tests are not criminal proceedings. No one is in danger of being imprisoned. The Fifth Amendment is inapplicable.

Rather, the issue is whether (prospective) employees should have to disclose information that enables employers to make a rational assessment of the employees' suitability for the job. The answer, I would have thought, is yes. Were that not so, employers could not require applicants to submit school transcripts, employment records, and letters of recommendation—since these are, for most purposes, properly considered private. In summary, it is appropriate for employers to ask applicants to divulge any information, including information about drug use, if it is relevant to job performance.

Employers may thus reasonably want to know whether their employees use drugs, if that use would affect employee performance. But this does not yet establish that employers may use mandatory drug tests as a way of discerning use. For the issue is not merely about what information an employer may reasonably desire, but the means she may use to obtain it. To consider an earlier example, the local parish may ask prospective priests about their religious views. After all, such beliefs are relevant to job performance. But the parish cannot demand that applicants submit to lie detector tests; nor may it tap their phones or eavesdrop on them to determine if, in fact, their views are as they say.

Likewise, employers may ask an employee about drug use if that employee's work could be adversely affected by use. Perhaps, too, they might legitimately dismiss any employees they discover using drugs. However, employers should not automatically conclude that mandatory drug testing is an appropriate means of discerning use. We must still protect employees' privacy. Testing is not a justified means of identifying drug use unless, in addition to being relevant to job performance, a) use is of substantial and direct risk to others and b) testing is a reliable and relatively unintrusive way of limiting use. Or so I shall argue in the next section.

The Rationale for Mandatory Testing

The Theory

The principles discussed in the previous section appear to provide the rationale for a mandatory drug-testing program established under a 1988 ruling by the Department of Transportation. That ruling specified that nearly four million private-sector employees with safety or security-related responsibilities (e.g., airlines personnel, truck drivers, certain railroad and mass-transit employees, and employees who handle pipelines carrying natural gas or hazardous substances) will be subject to mandatory random drug and alcohol tests. These regulations require employers to test all job applicants, to randomly test current employees, and to specifically test any employee involved in an accident.

The ruling further specified that "testing of employees is conducted in a manner that protects the privacy and dignity of individuals, while at the same time insuring the integrity of the sample." People who test positive must be removed, although they can be reinstated if a medical officer certifies they have been rehabilitated. (Bakaly, 1990, p. 344)

The stated purpose of these tests is to protect the safety of innocent people whose lives may be endangered by the inappropriate behavior of transportation workers. That purpose is most noble. However, before we endorse testing, we must determine if testing is the most reasonable and relatively unintrusive way of achieving that purpose.

To bring the previous discussion together, I propose that testing is permissible if and only if all of the following conditions are satisfied:

1. The job is such that its improper performance can have immediate, serious, and irreversible consequences for others (which others I shall discuss later).

2. Use of certain drugs is relevant to job performance in the following way: drug use demonstrably increases the chance that an employee will perform in ways that harm others.

3. It is unlikely that we can prevent the harm without random testing.

4. Testing is a reliable way of discerning the presence of drugs,

5. Without being unduly intrusive.

If each of these conditions is satisfied, then testing is the only plausible way to protect people from harm, and is, therefore, justified. Moreover, I think that were such criteria *demonstrably* satisfied, well-intentioned members of the profession in question would agree to mandatory drug testing. They would recognize that testing would increase the likelihood that their fellow professionals acted responsibly and in the best interest of the public they serve. Surely that is a goal of all responsible professionals.

Someone might object that such testing, even for this noble purpose, is not permissible because it inappropriately intrudes into employees' private lives. Most assuredly we must protect employees' privacy. It is *very* easy for policy makers and executives to lose sight of these concerns in their quest to protect the public—or to enhance the company's public image. If, however, these conditions are satisfied, drug use would not be private for employees in these jobs.

Rather it would be public. It would be public even by the guidelines set down by the staunch defender of individual liberty, J.S. Mill. "[T]he only purpose for which power can be rightly exercised over any member of a civilized community, against his will, is to prevent harm to others." However, if an activity is likely to harm another person, then for those actions each of us "is amenable to society." (Mill, 1978, p. 9) We cannot draw a distinction between the public and the private in the abstract. An action which is generally considered private, would, under certain conditions, be public because of its potential affects on others. However, we can only determine if that action is public in the relevant sense, if it potentially harms others. In summary, employees' private lives should be free from intrusion, including any intrusion from employers. However, for people in jobs which satisfy the stated criteria, drug use is not, properly speaking, private.

The Practice

I have argued that testing is theoretically justified: that testing is permissible *if* five conditions are satisfied. Whether testing is *actually* permissible, however, depends in substantial degree on whether these criteria are satisfied. We cannot merely assume they are satisfied. We must demonstrate that they are, else testing will be unacceptably intrusive.

How likely is it that a professional who uses drugs will perform her tasks in ways which harm others? Perhaps the chances are extremely remote. If so, testing would not prevent harm to others and therefore would be unnecessary. Perhaps there are more effective or less intrusive ways of achieving these same results. If so, testing would be unacceptably invasive. If on the other hand these criteria are clearly satisfied, then testing is not only permissible but mandatory—after all, we have a duty to protect innocent people from harm.

Philosophers, however, are not especially equipped to determine when the criteria are satisfied, although they may be adept at specifying what would count as evidence. Thus, I cannot state univocally that the criteria are satisfied. Nonetheless, it is plausible to believe they are satisfied in at least some instances. Both anecdotal and scientific evidence suggests that use of certain drugs will seriously hamper performance of some tasks in ways which would be extremely dangerous to others. Consider, for example, a pilot for a commercial airline. Pilot error could have immediate, disastrous, and irreversible consequences for all passengers (criterion 1). Also the presence of certain drugs in the bloodstream (including alcohol) will substantially increase the possibility of an accident. Perhaps, too, previous experimentation with certain drugs (like LSD), even if not currently in the bloodstream, might increase the likelihood of such accidents (criterion 2).

Moreover, by all accounts, there is no feasible way of detecting use of some drugs except by testing (criterion 3) and testing appears to be a reliable means of identifying drug use (criterion 4).[4] Finally, it appears standard procedures for administering tests—procedures like those established by the DOT—are not unduly intrusive (criterion 5).

If these suppositions are plausible, and if there is reason to believe people in said profession are susceptible to drug use,[5] then testing is a reasonable way to prevent harm and is therefore permissible.

It is important to note that this argument for drug testing does not imply that drugs ought to be illegal. Although I have not settled this issue to my own satisfaction, I am sympathetic with the claim that people should have a right to take any drug they want, particularly if by so doing they harm no one except themselves.(Szasz, 1972) But these arguments for legalizing drugs are irrelevant for those who have voluntarily undertaken careers where their actions could have dramatic and irreversible consequences for people under their care. *Ex hypothesi*, this behavior no longer concerns just themselves; on good Millean grounds we should support limited testing.

Limits on Testing

But limited testing it must be. I do not endorse extensive testing programs. However, I fear on historical grounds that testing will be used far more widely than is necessary. There are any number of ways in which managers could mistakenly apply or inappropriately interpret this rationale. Unless carefully monitored, executives could blithely assume that all of the criteria have been satisfied when, in fact, they have not. This would lead to far more extensive testing than is justified. Were this to happen, some of us might come to oppose *all* drug testing even when the five criteria *are* satisfied.

For instance, it is likely that some employers will establish testing programs merely to insure that employees adhere to the com-pany's views of appropriate behavior. That is morally abhorrent and politically frightening. I am in strong sympathy with Justice Scalia's biting dissent to the majority's holding in *National Treasury Employees Union*. Scalia had approved the Court's ruling in Skinner since a) it involved testing a few people (railroad employees involved in train accidents) and b) there was evidence of substance abuse in the targeted class. He claimed, however, that the circumstances in *National Treasury* were relevantly different. "I decline to join the Court's opinion in the present case because neither the frequency of use nor connection to harm is demonstrated or even likely. In my view the Customs Service rules are a kind of immolation of privacy and human dignity in symbolic opposition to drug use."(1398)

Or, as he stated later in the opinion, "The Court's opinion in the present case, however, will be searched in vain for real evidence of a real problem that will be solved by the urine testing of Customs Service employees."(1399) In such cases, testing programs are clearly inappropriate and indefensible. Testing under these conditions would be nothing more than an inappropriate intrusion by employers into the private lives of their employees—an intrusion endorsed by the courts.

Scalia objects to testing programs that are motivated by something other than the desire to protect public safety. I likewise object to such programs. But I also object to testing, which, although appropriately motivated, is unwarranted nonetheless. Consider, for a moment, automakers, bridge builders, construction workers, etc.—workers with jobs whose ill-performance could lead to substantial and irreversible harm to others. Despite the potentially disastrous effects of employee malfeasance, I would be loathe to endorse a full-scale mandatory drug program for people in these professions.

What distinguishes these cases from the previous ones? Several of the proffered criteria are not satisfied. For instance, any harm which might occur, although serious, is not immediate in the sense required. Workers may later discover and correct their own errors. If they do not, company supervisors or inspectors should find them. Thus testing is not the only way—and probably not the best way—of protecting people from harm.

It is not merely that such errors *might* be detected. We expect companies to detect them. We would expect construction companies to carefully scrutinize employees' work even if none of their employees used drugs. Companies should scrutinize their work to identify flaws resulting from poor materials or from employee inattention, mistake, or ignorance. In the process, the company should also identify any flaws attributable to employees' drug use. Hence, drug testing is unnecessary since any harm which might eventuate from employees' drug use should be prevented by normal supervisory monitoring of work. Since intrusive drug tests are unnecessary, they are unjustified.

This discussion helps us focus on an ambiguity I have heretofore glossed over. The first criterion states that testing is permissible if employee behavior is likely to harm others. Until now I have not specified who counts as "others." My comments implied that "others" referred to individuals outside the company who could be harmed by the employees' actions: passengers on a train or plane, people who live along a gas line, etc.

Should employers likewise be counted as "others"? Can a company legitimately test employees to prevent harm to it? I argued that a bridge company cannot legitimately test its employees as a means of preventing harm to those who may use the bridge, since drug-induced errors should be detected by normal company inspections. However, can those employers legitimately prevent harm to themselves by forcing employees to undergo drug tests?

The answer, at least in most cases, is "No." Supervisors should inspect work at each level of construction: e.g., when laborers pour the footings or erect major beams, etc. Thus, even if drug use does lead to mistakes, those mistakes could be discovered quickly and the cost of correcting them would be relatively minimal. Perhaps in rare cases the financial damage to the company could be substantial. If so, then assuming all five criteria were satisfied, testing employees to prevent harm to the company would be justifiable. I suspect, however, that such cases are rare indeed.

Fairness in Testing

Although my proposal seems theoretically defensible, it is vulnerable to the charge that it is politically naive. For the powers that be will use this argument to require large numbers of workers, especially manual workers, to submit to drug tests. Once again executives will foist an intrusive procedure on the "little people" while they, the rich and powerful, escape unscathed.

This criticism bothers me considerably, for there is more than a mite of truth in it. Most of the substantial, long-term ills in this world are wrought by high-paid executives sitting in plush offices. These executives—like old politicians who will not have to die in the wars they declare—are never subject to the indignities they cavalierly impose on workers. Since they do not have to suffer these indignities, they will likely ignore the need for evidence and merely assume the five conditions are satisfied. They will subsequently establish far more extensive testing programs than are justified as a means of preventing harm.

In the name of fairness should we thus require these executives to be subject to tests they inflict on their employees? Although I find this proposal appealing, it cannot be justified on the grounds mentioned earlier. There are three reasons why. First, executives' and politicians' work *is* scrutinized by others, and thus, any harm they could cause is preventible by the actions of others. Stockholders can fire CEOs; voters can toss out politicians at the next election. Second, there are genuine disagreements about how politicians or executives should behave; there are no similar disagreements about how airplane pilots should behave. Thus, we have no test which can straightforwardly identify executive or political behavior likely to cause harm. Any test we could construct would prematurely resolve ongoing debates over important political questions. Finally, and most importantly, evils wrought by politicians or executives are rarely the results of drug use, but of greed, insensitivity, ignorance or shortsightedness. Such evil is indeed evil. However, these evils are not preventable by mandatory drug tests. In summary, the criteria which justify forcing some workers to have mandatory drug tests are inapplicable to executives.

Nonetheless, it *does* seem unfair to allow executives to exempt themselves from drug testing, particularly given a propensity to exaggerate testing's benefits and to downplay its inconveniences. Consequently, I propose we adopt the following adjunctive principle: an executive cannot mandate that her employees be tested unless she undergoes testing herself.

The rationale for this principle is a variation on (although certainly not identical with) the five criteria stated earlier. Unjustified testing programs would harm innocent people (the workers); we should prevent harm. The most effective and least intrusive way of preventing that harm is to demand that those who institute testing programs subject themselves to the same tests, and in the same manner. Were such executives to submit to the same tests as employees, then we could reasonably assume executives would be unlikely to endorse testing unless they were *convinced* each of the criteria were satisfied.

Likewise for legislators who pass laws mandating testing. They should be subject to the tests they mandate for others. If they were, then they would fully appreciate the imposition testing involves. Therefore they would be less likely to institute testing unless they were convinced the criteria were satisfied. That would fulfill the goals of testing without unduly interfering with workers.

There is an obvious objection to this suggestion. If we adopt this adjunctive principle, only executives and legislators who themselves do not use drugs would require drug tests. That would be bad for two reasons: (1) some innocent people who would have been protected by drugs tests on certain workers, e.g., airplane pilots, will no longer be protected, and (2) executives' and legislators' drug use would still escape detection. Hence, the principle's goal would have been thwarted and the benefits of the initial program curtailed.

This objection isolates a significant flaw in my proposal, albeit a different flaw than the objector supposes. Moreover, once this defect has been corrected, we will be able to plausibly retain this adjunctive principle. Here's how. This objection arises because employers are the ones who decide when and if mandatory drug testing is instituted. However, that makes testing and its potential benefits, entirely dependent on the conscientiousness of employers. That is unacceptable—whether the executives themselves use drugs or not.

As I argued earlier, if all five conditions are satisfied, then testing is not only permissible, but required. After all, it is (presumably) the only feasible way of protecting innocent people. Hence, to achieve the goals of testing, legislatures must mandate testing for any job which satisfies the five criteria. Executives, as well as workers, in such professions would be tested. Requiring executives to be subject to these tests would insure that they were vividly aware of the indignities accompanying testing. They would thus be more likely to conduct testing in a manner sensitive to the interests of workers. That would maintain the benefits of mandatory testing while lessening the intrusion on workers.

Of course legislators who use drugs might then refuse to mandate testing as a way of hiding their own use. If they do, however, voters desirous of protecting themselves from drug-induced employee error could toss legislators from office during the next election. I suspect that is exactly what voters would do.

In summary, by establishing mandatory drug testing, we will protect the lives of others who may be put at risk by drug-induced employee error. By requiring executives and legislators to undergo any testing they mandate, we substantially increase the likelihood that they will not require intrusive procedures which do not satisfy the five stated criteria. The public and the employees are protected. What more could we ask?

NOTES

*Copyright © 1994 Burton M. Leiser. Reprinted by permission.

1. There have been points in history when, because of unusual conditions, employers were at a decided competitive disadvantage compared to employees—and the powers that be forbade workers from exploiting the situation. For example, following the Black Plague, when there were relatively few workers in Europe, King Edward passed the Statute of Laborers which capped worker's salaries. (Bakaly, 1990, p. 3)

2. The Court recently extended the application of the Fourth Amendment so that it is relevant, at least in principle, to mandatory drug testing. However, this is not the Amendment's primary focus. Moreover, the extent to which it *is* now applicable to drug testing is derivative from the more general constitutional concern with privacy. That is, it was only after *Griswold*, which first identified the right to privacy, that the courts began to extend the application of the Fourth Amendment. These more general privacy rights I shall discuss shortly.

3. Obviously there are *some* cases where such intrusion is justified, for example, when an employer has systematically discriminated

against people of color. But such intrusions must be justified. They are not the norm.

4. Some of the available tests are extremely accurate. Other versions are notoriously unreliable. This criterion will be satisfied only if the more reliable forms are used.

5. If there is no reason to believe members of said profession will use these drugs, then testing would not only be silly but also a violation of employees' privacy. For, as I have argued, employers cannot intrude into the private lives of employees unless the matter is directly relevant to job performance.

REFERENCES

Bakaly, C. et. al. *The Modern Law of Employment Relations*. Englewood Cliffs, NJ: Prentice-Hall, 1990.

Israel, J. and W. LaFave. *Criminal Procedure*. St. Paul: West Publishing Company, 1975.

Mill, J.S. *On Liberty*. Indianapolis, IN: Hackett, 1978.

Szasz, T. "The Ethics of Addiction: An Argument in Favor of Letting Americans Take Any Drug They Want," *Harpers*, April, 1972.

Against Mandatory Drug Testing

Daniel Shapiro

At first glance, mandatory drug testing seems justified, at least for certain types of jobs. There are jobs or professions, primarily in transportation industries, the improper performance of which can produce serious and immediate harms to others: pilots, train engineers, truck drivers, etc. Clearly those who run such industries have a responsibility to try to prevent accidents and other serious harms, and if mandatory drug testing was a necessary means to this aim, and if the testing was fair and did not violate individual rights, then no one could reasonably oppose it. Similarly, an extremely uncontroversial justification for legal coercion is to prevent serious and immediate harm to others, particularly if (1) the harm could not be prevented without the coercion, and if (2) the coercion does not conflict with or violate other moral requirements. Thus if drug testing in dangerous jobs (those whose improper performance pose a genuine risk of serious and immediate harm to others) met (1) and (2), then it's hard to see how one could oppose legislatures mandating testing in these jobs. Hugh LaFollette argues, in essence, that in the case of dangerous jobs, but only in the case of those jobs, mandatory drug testing and laws requiring this testing are justified for these reasons. In this essay, written partly as a response to LaFollette, I shall argue that, with one exception, mandatory drug testing cannot be justified by the aim of preventing serious and immediate harm to others, and that any legislation mandating drug testing will very likely violate important moral requirements. As for mandatory drug testing for those jobs the improper performance of which does not pose serious and immediate harm to others, I shall follow LaFollette in opposing such testing, though my arguments here will be significantly different from his.

Before I begin my argument, I shall mention the exception to it that I alluded to above. There are three kinds of drug tests: pre-employment screening, random testing, and for-cause testing. For-cause testing refers to testing after an accident, or when there is good evidence of impaired performance or suspicious behavior on the job. For-cause testing in the case of dangerous jobs is often justified. When serious harm like an accident occurs, it is legitimate to determine if anyone is culpable, and drug testing can help in this regard (particularly if there is independent evidence that the accident could have been avoided). And since impaired performance in dangerous jobs poses a genuine risk of immediate and serious harm, then it is legitimate to take actions which are necessary to prevent that harm, provided of course such actions do not violate other moral requirements. Non-intrusive drug testing could very well be appropriate in these circumstances as well.[1] In my arguments against mandatory drug testing that follow, then, I am excluding for-cause testing for dangerous jobs.

Preventing Serious and Immediate Harm to Others

LaFollette argues that random drug testing is required if and only if all of the following five conditions are met:

1. The job[2] is such that its improper performance can have immediate, serious, and irreversible consequences for others (where "others" refers to those outside the company.)

2. Use of certain drugs demonstrably increases the chance that an employee will perform in ways that harm[3] others.

3. It is unlikely that we can prevent the harm without random testing.

4. Testing is a reliable way of discerning the presence of drugs.

5. The tests that are a reliable way of discerning the presence of drugs can be done without being unduly intrusive.

LaFollette makes three errors in setting out his conditions. First, condition #2 mischaracterizes the way in which probability is relevant. Even if the use of certain drugs does demonstrably increase the chance that an employee will cause harm to others, this would not justify drug testing unless the probability that harm will occur is at least non-trivial. If the probability that harm will occur is increased from virtually zero to a level that is still extremely low, then the fact that drugs *increased* the probability of harm occurring is quite irrelevant. What is relevant is whether that level is significant or at least not trivial.

Another problem with the second condition is that it's not the use of drugs per se that has a significant chance of producing serious harm. There is no drug any amount of which would affect one's performance on the job such that it will likely produce serious harm; it depends, in part, on the amount of the drug in one's system. It also depends on the nature of the individual and the environment within which one takes the drug and feels its effects: e.g., whether one is an experienced drug user or a novice, whether one takes the drug for relaxation or to escape one's problems, whether one takes the drug in a social setting or alone, etc., can help determine how drugs will affect you.[4] Since these factors differ from person to person, and since we need some kind of general standard, the best thing to do is to refer to the effects that a certain level of drugs will have on the average person. Let us then revise condition #2 so that it reads:

2'. There is a significant probability that the use of a certain amount of drugs by an average person will cause that person to perform in ways that seriously and immediately harm others.

The third problem is that, contrary to the fourth condition, the issue is not whether testing is a reliable way of discerning the presence of drugs, but whether it is a reliable method of determining whether the level of drugs in one's system while one was at work was likely to have impaired one's performance on the job such that serious harm arises. Let us then revise condition #4 so that it reads:

4'. Testing is a reliable way of discerning whether there is a significant probability that someone's use of drugs had, does, or will impair his performance on the job, such that his or her performance did, does, or will cause serious and immediate harm to others.

Condition #5, which concerns whether drug tests that discern the use of drugs are invasive, would also have to be revised so that it mentions drug tests that discern impairment.

Thus LaFollette's conditions, suitability revised, now read:

1. The job is such that its improper performance can have immediate and serious consequences for others (where "others" refers to those outside the company.)

2'. There is a significant probability that the use of a certain amount of drugs by an average person will cause that person to perform in ways that seriously and immediately harms others.

3. It is unlikely that we can prevent the harm without random testing.

4'. Testing is a reliable way of discerning whether there is a significant probability that someone's use of drugs had, does, or will impair his or her performance on the job, such that his or her performance did, does, will or cause serious and immediate harm to others.

5'. The tests that are a reliable way of discerning whether drug use had, does, will, or did cause impaired performance can be done without being unduly intrusive.

These conditions cannot be all met. (4') fails because random drug tests are an exceedingly unreliable way of determining impairment on the job: the correlation between the amount of drugs in one's urine and impairment is very poor. For example, the presence of marijuana can show up in urine days after one has ingested it; the same is true for cocaine, opiates, barbiturates, amphetamines, and in the case of alcohol, it can be detected in the urine up to a day after consumption. Alcohol intoxication, it should be noted, can be reliably determined by blood[5] tests; while most drug tests are at present urine tests, since these are cheaper and easier to analyze, someone convinced by LaFollette's conditions might favor abandoning drug testing except for alcohol, if that is the only drug for which reliable information about impairment can be obtained. However, blood tests for alcohol intoxication violate condition #3, since the amount of alcohol that would likely produce immediate and serious harm can be detected without random drug testing. Alcohol intoxication often betrays itself in suspicious and erratic behavior, and supervisors and co-workers who are trained and obligated to report such behavior can get intoxicated drivers off the job. (Intoxication can then be confirmed, if necessary, by a drug test—but in that case we have for-cause testing, rather than random testing, and the former is not, as I argued earlier, objectionable.) An additional check on co-worker and supervisor detection of intoxication is quick tests of motor skills prior to flying a plane, driving a train, etc.; these are often useful in detecting the kind of impairment that is likely to cause an accident.[6]

The difference between testing for, and being alert to, impairment, rather than drug use, is worth stressing, for it is the Achilles' heel of LaFollette's argument. Harm to others in dangerous jobs results from impaired behavior, and as such it makes more sense to monitor and test for impairment than drug use. In fact, monitoring suspicious and erratic behavior and using motor-skill testing have clear advantages over random drug tests. First, by testing directly for impairment, one can flag people who are impaired due to stress, lack of sleep, and other causes having nothing to do with drugs. Second, random drug testing tends not to be done very often, while monitoring and testing for impairment can be done on a continual or nearly continual basis; clearly an occasional means of detection is less effective than a continual means in catching and deterring impairment due to drug use.[7]

It might be thought that my argument depends quite heavily on present drug-testing technology; as the technology improves, so might the correlation between drugs detected by drug tests and impairment. However, there is nothing wrong with letting arguments in political philosophy or public policy depend on the facts. The issue is whether drug testing is justified now or in the foreseeable future; whether it would be justified under some possible conditions is not terribly important. More importantly, improving drug-testing technology will not help. Improved technology will help provide more accurate detection of drugs, but the question is not the use of drugs per se but when such use impairs performance to the extent that it is likely to produce serious and immediate harm. Unless there is a very strong correlation between the amount of drugs detected and present or very recent impairment, and unless impairment cannot be detected without drug testing, then improving drug-testing technology will not help.

Suppose, however, for the sake of the argument that I am wrong and LaFollette's five conditions, suitably modified, can meet the problems noted above. (Suppose for example, drug testing is able to determine *subtle* impairment due to drug use that cannot be detected by other means.) As LaFollette rightly recognizes, this does not yet settle the issue, for there is still the quite important question of whether mandating drug tests might lead to abuse. LaFollette is worried about two levels of abuse. First, at the level of business, he worries that executives and managers will mandate drug tests that have little to do with the issue of preventing serious and immediate harm and which will be unduly invasive. Second, he worries that legislators who require that drug tests be administered in certain industries will mandate tests in cases which don't meet his five conditions. To avoid these problems, LaFollette proposes what at first glance seems like a cogent solution: legislators should only mandate tests that they themselves are willing to undergo and they should be mandate that everyone in the relevant industry undergo such tests.

Unfortunately, LaFollette's solution does not succeed in meeting the goal of preventing abuse in drug testing. It is true that if legislators know that they will be subject to any tests they mandate, then they will mandate as non-intrusive tests as possible, thus satisfying LaFollette's fifth condition. But nothing in his proposal insures that legislators will mandate tests only for those industries or professions where being impaired by drug use on the job is likely to produce serious and immediate harm. That legislators are subject to the same tests they mandate for others is a safeguard against abuse in the *methods* which will be mandated, but this is completely separate from the issue of *which jobs* should be tested. After all, if the legislators will be subject to drug tests regardless of whether they mandate them for, say, athletes or autoworkers, rather than, say, pilots or train engineers, they have little or no incentive to refrain from mandating testing for the former.[8]

LaFollette might concede that his proposal does not provide legislators incentives to avoid mandating testing where it is not justified, but go on to argue that there is no perfectly designed legislation, and that the alternative to not having legislators mandating drug testing is to leave it up to business discretion, and this itself can lead to abuse as well. This could lead to businesses mandating testing in jobs in which impaired performance does not pose any significant risk of immediate and serious harm to others (perhaps businesses will test merely to try to impose a puritanical moral code on their employees) or it could lead to a failure to test where it would be appropriate.

Notice that were LaFollette to respond this way, the justification of his proposal would then rest on a judgment that there is likely to be more abuse if drug testing is left up to business discretion as opposed to legislative mandate. There are, however, some good reasons to believe that the *opposite* is true. If legislatures wrongly mandate testing for certain jobs, then all people who hold those jobs are affected; but if a certain business or businesses wrongly mandate testing, then not everyone in that profession is affected. This wouldn't be a significant difference if all businesses had similar policies about testing, but there is a fair amount of evidence that this is not the case. Even today, the majority of businesses do not engage in drug testing,[9] and most businesses do not engage in random drug testing.[10] More importantly, many of the businesses that do engage in drug testing did so in large part in response to legislative and social pressure that arose because of the "War on Drugs";[11] this indicates that many businesses do not have a burning desire to do drug tests, and that if left to their own devices, there would not be universal over-testing. As for the question of whether if testing was left up to business discretion there would be too little testing—i.e., widespread failures to test where this would be justified by the aim of harm prevention—businesses have some strong incentives not to do this, namely that failure to do so could cost them a significant amount of income and perhaps produce bankruptcy. Thus LaFollette and any advocate of mandatory drug testing who is worried about drug tests being used in improper ways would do better to leave testing up to business discretion than to legislatively mandate it.[12]

An additional problem arises when we consider the meaning of the term "drugs." As this term is used today it often means or refers to only illegal drugs. Yet when the issue is preventing harm, it doesn't matter whether the drug is legal or illegal: impaired performance on the job from either kind of drug can cause serious and immediate harm in certain professions or industries. Presumably, then, LaFollette would want legislators to mandate testing for *any* drug which can cause impaired performance resulting in immediate and serious harm. However, there are limits on the number of drugs for which testing is feasible and reasonably cost-effective,[13] so some decision will have to be made by the legislators concerning which kind of drugs they want detected. In the current climate of drug prohibition, it is extremely likely that the legislators will focus on testing for illegal drugs, regardless of whether these are in fact the drugs most likely to cause impaired performance on the job resulting in immediate and serious harm. This means that LaFollette's legislative proposal, assuming it is meant as a proposal for today's situation, is likely to produce significant unfairness. It is unfair for someone to be subject to sanctions for drug use if that use was unlikely to produce serious and immediate harm when others who are using drugs in ways that are more likely to produce such harm are not subject to sanctions—and this is what could easily occur if legislators focus on tests for illegal drugs rather than tests for drug use that is likely to cause such harms. For example, those heroin addicts who are on a stable "maintenance" dose (a small dose sufficient to avoid withdrawal symptoms) have normal motor skills and are far less likely to cause serious accidents than heavy drinkers, yet it is probably fair to predict that legislators in today's climate will be more likely to mandate testing for heroin than alcohol.[14]

LaFollette might respond here along the lines I discussed earlier, namely by arguing that leaving testing up to business discretion could produce the same kind of problems. I would respond to this point in a similar manner as I did before, and point to the difference between legislators universally mandating a policy that is unfair and some businesses following unfair policy.

I have shown that LaFollette's arguments have three serious problems, which I will now summarize, and indicate why these problems have broad applications. First, the conditions under which LaFollette argues that drug testing would be required do not justify such testing. LaFollette argues that such testing would be justified only if (among other things) it is a reliable way of discerning drug use, but it is not drug use per se that is likely, in certain industries or professions, to produce serious and immediate harm, but rather a certain level of drug use that produces impairment. However, there is a very poor correlation between drug use detected by drug tests and impairment, with the possible exception of blood tests for alcohol (and impairment in that case can be determined without drug tests.) The large gap between testing for drug use and discerning impairment on the job is a problem that will affect any attempt to justify mandatory testing by the aim of preventing serious and immediate harm.[15] Second, LaFollette's proposal for avoiding abuse in drug testing fails to do that, since it provides no incentive for legislators to avoid mandating testing in industries or professions where there is little risk of a drug impaired person causing serious and immediate harm. In general, when it comes to drug testing in a profession, the uniformity of legislative mandates versus business diversity means that there is likely to be more abuse if legislators mandate drug tests than if we leave such tests up to business discretion. Third, in the present climate of drug prohibition, LaFollette's proposal is likely to lead to unfairness, in that it is likely to lead to people being penalized for drug use which is unlikely to cause serious harm to others, while the use of legal drugs which could cause such harms is likely not to be detected by drug tests. Again, this seems to be a general problem which would affect any proposal to mandate drug testing in today's political climate.

Since even LaFollette's careful and quite limited endorsement of mandatory testing is not a success, and since these problems seem to have broad applications, we may be tempted to conclude that no argument for drug testing can succeed. But before we conclude that, we need to examine whether justifications for drug testing based on grounds other than preventing serious and immediate harm to others can succeed. I shall discuss three other possible justifications for mandatory drug testing: that it is necessary to prevent harm to others, where "harm" and "others" are understood more broadly than preventing serious and immediate harm to those outside of the company; that it is necessary to prevent harm to the drug users; and that it is necessary to prevent immoral behavior.

Preventing Harm to Others, in a Broader Sense

A broader sense of harm would be one that covers all serious harm, without that harm needing to be immediate. A broader sense of "others" would include not just those outside the company who would be directly affected by impaired performance on the job (e.g., accident victims), but the company itself (its financial interests) and the general effect that drug use might have on society at large (over and above whatever effects would occur in virtue of accidents, etc.). If we combine these ideas, we get three senses of harm to others that drug testing might prevent and which haven't been discussed yet: (1) serious though not immediate harm to those outside the company who would be directly affected by impaired performance on the job (e.g., accident victims); (2) serious and immediate harm to the company and society at large; and (3) serious though not immediate harm to the company and society at large.

Concerning (1), as LaFollette pointed out, if the potential harm from drug use is serious but not immediate (as in the case of defective work in making a bridge, a car, etc.), then supervisors and co-workers can and should detect the error before the product is used by the public. (2) also can be quickly dismissed. Any immediate harm to the company or society at large that is likely to occur is due to accidents, and we have already discussed that question. Any harm to society at large over and above effects from accidents, etc.—effects due to reduced productivity, less of a work ethic, etc.—is unlikely to be immediate.

This leaves us with (3). One might argue that drug use, even if it doesn't cause impairment, can lead to a reduction in productivity and to sloppiness in work that can over time have a significant effect on a firm and perhaps put it out of business. Since it is legitimate for a firm to try to insure that its employees do not engage in sloppy work, are extremely productive, etc., then if drug testing would help in this regard it would seem to be justified. As for society at large, one might argue that the issue of accidents to one side, over time widespread use of drugs can cause insidious harm to the public. Lack of pride in one's work, a lackadaisical attitude towards one's responsibilities, an emphasis on getting high or just getting through the day rather than being a productive member of society—all of these are clearly harms to society at large. If drug testing could help prevent them, it would seem hard to object to it.

I grant that if there was some kind of significant relationship between drug use and lost productivity, etc., and if mandatory drug testing would be an effective way of detecting and preventing that use, then it would be justified for businesses to require their employees to be tested. But these are both big "ifs." Whether drugs cause one to be a less effective or productive worker than one would otherwise be depends on a variety of factors: the dose of the drug that is in one's system while at work, the type of drug, how often one uses the drug and one's experience with the drug, the conditions under which one took the drug, etc. (In fact in some cases, drug use can boost productivity: caffeine does so for some people in certain jobs, marijuana can make boring jobs more interesting, heroin can make anxiety-producing jobs more manageable,[16] etc.) There is no simple relationship between drug use and loss of productivity, except in the case of chronic uncontrolled use. Drug testing, however, is a poor vehicle for tracking uncontrolled drug use. A positive result of a drug test does not distinguish between casual or controlled use on the one hand and chronic or uncontrolled use on the other. Of course we could use drug testing to just determine chronic use, by keeping track of how often a person registers positive for a drug test and what levels were detected, but this has the problem that such use is likely to be detected without drug tests. These same points hold true for the insidious harms to society that were discussed earlier.

Preventing Harm to Self

Having shown that mandatory drug testing cannot be justified on the grounds that it is necessary to prevent harm to others, the next step is to see whether preventing harm to the drug user would be an adequate justification. The view that it is legitimate to use legal coercion to prevent serious harm to one's self, i.e., to the person engaging in or performing the action, is called legal paternalism. It is quite difficult to justify mandatory testing by legal paternalism for three reasons. First, the link between drug use and serious harm to one's self is weak for the same reasons that the link between drug use and harm to society at large is weak: only in the case of chronic or uncontrolled use is there a clear link, and in that case we could determine the harm without the tests. Second, paternalist justifications for coercion are suspect in a free society. A free society treats sane adults as responsible for their actions, and tends to follow the maxim of law *volenti non fit injuria*—to one who consents no wrong is done. The idea, applied in the present context, is that if a sane adult consents to an activity or behavior which turns out to harm him or her, then that is his or her responsibility, and it is none of the law's business. Of course, the *volenti* maxim is not universally followed in free societies, but it is generally followed, and so paternalist interferences with sane adults face a fairly strong burden to overcome. The cases where paternalism is most clearly justified is when someone does not genuinely consent to the harmful activity. One might argue that drug addicts do not consent to their addiction and thus that the *volenti* maxim is no obstacle to justifying drug testing. However, while it may be correct that addictive use of drugs is not consensual, most users of drugs are not addicts[17] so the *volenti* maxim still stands as a general bar to justifying drug tests. Third, in the spirit of LaFollette's remarks about what is and is not legitimate for employers to inquire about, it would seem at the very least unclear why those in business and others who oversee employees should have the special task of preventing people from harming themselves by using certain drugs. Business is not supposed to oversee the overall health and well-being of its employees.

Preventing Immoral Behavior

Another possible justification of mandatory drug testing is legal moralism. Legal moralism is the view that it is a legitimate function of law to prevent immoral behavior—where "immoral" is understood to be broader than merely causing harm to others or one's self. I suspect legal moralism is what explains most mandatory drug testing. Though the large gap between drug use and harm to others (or self) makes it difficult to justify drug testing on grounds of harm prevention, if drug use was immoral, and if it was the law's business to prevent immoral behavior, then drug testing would make perfect sense.

Explanation, of course, is not the same as justification. In order for legal moralism to justify mandatory drug testing, it must be clear what kind of drug use is considered immoral and why—for unless one adopts the religion of Christian Science, drug taking per se cannot be considered immoral. Perhaps the view is that illegal drug use is immoral, because one has broken the law, or more plausibly, that one has broken a legitimate law or a law in a democratic society. Mandatory drug testing would then be a way of ferreting out law breakers. This argument fails because (among other reasons) it would rationalize the totalitarian idea that people are to be investigated to see if they have broken a law without probable cause. There is the additional problem that employers are not the guardians of law enforcement.

A more plausible view is that it is wrong to take certain drugs for certain reasons or to use drugs in an uncontrolled manner, apart from the issue of whether harm is caused to others or one's self. I have a good deal of sympathy for this view: generally uncontrolled drug use indicates an irresponsible attitude towards others and oneself. If using drugs has become a major preoccupation of one's life, then it is likely that one is neglecting many of the good things in life as well as failing to meet one's obligations to others. But while it can be granted that uncontrolled drug use is immoral, this will hardly help justify mandatory drug testing, for reasons similar to those already given. Uncontrolled drug use is not easily detected by drug tests, unless one tests very often, and in any event such use can be detected without drug tests. And once again there is the question why employers should have as their job preventing immoral behavior.

I conclude, then, that mandatory drug testing, except in the special case of for-cause testing for dangerous jobs, is wrong. Neither preventing harm to others, harm to the drug user, or preventing immoral behavior can justify this widespread practice.

NOTES

1. However, for reasons I shall discuss later, drug tests in these cases are only helpful if they discern high levels of drugs in the blood, urine, etc., for otherwise, it is difficult to be confident that the drug use would cause or did cause an accident.

2. It's worth noting that it is unclear why LaFollette limits his discussion to testing people *at work*. The arguments he gives, if sound, would appear to justify random drug testing of automobile drivers. I will not pursue this point, and with LaFollette, limit myself to the question of drug testing at work.

3. I presume that the harm referred to here concerns the consequences mentioned in the first condition. In what follows I ignore the reference in the first condition to irreversible consequences, for it's quite unclear why if a harm is serious and immediate it matters whether it is irreversible. (If the harm was almost immediately reversible then it might matter, but in that case it probably doesn't count as a *serious* harm.)

4. I follow here Norman Zinberg who has emphasized in a number of works that the effects of a drug depend upon drug, set, and setting—i.e., the nature of the drug, of the individual, and the environment within which he takes the drug. See *Drug, Set and Setting: The Basis for Controlled Intoxicant Use* (New Haven: Yale University Press, 1984).

5. Franklin E. Zimring and Gordon Hawkins, *The Search for Rational Drug Control* (Cambridge: Cambridge University Press, 1992), pp. 125–6. Also see Robert E. Willette, "Techniques of Reliable Drug Testing," in *Drug Testing*, ed. Robert H. Coombs and Louis Lolyon West (NY: Oxford University Press, 1991), pp. 81–2.

6. The same point applies to urine tests and drugs other than alcohol. We could avoid the problem of a lack of correlation between drugs in the urine and impairment by having these tests flag only very high concentrations of drugs in the urine. However, if the concentration was that high, it's likely we could detect the impairment without the test.

7. I owe this point to Stanton Peele, "Asleep at the Switch," *Reason* 23 (December 1991), p. 65.

8. LaFollette does not make clear whether his proposal means that the legislators will only be subject to the same *kind* of tests they mandate for others, or whether they also will be subject to the same *amount* of testing they mandate for others (so that, for example, if they mandate drug testing for ten industries or professions, they will be tested ten times during a certain time period.) If it is only the former, then the legislators have no incentive to avoid mandating widespread drug testing, since the legislators will be tested the same amount regardless of whether they mandate testing for one industry or profession or for all of them. If it is the latter as well, then the legislators have some incentive to limit the amount of testing, but this does not provide an incentive to limit testing to those professions where impairment by drug use is likely to produce serious and immediate harm.

9. In 1991, 40% of Fortune 500 companies did some kind of drug testing. However, most people don't work for Fortune 500 companies. In a 1988 Gallup Poll, 28% of all businesses said they did some kind of drug testing. See Deborah Ackerman, "A History of Drug Testing," p.16 in *Drug Testing*.

10. Helen Axel, "Drug Testing in Private Industry," p. 149 in *Drug Testing*.

11. This is strongly suggested by Robert Coombs and Louis Lolyon West in their introduction to *Drug Testing*.

12. An alternative to business discretion and legislative mandate is legislative restriction. That is, rather than leaving it up to businesses whether to test, or having the legislature mandate when to test, legislatures could simply restrict business' ability to use drug tests by making it illegal to use drug testing in professions where improper job performance does not pose a genuine risk of immediate and serious harm to others. If one accepts LaFollette's argument that it is wrong for employers to inquire about behavior or beliefs which are irrelevant to job performance, then legislative restrictions on drug testing may seem plausible. However, one cannot fully determine whether it *is* plausible without a theory about what rights employers should have vis-a-vis em-

ployees, for whether it is wrong for employers to use drug testing, and whether they have a right to do it, are two separate issues. (One can have the right to do the wrong thing, e.g., join a racist political organization.) Obviously, space limitations prevent me from discussing what rights employers should have vis-a-vis their employees.

13. Deborah Ackerman, "A History of Drug Testing," p. 11.

14. In fact, most drug tests in the workplace today do not test for alcohol. See Deborah Ackerman, "A History of Drug Testing," p.18, and Helen Axel, "Drug Testing in Private Industry," pp. 150–1. On the effects of heroin on motor skills, see E. Leong Way, "Pharmacologic Assessment of Dependence Risks," pp. 394–5 in *Searching for Alternatives: Drug-Control Policy in the United States,* ed. and intro. by Melvyn B. Krauss and Edward P. Lazear (Stanford, CA: Hoover Institution Press, 1991), and Richard Lawrence Miller, *The Case for Legalizing Drugs* (NY: Praeger Publishers, 1991), pp. 6–7. Way notes that heroin addicts in Hong Kong work as high-rise construction workers, and use heroin to calm their fears. In all fairness, it should be noted that not everyone agrees that heroin users have normal motor skills. John Kaplan, *The Hardest Drug* (Chicago: University of Chicago Press, 1983), p. 23, says that heroin slows down the speed of performance, though not its accuracy. In the context of transportation jobs, slower speed amounts to impaired motor skills.

15. The problem is even greater in the case of pre-employment screening than in the case of random testing, since there is a considerable difference between using drugs at a certain time before being employed and being impaired on the job.

16. See note 14.

17. Concerning marijuana, no serious scholar who studies drugs would deny that most people's use of it is, or has been, responsible. See Arnold Trebach, *The Great Drug War* (NY: Macmillan, 1987), pp. 81–5, and Ethan A. Nadelmann, "The Case for Legalization" in *The Crisis in Drug Prohibition,* ed. David Boaz (Washington, DC: The Cato Institute, 1990), pp. 37–8. Despite cocaine's recent reputation as a drug that few, if any, can use or did use responsibly, this is not borne out by the government's own figures on cocaine use. See James Ostrowski, "Thinking about Drug Legalization" in *The Crisis in Drug Prohibition,* pp. 65–6, and the interview with Michael Gazzaniga, Professor of Cognitive Neuroscience in the Department of Psychiatry at Dartmouth College, "The Federal Drugstore" in *National Review* (February 5, 1990), pp. 38–9. On the number of heroin users being greater than the number of heroin addicts, see John Kaplan, *The Hardest Drug* pp. 33–4 and the references he cites therein, and Arnold Trebach, *The Heroin Solution* (New Haven:

Yale University Press, 1982), p. 246. Trebach estimated that there were 3.5 million heroin users; and there is widespread agreement that the heroin-addict population has been stable for some time around ½ million. On the latter point, see James Wilson, "Against Legalizing Drugs," *Commentary* (February 1990), p. 21.

Foreign Policy

International Narcotics Control:
A Challenge and an Opportunity

James M. Van Wert

Introduction

Drug abuse is a complex social phenomenon that defies simplistic definition and solution. Americans use drugs for a variety of psychological and socioeconomic reasons. Increased mobility and demographic change, erosion of cultural values and norms, economic instability, increased disposable income, and mass media are major determinants of drug abuse. Most Americans agree that reducing domestic drug demand must be a central component of U.S. drug policy. Yet, changing attitudes is a long-term proposition, requiring at least a generation of preventive education, treatment and rehabilitation, and drug research. In the meantime, because an estimated 95 percent of all heroin and cocaine abused in the United States is of foreign origin, the U.S. Government (USG) has developed and must continue to implement an international "supply reduction" component in its National Drug Strategy.

During the past decade, no other issue has generated more public debate, interagency Federal Government involvement, or dogmatic solutions than international narcotics control. Often perceived as an unrealistic goal, the elimination of drug abuse has led policymakers to formulate extreme positions, such as legalization and zero tolerance. Balance and long-term, multifunctional efforts are required to solve complex public problems.

Moreover, how officials frame the drug-policy debate and define the problem can influence one's moral and legal position regarding international narcotics control.

In the spring of 1988, drugs joined deficit reduction, defense, and day care as a major presidential campaign issue for George Bush. The Congress, the Executive, and the public worried about increasing drug abuse. Until the Persian Gulf War erupted in August 1989, respondents to a Gallop Poll identified drug use as the greatest threat to the nation. In 1992, drug control was *not* a major election issue, but reduction of drug abuse and related violence continues to be an important public health and safety goal of the United States.

Efforts to reduce drug abuse inspired the U.S. Congress to pass the 1988 Omnibus Drug Bill. This law created the Office of National Drug Control Policy (ONDCP) to formulate and coordinate the government's overall drug policy and programs, increased the financial resources of a number of Federal agencies, and broadened drug control program responsibilities in nontraditional drug agencies. During the Bush Administration, federal drug budgets nearly doubled, from $6.6 billion (FY 1989) to $12.7 billion (FY 1993).

At the outset of this essay, I want to state my contention that there is no legal or moral basis for *unilateral* intervention by enforcement officials in the internal affairs of another country. I do believe, however, that strategic and tactical intelligence gathering, technical support, and diplomatic "pressure" to achieve drug control is appropriate and often in the USG's best interest. But more germane to the policy debate is the question: "Is it cost effective for countries to *cooperate* in drug control, or supply reduction, programs?"

It is my view that countries can and should cooperate, bilaterally and/or multilaterally, in effective law-enforcement programs to control narcotics, just as they cooperate in world health efforts to vaccinate against smallpox and measles, preserve the environment, eliminate terrorism, develop healthy macroeconomic systems, and a host of other transnational issues. Most countries have signed and ratified international drug conventions, which commit them to work toward the elimination of illicit drug production, trafficking and abuse. I contend that securing *true* consensual agreement of a country's elected representatives to cooperate with the United States or any other nation is key to ensuring the Jeffersonian ideals of "rule of law and human dignity." Respect for the law and moral behavior are at the heart of free, democratic societies.

Moreover, I contend that cooperative international efforts to reduce illicit drugs are not counterproductive, but, in fact, they actually strengthen Third World political systems and support long-term economic growth and development. With democracies currently functioning throughout Latin America and radical political change unfolding in the republics of the former Soviet Union and Eastern Europe, global economic growth and development, particularly in this hemisphere, has become a more central USG foreign-policy goal.

In this essay, I intend to do three things: (1) trace several broad historical shifts in the USG's international narcotics-control strategy and describe supply reduction tactics; (2) describe the complexities of implementing effective source-country control programs; and (3) provide a normative, albeit cursory, set of prescriptions for USG drug-control policymakers to improve bilateral drug-control programs.

Historical Drug Policy Shifts

From a public-policy viewpoint, the United States has experienced great swings from "isolationism to activism" in its international narcotics control (INC) policy and tactics. Yet, as David Musto relates in his history of drug policy, *The American Disease*, there are two constants in international drug control: (1) drug control will always be subservient to USG security concerns, perceived or real, and (2) progress depends on disparate events that often have little or no relationship to one another.

For instance, in the 1980s, the USG viewed Latin America through "East-West" eyes: security concerns submerged all other bilateral interests. If viewed from this perspective, our anti-Marxist policy toward Chile and Central America becomes much more understandable (particularly the USG long-term relationship with Noriega). With the end of the Cold War, however, the

USG can now look at Latin America with primarily an economic, and not a politico-economic, framework. With the fall of Soviet Communism, making free-market–oriented systems and democracy work better has become the principal foreign-policy challenge for the USG.

Historically, the evolution of a policy issue is often the result of completely disparate and separate events. For example, three different countries and three distinct events led to the signing of the Shanghai and Hague Opium conventions in 1909 and 1912, marking the birth of the modern international narcotics-control movement. The Chinese appetite for opium consumption, the British desire to have free trade in opium from India to China, and the USG's interest in protecting the Philippines led to the Shanghai and Hague meetings of the early 1900s. Again, pre– and post–World War I attitudes varied widely and fluctuated between belief in the need for international cooperation versus skepticism over the ability to achieve such cooperation. Experience with two world wars led the USG to distrust global treaties and helped to create a sense of isolationism in international affairs.

For forty-five years after World War II, or from 1946 to 1991, the "Cold War" dampened true international cooperation. The image of superpower countries as exploiters, functioning from a "win-lose" framework, inhibited regional and multi-lateral cooperative efforts. Since 1989, however, the massive changes in the political world order have created a new era of possibility. With the collapse of the Soviet Union and its State-dominated political and economic systems, historians will not find a more optimistic period when the major "players" can co-operate on global issues (e.g., environmental health, economic growth, peace, and security), and when the national interests of the new republics of the former Soviet Union, China, and the United States are converging. After all, the vast majority of the world's opium is grown on land between the "cold warriors" with consumption (markets) expanding in all three. Concern over increasing drug abuse in the former Soviet Republics and China provides USG policy officials with a viable target of opportunity for strengthened international cooperation.

Historian William Walker (1990) writes that, since World War I, the USG drug-policy debate has been dominated by supply reduction antagonists who developed certain world assumptions, which have not always held true.[1] For example, there was an inherent belief that other governments would act as the USG acts and that most governments would accept and develop drug-control programs willingly if appropriate means were made available.

In 1969, however, this dominant attitude changed with an event called "Operation Intercept." Based on mounting frustration over increased Mexican heroin smuggling across the southwest border of the United States, the U.S. Customs Service initiated a three-week operation to search every passenger and vehicle crossing the border into the United States. The result was predictably inordinate delays at the border, which disrupted both commerce and tourism—major income generators for residents on both sides of the border. Catching the attention of Mexican and American political and business leaders alike, this operation was a critical event in United States–Mexican drug relations. Political scientist Richard Craig (1980)[2] writes that Operation Intercept was immediately unpopular and stimulated efforts on both sides to terminate the search. More importantly, "Intercept" sent a clear message to the government of Mexico that drug production and trafficking was primarily a "foreign problem" and that the USG policy goal was to assist drug-source countries to recognize that illegal drugs represent an *internal* legal, moral, and social problem requiring host-government action.

More than twenty years later, the USG continues to formulate drug policy in the 1990s with the same belief. The U.S. Congress passed the 1986 Certification Law, which forces foreign source countries to condemn and take action to abolish drug production, trafficking, and abuse. Those drug source and transit countries that are not certified as "fully cooperative" may suffer the consequences of reduced or eliminated U.S. foreign aid. By signing international drug conventions in 1961, 1971, 1972, and 1988,[3] most drug-source and transit countries not only began to deal with illegal drugs as an internal problem, but also admitted a shared, global responsibility to "cooperate fully with the

United States" in reducing illicit drug production, trafficking, and abuse.

The USG believes drug-source countries have an international responsibility to reduce drug production and trafficking. To reinforce this belief, Congress linked foreign aid and drug-control performance when it drafted the Certification legislation. Yet, judgments on a country's relative capability to perform, as well as its importance to the USG "national interest" for other non-drug reasons, are important factors in making certification decisions. Congress introduced the concept of variability by using terms such as "cooperated fully," "taken adequate steps," and "maximum achievable reductions." Definition and interpretation of these terms generate lively debate between the executive and legislative branches of the USG each year—particularly when some countries are certified based not on their drug-control performance but because they are important to USG "national interests" for other reasons.

Multilateral Drug-Control Conventions

In 1961, the United Nations (UN) Convention on Drug Abuse stipulated that in twenty-five years (i.e., by 1986), the signatories would have cooperated on a multilateral basis to eliminate all coca and opium production that exceeded licensed commercial levels. Again, in 1971 the UN demonstrated its collective concern over abuse of certain substances and reaffirmed the tenets of the 1961 Convention by drafting the Convention on Psychotropic Substances. In 1972, the world body amended the 1961 Convention and stated that ". . . all Parties shall endeavor to limit the cultivation, production, manufacture and use of drugs to an adequate amount required for scientific and medical purposes, to ensure their availability for such purposes and to prevent illicit cultivation, production and manufacture of, and illicit trafficking in and use of, drugs." Finally, in 1988, the UN promulgated a Convention against Drug Abuse and Illicit Trafficking, which recognized that "eradication of illicit trafficking is a collective responsibility of all States and that, to that end, coordinated action within the framework of international co-operation is necessary."[4]

Signatories and ratifiers of these international conventions agreed to take appropriate measures, within their own legal and administrative systems, to prevent illicit cultivation of drug crops in their territories and to conclude bilateral and multi-lateral treaties, agreements, or arrangements to enhance the effectiveness of international cooperation to reduce the world-wide availability of illicit narcotics. It should be noted that the 1988 Convention also concluded that "no Party shall undertake in the territory of another Party the exercise of jurisdiction and performance of functions which are exclusively reserved for the authorities of that other Party by its domestic law." In other words, the UN Convention reaffirmed the widely held belief that nations are sovereign and responsible first to their own internal legal and juridical systems.

Section 481(c) of the U.S. Foreign Assistance Act, more commonly known as the Mansfield Amendment, corroborates this international sentiment of sovereignty, by prohibiting any officer or employee of the United States to "directly effect" an arrest in any foreign country as part of any foreign police action except to protect life and safety in exigent circumstances.[5] Moreover, the Drug Enforcement Administration (DEA) has in its field operations and in congressional testimony interpreted the Amendment as a "ban on being present when direct police actions occur." Section 481(c)(2) revised the Mansfield Amendment to allow U.S. agents in a particular country to be present when foreign police officers are effecting an arrest or to assist foreign police officers who are effecting an arrest, if the Ambassador of the U.S. Embassy approves a waiver of the prohibition for that country. The express intent of USG administrative and legislative procedure was to prohibit intervention by USG agents into the internal affairs of another sovereign nation.

Source-Country Control Policy

For the past eighty years, the USG has formulated an international narcotics-control policy and fostered overseas drug-supply reduction programs for a number of reasons. First, policymakers believe that reducing global drug supplies *sufficiently* will result in less drug consumption in the United States; that is, if drug supplies are hard to find, expensive to buy, and risky to consume, fewer people will become drug abusers. Second, reductions in drug availability should result in less organized criminal behavior and lawlessness that accompany drug trafficking, and consumption. Finally, predicated on the belief that drug money corrupts, reducing drug production, trafficking, and abuse overseas will defend friendly governments against the insidious power and influence of the drug cartels.[6]

The history of drug use in the United States suggests a positive correlation between drug availability and the prevalence of use. Specifically, the Harrison Narcotics Act in 1914 led to a reduction in drugs supplies and a decline in drug use in the 1920s, followed by an increase in heroin use subsequent to World War II with the reopening of sea lanes in the late 1940s. Again, the Turkish opium ban in 1973 and the Mexican herbicidal opium-eradication program beginning in late 1975 both led to dramatic declines in heroin availability and use in the United States. Although data on heroin addicts are imprecise at best, the estimated number of heroin addicts dropped from approximately 700,000 in 1970 to 375,000 in 1978.[7]

"Source-Country Control" signifies those international drug-supply reduction efforts implemented in the drug-producing countries to achieve a net reduction in drug supply. Historically, these efforts have focused on crop reduction or control but, more recently, have emphasized law enforcement efforts to eliminate the trafficking organizations and their means of production. By immobilizing the organizations and their productive capacities, host governments will achieve a net reduction in illicit drug production.

The cultivation of illicit narcotics crops often represents the most viable economic alternative available to otherwise impoverished local residents. Eliminating drug crops at the source through crop eradication and/or income replacement has been a central, or at least an integral, part of the USG's international narcotics-control policy for the past twenty years. The source of the illicit drug is believed to be the most commercially vulnerable point in the chain from grower to user. Since 1989, however, USG policy officials have shifted away from crop control in favor of targeting major trafficking organizations and their principal assets/means of production, and enhanced interdiction.

As stated in the 1992 National Drug Control Strategy, the drug trade is most susceptible to disruption at the organizational center of gravity—the traffickers' home country of operations. Once the product leaves the production area and enters the distribution networks, it becomes more difficult to locate and control. Consequently, the USG's drug-supply reduction programs focuses major attention at the drug source, which represents the smallest, most localized point in the grower-to-user chain.

By eliminating *sufficient* amounts of raw material and the means of production at the source (e.g., the organization infrastructure, refineries, chemicals, drug product), the USG predicts that in the short run the retail street price of the refined drug will rise, the farm gate price will fall, and the consumption patterns both in producing and consuming countries will diminish. At that time, the drug producers will be more amenable to income replacements and crop eradication, if the economic incentives of production diminish sufficiently and the risks of production increase.

It is true that targeting the product at the farm gate may have little or no short-term effect on the price of cocaine in the United States—at least when done on a small scale. Rand economist Peter Reuter (1992) believes supply-reduction efforts that focus on parts of the distribution system distant from the consumer cannot affect the price paid by the consumer.[8] Source-country control, whether crop control or interdiction, is largely sector-specific (farmer, refiner, trafficker). Reuter believes that there are too many variables in the chain and too large a price differential for source country-control efforts to reduce drug availability in the United States; that is, traffickers can raise the price paid to the farmers significantly without necessitating concomitant increases in retail cocaine prices. Even with enforcement success "on the margin," Reuter believes that the suppliers would rather reduce exports to local consumers and/or other markets in Europe before they reduce exports to the United States. Eventually, they will also develop other growing areas as the traditional zones become "affected."

There are, of course, different political and economic effects resulting from targeting the different sectors of the trade: growers, versus the buyers, versus the traffickers and distributors, but the net effect in market terms is the same—a decrease in available supplies and an increase in the product price, which ultimately should drive down demand. Since 1989, believing that it was more palatable politically and cost-effective to target the trafficker rather than the farmer, the USG has shifted its international attention more on the organizations and their infrastructures as an indirect means of achieving a "net reduction in production." At least one senior Office of National Drug Control Policy staffperson thinks that crop eradication as a means of crop control is ineffective, politically destabilizing, and counter-productive for the farm sector.[9] Rather, USG efforts should bolster efforts to immobilize the organizations rather than "drive the peasants into the arms of the insurgents."

For the sake of argument, there may be circumstances when (short-term) reductions in cocaine availability in the United States can be gained by source-country supply reduction: (a) when significant reductions occur simultaneously, or in relatively close time spans, in key production zones of Peru, Bolivia, and Colombia; and, (b) when increased enforcement pressure on key organization activities reduces drug inventories. It is also true that cocaine can grow in many other locations outside the Andean source countries and the economic imperative that drives the farmer will eventually encourage displacement of coca growing to other localities. Yet, unlike heroin or marijuana, coca is a perennial plant that requires nearly three years of growth before it can produce cocaine commercially. Therefore, should significant acreage be destroyed, the impact on the supply system would be substantial—at least in the short-run.

Source-Country Control Policy Issues

The current source-country control approach poses a number of important questions which highlight the overall complexity of this issue. Raphael Perl describes three such issues: (a) Availability of resources, (b) "militarization" of the drug war, and (c) continuing foreign government cooperation.[10] First, can the USG afford the price tag or is it appropriate for the USG to pay nations to stop producing illicit drugs, either directly to the producers for stopping the production voluntarily or to the government in the form of economic and technical assistance? The risk, according to Perl, "seems comparable to that of paying nations to stop hijacking aircraft or taking hostages." Peter Reuter (1992) believes there are two problems with the "buy-out approach": it sets a floor (not a ceiling) on the earnings of coca farmers, and most farmers will "offer" up only those fields that are no longer productive and may already be too old to be of any value.

Second, can the introduction of military assistance into a law enforcement milieu inadvertently foster human-rights abuses because soldiers are not trained to respect the rights of civilians, and/or "undermine the authority of already beleaguered democratic civilian governments?" Given the history of corruption among the Latin American militaries and the antipathies between military and civilian forces in Peru and Bolivia, encouragement of the military to become more engaged in the drug-control effort may create additional tensions and problems.

Third, can the law enforcement interests of USG policymakers be melded with economic, trade and social interests of Andean policymakers, resulting in sustained foreign cooperative programs? That is, will the USG be successful in raising drug control high enough on the Latin American policy agenda to encourage active participation? All governments function in their own self-interest. With a number of more pressing social, economic, and political problems in source countries, the challenge will be to "make the drug issue important enough" to create the host-government political commitment necessary to implement effective control efforts.

USG Drug Policy in Latin America in the 1980s

The major Western Hemisphere foreign-policy issues in the 1980s were political democratization and debt reduction. In his February 1991 Appropriations testimony before the Congressional Foreign Affairs Committees, Secretary of State James

Baker listed five major foreign policy concerns of the Bush Administration: (1) promotion of peace and the end to regional conflicts, (2) creation of political stability and democratization, (3) development of healthy market-oriented economies, (4) reduction of transnational threats: terrorism and political violence, narcotics trafficking and abuse, global environmental degradation, and (5) provision of humanitarian assistance.

Throughout the 1980s and into the 1990s, the process of democratization continues to unfold around the world. In 1989, for the first time in decades, Brazil, Chile, and Paraguay had free presidential elections. (Only Cuba and Surinam in the Western Hemisphere still have State-dominated dictatorships.) In the 1970s, the Latin American region was characterized by aging dictators and ruling military juntas; by the end of the 1980s, civilian rule and democracy was the norm, not the exception. The fall of the Berlin Wall in 1989 represented a watershed event in global political change in Eastern Europe and the former Soviet Union. In short, democratic movements, often fueled by intense nationalism, continue to grow throughout the world.

Economic growth, however, has not enjoyed the same success as the creation of the new political world order. In the Western Hemisphere, economic problems continue to plague many societies, although there are some signs of hope. World leaders have admitted the need to base long-term economic development on free-market strategies and have begun to shift away from State-owned and dominated monopolies. From 1980 to 1989, the economies of Latin America were fraught with serious problems of inflation, debt, stagnation (except for Chile and Colombia), and inappropriate use of capital (for speculation rather than production). With more Draconian economic measures (Bolivia and Peru) and free-trade agreements (Mexico), the economic health of Latin America is beginning to improve. Yet, not unlike the economies of Eastern Europe and the former Soviet Union, the Latin American economies need to continue serious attempts at privatization and economic restructuring, informal wage and price controls, devaluation of currencies, shifts to export earnings, increase in investment potential, capital appreciation, bolstering the central reserves with hard currency, and reduced public sectors, many of which have grown so cumbersome that they suffocate private-sector growth. In several countries, a major portion of the gross national product is spent on meeting interest payments on the massive debt; for example, in 1989, nearly $420 billion in debt was outstanding in the five countries of Brazil, Argentina, Mexico, Peru, and Venezuela.

Against this backdrop of serious economic deterioration, where real incomes were less in 1989 than in 1980, Latin America experienced an expansion in coca production, trafficking, and abuse, with an increase in related violence. Although estimates of coca-leaf production grew from an estimated 294,000 metric tons in 1988 to approximately 337,000 metric tons in 1992, there appears to be some good news. During the past two years, the acreage under cultivation has reportedly decreased in the Andes,[11] perhaps signifying an increase in source-country commitment and belief that drugs have more negative than positive consequences.

Among the reasons cited for the increase in host-government commitment are the following. First, drug production harms the long-term, macroeconomic growth potential of developing countries. Second, drug production and abuse destabilize political institutions and create environments ripe for insurgency and anti-establishment sentiments. Third, drug abuse can ignite and spread, seriously affecting segments of the population and placing a burden on already-strained social welfare systems. In addition to the perceived negative aspects of drug production and abuse, countries also have a global responsibility to eliminate drug production and trafficking, as required under the precepts of international drug-control conventions, which make such activity illegal. By cooperating bilaterally and/or multilaterally in drug-control efforts, countries can create positive international relations with other nations.

Economic Significance of Drug Production

The illegal drug industry contributes to an increase in national income in most source countries, but it also generates negative economic and political effects that outweigh the positive ones. Drug cultivators earn money that enables the purchase of goods and services, but the net long-term economic effect on producing countries remains negative. With few exceptions, money earned through the drug trade does not return to the productive sectors of source countries, but remains in the consuming country or is invested in off-shore banks.

During the drug boom of the 1980s, drug-producing countries did not offer attractive long-term investment opportunities for business investors. Countries such as Peru, Bolivia, Burma, and Afghanistan have troubled economies and do not attract traffickers' investment portfolios. Typically, traffickers may spend money on food, arms, and security; or on luxury items (expensive automobiles, race horses, and gambling houses). Purchase of these items benefits only a few and does not offer positive economic-growth opportunities for the general economy.

The drug business does not mirror the typical economic cycle of jobs creation, which provides for consumption of goods and services; which in turn creates capital appreciation, investment possibilities, and additional jobs; and stimulates further growth, profitability and higher standards of living. For example, Colombian economist Francisco Thoumi (1987) writes that the drug boom of the 1980s hurt the development of agricultural and manufacturing activities, lowered the quality of investments (they became oriented to the short term), weakened government institutions by eroding public respect, and undermined the country's ability to have stable growth and compete in foreign markets.[12] For Colombia, economic costs of the drug war were estimated as high as $2.0 billion, or 6 percent of Colombia's GNP. Drug Consultant Rensselaer Lee III (1991) writes that between January and September 1990, foreign investment in Colombia plummeted by 68 percent. Tourism also suffered, as evidenced by decreases in restaurant sales, air traffic, and hotel occupancies. Residential home construction dropped by 20 percent. These effects on the Colombian economy were attributable at least in part to the rise in narcoterrorism during the government's eighteen month crackdown (1989–1991) on the Medellin cartel.[13]

In Southeast and Southwest Asia, drug production and trafficking offer a primary cash crop for food and support of antigovernment operations. Insurgent tribes in the Golden Triangle—and resistance groups in Afghanistan and Pakistan in the past—use the profits from the sale of opium to buy food and to fight the central governments. Politically speaking, illicit drug production and trafficking offer a viable means of acquiring wealth, which can be instrumental in buying power and influence. Drugs become the means for political destabilization, through the bankrolling of opposition parties and insurgent groups.

Source-Country Control Tactics

Since the first National Drug Control Strategy was published in September 1989, through the publication of the fourth Strategy in February 1992, the USG has increased its international focus on disrupting and dismantling the multi-national criminal organizations that support the production, processing, transportation, and distribution of drugs to the United States. It seeks to elicit the support of multilateral bodies, producing and consuming countries alike, to increase the effectiveness of law enforcement and security agencies to investigate and immobilize the trafficking organizations. Targeting the points of greatest value to the drug-trafficking organizations and networks (e.g., chemicals, assets, money, and key organization figures) was the core of the Bush Administration's international strategy.

Source-country control of the drug also complements domestic supply-and-demand reduction efforts and gives them a better chance of success. Under the Bush Administration Strategy, policymakers emphasized the importance of focusing law-enforcement efforts on the trafficking organizations. To eliminate the supply of drugs, cooperative international efforts must focus on "trafficking organization's leadership, operations centers, communications systems, shipping capability and transportation modes, processing facilities, chemical suppliers, and financial assets." Notionally, a drug network consists of centralized, coordinated *core* organizations (responsible for all phases of trafficking and usually international in scope), *secondary* organizations (responsible for subsidiary functions such as transportation, money laundering, or distribution within a region), and *local* organizations (responsible for local drug distribution and consisting of low- to mid-level street dealers). As the Strategy states: "The essence of the supply reduction strategy is to target particular networks of drug trafficking organizations, viewing them as multinational business enterprises, and attack them at all levels, from core organizations at international and national levels to local organizations at the neighborhood level." (cf 1992 National Drug Control Strategy, pp. 79–80)

Enforcement. The majority of funding in the international narcotics-control portion of the National Strategy is spent on increasing the efficacy of the host-government's criminal justice system. Effective cooperative law-enforcement support, to include investigation and arrest of major trafficking figures, interdiction of chemicals, forfeiture of assets, destruction of labs, seizure of drug shipments, and financial investigations to curb money laundering by drug organizations can result in effective source-country control. Pressuring the traffickers and raising the risk (and price) of doing business should result in a net reduction in drug production and increased control of illegal enterprises within the country.

Crop Control. The illicit crop probably constitutes the cheapest link in the narcotics chain. Producers devote fewer economic resources to prevent detection, and enforcement officials can find and destroy crops in the field more easily than they can find the finished product in the smuggling routes or on city streets of the United States. Yet, in some countries, targeting the grower can destabilize the political leadership and increase the ranks of antigovernment insurgent forces. Therefore, the 1992 Bush Administration strategy states that "eradication programs will be undertaken only after an assessment of their effect on total country production, their costs and benefits when compared with other drug control programs in the same country or areas, and the likely political consequences."

Historically, the USG has had varying degrees of success in supporting bilateral herbicidal eradication programs in Mexico, Colombia, Belize, and Burma and manual eradication efforts in Bolivia, Jamaica, and Thailand. In the mid-1970s, Mexico began an aerial herbicidal eradication program on both opium and marijuana and reduced the cultivation of these illicit substances significantly. In 1991, Mexico reportedly destroyed 6,500 of its

10,000 hectares of opium and 11,000 of its 29,000 hectares of cannabis.

In the early 1980s, the Colombian government used glyphosate to eradicate most of its marijuana in the north coast region. Today, Colombia is using the same herbicide on the newly discovered opium plots in the Cauca and Huila departments. In 1987, the USG supported the government of Belize in an aerial herbicidal eradication program, which resulted in a 90 percent decline in cannabis production.

In the 1987–1988 growing season, the Socialist Republic of the Union of Burma (now called Myanmar) destroyed an estimated 12,500 hectares (31,000 acres) of opium poppy. This herbicidal eradication program was stopped late in 1988 when the ruling military accommodated certain trafficking insurgents (i.e., Wa and Kokang Chinese who were fighting one of the Burmese government's principal enemies, Khung Sa and his Shan United Army).

Manual eradication of drug crops also continued in 1991 in a number of countries, including destruction of nearly 30 percent of Thailand's 4,200 hectares of opium, approximately 10 percent of Bolivia's 53,000 hectares of coca, and a little less than half of Jamaica's 1,800 hectares of cannabis.

Area Development and Income Replacement. A third tactic to reduce drug supplies is an indirect one, i.e., area development with or without an alternative crop component. Replacement of opium, coca, or marijuana production with a licit agricultural commodity, by itself, can never be successful because of the immense profit margins of illicit narcotic cultivation in source countries. A more broadly defined income-replacement approach, however, coupled with strong law enforcement, may succeed in making it possible for drug growers to stop the illicit cultivation.

In the early 1980s, the USG–Pakistani efforts to implement a fully integrated, rural-development project in the Malakand District of Pakistan's Northwest Frontier Province (NWFP) resulted in a net reduction in opium poppy production. Providing economic development support for the 300,000 inhabitants of the Malakand District, such as providing roads, water, electrification, and agricultural substitutes (peanuts, apples), enabled local residents to earn an income, thus making the cultivation of opium poppy unnecessary. An ancillary side benefit of the development efforts was the creation of valuable infrastructures to raise the standard of living throughout the region and encourage the nomadic populations to establish roots and achieve more stable living conditions.

In Southeast Asia, the Highland Village Project in northern Thailand has provided similar benefits to the culturally diverse, opium-producing hill tribes and has resulted in decreased opium cultivation consistently over the last three years. In Laos, the Houaphanh project near the remote border region with Vietnam began to provide area development incentives in 1990 (e.g., improved water, roads, medical, and educational benefits) for growers who opted to cease planting opium.

In the Western Hemisphere, a principal component of the Andean strategy to eliminate illicit coca in Peru and Bolivia has been the offer of economic assistance to entice the growers away from coca cultivation. A major goal of the Andean effort is to strengthen and diversify the legitimate economies to cushion against the destabilizing effects of eliminating cocaine money. Provision of hard currency to improve balance of payments, trade and investment incentives, debt restructuring and/or debt forgiveness, and loan guarantees can be effective macroeconomic tools to encourage host governments to cooperate in source-country production control.

In the broadest sense of the term, "crop substitution" or crop control worked effectively in Turkey in the early 1970s when a government cash subsidy permitted the farmers to harvest the opium poppy *before* the plant had produced the opium gum. In this way, the traditional cooking and ceremonial uses of the opium poppy could be maintained through the "poppy straw process," as it is called, but the flower could not be harvested for illicit opium gum, the raw material of heroin.

Supply Reduction Program: Success or Failure?

Despite the shift in focus during the last three years, which has generated statistics on seizures, arrests, assets forfeited, etc., much of the literature still reflects a sense of pessimism and failure over any form of source-country control.[14] A number of articles support the contention that such control efforts are ineffective at best and counterproductive at worst (e.g., threatening societal security and increasing human-rights abuses). In its assessments, the General Accounting Office (GAO) stops short of concluding that interdiction efforts are counterproductive, but states that law enforcement has had only a negligible impact on reducing cocaine supplies in the United States. In much of the literature, it is stated that interdiction cannot raise the traffickers' costs and risks high enough to make a difference in U.S. prices and, therefore, consumption habits.

Pessimism also extends to source-country control efforts because of conceptual, political, and technical arguments. Opponents of control programs, including eradication, believe that the reduction of foreign drug supplies is probably not achievable, or short term at best; and, even if it had a longer-term impact in the source country, it would not have a meaningful effect on levels of illicit drug consumption in the United States. The domestic consumer would simply switch to other available drugs. Moreover, some fear that inordinate environmental damage may result from herbicide use, if aerial spraying were widely used. Others question whether a global policy of crop control is feasible politically, because many growing areas are beyond government control, often located in insurgent-controlled territory. Even when there is government jurisdiction, crop eradication becomes impractical because of the grower's ability to shift areas of cultivation continually. Some also argue that instituting effective eradication efforts in some source countries, such as Peru, might also drive the growers and the insurgents, who co-locate with the drug traffickers, into threatening alliances that undermine the central government authority even further. Finally, some question the value of supply-reduction efforts at the source altogether, since world production and supply of illicit drugs vastly exceed world demand. If worldwide supply were reduced dramatically, it might not be felt in the United States until the supply had dried up throughout the rest of the world, because until 1990–1991, domestic consumers often paid higher prices than any other consumers and U.S. dollars were the preferred narco-currency.

Peter Reuter (1992) believes that the apparent failure of source-country coca control lies not so much in the difficulties of program implementation, but rather in the basic structure of the drug industry. In other words, leaf price at the farm gate accounts for a minuscule share of the retail cocaine price paid in the United States.[15] Reuter believes that it is possible to eradicate substantial coca in the wide-open, exposed areas of Peru's Upper Huallaga Valley and Bolivia's Chapare, but, once there is a modicum of success, the farmers will begin to plant in more unobtrusive places to avoid detection and destruction. The Mexican experience in the late 1970s and early 1980s demonstrated the resilience of the opium farmers to plant the crops in smaller plots, in deep valleys, and expand into nontraditional cultivation areas.

Coca grows in the Andean countries because of cheap labor and, at least to date, only minimal risk of government prohibition and retaliation. Effective enforcement could bring out the adaptive capabilities of the economically-strapped farmers. Even with "substantial eradication success," however, Reuter contends that it will not affect availability in the United States because of (presumed) stockpiled inventories and the traffickers' ability to shift European-bound cocaine to U.S. markets. Yet, if cocaine functions like any other commodity market system, I fail to understand the economic advantage of redirecting supplies from more lucrative European markets to the cheaper United States markets, i.e., in 1992 the price per kilogram of cocaine was nearly three times more expensive in Madrid than in Miami. In January 1992, a kilogram of cocaine in Miami sold for $14,000–$18,000, down from $22,000–$25,000 a year ago. The same kilogram of cocaine could bring nearly $50,000 in Europe.

It is true that source-country control efforts have not succeeded in decreasing substantially domestic narcotics availability. As stated in a Congressional Subcommittee Staff Report, entitled "The Andean Initiative: Squeezing a Balloon" (February 25, 1992), because the supply has not been cut significantly, cocaine is as cheap, as potent, and as readily available as ever on American streets. Despite notable "successes" such as the partial suppression of the violent Medellin cartel, interdiction of hundreds of tons of cocaine destined for the United States, and destruction of illicit drug fields, there has been a "balloon or spill-over effect." That is, eradication has led to the cultivation of smaller, more remote plots; destruction of labs and processing pits has led traffickers to build them elsewhere. When one trafficking cartel is weakened, another takes its place; some smuggling routes are discovered and blocked, others open up.

Despite the resilience of the drug traffickers to thwart the supply-reduction efforts, however, it is my view that source-country control efforts have raised the public consciousness of drug-producing nations to admit they have a difficult problem to solve. Secondly, supply reduction will succeed only when done simultaneously in several regions, using all the various tactics at the same time (especially economic assistance and crop control). Increased enforcement, independent of substantial economic incentives and eradication, will not create enough source-country political commitment and, therefore, will not decrease drug supply sufficiently to affect the consumer in the United States. In this sense, true supply reduction has never been tried, i.e., using all the tactics in a coordinated fashion in many source areas simultaneously.

Melvyn Levitsky, the former Assistant Secretary for the State Department's Bureau of International Narcotics Matters (INM), believes that there have been small but real successes during the past few years. He states: "The war on drugs is a war of small, but important advances and is like fighting a forest fire. The area burning attracts the cameras, while what counts is the ground gained." Some small but significant advances include the stabilization of coca growth in Peru and decrease in coca cultivation (for the second year in a row) in Bolivia and Colombia; the crippling of the "once powerful" Medellin cartel in Colombia; and a tripling of cocaine seizures in Mexico.[16]

Supply reduction is not a quick-fix venture; it represents a long-term cooperative effort on the part of the host government and the international community. Even though supply reduction has been a core part of the Strategy for over a decade, it is only in the past several years that economic incentives have been offered to make it feasible for drug producers to "detoxify" from the dependence on cocaine money.

Conclusion

Promoting democracy and healthy economies, key strategic foreign-policy interests of the United States throughout the world, and eliminating drug abuse, one of the premier domestic issues with foreign-policy implications, both require an active partnership between consuming countries and drug source countries. Neither objective can be reached without substantial progress in containing the insurgencies endemic to much of the drug-producing world and in advancing rational economic policies that will allow drug regions to function as stable parts of the international financial and trade system. A twenty-year history of international narcotics control has taught us a number of lessons. Stable political systems and healthy economies are indispensable elements to even the possibility of effective narcotics control. Narcotics and violence often are interrelated phenomena requiring coordination of our drug and security-assistance policy and foreign assistance efforts. Drug traffickers and insurgents do pose severe strains on democratic systems, even when they do not operate in tandem.

I have argued that, if *sufficient* source-country drug-supply reduction can be achieved, i.e., by raising the cost and risk of production, the price of narcotics to United States consumers will inevitably rise, driving down the level of consumption. All supply-reduction tactics, such as chemical controls, drug interdiction, trafficker immobilization efforts, alternative development assistance and income replacement, should result in the same increase in street price, reduction in retail street purity, and less drug abuse. This tenet, of course, assumes normal functioning of macroeconomic laws, such as relative elasticity of demand, heterogeneity of market supply, and competition. Of course, given the immense profits inherent in drug production and trafficking, no supply-reduction strategy by itself can achieve the ultimate goal of the USG; namely, reduced drug abuse. At the same time, the USG must focus more attention and resources on reducing domestic demand for drugs through education of its consuming populations.

Complexities of INC Efforts

A number of difficulties inherent in source-country crop control and law-enforcement approaches have led to the sense of pessimism described earlier in this essay. First, many of the growing regions are located in remote, inhospitable areas outside central government control. The presence of insurgents and threat of violence in some of the growing areas (e.g., Peru, Colombia, Burma, Laos, Afghanistan) create an unfavorable climate for bilateral and/or multilateral programs.

Second, in a free-market economy, no legitimate crop can compete with either coca or opium as an income-producing agricultural commodity. Even if there were competitive substitutes, with the immense profit margin in the drug trade, the drug traffickers could continue to raise the price and provide attractive incentives to compete for willing cultivators.

Third, much of the land in the growing zones cannot support legitimate agricultural products, or not sufficiently to support the farming population. The two largest illicit coca-growing regions in the world, the Upper Huallaga Valley in Peru and the Chapare region in Bolivia, are not considered suitable for many agricultural products.

Fourth, there are not many international markets to accept the substitute crops that could be grown. For instance, in the Bolivian Chapare region, oranges and coffee are viable agricultural products, but the international coffee cartel and U.S. citrus growers do not support Bolivian products competing for shares of existing markets. Even were viable markets available, a large number of coca cultivators are not farmers and know nothing about agriculture. Many are unemployed, displaced urban dwellers and laborers who moved to the coca-growing regions to seek a viable living. The collapse of the tin market in the late 1970s and early 1980s sent unemployed Bolivian miners into the Chapare to plant coca. In the long run, regional development efforts in the urban areas may be required to attract the cultivators back to their places of origin.

Fifth, successful crop substitution takes years of agro-research, infrastructure development, training and marketing and may take too long for subsistence and/or cash-crop producers.

In Pakistan's Malakand project, it took more than five years to develop the agricultural component of the project. Some argue that in the absence of strong law enforcement and control, crop substitution only provides an *additional* income generator, but not a true substitute. The growers will accept the substitute and continue to cultivate the illicit drug crop.

Perhaps the most serious impediment to effective source-country control is corruption. In many countries, the police and regulatory institutions, e.g., judges, magistrates, license bureaus, are the most susceptible to corruption because they are generally the lowest paid and have the most to provide in the way of favors. For instance, the Customs official in La Paz who makes $50 per month can with one act of omission, such as turning his head at an appropriate moment in the clearance process, increase his monthly income more than forty times. Institutional and individual corruption exist throughout the world, making effective narcotics control an extremely complex endeavor.

Future Prospects

A number of normative recommendations can be made about our current drug-control policy. First, the USG must take a multifunctional, long-term approach and resist any "quick-fix" solutions. Behavioral change occurs slowly and drugs are produced for a variety of reasons that need to be addressed. We must assess our policy options and design strategies that deal with reducing both the demand and supply of illegal drugs, emphasizing what works and modifying what does not.

Second, the USG must take a multilateral approach to this international problem. That is, regional approaches to the issue should be used more effectively, such as involvement of the Organization of American States (OAS), Association of Southeast Asian countries (ASEAN), UN, European Community (EC), and other developed countries and multinational private-sector interests, to reduce the perception that the United States is the only entity interested in the problem or the principal causative agent. It is also important to utilize the resources and political acceptability of the United Nations. The UN needs to be involved in much broader macroeconomic incentive packages for source countries.

Third, the international community needs to buttress the foreign governments' will and capacity to reduce available supplies of illicit narcotics. This can be done in part through developing macroeconomic incentives which permit countries to "detoxify" from their dependency on drug money. A number of tactics should be considered under this economic-incentive rubric, such as continued debt forgiveness, trade incentives, private sector inducement both in the United States and in producing countries, hard-currency support, and targeted development assistance which use "grass roots" organizations. Moreover, the international community should work to bolster the judicial systems and develop legislative initiatives that can assist producing countries reduce their drug supplies more effectively.

Fourth, law-enforcement efforts must become more effective, efficient, and less externally motivated. Strengthened chemical controls, asset forfeiture and seizure incentives, better money-laundering statutes, and improved use of targeted intelligence will improve interdiction and investigative efforts. Destroying the organizational infrastructure and immobilizing major traffickers will have a far more profound impact on drug supplies than interdiction of the drugs and arrest of low-level dealers.

Yet, despite the best cooperative efforts of the drug warriors, reduction in global drug abuse will not result from source-country control efforts alone. USG policy must urge greater effort on education to reduce domestic demand and place less reliance on international law-enforcement efforts. The USG should continue to support effective bilateral source-country drug-control programs because they raise the price of drug production and trafficking and the cost of "doing business." If these programs can make it (even marginally) more difficult to obtain illegal drugs, then they will have achieved their purpose.

Finally, a broader question has evolved to challenge the global community in the 1990s: namely, to what extent are societies outside the industrialized world likely to become viable drug markets? If, indeed, production of illegal drugs is high, and the American market is saturated (due in part to successes in reducing demand), and trafficking organizations are aggressively developing new markets in developing countries and in the former communist bloc, then it is critical for the global community to develop effective and enlightened cooperative programs to reduce both the supply and the demand for illicit substances.

NOTES

1. Remarks made by William Walker at a policy conference on drugs sponsored by the Center for Strategic and International Studies (CSIS), in Washington, DC, on April 1, 1992.

2. Richard Craig, "Operation Intercept: The International Politics of Pressure," *The Review of Politics*, Vol. 42, 1980, pp. 556–580.

3. In addition to the Hague and Shanghai Opium conventions of 1909 and 1912, there are three principal international drug-control treaties, which signify international consensus on the shared global concern over drug abuse and the need for strong international control efforts: (a) 1961 Single Convention on Drug Control and its 1972 amendments; (b) 1971 Convention on Psychotropic Substances; and (c) 1988 Convention on Illicit Trafficking.

4. 1988 Convention on Illicit Trafficking, p. 1.

5. The Mansfield Amendment has been part of the Foreign Assistance Act for nearly 20 years and was created to limit the role DEA agents play in foreign sovereign territories.

6. Mark Moore, "Supply Reduction and Drug Law Enforcement" in *Drugs and Crime*, ed. Michael Tonry and James Q. Wilson (Chicago: University of Chicago Press, 1990).

7. The prevalence of heroin addiction is extremely difficult to measure. The reliability and validity of the estimates are limited at best. In the early 1970's, a linear approach was used by Joseph Greenwood, Bureau of Narcotics and Dangerous Drugs, who used the Addict registry to extrapolate a broader population from single sampling. This approach used a "capture-recapture" rate to estimate a range of heroin addicts. The highest number in the range was 700,000.

Another methodology used during the past 15 years has been a multivariate approach first developed by Retka, Pearson, *et al.*, which assumed that heroin addiction was a hidden phenomenon that could be estimated only indirectly by measuring effects. By measuring a family of indicators (e.g., price, purity, overdose deaths, treatment episodes, and emergency-room mentions) across standard metropolitan statistical areas, one can use a principal component analysis methodology to develop an index (heroin-problem index) that could then be used to develop a range of estimates for each metropolitan area. With this methodology, NIDA estimated that the number of heroin addicts in this country had been steadily decreasing from a high of 593,000 in 1973 to a high of 508,000 in 1978. Variants of the same multivariate analysis have been used by NIDA during the past decade. NIDA continues to develop new methodologies to estimate the number of heroin addicts.

For a more complete description of the history of heroin prevalence estimation techniques, see Mark Brodsky's article in *NIDA Research Monograph 57,* "Self-Report Methods of Estimating Drug Use," Rockville, Maryland, 1985.

8. Peter Reuter, "The Limits and Consequences of U.S. Foreign Drug Control Efforts," *The Annals of the American Academy of Political and Social Science,* 521, May 1992.

9. This sentiment was exhibited by Office of National Drug Control Policy (ONDCP) analyst Arthur Houghton, III, at a CSIS-sponsored drug conference held in Washington, DC, April 1, 1992.

10. Raphael Perl and Roy Surrett, "Drug Control: International Policy and Options." Issue Brief # IB88093, Congressional Research Ser-vice, Washington, DC, August 31, 1988.

11. 1992 International Narcotics Control Strategy Report, p.15.

12. Francisco E. Thoumi, "Some Implications of the Growth of the Underground Economy in Colombia," *Journal of Interamerican Studies and World Affairs,* Vol. 29, No. 2, Summer 1987, pp. 35–55.

13. Rensselaer W. Lee, III, "Making the Most of Colombia's Drug Negotiations," *Orbis,* Vol. 35, No 2, Spring 1991, pp. 235–52; and *The White Labyrinth* (New Brunswick, NJ: Transaction Publishers, 1989); and "Why the U.S. Cannot Stop South American Cocaine," *Orbis,* Fall 1988.

14. The following references reflect the growing pessimism over the ineffectiveness of source-country control efforts:

Institute of the Americas and the Center for Iberian and Latin American Studies, "Seizing Opportunities: Report of the Inter-American Commission on Drug Policy" (San Diego: University of California, 1991).

GAO Report, *Drug Control: Impact of DOD's Detection and Monitoring on Cocaine Flow*, September 19, 1991.

A Report of the Global Policy Project, The United Nations Association of the United States of America, "New International Approaches for Controlling Narcotic Drugs," New York, 1991.

Committee on Government Operations Report, "Stopping the Flood of Cocaine with Operation Snowcap: Is It Working?" Washington, DC (August 1990).

Peter Reuter, "The Limits and Consequences of U.S. Foreign Drug Control Efforts," *The Annals of the American Academy of Political and Social Science* 521 (May 1992).

Bruce M. Bagley, "Colombia and the War on Drugs," *Foreign Affairs* (Fall 1988), pp. 70–92.

Rensselaer W. Lee, III, *The White Labyrinth* (New Brunswick, NJ: Transaction Publishers, 1989), and "Why the U.S. Cannot Stop South American Cocaine," *Orbis* (Fall 1988).

15. Reuter, *Ibid.*, p. 155 states that leaf price accounts for less than 1 percent of the price paid by U.S. consumers for cocaine. It costs $750 for one pure kilogram equivalent at the farm gate, whereas the retail price in the United States (one gram units) brings in $135,000 per kilogram after the exporter, importer, wholesaler, and several retailers have factored in their costs and risks, and have cut the product several times.

16. Melvyn Levitsky, Letter to the Editor, *The Foreign Service Journal*, Washington, DC, June 3, 1992.

Contributors

Block, Walter	College of the Holy Cross, Worcester, Massachusetts
Brown, W.M.	Trinity College, Hartford, Connecticut
Edwards, Rem B.	University of Tennessee, Knoxville, Tennessee
Hough, Sheridan	University of Houston, Houston, Texas
LaFollette, Hugh	East Tennessee State University, Johnson City, Tennessee
Leiser, Burton M.	Pace University, New York, New York
Narveson, Jan	University of Waterloo, Waterloo, Ontario
Nathanson, Stephen	Northeastern University, Boston, Massachusetts
Reiman, Jeffrey	The American University, Washington, DC
Scribner, Phillip	The American University, Washington, DC
Shapiro, Daniel	West Virginia University, Morgantown, West Virginia
Simon, Robert L.	Hamilton College, Clinton, New York
Steinbock, Bonnie	University at Albany, State University of New York, Albany, New York

Van Wert, James M.   Small Business Administration, Silver
                      Springs, Maryland

Vihvelin, Kadri   University of Southern California, Los
                      Angeles, California